D0849516

Illinois in the Civil War

Victor Hicken

ILLINOIS IN THE CIVIL WAR

Foreword by E. B. Long

SECOND EDITION

UNIVERSITY OF ILLINOIS PRESS
Urbana and Chicago

This work has been supported in part by a grant from the Robert R. McCormick Charitable Trust and the Illinois State Historical Society.

The illustrations in this work are published with the permission of the Illinois State Historical Library.

Manufactured in the United States of America
1 2 3 4 5 C P 5 4 3 2 1

This book is printed on acid-free paper.

Library of Congress Cataloging-in-Publication Data
Hicken, Victor, 1921–
Illinois in the Civil War / by Victor Hicken; foreword by E. B. Long. — 2nd ed.
p. cm.
Includes bibliographical references and index.
ISBN 0-252-01772-2 (cl.). — ISBN 0-252-06165-9 (pbk.)
1. Illinois—History—Civil War, 1861–1865. 2. United States—History—Civil War, 1861–1865—Campaigns. I. Title.
E505.H5 1991
973.7'473—dc20 90-41288
CIP

Contents

Foreword

They came from the prairies and the lakeside, from the river valleys and the hills, and they marched off together into a wild and unknown life. Few Americans and certainly few from the "western" state of Illinois knew about war. Few indeed had ever been far from their farms, villages, or small cities.

The Illinois country was not exactly new in 1860, for it had seen the French and the British, the early forts and trading posts. It had been a separate United States territory since 1809. Upon admittance to the Union in 1818 there were some 40,000 scattered settlers in the state. Illinois men had taken part in the Black Hawk War of 1832, but it had been a pretty tame affair, local in scope. In 1846–48 the men of the state—six regiments in all—had once again gone to battle, this time to far-off Mexico.

By 1860 many of the 6,123 Mexican War volunteers were still about, and they told of war in places with melodious names where many of their fellow soldiers had died in battle or of wounds. And now it had come again, that dread and yet romantic, beckoning word "war." This time it was not war against Indians or an unknown people across a far away border. It was against their own, against the South.

Illinois, through the accident of geography, lay with its southern tip pointed like a sword at the heart of the new-formed Confederacy. A number of its residents had come from the Southern states and an even larger percentage had parents who had migrated from Kentucky or Virginia. In southern Illinois, particularly, where pro-South sentiment naturally flourished, the schism of internecine war cut deep and the anguish there was bitter and strong. Elsewhere in the state there were pockets of violent abolitionists, striking out with all the reformer's zeal. The majority of citizens, however, held opinions somewhere in between these extremes, or were without confirmed judgments on the issues of the struggle. From this variance of feeling and typical western and American individualism had to come not only the Illinois soldier, but his moral, economic, political, and emotional support.

While old in the land itself, Illinois was stilll young, just moving into its teenage growth, slowly finding its way out of the early frontier into the more mature stature soon to be labeled "mid-western." Ferment had been growing long before the Civil War actually began, and the issues involved were discussed and sometimes contested violently. Antislavery factions had agitated vigorously, fulminated against by those who, while not necessarily advocating slavery, had their hearts in southern principles. Then, too, there were others who saw more to the issue than just slavery, who were concerned about the individual rights of the people as opposed to government. The Senate race of 1858 between Democrat Stephen A. Douglas and Republican Abraham Lincoln, the increasing turbulence and widening rifts of opinion, the Republican presidential convention of 1860 in Chicago, and the election itself had made Illinois conscious of the leading role it now must play in the national arena. After all, the state could claim two of the four presidential candidates of 1860—Douglas and Lincoln—and was the homeland of the winner!

While war itself was new, except for those fading memories of Mexico and the marches after Black Hawk, Illinois manhood itself was keenly cognizant of the crisis. The state was booming, boasting a population of 1,711,961 in 1860, over twice as many as the 851,470 of ten years before, and startling when compared to the 12,282 of 50 years previously. While much of its strength still lay in the farmlands and small villages, there was a swelling city growth as well. Chicago was burgeoning with 109,260 people, followed by Peoria, Galena, Alton, Quincy, Freeport, and Rock Island. Foreign immigration was increasing, and of the total population 7,628 were Negroes.

The cash value of Illinois farms was fourth in the nation, but the value of manufactured products was only fifteenth. The rapidly spreading railroads and the economically strategic geographical position of the state were soon to alter these statistics. The state was indeed a "conscious" one, not only in politics and business, but in the already sometimes frenetic energy of its people. And now it was to go to war—unready, inexperienced, but generally eager. In many ways Illinois was not too much different in its war effort from other northern states—they all did a share. It was in the subtleties, perhaps, or the chance of events that gave the Illinois soldier a distinctive character. We have to go back to the war times, to the newspapers, the letters, the diaries, to find the Illinoisan of that day.

In doing this we see the mass of the 259,092 men of the state in the army and navy, and also the men and women at home backing them up, at least in most cases. And at the same time we are appalled by the gory casualty lists plastered on bulletin boards at wayside crossings and in crowded city squares—lists that in the end totaled nearly 35,000 dead in battle, of wounds, disease, or in faraway prison camps. Nevertheless, in homefront Illinois it was possible not only to fight a war but to advance the state as well, for Illinois spurted during the 1860s to come out with a running start in the postwar expansion. A major contribution of Illinois was in leadership, and it is a truly impressive list: President Abraham Lincoln, Senator Stephen A. Douglas, General Ulysses S. Grant, and on down the list of the great and near great in uniform and out. Of course there are a few, too, who can only be listed as the not-so-great.

Most of the soldiers were volunteers and most of them were young. The majority were between 18 and 25, but some 237 were 50 years of age or over, and five were boys of 13. They took part in major campaigns, gigantic, awesome battles in the West, and some in the East. They fought in so-called lesser engagements, and they fired their weapons in countless tiny outbreaks of combat, some of which are not even in the records.

Of the roughly 10,500 military events of the Civil War it is impossible to determine just how many involved men of Illinois, but a goodly total it was. In addition, there were other not-so-glamorous duties such as the guarding of towns and cities, protecting railroads and bridges, forwarding supplies, and just being there in case of need.

Most of these men were in the conflict without an idealistic purpose—just a general conviction that the Union was in trouble and something had to be done. For some it would evolve into more; for a few it would become a crusade; for others it would remain largely a personal adventure into which they were more or less forced, for it was the thing to do. They entered into all this with an élan and an attitude of camaraderie that the United States had not seen before and was perhaps not to see again. They joined the fray with almost a college spirit—their regiments were to become their alma maters. The regiment was something new and yet something old, something they could cling to, something that gave the humblest of them a place of importance. Small enough and usually composed of men from the same general area of the state, the regiment gave the youthful and sometimes frightened and homesick soldier an identity and a refuge. Oh, certainly, they were proud at times of brigade, division, corps, army, state, and nation. But nearly always closer to their hearts was the old regiment. These regiments developed distinctive personalities, drawing their names and reputations from their records and from the predominating composition of the outfit, whether of preachers, teachers, businessmen, city boys, "foreigners," or what have you. "Esprit de regiment," one might properly say—a spirit unique to the Civil War.

All of this was so long ago—a century or more now—and the men who marched out on their great adventure and the women who cheered them and wept for them are gone. The face of the world, the nation, the state, and perhaps the individual has changed almost out of recognition. So why bother to remember? What difference does it really make to us now?

The historian knows why it makes a difference, and to express this he has written billions of words. Without history we could barely exist at all, for we would not have the tools of life! The Civil War was one of the tasks of our historical existence. We all lived through it. When the fact that a century had passed became apparent, those in Illinois who do believe that history counts organized an able and distinguished commission to determine how best to re-illuminate the events of those days.

As the fevers of the centennial observances mounted throughout the nation, this commission searched for an appropriate way to commemorate the Civil War. No great battles were fought in Illinois to re-enact; there was no desire to celebrate and boast about the northern triumph. There was a desire instead to memorialize properly and to understand what the sturdy people of Illinois did in the Civil War, and what effect those years had on the development of our homeland. An extensive program of historical markers, dignified observances, and publication was inaugurated. The Illinois Civil War Centennial Commission was unanimous in believing that the emphasis of the Illinois efforts should be on the lasting, the worthwhile, the scholarly, and at the same time the reasonably popular. With this laudable goal in mind, a bibliography of manuscript sources in the state relating to the Civil War was prepared. This will stand for years to come as a tool for the serious historian and will save countless hours of work and travel, as it enables the scholar more readily to make use of the many fine archives of the state.

At the same time, the Commission was aware that today's average interested citizen had little, if any, knowledge of what the men of Illinois did in the Civil War and how the conflict looked to them. There existed a few general volumes, not easily available, and most of them dull and dry. Just what did the Illinois soldier do? Beyond that, what kind of a fellow was he? What were his emotions as he faced the enemy's fire? How did he behave in camp? What type of a life did he lead? What record of his experiences has he left us?

The task of bringing the trials and triumphs, and a few failures, of those years to current memory was wisely entrusted by the Illinois Civil War Centennial Commission to Victor Hicken of Macomb. Dr. Hicken, a native of Illinois, has devoted much of his career as a historian to exploring the story of his region. Born in Witt, he was educated in the public schools of Gillespie. After attending Southern Illinois University, he received his doctorate from the University of Illinois, and has been a member of the faculty at Western Illinois University at Macomb since 1947. Rising to the rank of full professor, Dr. Hicken was named "outstanding professor" by the student body in 1964. He has been active in numerous educational professional bodies and has written many articles for the *Journal of the Illinois State Historical Society*, the *Chicago Tribune*, and other publications. His writings and research have included such subjects as mining history, pre–Civil War politics in Illinois, and of course the war itself.

The Commission, in choosing Dr. Hicken to relate the story of the Illinois soldier, could not have found a man better qualified or more dedicated. Dr. Hicken, in essence, moved back a century and personally joined the volunteers from Illinois at their enlistment camps, en route to the theaters of war, on the battlefield, in the bivouac, in the prison camps, and at the end followed them to their homes again. Not content with secondhand sources, Dr. Hicken sought out the soldiers themselves and came to know them through their published and unpublished diaries, letters, memoirs, and regimental histories. Tireless in his research, he rediscovered the usual and unusual, gathered it together, and then sat down to write what really cannot be called just a mere recounting of the facts of the history of Illinois in the war, but can more aptly be described as a composite eyewitness report of the Illinois volunteer as he was.

The author has achieved the requisite humility of a true historian. He has recognized that the soldiering and fighting these young men underwent was perhaps the most important experience of their lives. He knew that when they did come home to live the long years afterward there was always the shadow of "the War" upon them. They wanted to share that epic time, and now they have been given the opportunity once more.

Dr. Hicken heard again the fearful sound of the guns, the anguished cries of the wounded and dying. He shared in the tearful farewells and joyous returns. But it is clear that this is not entirely Dr. Hicken's book. It belongs to the men and women of Illinois, for it is their story. It is a people's tale, be they generals or privates. Through their words we can become comrades-in-arms with them all.

We can evoke, in memory at least, the glories and disasters of those destiny-packed years. We can don the blue and march out with ardor or in fear, shout and shoot our way into the deepest Southland with the men of Illinois, see strange new sights and endure unfamiliar hardships. And when it is over we, at least, can come back to our world, and perhaps we, too, like the generation of that day, will never be the same again. We have, through the trials of others, fought and won a war, and, it is hoped, found renewed strength for the struggles of the future that we all must face.

E. B. LONG
Oak Park, Illinois
December, 1964

Preface to Second Edition

Almost three decades ago, when the Illinois Civil War Centennial Commission planned to celebrate the centenary of that great conflict, plans were made for the publication of several volumes dealing with the war. One was to be a book about Illinois soldiers in combat, which was commissioned to me. The second was to deal with Illinois on the home front during the four years of war, and that was commissioned to Harold Sinclair, an Illinois novelist who had gained fame with a novel called *The Horse Soldiers,* an exciting story that was eventually made into a successful movie. Though my book, *Illinois in the Civil War,* was published in 1966, the Commission saw fit not to have Sinclair's work reach publication. One unfortunate result of its decision was that one of the few criticisms of *Illinois in the Civil War* was based on the misunderstanding that it should have covered the civil aspects of the war as well as the military.

When I commenced the research for my book, I became entranced with the nature of the work. Like Carl Sandburg, who was commissioned to write a child's biography of Lincoln in the 1920s and fell so in love with his subject that he changed the nature of the work, I fell in love with the character of the citizen-soldier of 1861–65. First of all, I discovered that the aging correspondence, diaries, and reminiscences I ruffled through were filled with literately written insights and stories of the war. Second, they proved that humanity and war had not changed much in the years between "Billy Yank" and my own experiences in World War II. Except for a few shadings here and there, mostly in the manner of expression, the letters of the men who wore the blue and the women who wrote to them were essentially the same as the letters of the G.I.s and the women who wrote to them. I ought to know, having been a censor for some time during World War II.

I quickly gained a true respect for the educational system of pre–Civil War days. Whether they were college or academy students, such as the members of the 33rd Illinois, or they had received only grade school educations, these soldiers could write with a flourish. This is not to say that I did not find some terribly illiterate scrawlings from time to time, but most of their writings were impressive. I always come back to one Leander Stillwell, a farm boy who lived with his family on the outskirts of Otterville in southwestern Illinois. In the summer of 1861, Leander was sweating out his days helping his father with the farm chores. The draft was breathing down his neck, and odium was associated with any young man who allowed himself to be taken into the service in that manner. So he and his father brought in the harvest, and Leander went into town and joined up with the 61st Illinois Infantry Regiment. When he came home in 1865, his education had consisted of a few years in grade school and the war itself. Years later, he wrote it all down in what is a minor literary classic, which he called *The Story of a Common Soldier of Army Life in the Civil War, 1861–1865*. Nowhere does one find better descriptions of the war, especially of that awful struggle at Shiloh Church. Leander awakes on that warm April morning to the sounds of shouting and shooting. He sees alien banners streaming through the underbrush. Bewildered, he stands like a statue until his superior officer shouts in his ear. Just shoot your gun—at anything—but shoot, the officer says. Leander does just that. War was a long way from pitching hay.

Many Civil War writings are filled with the mundane events of camp life: the weather, complaints about the food or the officers, and observations about the quality of the land, a natural topic since so many of the soldiers are farm boys. There are also precious vignettes: insights into life in the service or life at home. General John Palmer, to save writing paper, wrote letters vertically and horizontally on each page. It is exasperating and difficult to read them, but in one letter to his wife in Carlinville, Illinois, he tells a fascinating story about one of his men who went home on leave without telling his wife in advance. Unfortunately for all concerned, the soldier was already coming up the walk when his wife and her lover discovered his arrival. The interloper had no chance to dress completely. With the husband in pursuit, he only had time to dash out of the back door and into the outhouse. In the relative safety of a locked outhouse, he engaged the husband in a hot debate, during which the outhouse was pushed over on its doorside, leaving only two exits for the imprisoned lover. It is best to end the story there, but Palmer obviously took much glee in telling the story, and the townspeople of Carlinville probably took even more glee in retelling it.

Usually collections of Civil War letters are made up of missives sent by soldiers from the field and lovingly saved by their wives. Unless the ordinary soldier was well billeted, it was extremely difficult for him to save letters from home. There are some exceptions, however, and the Chipman Collection in the Illinois State Historical Library is one. Albert (of the 76th Illinois infantry) and Sophonia Chipman maintained an active correspondence during the war. His letters detailed life in camp and descriptions of battles; hers told of developments at home. Despite their obvious affection for each other, their letters, like most correspondence between husbands and wives at that time, were short on expressions of love and affection. We must assume that such feelings were taken for granted during this mid-Victorian era. To use a contemporary term, a commitment then really meant just that—a union held together by hardship, danger, hard work, and even separation.

One of the more interesting series of letters on the Civil War is to be found in the Wallace-Dickey Collection, located at the Illinois State Historical Library. In 1860, William Harvey Lamb Wallace was a highly successful lawyer in La Salle County, Illinois. His marriage to a lovely member of the prominent Dickey family was a true romance, and the young couple's home, Robins' Nest, near Ottawa, Illinois, was the center of much social activity. When the war began in 1861, Wallace, by then a father, was mustered in as colonel of the 11th Illinois Infantry. He quickly learned the military arts, and, by the time of the Battle of Fort Donelson, he had become a brigade commander. By late March, 1862, he had won his appointment as brigadier-general.

His letters to Robins' Nest at this time are filled with longings to see his wife and child. These early days of April brought spring, and a deceptive calm descended on Pittsburg Landing on the Tennessee River. Both General Grant and General Sherman were confident that the Confederate army was miles away and that no battle was at hand. Also assured of this, Wallace sent for his wife.

On April 6, the Confederates struck, and Wallace's 2nd Division was soon heavily involved in the fighting. At almost that very same moment, Mrs. Wallace arrived at Pittsburg Landing. Late in the afternoon, Wallace, while attempting to lead some of his troops out of the "Hornet's Nest," was struck in the head by a piece of shell. All that frightful and rainy night he lay behind Confederate lines, to be found on the following day by the advancing troops of Grant's counterattack. With no real chance of recovery, he was brought back to Pittsburg Landing and to his wife. Wallace never regained consciousness, and he died a few days later at Savannah, Tennessee.

The Wallace-Dickey Collection does not end there, however. There are other war related casualties in the family. Years pass, the Wallace daughter grows up and weds, and, by the 1920s, another descendant of the Wallace-Dickey union finds her way to Hawaii and marries into the rich and powerful Dole family, which virtually controlled the pineapple industry. There the letters end. The Wallace-Dickey Collection contains such a marvelous family history of national and social change that I have often wondered why it has not been edited by some ambitious historian and published.

The inescapable conclusion one reaches after researching Civil War collections is that the ordinary Union soldier understood the necessity for the great adventure in which he was involved. That might not have been true of many American soldiers in World War II, Korea, or Vietnam. But Billy Yank knew that his failure would mean the dissolution of the Union, the end of the nation. The conflict was related to national issues and not to some far off place in Asia or Europe. Each company was raised in a specific community—Macomb, Carbondale, or one of hundreds of such places throughout the state—and the soldiers in each company had a common background. Perhaps they were Germans from Peoria, or miners from Galena, or farmers from Macoupin County. Whatever the nationality, whatever the background, there was a bonding between the men. One man's patriotism permeated a company and then a regiment. A regiment could raise the combative efforts of a division, and so on up the hierarchy of the army. The regiments, according to their experiences in the field, developed pride in a number. Take the 59th Illinois, for instance. Raised originally as a Missouri regiment, it was eventually accepted in the Illinois quota. It fought in so many battles and campaigned in so many areas that, through deaths, wounds, and attrition, the number of men in the regiment dwindled to a few hundred. There were attempts to blend these survivors into another regiment, but they would not accede; when the war ended, the 59th was still in existence.

Another storied regiment was the 55th Illinois Infantry. Commanded by Colonel David Stuart, a politician from northern Illinois, the regiment was composed of companies from both northern and western Illinois. The unit had two other distinctions. First, an extraordinary number of brothers had enlisted in the regiment. Second, as the war wore on, the regiment became harder and harder to handle. They might have been the type that the old German drillmaster, Friedrich Wilhelm Von Steuben, had described during the American Revolution. "You just can't order them to do something," Von Steuben said. "You have to tell them why."

One of the problems lay in the command. Stuart, who was not destined to stay long in the army mainly because of the very nature of the 55th, was particularly inept. During the fighting on the Union left at Shiloh, Stuart attempted to form his unit into a hollow square, an antiquated maneuver dating back to 1776. In the gullies and ridges at Shiloh, the square naturally fell apart, and the regiment had to conduct a fighting retreat to the banks of the Tennessee. By this time Stuart had tipped his hand to his soldiers, and they paid little heed to his orders, preferring instead to obey the fighting chaplain of the regiment, Milton Haney. Haney, who came from Bushnell, Illinois, was one of the two chaplains to be awarded the Congressional Medal of Honor, which he won in the Battle of Atlanta. Haney's Sunday sermons to the 55th, by the way, usually ran along the line of routinely consigning all Democrats to hell. At Shiloh, Haney, a Presbyterian, rounded up a barrel of whiskey and went up and down the line of the 55th dispensing drinks.

After the battle, Stuart went home and was replaced not by Haney, whom the troops wanted, but by a Danish officer by the name of Oscar Malmborg, who likewise found the regiment hard to handle. In 1864, the regiment refused to reenlist unless Haney was appointed their leader. All worked out in the end, however. Haney remained as chaplain, Malmborg went home, and a more likable officer was named to lead the 55th. The 55th then went on to finish the war as one of the best regiments in the entire army.

Of an entirely different nature is the story of the 109th Illinois.

Raised in Union, Johnson, Pulaski, Jackson, and Alexander counties, where for a while pro-slavery arguments found some logical relationship to save-the-Union contentions, the regiment held together until early 1863. When Lincoln's emancipation policy went into effect, the logic broke down. Saving the Union apparently became less important than retaining slavery, and by the end of January only a few sergeants and enlistees were showing up for muster. The rest had gone home. Those troops who remained loyal were amalgamated into the crack 11th Illinois.

All in all, the thousands of Union troops who carried the North to eventual victory were rather remarkable. The war itself, like most wars, was made up of long periods of idleness, severe campaigning, and battles or skirmishes. In the latter, lines of opposing infantry armed mostly with single-shot rifles advanced toward each other, while artillery gave whatever support it could. Fighting was mostly of a stand-up variety, since it was much easier to ready a muzzle-loader that way. It took a good deal of nerve to go through the process of pouring down the powder, tamping the cotton wadding, and ramming down the ball while some forty or fifty yards away an opposing soldier was readying to fire. Sometimes fighting became hand-to-hand, as during the Battle of Franklin in 1864. At one point during this struggle, Confederates and Yanks clubbed each other with their rifles and, with knives in hand, wrestled one another to the ground. In a later battle involving Illinois troops, a Union officer struggled with an opponent down an incline until he was able to free his saber and lop the hand of his enemy.

What is generally overlooked by Civil War historians, who tend to isolate battles, is an important element in campaigning—the seemingly endless marching in search of a battle. This quite often is what Billy Yank described in his letters home. Early in the war, in 1861 and 1862, Illinois regiments trudged east and west and north and south throughout Missouri in search of either Sterling Price's Confederate army or some other rebel unit, or on the track of countless guerrilla bands. Although they were good Union men, they were not quite soldiers yet, and their letters home revealed that fact. A 14th Illinois Infantry soldier, who had marched three hundred miles in just a few days, wrote that he was done in. Like novice G.I.s in World War II, they carried too much of home with them—impedimenta of all sorts. But, like a latter-day soldier, Billy Yank soon learned to discard and to organize. By wrapping a blanket in the right manner, he could sling his gear about his shoulders and maintain an easier and longer stride.

It paid off in the end. These same soldiers covered long distances through Tennessee on to Chattanooga. They streamed through mountain passes, outflanking the Confederate army attempting to hold Georgia. As they wrote their wives or friends, the march from Atlanta to the sea was a real lark. Swinging along red clay roads and eating their way through abundant crops of peanuts and yams, they made a mockery of distance. Their faces were turned black by tar from the burning pine woods of South Carolina. Yet the real test of stamina was yet to come. When Lee and Johnston surrendered, someone in Washington, perhaps the new President, Andrew Johnson, got the idea that a grand march ought to be held in the capital city. The Army of the Potomac was virtually there already, but some of Sherman's rangy veterans were hundreds and hundreds of miles south. By forced marching, with some men collapsing by the side of the road or bleeding from the mouth or feet, this redoubtable army made it in time.

On the first day of the Grand Review of the Armies, the Army of the Potomac, boots polished and shined, some units wearing white gloves and collars, gave a marvelous show. It was so impressive that General Sherman remarked to his opposite, General Meade, "I'm afraid my poor tatterdemalion corps will make a poor appearance tomorrow when contrasted with yours."

On the following day, 65,000 men of Sherman's army, many of them Illinois men, followed their generals down the same route traversed by the Army of the Potomac. Sherman, looking back, was overcome with pride. He would later write that "the sight was simply magnificent. The column was compact, and the glittering muskets looked like a solid mass of steel, moving with the regularity of a pendulum." It was a leaner and rangier army, and, as one observer put it, their faces seemed to bear a "glory look." They had even beaten the Army of the Potomac in its most prideful métier—the dress parade. Well they should have. Missouri, Kentucky, Tennessee, Georgia, South Carolina, North Carolina, and Virginia—they had campaigned and walked the whole distance. It is little wonder, then, that in years to come the war would remain the great adventure of their lives, the one rite of communion at their annual regimental gatherings, their basis for loyalty and comradeship to the end of their days.

Preface to First Edition

The Civil War was, without question, the great and overwhelming drama of American history. During these trying years of turmoil, the nation struggled to maintain an identity which it had achieved at great sacrifice less than a century before. It was a time of nobility, patriotism, and devotion to cause, the like of which would be difficult to match in any other period. In the end, of course, the national union was preserved, though not without tremendous sacrifice.

Of the various states which contributed to the total victory, none gave more willingly and more unsparingly than Illinois. Lincoln, the towering figure of destiny, began his trial of national office when he stepped aboard the train at Springfield. Grant, who was destined to lead the Federal armies to eventual victory, offered his first significant service to the cause from Galena. There were others, many others, including John A. Logan and John A. McClernand, and scores of general and lesser officers who led troops from the cities, towns, and hamlets of the Prairie State in the cause of liberty.

But such leaders were only part of the total contribution. What of the hundreds of thousands of young Illinoisans who placed themselves behind the colors and marched voluntarily off to war? And what of the 34,834 Illinois men who never returned to their homes in 1865, but lay scattered about battlefields and cemeteries from Texas to Virginia?

This is the story to be told: the contributions of Illinois to the fighting forces of the nation from 1861 to 1865. In the pages which follow, therefore, an attempt is made to relate the narrative of the Illinois soldier from the beginning of the war, his enlistment in a regiment, his participation in various conflicts, and his return home again. As will be seen, the author has placed considerable reliance upon regimental histories and soldiers' reminiscences, diaries, and correspondence.

Without the consideration of the Civil War Centennial Commission of the State of Illinois, this study could never have been made. Beyond this, however, further appreciation must be offered in a number of quarters. Mr. Clyde Walton, the Director of the Illinois Historical Library, gave the author unlimited use of facilities and material under his charge, and for this he must be thanked. Gratitude must also be offered to Miss Margaret Flint of the Illinois Historical Library, Mrs. Helene Levene and Miss Mary Lynn McCree of the Centennial Commission, Mrs. Ellen Todd Whitney of the Illinois State Historical Society, and to various other individuals who gave both of time and patience in helping me to find materials.

I must also offer appreciation to Professor Robert Sutton of the University of Illinois and to Professor Glenn Seymour of Eastern Illinois University for their encouragement and confidence. And one last expression of gratitude must be extended to Dr. Arthur L. Knoblauch, President of Western Illinois University, for his understanding of the problems involved in working upon such a project as this.

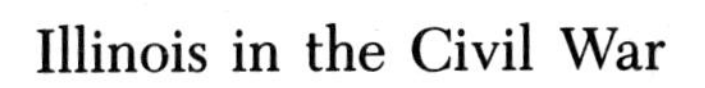

Illinois in the Civil War

CHAPTER I

Illinois and the War in 1861

April of 1861 was a month of big and little decisions. Some of them were official in nature, and part of the organization and logistics of war. Others, individual and personal in scope, involved the national reaction to the coming conflict. Yet all of them were tied together into the same exact pattern of history. Thus it was that when President Lincoln issued his call for volunteers, Governor Richard Yates of Illinois translated it into an appeal for a gathering of regiments.[1] And more directly were decisions made when thousands of young men swarmed to the recruiting booths so that they might march for the grand old flag.

The governor's call on the fifteenth of the month was for 6,000 volunteers. In response, military companies were quickly organized on a local basis and offered to the service of the state. The *Chicago Tribune* noted that the whole state seemed to be ablaze with military activity, and that young men were drilling everywhere. In Springfield, the *Illinois State Journal* proclaimed that 100,000 volunteers could be found within the boundaries of the state. Mass meetings, planned and spontaneous, were held in almost every town. One such gathering in Quincy brought forth seven companies of home guards. Little Petersburg, rallying on the same day in late April, raised enough men to form a single

---

[1] *Report of the Adjutant General of the State of Illinois*, rev. Brig. Gen. J. W. Vance (8 vols., Springfield, 1886), 1, 5–7.

company. Down in the Springfield area, one man, hearing of the call for volunteers, walked over 20 miles in order to enlist.[2]

The original request of the War Department was for six Illinois regiments, but the General Assembly, in a characteristic excess of patriotism, authorized ten. The initial six, numbering from the 7th to the 12th regiments, were quickly accepted into service. The remainder, including the various artillery and cavalry units also raised in April, were accepted by the War Department in June. The decision to accept such unrequested regiments was due partly to pressures brought upon the federal government by Representative John A. McClernand, a loyal southern Illinois Democrat, and the governor himself, and partly by the exigencies of the war.[3]

After the July and August defeats at Bull Run and Wilson's Creek, Congress authorized the President to call for 500,000 additional troops. Once again Illinois turned itself to the task of filling its quotas. By the first few days in August, the state had regiments in the field as high in number as the 55th Illinois. Many of these new regiments came from southern Illinois, an area considered by many to be of doubtful loyalty to the Union cause. Overcoming an early repugnance to the war, volunteers continued to come from that part of the state in an ever-increasing flood. "Southern Illinois known as Egypt," wrote one well-known eastern correspondent, "is turning out men . . . with surprising liberality. . . ."[4]

The amazing fact of the fall of 1861 is that there were more volunteers for the service than the state could handle. The problem, attendant to the enthusiasm for the war, was complicated by other factors. Many of the strong Union newspapers in the state urged young patriots to go directly to Springfield and present themselves to the Adjutant General. Several thousand indi-

---

[2] *Chicago Daily Tribune*, April 19, 1861. *Illinois State Journal* (Springfield), April 15, 1861. *The Diary of Orville Hickman Browning*, ed. Theodore C. Pease and James G. Randall (2 vols., Springfield, 1925, 1933), I, 464.

[3] Richard Yates to Abraham Lincoln, May 15, John A. McClernand Collection, Illinois State Historical Library, Springfield. (This library is hereinafter referred to as ISHL.) Yates to McClernand, May 18, 1861, McClernand Collection.

[4] Albert D. Richardson, *The Secret Service, the Field, the Dungeon, and the Escape* (Hartford, Conn., 1865), 186.

viduals, disdaining such poor advice, took the earliest opportunity to enlist in Kentucky and Missouri regiments. At the crossroads hamlet of Tennessee, Illinois, for example, a company was quickly organized in April, but it could not gain acceptance into any authorized Illinois regiment. When a recruiting agent for the 9th Missouri passed through the town, the company simply volunteered to fight under that banner. In fact, virtually all of the 9th Missouri consisted of Illinois men, and later in the war the regiment was rightfully transferred to the Illinois quota.[5]

In December recruiting was ordered to a halt, only to be reopened again the following summer in order to replenish regiments decimated at Pea Ridge, Donelson, and Shiloh. The President's July, 1862, call for 300,000 more volunteers soon followed, but it was met with something less than enthusiasm on the part of the general public. Many of the older regiments such as the 9th Illinois, which had suffered badly at Shiloh, met great difficulty in filling up its ranks. Even the appeals of General John A. McClernand, especially assigned to recruiting duty in Illinois, fell upon deaf ears.

In August the drought in recruiting was brought to a close when state and national authorities threatened open conscription and a draft of militia units throughout the North. Faced with the choice of being drafted or volunteering, Illinois men quickly chose the latter. As it was aptly expressed by one Morgan County correspondent of Governor Yates: "The war fever is raging here; the intimation of a *Draft* seems to fetch them to their milk." Veterans of older combat regiments contributed their part in spurring enlistment by urging their friends back home to volunteer so that the state would not face the "disgrace" of a draft.[6]

By the end of August, 1862, regiments up to and including the 116th were either under arms or being organized. September brought a continuance of the flood, with the 125th Illinois in the field, the 123rd armed and awaiting orders at Mattoon, and the

---

[5] *Warfare Along the Mississippi: The Letters of Lieutenant Colonel George E. Currie*, ed. Norman E. Clarke, Sr. (Mt. Pleasant, Mich., 1961), 3–4.

[6] J. S. Crane to Yates, August, 1862, Richard Yates Papers, ISHL. David Givler, "Intimate Glimpses of Army Life During the Civil War" (unpublished typed transcript, ISHL), 90.

129th in the recruiting stage. The final completion of the fall harvest in October brought another surge of enlistment in the rural areas. When the weather turned in late November, Illinois was able to claim a total enlistment of 125 infantry regiments, 16 regiments of cavalry, 30 batteries of artillery, and a quota excess of over 20,000 men.[7]

Despite such efforts by other western states, the total national enlistment was not enough to meet the demands of the war, and on March 3, 1863, President Lincoln approved the Conscription Act. Illinois managed to avoid the application of the draft through the summer of 1863, however, by establishing credits for Illinois volunteers serving in the regiments of neighboring states, and by tapping hitherto unused segments of the population for volunteers.

In the latter respect, the first Illinois Negro regiment, eventually called the 29th U.S. Colored Infantry, was authorized in the fall of 1863. Though enlistment in this regiment was unduly slow, because of the lower pay and bounty for the Negro private soldier, the 29th was able to leave its Quincy camp by April, 1864. Other Negroes from Illinois had enlisted in over 22 separate national military units also, and these too were eventually credited to the Illinois quota.[8]

To the regret of most state officials, the draft was finally applied to most Illinois districts by the fall of 1864. By the following March conscription was in motion in all but a few scattered areas — this despite the great resistance given to drafting officers everywhere. Especially was the latter true in southern Illinois, where not a few of these officials were caught by mobs and whipped. Yet despite the great turmoil over the draft, figures show that the need for conscription in Illinois was slight. Only 3,538 men were placed in uniform by this process, and only 55 individuals in the state paid the $300 commutation fee to avoid military service.

The few thousand men conscripted into the service seem rather insignificant when measured against the total military contribu-

[7] *Chicago Tribune*, Aug. 8, 25, Sept. 19, 1862. Leander Stillwell, *The Story of a Common Soldier of Army Life in the Civil War, 1861–1865* (2nd ed., Kansas City, Mo., 1920), 13.

[8] *Quincy* (Ill.) *Herald*, Dec. 8, 1863, Jan. 28, 1864. *Chicago Tribune*, Dec. 10, 1863. George W. Williams, *A History of the Negro Troops in the War of the Rebellion, 1861–1865* (New York, 1888), 133.

tion of 259,092 men. Of this latter number, 255,057 were white troops who served in 150 regiments of infantry, 17 regiments of cavalry, 2 regiments of light artillery, 8 independent batteries of artillery, and several small special units. Of the remaining number, 2,224 served as sailors or marines, and 1,811 were enlisted in the aforementioned various colored regiments.

There are other facts which tell the story of the Illinois contribution to the war effort. The state followed only New York, Pennsylvania, and Ohio in total enlistments and, fortunately for the Union, gave its men when they were most needed. By October, 1861, for example, Illinois had more regiments in the field than New York, despite the vast population advantage of the latter state. There were many who even argued that the draft should never have been applied to Illinois, and that poor enrollment and errors in tabulations caused the state to be taxed in manpower beyond what was required.

Some counties in the state exceeded in providing soldiers for the cause. One authority has stated that Massac County enlisted five-sixths of its entire voting population, and that some counties in "little Egypt" oversubscribed their quotas by nearly 50 per cent. Henderson County, a little section of land wedged against the Mississippi River in western Illinois, reported a population of 9,499 in the census of 1850; yet it supplied 1,157 men to the Union army.[9]

The meeting of the War Department quotas for troops was only one problem faced by Governor Yates in raising and equipping the regiments.The numerous soldiers required housing and training before being sent to the front. In the matter of accommodations, the larger cities within the state offered the best possibilities. In the early days of the war, for instance, Chicago was able to house several regiments at a time within the spacious confines of the "Wigwam," the convention hall in which Lincoln was nomi-

---

[9] William F. Fox, *Regimental Losses in the American Civil War* (Albany, N.Y., 1889), 532. U.S. War Department, *The War of the Rebellion: A Compilation of the Official Records of the Union and Confederate Armies*, prepared under the direction of the Secretary of War, by Bvt. Lt. Col. Robert N. Scott, Third U.S. Artillery (70 vols., Washington, D.C., 1880–1901), Ser. III, Vol. IV, 1264–70. (These records are hereinafter referred to as *Official Records.*) Arthur Charles Cole, *The Era of the Civil War, 1848–1870*, Vol. III of *The Centennial History of Illinois*, ed. Clarence W. Alvord (5 vols., Springfield, 1919), 274–275.

nated by his party in 1860. Other Chicago regiments were briefly housed in these early months in such outdoor locations as Camp Long, Camp Blum, and Camp Mather.

There was another Camp Mather at the fairgrounds in Peoria, where the old agricultural and cattle display buildings were cleaned up for the new recruits. Springfield was able to provide a fairgrounds location known as Camp Yates as a troop rendezvous. Though Camp Yates was far from being an ideal spot for the housing of soldiers, it was a virtual paradise by comparison to another campsite located in a nearby brickyard and called Camp Taylor. Other establishments were quickly set up in such larger towns as Quincy, Carrollton, and Aurora. All, like Camp Taylor, were products of expediency, and barely suited for continued use as troop locations.[10]

As the years of the war rolled on, the principal places for the mustering of Illinois regiments became Camp Douglas in Chicago and Camp Butler in Springfield. The former, located near the grave of the statesman from whom it took its name, eventually grew into one of the larger military establishments in the North. By the end of the war it had close to 158 buildings, each of them capable of housing 150 men. Not only was it able to provide for many newly organized Federal regiments, but in time it became one of the largest prisoner-of-war camps in the Union.

While Camp Douglas would have a reputation which was better than average among most Federal soldiers, Camp Butler would rank close to the bottom of any list. Here the barracks were poorly kept and were generally vermin-ridden. New troops required days in order to clean their new quarters for use. There was such a transient military population within its log stockades that thievery both inside and out of the camp was notable. One soldier, a member of the 124th Illinois, wrote home that since corn shucks provided the best contents for mattresses, most of the farmers in the area were destitute because of nocturnal attention given by soldiers to their fields. Other soldiers located in Springfield at vari-

[10] *Chicago Times*, June 26, 1861. George Paddock, "The Beginnings of an Illinois Volunteer Regiment in 1861," in *Military Essays and Recollections: Papers Read Before the Commandery of the State of Illinois, Military Order of the Loyal Legion of the United States* (4 vols., Chicago, 1894), II, 258. (This collection is hereinafter referred to as *Military Essays and Recollections.*)

ous times during the war wrote of a different kind of depredation — the high prices charged by Springfield merchants for food and clothing.[11]

The composition of the various regiments which passed through camps Butler and Douglas varied in accordance with the areas of the state from which the men were recruited, and the officers authorized to do the recruiting. There were a number of German regiments, for instance, including the 24th or "Hecker Regiment" and the 43rd or "Koerner Regiment." Other Germans composed individual companies within various regiments, and many Illinois Germans offered their services to specific German regiments organized in Missouri. It was estimated that in the first six months of the war there were over 6,000 Germans from Illinois in the entire Union army.

Other Illinois regiments were also organized by nationality or profession. Scots joined the 12th and 65th regiments, known respectively as the "First Scotch" and the "Second Scotch." Irish volunteers rushed to fill such regiments as the 23rd, which was organized by Colonel James A. Mulligan, and the 19th, which was organized by Colonel John Basil Turchin. While Mulligan was Irish, Turchin was not — a fact which did not deter immigrants from the Emerald Isle from entering the 19th Illinois.

The 45th Illinois, which eventually became one of the excellent regiments in Grant's Army of the Tennessee, was composed of lead miners from Galena and was known as the "Lead Mine Regiment." The 34th, organized originally by farmers in the Dixon area, called itself the "Rock River Rifles," an interesting and attractive name for young recruits. The 73rd or "Persimmon Regiment" was gathered by a Methodist minister, James Jaquess, and contained so many men of the cloth that it was also referred to as the "Preacher's Regiment." There were so many Catholics and Lutherans who paradoxically volunteered for the 73rd that a "Second Preacher's Regiment" was authorized under the command of the Reverend Jesse Hale Moore. It is interesting to note that the

[11] Pvt. J. G. Given to his brother, Sept. 13, 1862, John G. Given Papers, ISHL. Joseph L. Eisendrath, Jr., "Chicago's Camp Douglas," *Journal of the Illinois State Historical Society*, LIII, No. 1 (Spring, 1960), 41–44. (This journal is hereinafter referred to as *Journal.*) [Lucien B. Crooker *et al.*], *The Story of the Fifty-fifth Regiment Illinois Volunteer Infantry* . . . (Clinton, Mass., 1887), 20–21.

latter regiment, the 115th, was once reprimanded and placed under arrest by its division commander on the charge of stealing, a condemnation which was lifted after the brilliant performance of the regiment at Chickamauga.

One of the more unusual regiments was the 33rd Illinois, a unit originally raised on the campus of the Illinois State Normal School near Bloomington. Though formed principally of college students, the average age of the soldiers of the 33rd was so low that one soldier would later recall that in his particular company there were only four who could truly qualify as men. The standard joke concerning the regiment was that the privates who were discharged from the unit due to mental incapacity were quite eligible to become officers in other regiments. There was more than a grain of truth in this; in one of the companies of the 33rd there were 13 college graduates – and they were all privates.[12]

Few of these new soldiers, even in the "Teacher's Regiment," had any real understanding of military behavior. As a member of the 10th Illinois was to describe it later, the imagination of the ordinary recruit was stocked with the feats of Napoleon and mental images of Santa Anna surrendering to the Texans. There were times in 1861 when early attempts at soldiering approached the ridiculous. An officer of the 14th Illinois, a regiment raised in Macoupin and Morgan counties, noted with some surprise that many of the officers of his unit wore the wrong insignia, and that some companies were drilled in the "goose step." Another veteran, a member of the 47th Illinois, would later recall that his early training at Camp Mather in Peoria was scarcely more than learning how to cook and to build tables. The occasional marching was done with hickory sticks rather than rifles, and even that was constantly interrupted by well-meaning women from nearby towns who deluged the troops with flags, Bibles, cakes, and thread.

Rudimentary forms of training could be observed in some of the regiments from the Chicago area. The influence of Elmer Ephraim Ellsworth, the organizer of the "Chicago Zouaves" who became an early war casualty, was felt throughout the area. Such

[12] J. H. Burnham, "The Thirty-third Regiment Illinois Infantry in the War Between the States," *Transactions of the Illinois State Historical Society for the Year 1912*, No. 17 (Springfield, 1914), 80–81. (These records are hereinafter referred to as *Transactions*.)

units as the 19th and 39th Illinois contained former subordinates of Ellsworth, and at the camps at which these regiments were quartered there could be heard the peculiar chant of the Zouave cadence: "One, two, three, four, five, six, seven—Tiger!" The tune to which these exercises were usually performed was "The Girl I Left Behind Me." [13]

Each regiment was faced with problems peculiar to its own organization. The medical examinations, which were given by barely trained frontier doctors, consisted of scarcely more than two or three taps on the chest. Since this routine was practiced on fully dressed recruits, it is true that a few women were actually mustered into the service with Illinois regiments. Mary Livermore, whose work with the U.S. Sanitary Commission in Chicago brought her into contact with Illinois soldiers, claimed that a surprising number of women passed as soldiers during the war. Miss Livermore later claimed that she personally discovered such a case in the 19th Illinois, one of the toughest and best disciplined Chicago regiments. In another instance, Albert D. J. Cashier, who served in the 95th Illinois and who participated in the battles of Brice's Crossroads, Spring Hill, and Franklin, was found to be a woman—but only on her deathbed, long after the war had ended. Cashier was revealed to have been a Miss Jennie Hodgers, a girl who had emigrated from Ireland prior to the conflict.[14]

In a real sense, the introduction of each regiment to military life depended upon those called to lead it. Throughout the war, the colonel of each new regiment was that individual who had been authorized to raise it. At the beginning of the struggle, lesser commissioned officers were most often chosen by balloting in each company, or by the colonel himself. Noncommissioned officers also were almost always chosen by election. Commissioned or noncommissioned, soldiers elected for these positions were often individuals who had experience in either the Mexican or Black Hawk wars.

[13] Matthew H. Jamison, *Recollections of Pioneer and Army Life* (Kansas City, Kan., 1911), 150. "The Diary of Colonel William Camm, 1861 to 1865," ed. Fritz Haskell, *Journal*, XVIII, Pt. 2, No. 4 (January, 1926), 802.

[14] Gerhard Clausius, "The Little Soldier of the 95th: Albert D. J. Cashier," *ibid.*, LI, No. 4 (Winter, 1958). Mary Livermore, *My Story of the War: A Woman's Narrative of Four Years Personal Experience* (Hartford, Conn., 1889), 114–115.

The great difficulty with such experience, however, was that what had happened 20 or 30 years previously was of no real practical benefit in 1861. Private Leander Stillwell, an Otterville soldier of the 61st Illinois, remembered one so-called veteran officer who was not only illiterate, but whose command for a left or right wheel, a fundamental military maneuver of the time, was: "Swing around, boys, just like a gate." Another Illinois soldier, writing in 1861 about his superior, commented: "The Major . . . has drilled us but once since having command and has made somewhat of a failure. He sits a horse about as gracefully as a sack of flour, but after all I think he will do better than some expect. He has good sense even if it is tinctured with Mexico." [15]

The backgrounds of the various colonels authorized to raise regiments differed greatly. Some were men like David Stuart, the colonel of the 55th Illinois, who had been involved in personal scandal in Chicago and who wished to recoup his political fortunes with a good military record. Stuart, like many officers with political aims, knew a minimum of drill technique and considered any study of tactics as beneath his character. While Stuart was one political colonel who was never to overcome his deficiencies in this respect, there were others who did. John A. Logan, a southern Illinois Democratic politician, not only compiled a brilliant war record, but looked the part of a military leader as well. One may be impressed with the comment of one Confederate soldier after seeing Logan for the first time. "Don't he look savage!" the young southerner whispered.[16]

Whether inspired by political motives or others of a different nature, many of the younger regimental officers were exceedingly ambitious – a fault which caused many of them to obtain commands far beyond their basic courage and ability. Colonel Michael Lawler, the commanding officer of the brawling 18th Illinois, complained in September, 1861, that five of his younger officers were virtually worthless.[17] In another instance, a young ser-

---

[15] Stillwell, *Story of a Common Soldier,* 12. Samuel West to P. S. Post, April 4, 1862, Philip Sidney Post Papers, ISHL.

[16] [Crooker *et al.*], 22. Edmund Newsome, *Experience in the War of the Great Rebellion by a Soldier of the 81st Regiment Illinois Volunteer Infantry* . . . (Carbondale, Ill., 1880), 79.

[17] Lawler to McClernand, Sept. 7, 1861, McClernand Collection.

geant of the 95th Illinois wrote: "Old Tom (gd Dn him) is so afraid that he will fail in obtaining Stars that he would willingly Sacrifice every man in the *Brig*, if he had the honor to obtain that one thing . . . a *Star*." Sometimes such ambition seemed to have an infectious quality. An officer of the 94th Illinois, who based his hopes for promotion on a personal association with President Lincoln, wrote: "I have already been attacked by a serious camp disease: viz. a desire for promotion and I have laid the plans to obtain a Brigadier General's commission: how well my plans may succeed I cannot guess."[18]

It required little time for a soldier to perceive the inadequacies of a superior officer. In many cases the very qualities which had brought about an officer's election served him poorly in his command. A soldier of the 118th Illinois, for instance, described his ebullient young captain as "so young and boyish he does not command much respect from the company." A private of the 86th Illinois, in describing the same problem, wrote his father: "The officers of our regt are nearly all green, just from the prairie plow. . . ." The regimental bugler of the 7th Illinois deprecated his immediate superior officer as proficient only in "horse stealing and horse racing."

Not infrequently did such inexperience on the part of officers lead to insubordination on the part of their men. During a river expedition in 1862, the private soldiers of the 20th Illinois became so angry at their own constant exposure to the elements that they rousted the regimental colonel from his warm bed and threatened to throw him overboard. Such behavior shocked visitors from eastern armies, but it served a purpose in the West. In time many of these incompetent commanders resigned their commissions and went home, leaving the field to more able men.[19]

Illinois furnished 53 brigadier generals during the war, nine of whom were raised to major general rank, and one to lieutenant

---

[18] *The Civil War Letters of Sergeant Onley Andrus*, ed. Fred Shannon (Urbana, Ill., 1947), 71. W. W. Orme to his wife, Sept. 5, 1862, William Ward Orme Papers, ISHL.

[19] Samuel Gordon to his wife, Sept. 16, 1862, Samuel Gordon Papers, ISHL. L. A. Ross to his father, Sept. 26, 1862, Levi Adolphus Ross Papers, ISHL. Givler, 117. Ira Blanchard, "Recollections of Civil War Service with the 20th Illinois Infantry" (unpublished typed manuscript, ISHL), 25.

general. Beyond these, there was a whole host of brevet brigadiers. Among the fully commissioned general officers from northern Illinois were such men as U. S. Grant, John E. Smith, Jasper A. Maltby, Augustus Chetlain, John M. Schofield, Stephen A. Hurlbut, Thomas Lawler, John Franklin Farnsworth, John McArthur, John A. Rawlins, John Basil Turchin, Napoleon Bonaparte Buford, W. H. L. Wallace, and James A. Mulligan. Southern Illinois generals included John A. Logan, John A. McClernand, Richard Oglesby, John M. Palmer, John Pope, Wesley Merritt, Benjamin Prentiss, Benjamin H. Grierson, Giles A. Smith, Isham N. Haynie, Michael Lawler, and James H. Wilson.

The first list of general officers from Illinois was based upon both political and military considerations. Names were presented to a caucus of Illinois politicians in Washington in July, 1861, and after some deliberation the group decided to support commissions for Ben Prentiss, Stephen A. Hurlbut, Eleazer Paine, John Palmer, John McClernand, Grant, and W. H. L. Wallace. Only four of these names were immediately accepted by the administration, and the dates for these commissions were set back to the preceding May.[20]

Of the first four appointments, only Grant had experience of significance, having fought with distinction in the Mexican War. Prentiss had flirted with military experience in the same conflict, and Hurlbut's experience went back to the Seminole War. Though McClernand saw some service in the Black Hawk War, his appointment was based purely upon his important influence in southern Illinois, a section of the state with questionable loyalty in 1861.

All through the early months of the conflict, leading politicians of Illinois had received disturbing information about disunionist sentiment in the Marion and Carbondale areas, a condition which prompted a Dongola resident to warn Senator Lyman Trumbull that the "state of the people here is very unfavorable." Two downstate newspapers, the *Jonesboro Gazette* and the *Cairo City Gazette*, were indeed openly secessionist. Thus was McClernand's appointment an appropriate one. Soon he was back in Illinois,

[20] Smith Atkins, "The Patriotism of Northern Illinois," *Transactions, 1911*, No. 16 (1913), 82–83. Bluford Wilson, "Southern Illinois and the Civil War," *ibid.*, 103. Wilson claims John Rawlins as a southern Illinois general.

heeding Lincoln's admonition to "keep Egypt right side up," and encouraging the formation of an "Egyptian Brigade." [21]

Despite McClernand's important effect upon southern Illinois, there was one Confederate company, consisting of about 45 men, which enlisted in 1861. Late in May the company crossed the Ohio to Paducah, Kentucky, where it was presented with a Confederate flag. Mustered into the 15th Tennessee as part of Company G, it suffered heavy casualties in fighting at Belmont, Chickamauga, Missionary Ridge, and the Atlanta campaign. By late 1864, however, most of the men had returned home, and at the end of October there were only one sergeant and one private present for duty.[22]

Most of the southern Illinois problem was solved earlier, however, due to quick action by Governor Yates. Warned by the War Department of the strategic importance of Cairo, he forwarded 595 men from various local militia units to the junction of the Ohio and Mississippi rivers. Shortly thereafter General Prentiss arrived in Cairo with more troops, and was soon able to announce that he would hold the city until "hell freezes over." Such quick action coagulated the loyalty of most southern Illinoisans. As one farmer of the area expressed it: "I tell you what it is, them brass missionaries has converted a heap of folks that was on the anxious seat." [23]

By September such Illinois regiments as the 9th, 30th, and Logan's 31st were in Cairo proper. The Illinois 12th was encamped on the Kentucky side of the Ohio, and the 11th, 22nd, 24th, and 41st Illinois were well situated across the Mississippi at Bird's Point, Missouri. Troops were also stationed along most railroads which ran through that part of the state, particularly in the area of the Ohio and Mississippi Railroad east of St. Louis. By November other regiments were in Missouri—the 7th under Colonel

[21] *Jonesboro* (Ill.) *Weekly Gazette*, April 27, May 26, 1861. Adam Earhart to Yates, Aug. 12, 1861, Yates Papers. Henry Clay Whitney, *Life on the Circuit with Lincoln* (Caldwell, Idaho, 1940), 372.

[22] Richard P. Weinert, "The Little Known Story of: The Illinois Confederates; They Lived in the North but Fought for the South," *Civil War Times Illustrated*, I, No. 6 (October, 1862), 44–45.

[23] Alexander Davidson and Bernard Stuvé, *A Complete History of Illinois from 1673 to 1884* (Springfield, 1884), 734–735. Thomas Mears Eddy, *The Patriotism of Illinois* (2 vols., Chicago, 1865–66), I, 100.

John Cook, the 23rd or "Irish Brigade" under Colonel James A. Mulligan, the 33rd under Colonel C. E. Hovey, and the 36th under Colonel Nicholas Greusel. One must also add the 9th Missouri, soon to be renamed the 59th Illinois and to be placed under the command of Colonel Philip Sidney Post. Post, Greusel, and Mulligan were all to become significant in the next few years.[24]

Virtually every one of the new regiments, despite their proximity to combat, faced an early shortage in the supply of adequate firearms. The original supply of guns located in Illinois armories, which included a few old muskets, rifles, and musketoons, was insufficient in quality as well as quantity. The situation was somewhat relieved in late spring, when Chicago merchants cleared their shelves of firearms, and Captain James Stokes of Chicago rescued 10,000 weapons in a daring night raid on the St. Louis Arsenal. The latter equipment was at one time in actual danger of seizure by pro-Confederate mobs which roamed the streets of that city.[25]

Shortly after his arrival in St. Louis, General John C. Frémont, Commander of the Western Department, purchased a large number of ancient European firearms as well as a quantity of Harper's Ferry muskets. The former were in extremely bad shape, and many were of such an exotic nature that many Illinois troops could not divine their origin. Soldiers of the 78th Illinois, for instance, wrote of acquiring "Mexican" guns with such a large bore that privates of the regiment called them "Bennisons," after the disliked colonel of the unit. The 33rd Illinois found that its Austrian muskets would often fire when held at parade rest; and the 55th Illinois, a high-spirited regiment, threatened a march on Springfield after a number of men in that outfit suffered wounds from unreliable guns. Still, there were other more fortunate regiments which, having politically apt colonels, were able to acquire light and accurate Springfields or good British Enfields.[26]

---

[24] Davidson and Stuvé, 746–756.

[25] Grant to Gen. Henry W. Halleck, Nov. 21, 1861, *Official Records*, Ser. I, Vol. VII, 442. Davidson and Stuvé, 743.

[26] Diary of John Batchelor, ISHL, 2. *Report of Proceedings of the Reunion of the 33rd Regiment* (Bloomington, Ill., 1875), 10–11.

In late summer of 1861, Governor Yates made several trips to New York and Washington in search of arms and equipment, and in July he obtained a promise of 7,000 new guns, plus battery and field pieces. Three months later he persuaded the federal government to forward 6,000 rifled muskets, 500 rifles, 14 batteries of artillery, and 84 pieces of James' rifled cannon. All of these, plus some large Columbiads and 10-inch mortars, not only served to afford protection for Cairo but allowed for an aggressive extension of the war.[27]

In order to carry the war to the enemy, Kentucky and Missouri needed to be occupied. With regard to the latter state, it may be stated that Missouri was never completely assured for the Union, and that the war in that area developed a character all its own. The terrain particularly called for considerable marching and countermarching in 1861, and though the early battles were small, they were savagely fought.

Confederate guerrillas presented a constant danger everywhere, for the "bushwhackers," as Illinois soldiers called them, were apt with rifles at long range. Horses frequently returned from cavalry patrols with blood-stained saddles, their riders ambushed by the enemy. In January, 1862, when Bird's Point was almost overrun with Illinois regiments, four pickets were shot within sight of the regimental camps. This action, plus other incidents, forced General Grant to clear all nonmilitary personnel from within six miles of the Bird's Point headquarters.[28]

The guerrilla warfare in Missouri did force Illinois troops to harden to the service, however. Any patrol, on horse or foot, was likely to be attacked. Lieutenant C. E. Lippincott of the 33rd Illinois experienced one such incident, when, during a melee with a number of Confederates, he punched his sword between the ribs of an enemy officer. The enemy soldier, still alive, cried: "Shoot the damned Yankee!" "Born in Egypt," Lippincott wrote, "I could not stand the insult – so I wheeled and dropped one

[27] *Chicago Tribune*, July 26, Oct. 19, June 7, 1861.

[28] *Army Life of an Illinois Soldier, Including a Day by Day Record of Sherman's March to the Sea; Letters and Diary of the Late Charles W. Wills* . . . comp. and pub. by his sister [Mary E. Kellogg] (Washington, D.C., 1906), 36–40. "Memoirs of Lemuel Adams" (unpublished typed manuscript, ISHL), 37. Grant to E. A. Paine, *Official Records*, Ser. I, Vol. VIII, 494–495.

bullet from his own pistol — just under his shoulder blade." [29] Lippincott had indeed come a long way from his classroom at the Illinois State Normal School.

In the years following the war, it was the marching which veteran soldiers remembered most about Missouri. "There were just enough rebels lying around to make things a little spicy," recalled one soldier. "The entire campaign in northern Missouri was war in poetry and song, and set to music." A member of the 9th Missouri, later the 59th Illinois, would remember that Missouri gave most Illinois soldiers the idea that the "rebellion was a bladder, the war a bottle of smoke, and that both . . . were about to collapse." Another soldier, Private Payson Z. Shumway of the 14th Illinois, wrote home to Taylorville in November, 1861, that he was sick of marching; that his regiment, which had left Rolla just a few days before, had marched 350 miles, only to find itself 100 miles from the point of departure.[30]

Other Illinois soldiers registered the same complaint. The bugler of the 7th Illinois wrote that he had joined the army in order to teach the enemy that "the way of the transgressor is hard," only to find that life had been harder upon the teacher. Private Edward H. Ingraham of the 33rd Illinois wrote his relatives in May, 1862, that he was almost "gin out"; yet he concluded: "Who would not be a soldier!" Lyman K. Needham, a soldier of the 42nd Illinois, complained that he would "rather be shot and done with it, than to kill myself carrying so much." [31] But the marching produced lessons and experience which would serve in good stead in years to come. The young Illinois recruit soon learned that one only carried the essentials, and that all of these could be wrapped in a blanket and slung about the shoulders. It wasn't exactly old army, but after all this wasn't an old-style war.

The ordinary soldier could adapt his dress and marching ca-

---

[29] Lippincott to Newton Bateman, Oct. 19, 1861, Newton Bateman Papers, ISHL.

[30] Oliver W. Nixon, "Reminiscences of the First Year of the War in Missouri," in *Military Essays and Recollections*, III (1899), 427. George W. Herr, *Nine Campaigns in Nine States* (San Francisco, 1890), 444. Shumway to his parents, Nov. 8, 1861, Payson Z. Shumway Papers, ISHL.

[31] Givler, 76. Ingraham to his niece, May 12, 1862, Edward H. Ingraham Papers, ISHL. Needham to his brother-in-law Eli B. Gilbert, Oct. 20, 1861, Lyman K. Needham Papers, ISHL.

dence to the requirements of the Missouri countryside, but it was much more difficult to contend with officers who tried to live by the rulebook, or whose inexperience precluded common sense. The 33rd Illinois, for example, bivouacked in a deep Missouri ravine in the rainiest month of the year, awoke one night to find that its tents and equipment had been washed away in a cloudburst. Major John C. Black of the 37th Illinois wrote his father in September, 1861, that his own superior, his colonel, "might prove to be a soldier in peace, a citizen in war. . . ." A member of the 33rd Illinois would later describe General William P. Benton, his brigade commander during the Missouri campaigns, as a man lacking in fundamental requisites of leadership. Benton's marriage to a Missouri widow after a ten-day courtship, so said the veteran, was the "most courageous thing we ever knew him to do." [32]

The long marches, the logistical disorganization of the army in Missouri, and the inexperience of soldiery at all levels brought on an abnormal amount of sickness and death. Lingering coughs and diarrhea were the common complaints. One Illinois private, complaining that he did not want to die such an inglorious death, wrote: "We are so much fooled around with that not only myself but all our boys get disgusted with the war." A high-ranking Illinois officer wrote in October, 1861: "Our men lay sick by the hundreds, chiefly confined at the start by diarrhea and chills then through criminal neglect . . . they grow worse and worse. . . ." Still, as in all armies, there were occasional humorous situations. The troops of the 33rd Illinois, that self-styled community of scholars, laughed long at the reaction of one of their numbers trapped by guerrillas as he filled his canteen at a stream. "Please, gentlemen," the young private pleaded, "don't shoot, I'm not well." [33]

Amidst all of this complaining and illness, there were some small but savage battles in Missouri interspersed with numerous small skirmishes. The latter, called battles just after their occurrence, were rightfully regarded a year later as minor brushes with

[32] Virgil G. Way, *History of the Thirty-third Regiment Illinois Veteran Volunteer Infantry* . . . (Gibson City, Ill., 1902), 30, 32. Black to his father, Sept. 28, 1861, John C. Black Papers, ISHL.

[33] *Macomb* (Ill.) *Journal*, Jan. 31, 1862. Black to his father, Oct. 25, 1861, Black Papers. Way, 24.

the enemy – particularly after Donelson and Shiloh. Prior to the Confederate victory at Wilson's Creek on August 10, there was a rapid succession of these smaller clashes. On July 9–11 the 16th Illinois, under Colonel Robert F. Smith, drove in a number of Confederate guerrillas at Monroe Station. In August the 22nd Illinois, under Colonel Thomas E. G. Ransom, smashed a gathering Confederate force at Charleston. In this brief engagement Ransom demonstrated some of the characteristics which would gain him considerable fame in years to come.

Another sharp engagement took place on October 21, when the 11th Missouri, basically an Illinois regiment, and the 17th Illinois met a Confederate force at Fredericktown. As the troops on both sides prepared for battle, it appeared for a while that the engagement would be a major one. In the end, however, there was not much to it; just a brisk little affair after which the clever Jeff Thompson, commanding the enemy elements, disappeared into the underbrush from which he had come.

When conditions were right, fights which began as mere guerrilla clashes occasionally developed into full-fledged battles. In September the Confederate leader Sterling Price marched northward through Missouri toward Lexington, a wealthy shipping center on the Missouri River. Colonel James A. Mulligan, the commanding officer of the 23rd Illinois, the "Irish Brigade," was ordered out from Jefferson City to meet Price's challenge. Mulligan did not have much of an effective fighting force: the 2,800 men consisted of his own regiment and some Missouri Home Guards, whom Mulligan described as "in peace invincible; in war invisible."

Mulligan reached Lexington ahead of Price and built breastworks on the outskirts of town around the Masonic College. The Confederates laid siege, arriving September 12. On the morning of September 18, an extremely hot day, the actual battle began. Short of water but expecting help, the Federals gave a good account of themselves for several days. On September 20 Price's men opened an advance upon the Union trenches behind an ingeniously contrived line of wet hemp bales which the Confederates rolled ahead of their advance. His position now untenable, Mulligan had no choice but to surrender to an enemy force which outnumbered him three or four to one.

The defeat at Lexington did not mean the end of the war for the handsome Mulligan, who was only 32 years old. He was exchanged, helped to reorganize his regiment after its parole by the Confederacy, and in June, 1862, he was sent east with his unit to Virginia. From the time that it entered that area of conflict, the "Irish Brigade" was involved in a series of vicious battles, one of the worst of which occurred at Second Kernstown, Virginia, in July, 1864. Here the regiment lost half its number, and Mulligan himself, now commanding a division, was mortally wounded. It was part of his nature that in his battlefield agony, when his troops attempted to move him out of the line, he shouted: "Lay me down and save the flag!" His men obeyed, and he died in enemy hands.[34]

While Mulligan was futilely defending Lexington in northern Missouri, troops continued to pour into Cairo, where Grant was in command. On September 6, Grant, with the 9th and 12th Illinois, moved from Cairo to capture strategically important Paducah, Kentucky, without opposition. By the end of October Grant was able to account for five brigades, mostly soldiers from Illinois, totaling over 11,000 men. These five brigades were strategically placed about the area: McClernand's was at Cairo; Colonel Richard Oglesby's and Colonel W. H. L. Wallace's were at Bird's Point; Colonel Joseph B. Plummer's was located at Cape Girardeau; and Colonel John Cook's was camped at Fort Holt in Kentucky.[35]

On November 2 Grant received instructions from Frémont's headquarters that Jeff Thompson was again acting up in southeast Missouri, and that he was to assist other Union troops moving up from Pilot Knob in driving the enemy commander back into Arkansas. Grant moved immediately, ordering Oglesby up the west bank of the Mississippi with the 18th Illinois under Lawler, the 29th under James S. Reardon, four companies of the 11th Illinois, and his own regiment, the 8th Illinois.

On November 5 Grant again received instructions from department headquarters, these ordering him to demonstrate against

[34] Eddy, I, 171. Jay Monaghan, *Civil War on the Western Border, 1854–1865* (Boston, 1955), 185–192.

[35] Kenneth P. Williams, *Lincoln Finds a General: A Military Study of the Civil War* (4 vols., New York, 1949–56), III, 75.

Columbus, the Confederate stronghold on the Kentucky side of the Mississippi. Grant in turn requested that General Charles F. Smith, who commanded Union troops in the District of Western Kentucky, at Paducah, carry out the order. For his own part Grant sent Colonel Wallace to Oglesby with instructions for the latter to make a slight demonstration toward New Madrid, another Confederate strong point in Missouri. Cook was ordered in the direction of Columbus. Grant himself organized McClernand's brigade and two other regiments brigaded under Colonel Henry Dougherty for the purpose of making a feint against the Confederate camp at Belmont, Missouri, across the river from Columbus. All of this seemed intricate indeed, but the disposition of the Cairo troops resulted basically from two causes: Grant's concern over Oglesby's expedition, and a wish on his own part for some kind of military action against the enemy.[36]

McClernand's brigade, completely Illinois in character, consisted of the 27th under the command of the cocky and erudite Colonel Napoleon B. Buford; the 30th under Colonel Philip B. Fouke, soon to be elected congressman from Illinois; and the 31st, or, as its redoubtable Colonel John A. Logan called it, the "dirty-first." Dougherty's brigade, as the casualty lists for the battle at Belmont later showed, carried the brunt of the fighting. It was composed of his own regiment, the 22nd from southwestern Illinois, and a hard-fighting Iowa regiment, the 7th. All in all, the force, which also included two companies of cavalry and a six-gun battery, totaled 3,114 men.[37]

The troops were loaded upon four transports at Cairo, the finest of which carried the name of *Belle Memphis*. As the afternoon of November 6 waned, the steamers moved nine miles below Cairo and nudged their bows against the Kentucky shore for the night. Early on November 7 Grant received a message from Wallace which indicated that the enemy had been moving troops from the Kentucky to the Missouri shore in an attempt to trap Oglesby's probe into Missouri.

Grant's decision was in keeping with his character. He would

---

[36] *Official Records*, Ser. I, Vol. III, 267–268, 269, 273.

[37] *Ibid.*, 268–270. Richard L. Howard, *History of the 124th Regiment Illinois Infantry Volunteers, Otherwise Known as the "Hundred and Two Dozen"* . . . (Springfield, 1880), 66.

strike hard at Belmont in the hope of saving Oglesby rather than carry out a demonstration. Grant's night was a sleepless one, and his troops were nervous and apprehensive. One soldier, Private Trueman of the 27th Illinois, felt "dark forebodings" about the coming day, and as he observed the rising morning sun, it seemed to be bathed in blood.[38]

By nine o'clock on the morning of November 7, the Union troops were ashore three miles above Belmont, ready to march on the Confederate camp. Leaving five companies in reserve near the landing, Grant led the remainder in the direction of the enemy tents. For all but a very few, this was the first of many battles the soldiers would endure. For most it was the culmination of all of the military romanticism they had ever known. Raised upon the legend of Napoleon and the glories of the Mexican War, they now faced real combat. One of them, a captain of the 22nd Illinois, overcome by it all, called his men together and said: "I wish to remind you of the fact that Illinois troops became famous in the war with Mexico, and that today the eyes of Illinois are upon us and we must . . . preserve the escutcheon unsullied." All of this glory for such an unpretentious little spot—a cluster of three houses set in a clearing, and surrounded by tanglewood and canebrake.[39]

McClernand's three regiments took the lead in the advance on Belmont. The 31st, Logan's southern Illinois men, suffering terribly from the lowland humidity, threw off their overcoats, an action followed by each regiment in line. When the clearing was finally reached, the Confederates were already in line of battle, their leader, Gideon Pillow, exhorting them to stand fast. McClernand still in the lead, the Union soldiers filed across the field, the 27th Illinois on the far right, the 31st to its left and slightly out of line, and the 30th holding the left wing of brigade formation. Dougherty's brigade, the 22nd Illinois and the 7th Iowa, was still farther to the left in line of battle.

There was some delay as Logan refused momentarily to get into

[38] *Official Records,* Ser. I, Vol. III, 269. Trueman to Elizabeth Simpson, Nov. 11, 1861, Elizabeth Simpson Papers, ISHL.

[39] John Seaton, "The Battle of Belmont," in *War Talks in Kansas: A Series of Papers Read Before the Kansas Commandery of the Military Order of the Loyal Legion of the United States* (Kansas City, Mo., 1906), 306–316.

proper alignment. "I don't care a d——m where I am," replied the swarthy colonel from Carbondale, "so long as I get into this fight!" Soon, however, Grant gave the order to advance. "In this charge," wrote Logan, "I saw General McClernand, with hat in hand, leading as gallant a charge as ever was made by any troops unskilled in the arts of war."[40]

Thus did the battle develop in the simplest possible form; two forces equal in number encountered in parallel lines. Firing quickly grew intense, and it soon appeared obvious that sheer nerve alone would determine the victor.

For all of its simplicity, however, it was a brutal affair. "This kind of warfare is not the kind for me," a soldier of the 27th Illinois would write after the battle. Casualties among officers were particularly heavy. Captain Alexander Bielaski, a Pole who was a member of McClernand's staff, fell dead in the first charge. When another member in McClernand's entourage fell wounded from his horse, McClernand's Negro servant, William Stains, placed the officer on his own horse and went off afoot to cheer the Illinois boys on.[41]

Eventually the Confederate line cracked wide open, and with no reserves the enemy fled into the nearby woods. Now the Federal soldiers swept into the camps of the retreated, where fires still blazed under pans of frying bacon. The battle seemed to be over, and yet it was not. The civilian past caught up with officer and private alike. McClernand halted his men, theatrically mounted a captured cannon, and ordered them to give three cheers for the Union. Small but determined regimental bands broke out with the *Star Spangled Banner* and *Dixie*, and Union soldiers danced in gleeful abandon.

What the Federal troops did at Belmont was, for Grant, a lesson which he never forgot. The victory of those first hours almost turned to defeat, as the retreating Confederates halted and reformed. With fresh regiments sent over from Columbus, they now attempted to drive a wedge between the Union troops and

[40] Barbara Burr, "Letters from Two Wars," *Journal*, XXX, No. 1 (April, 1937), 151. George F. Dawson, *Life and Services of Gen. John A. Logan, as Soldier and Statesman* (Chicago, 1887), 19.

[41] L. P. Clover to McClernand, Nov. 8, 1861, McClernand Collection. *Chicago Tribune*, Nov. 13, 1861.

their boats. The try was narrowly unsuccessful, and Grant's regiments got aboard the steamers just ahead of the Confederate trap. One Illinois regiment, the 27th, which was commanded by Buford, did get cut off and followed a detour, to be taken on board farther upriver.[42]

The boisterousness of the early phase of the battle was nowhere present on the return to Cairo. Most of the men had lost their blankets and overcoats, and this, combined with powder-blackened faces, gave them a bedraggled appearance. The wounded whom the soldiers had managed to bring along lay moaning alongside the dead, who were covered with blankets. An officer of the 27th Illinois sat conspicuously alone on one of the boats, saddened by the knowledge that one of the Confederate dead found on the battlefield was his brother.

Losses, considering the brevity of the conflict, were heavy. The 7th Iowa, suffering the greatest, lost 119 men; the 22nd Illinois, the other regiment in Dougherty's brigade, lost 97. McClernand's brigade got off comparatively easy: the 27th Illinois lost 37, the 30th Illinois 15, and Logan's 31st 18. Total Federal losses were 80 killed and 322 wounded, plus some missing.[43]

The seven hospitals in the Cairo command were strained by the burden placed upon them by the unexpectedly high casualties. Fortunately, Dr. John Brinton, the chief surgeon of the district, had the assistance of a number of noble women from Illinois, certain members of the Sanitary Commission, and a group of Catholic nuns, the Sisters of the Holy Cross. It was during this episode that Mrs. Mary Bickerdyke gained an early reputation by working with the wounded returnees from Belmont. But there were others: Miss Mary Safford, a thin frail woman who could speak both German and French, and whose work eventually brought her to a nervous breakdown; and "Mother" Sturgis and "Aunt Lizzie" Aiken, both of whom had helped to form the Peoria Soldier's Aid Society, which later became the Women's National League.[44]

[42] Seaton, "The Battle of Belmont," 314–315.

[43] *Chicago Tribune*, Nov. 9, 1861. Fox, 358–362, 427.

[44] Mary Livermore, 218. "Memoirs of Lemuel Adams," 66–68, gives a good deal of credit to Mrs. Bickerdyke and Miss Safford. The reference to "Mother" Sturgis and "Aunt Lizzie" Aiken is found in Cloyd B. Bryner, *Bugle Echoes: The Story of the Illinois 47th Infantry* (Springfield, 1905), 11.

Belmont was, at one and the same time, a sad and necessary experience for Illinois soldiers. The old myths about war quickly disappeared, particularly as they watched the dead being carried off the boats at Cairo. "As we looked upon their pale faces, their hands crossed in eternal protest . . . ," wrote one soldier, "treason and rebellion assumed their true significance." New confidence was gained by most of the new recruits, however. There were few cowards on the field, a fact attested to by one Illinois soldier who wrote home after the fight that "only one or two in our company . . . wanted courage." Furthermore, they had performed well against a numerically superior enemy on his own soil. The whole lesson was best expressed by a Confederate, who, when asked about his opinion of western Federal soldiers, replied: "We thought this morning, when you were approaching, that we never saw such big men in our lives before. You looked like *giants*!" [45]

Throughout Illinois, the immediate reaction to Belmont was a violent one. The *Chicago Tribune* editorialized that it had no heart to comment on the fight. The paper claimed that the losses suffered in the fight were solely the fault of the organizer of the expedition, presumably Grant. Furthermore, the *Tribune* claimed, spies infested the Union camps at Cairo, and the Confederates had full knowledge of the impending attack before it occurred—a ridiculous charge, since Grant had decided to attack at Belmont after leaving Cairo.

In Springfield, the *Illinois State Journal* was even more bitter, charging that it hoped that in future expeditions, the generals of the North would "have a more worthy object in mind than a bloody fight." As the days rolled by, however, the Springfield paper and others changed attitudes about the Belmont battle. McClernand's long congratulatory order to his brigade, three times longer than Grant's statement to his whole command, and written in highly stylistic prose, earned much press coverage and served greatly to turn reproach into praise.[46]

While the furor over Belmont and Lexington was gradually dying down, other developments of major importance were tak-

---

[45] Jamison, 167. Pvt. Trueman to Elizabeth Simpson, Nov. 11, 1861, Simpson Papers. Seaton, "The Battle of Belmont," 314–315.

[46] *Chicago Tribune*, Nov. 9, 1861. *Illinois State Journal*, Nov. 12, 1861.

ing place in the West. General Frémont, because of his own actions, and upon complaints including those of western governors and the advice of such generals as John Pope and Samuel Ryan Curtis, was removed by the administration, which then began a sweeping reorganization of the western command. The old Western Department was divided into the Department of Kansas and the Department of Missouri. The new Department of Missouri was placed under the command of a new face in the West, Major General Henry Wager Halleck.[47]

Halleck was an experienced military man who, through the publication of various military textbooks and a steadily growing legend, had acquired the reputation for undaunted wisdom, hence the title "old Brains." As time would show, Halleck was a man with some virtues and considerable faults, the most significant being a lack of understanding of the western soldier. One finds also an interesting story in the relationship of Halleck with Grant. Halleck was old army; he was quite aware that Grant drank, and consequently he sometimes did not seem to trust his subordinate's actions or intentions. Halleck had, in fact, a natural distrust for many people, including McClernand, whom he disliked intensely.

The appointment of Halleck did mark an important change in the tempo of military activity in the West. After Halleck's arrival in St. Louis, both Grant and McClernand urged a more aggressive campaign in Kentucky. Despite these urgings, little was done in that border state except for scattered actions. The 34th Illinois, for instance, marching to Munfordville, encountered and fought a company of German soldiers from Texas. It was, as noted by a soldier of the 34th, a bright little affair which "caused a good deal of excitement in the camp, and had a wholesome effect on all." [48]

Early in January, 1862, Halleck decided on stronger action. At the end of the first week of the new year, he forwarded instructions to Grant that an expedition be sent into the area of Ken-

---

[47] Curtis to Lincoln and Pope to Gen. David Hunter, Oct. 12, 1861, quoted in J. G. Nicolay and John Hay, *Abraham Lincoln: A History* (10 vols., New York, 1890), IV, 431–432.

[48] Edwin W. Payne, *History of the Thirty-fourth Regiment of Illinois Volunteer Infantry* (Clinton, Iowa, 1902), 11.

tucky between Columbus and the Tennessee River. Halleck further cautioned Grant to refrain from engaging in any big fight, since the expedition was merely a reconnaissance in force.

Having received his orders, Grant ordered McClernand to lead the movement into enemy territory, but Grant went with him. By January 10, McClernand's troops, mostly from Illinois, had crossed the Ohio to Fort Jefferson. From here they marched southward, hampered all the way by "General Weather," as McClernand termed the climatical conditions. Two days later the tired troops returned to Fort Jefferson, complaining mightily that McClernand had obviously "lost his bearings or got 'off base' in some way."[49]

What each of those Illinois soldiers did not know was that the march into Kentucky was only a sign of events to come. Mounting pressure from Washington and rising Confederate strength made a clash in the West inevitable. The marching war of 1861 and the first few days of 1862 were coming to a close. Now men of all ranks were about to experience something far worse than Belmont or Lexington in the way of horror and death. Before it would all end over three years later, Illinois would lose 34,834 young men through death on the field of battle, in prison camps, or from wounds, disease, or individual incidents. This number was about 16 per cent of the total force sent into the field by the state.[50] Bad times were indeed ahead.

---

[49] McClernand's Report, *Official Records*, Ser. I, Vol. VII, 68–71. Alexander Raffen to his family, Feb. 16, 1861, Alexander Raffen Papers, ISHL.

[50] Fox, 526.

CHAPTER II

The Blooding of the Armies

In the months of the war between the Union defeat at Bull Run in July, 1861, and the end of January, 1862, regiments raised in Illinois were forwarded to two principal areas. The most important was Cairo, where the bulk of Illinois troops were concentrated in order to defend that city and to carry out offensive movements into Missouri and Kentucky. Most of these regiments would later follow Grant to Vicksburg, and then Sherman to Atlanta and the sea. The other regiments, fewer in number, were sent into central and northern Missouri. They were to fight there until the enemy threat appeared to be erased. Following this, many were sent into Kentucky and Tennessee, where some became part of the Army of the Mississippi or the Army of the Ohio.

This was all in the making, however. The months before January, 1862, saw little but probing and searching by the Union armies of the West—with occasional and almost accidental fighting with the enemy. Now, at the end of January, the face of the future began to form. The Union forces in Missouri made preparations for a move against the Confederate army. At Cairo, the scouting expeditions into Kentucky and the Confederate buildup had convinced Grant and others of the need for vigorous action. Furthermore, western governors and western newspapers called for it. The desire for a movement against the principal Confederate forts of Henry on the Tennessee and Donelson on the Cumberland found further expression down through the various ranks of Illinois soldiers who waited at Cairo. "I am urging that as soon as we get a couple more Regts," wrote one Illinois officer stationed in that city, "we float up the Cumberland some night and take the 2 forts for breakfast." [1]

Grant, continuing to press Halleck for a decision on his plan for the taking of Fort Henry, wrote to the department commander: "With permission, I will take Fort Henry on the Tennessee, and establish and hold a large camp there." Knowing his superior and his tendency for procrastination only too well, Grant was aided by Andrew H. Foote, the ranking naval officer at Cairo, in pressure upon Halleck. Foote, not a man to phrase his message to allow for a qualified reply, wrote: "Have we the authority to move for that purpose when ready." [2]

In defense of Halleck, in command far away in St. Louis, one may write that he had his reasons for delaying his decision. This early in the war, when any military strike seemed to be a hazardous one, a move against Fort Henry appeared quite risky. Furthermore, who really knew how many troops the Confederacy had in west Tennessee, or how many enemy regiments were on the way? All of these factors had their impact upon Halleck's naturally cautious character. On January 30 he sent Grant what may have been one of the more important messages of the war. The commander at Cairo was ordered "to take and hold Fort Henry." Later, more explicit instructions were sent out from St. Louis. Grant was to use all of the troops available to prevent Fort Henry from possible reinforcement, and to forestall any Confederate movements from the Cumberland River to the east, or from the enemy stronghold at Columbus.[3] Two comparatively new individuals became important at this time. General Charles F. Smith was a tough, straight-backed old soldier who had taught Grant at West Point and whom, sadly for the Union, the fates would take out of the war just before the battle of Shiloh.[4] He was brought into the picture by Halleck's instructions to Grant for the utilization of all available troops in the area. The second, Lieutenant Colonel James B. McPherson, was Halleck's chief engineering officer, sent down to Cairo in order to lend any assistance Grant might need.

---

[1] John Wilcox to his wife, Jan. 27, 1862, John Wilcox Papers, ISHL.

[2] *Official Records,* Ser. I, Vol. VII, 121, 120.

[3] *Ibid.,* 121–122.

[4] Kenneth P. Williams, III, 194. *Official Records,* Ser. I, Vol. VII, 122.

This officer was a bright and handsome young man whose leadership qualities were soon recognized with a promotion to general rank. How far McPherson might have gone had he not been killed near Atlanta in 1864 is not difficult to imagine. He had a talent which even his enemies recognized.

As the twilight of February 3 wasted away in a cold drizzle and darkness, Foote's steamers were well on their way up the Tennessee River with Grant and his 23 regiments aboard. In the early dawn of the following day, McClernand, who was to lead the movement upon Fort Henry, placed his division ashore at Itra Landing, eight or nine miles below the enemy fort. It was a poor spot for disembarkation, and Grant ordered the troops reloaded. This time Grant chose the landing location, a spot only three miles below the Confederate stronghold.[5]

The plan for the expedition upon Fort Henry was simple. In order to prevent enemy reinforcement from the west, Smith, who commanded one division, occupied the river bank opposite the enemy at Fort Heiman. The two brigades of McClernand's division were to move inland from the landing to a position astride the Fort Donelson–Dover road. This was to prevent the enemy from making any attempt to aid the beleagured forts from the east. Troops moved ashore on February 4, and supplies and ordnance followed on the next day. While the officers and men struggled to land their equipment at the landing, which McClernand had hastily named "Camp Halleck," Grant, McClernand, and Smith met in council aboard the flagship of the small fleet, the *Cincinnati*.[6]

On February 6 McClernand deployed his two brigades under Oglesby and W. H. L. Wallace toward the Dover road. Most of the Confederate troops who had occupied Fort Henry were already fleeing down that very road, however, and only Colonel Lyle Dickey's 4th Illinois Cavalry managed to tag the enemy rear guard. While Dickey, who was Wallace's father-in-law, had part of his men press the opposition up the Dover road, there were happenings on the river near the fort. At 11:45 the Federal gunboats moved up and began a brisk bombardment of the Con-

[5] *Ibid.*, 126–130, 581.

[6] *Cincinnati Gazette*, quoted in *Fort Henry and Fort Donelson Campaigns, February, 1862: Source Book* (Fort Leavenworth, Kan., 1923), 49.

federate stronghold. Scarcely two hours later, the white flag of surrender could be seen floating above the fort. General Lloyd Tilghman formally surrendered to Flag Officer Foote. McClernand's regiments, which had been nearby, marched into Fort Henry without a struggle. McClernand, who had a penchant for naming establishments, wrote to Foote that he was taking the "liberty of giving the late Fort Henry the new and more appropriate name of Fort Foote." The Illinois general also sent another letter to President Lincoln. "My division was the first into the Fort," he claimed, "and was the only one that pursued the enemy." Forgetting to mention that Smith was across the river, and in no position to share the spoils of victory, he wrote: "Whether considered with reference to the spoils captured or military consequences this is perhaps the most complete victory achieved during the war." [7]

The news of the victory at Fort Henry finally gave the northern cause something to cheer about. The *Illinois State Journal*, back in Springfield, reported that the victory on the Tennessee caused congratulations to be "passed from hand to hand" along the streets of the city. The national flag was run up the flagstaffs of all public buildings in the Illinois capital, and, on the Friday night following the news of the capture of the fort, booming salutes were fired from the guns of the state arsenal. The *Cincinnati Gazette*, giving the national view of the turn of events, called for "three cheers, and another, and yet another, and one cheer more!" "The soldiers of the Union have won another victory," it proclaimed, "and an important rebel stronghold has fallen into our hands." [8]

Despite the fact that most of the instigation and much of the planning of the conquest of Fort Henry was Grant's work, there was some tendency on the part of certain northern newspapers to deprecate the work of that general. Some reporters seemed puzzled about the reason for the entire operation, and others conjectured over the escape of enemy troops from the fort. The *Boston Journal* treated Grant's role with some sarcasm, and the *St. Louis Democrat* blamed Grant for the successful retreat of Con-

[7] Manning F. Force, *From Fort Henry to Corinth* (New York, 1882), 30–32. *Official Records*, Ser. I, Vol. VII, 129–130. McClernand to Lincoln, Feb. 8, 1862, Abraham Lincoln Papers (microfilm), ISHL.

[8] *Illinois State Journal*, Feb. 15, 1862. *Cincinnati Gazette*, quoted in *Fort Henry and Fort Donelson Campaigns*, 47.

federate forces. The latter paper gave him no credit for the more positive results of the feat. "The general comment on the fight at this place," wrote the *Democrat* reporter, "is marked by much complaint of General Grant. . . . Gen. Grant, it is thought, is much to blame for his inadequate transportation." [9]

It seems obvious that the first open break between Grant and McClernand had occurred after the affair at Itra's Landing. General Lew Wallace joined Grant's forces near Fort Henry at this time, and observed a scene which indicated the nature of the break between the two men. Grant had called a meeting with McClernand, Smith, Wallace, and his own adjutant, John A. Rawlins. Wallace, arriving late aboard the gunboat *Blackhawk*, immediately sensed the coolness and lack of cordiality between the various commanders. Grant opened the meeting with a discussion of the problem at hand, the proposed reduction of Fort Donelson on the Cumberland River. "The question for consideration, gentlemen, is whether we shall march against Fort Donelson or wait for reinforcements," he stated. "I should like to have your views." Smith replied quickly, saying: "There is every reason why we should move without a loss of a day." Grant then turned to McClernand, apparently expecting the same kind of brief reply. Wallace's report of McClernand's reaction reads as follows: "General McClernand, taking the sign next, drew out a paper and read it. He, too, was in favor of going at once. It had been better for him, probably, had he rested with a word to that effect; as it was, he entered into details of performance; we should do this going and that when we were come." [10]

If Wallace is to be believed, Grant and Smith, particularly the latter, grew increasingly impatient. When McClernand finally reached the end of his statement, Grant summarily ended the meeting with the terse pronouncement: "Let us go, by all means;

[9] *Boston Journal*, quoted in *The Rebellion Record: A Diary of American Events*, ed. Frank Moore (11 vols., New York, 1861–68), IV, 75–76. *St. Louis Democrat*, quoted in *Fort Henry and Fort Donelson Campaigns*, 67.

[10] Lewis Wallace, *An Autobiography* (2 vols., New York, 1906), I, 376–377. Wallace gives the name of the vessel as the *Tigress*. See *Fort Henry and Fort Donelson Campaigns*, 176, for the correct location of the meeting. Robert R. McCormick, *U. S. Grant: The Great Soldier of America* (New York, 1934), 34, dates the Grant-McClernand rift from the Itra Landing incident. A study of McClernand to Lincoln, Jan. 28, 1862, Lincoln Papers, would indicate an earlier break.

the sooner the better." Grant reported to Halleck on February 6: "I shall take and destroy Fort Donelson on the 8th and return to Fort Henry."[11]

Grant did not get his troops on the road to Donelson until after that day due to the heavy rain and because gunboats had to go back down the Tennessee to the Ohio and then up the Cumberland. The Confederates took the delay in the Union advance as an opportunity to strengthen the garrison within the fort, while Grant continued to receive reinforcements from Halleck. By the time he was able to move, his army had increased to 27,000 men. These included McClernand's division with three brigades: the first, under Oglesby, included the 8th, 18th, 29th, and 31st – all Illinois regiments; the second, under W. H. L. Wallace, included the 11th, now led by Lieutenant Colonel Thomas E. G. Ransom, the 20th, the 45th, and the 48th Illinois infantry regiments; the third, smaller in size, included the 17th and 49th Illinois, and was commanded by Colonel William R. Morrison. Also attached to McClernand's division were the batteries of Adolph Schwartz, Jasper M. Dresser, Ezra Taylor, and Edward McAllister, plus Lyle Dickey's 4th Illinois Cavalry and four independent companies of cavalry.

A second division, commanded by Smith, also contained a number of Illinois troops. The first brigade was commanded by Colonel John McArthur, and included the 9th, 12th, and 41st Illinois. The third, with the 7th and 50th Illinois, and fourth brigades were made up mainly of Indiana, Missouri, and Iowa troops, and were commanded by Colonel John Cook and Colonel Jacob G. Lauman respectively. The regiments of the second brigade were left at Fort Henry under the command of Lew Wallace. This unit was later sent by water in the direction of Fort Donelson. Thus three Illinois regiments, the 46th, the 57th, and the 58th, did not have to make the overland march.[12]

The weather in the week prior to the investment of Fort Donelson was bitter cold – so bad, in fact, that Colonel W. H. L. Wallace pessimistically wrote his wife in Illinois: "We are having terrible weather – rain, snow and sleet – the whole country mud

[11] Wallace, *Autobiography*, I, 377–378. *Official Records*, Ser. I, Vol. VII, 124.

[12] Force, 38–44.

and slush — the woods impossible almost for horse — movements with artillery impossible." On February 12, the President's birthday, the weather turned unseasonably warm. Arising early, Grant sent Halleck a message which began: "We start this morning. . . ." McClernand's division, preceded by Dickey's cavalry, pushed off at eight o'clock. By noon the day had grown so warm that the road along the line of march was strewn with overcoats and blankets cast away by the sweating soldiers. The road undulated through the harsh countryside which surrounded the fort, and the dense underbrush, which appeared to be everywhere, seemed to stifle the movement of air. Still the troops moved on, and by late afternoon they had reached the vicinity of the enemy fortification.[13]

Fort Donelson was much more formidable than Fort Henry. The Cumberland, sufficient barrier in itself, flowed in front of the heavy water batteries on the north side. Here substantial armament was located — nine 32-pounder guns, a 10-inch Columbiad, a Columbiad which was bored and rifled as a 32-pounder, and two 32-pounder carronades. The guns, surrounded by sandbags, lay protected in embrasures. West of the batteries was a flooded backwater, impossible for an enemy to traverse. To the south in a semicircle were the rifle pits, lines of logs and ditches which moved around to the east of the sleepy Tennessee town of Dover. In front of the rifle pits, which were atop a graduated ascent, were felled trees, so situated as to give an added handicap to any attacking force. Aided by the swollen creeks which fed into the Cumberland on both sides, the area was indeed a defensible spot.[14]

Brigadier General Simon B. Buckner, a strong-minded and noble Kentuckian, commanded the right wing with six regiments of Confederates. Buckner's division was also supported by two batteries. Brigadier General Bushrod R. Johnson, from whom Illinois troops would hear a good deal more before the end of the war, commanded the Confederate left, which comprised regiments from seven southern states. Colonel Nathan B. Forrest, another

[13] Wallace to his wife, Feb. 8, 1862, Wallace-Dickey Papers, ISHL. *Official Records*, Ser. I, Vol. VII, 612. Lewis Wallace, "The Capture of Fort Donelson," in *Battles and Leaders of the Civil War*, ed. Larned G. Bradford (New York, 1956), 66.

[14] Wallace, "Capture of Fort Donelson," 63–64.

name to be reckoned with, held the Confederate far left in front of Dover with his cavalry. In command of all was a man not so much to be reckoned with — Brigadier General John B. Floyd, who had arrived on February 13. Floyd had been Secretary of War under President Buchanan, and as such had been charged with questionable contract dealings and with being pro-secessionist.[15]

At dawn on February 13, the Union troops were moving into position at Fort Donelson. If one is to believe Lew Wallace's recollections of that day, "Birge's Sharpshooters," an element of the 66th Illinois, were given a special assignment. Ordered to "hunt your holes, boys," they were sent out to pick off any unthinking Confederate soldier who might expose himself. Soon Smith's and McClernand's divisions began their movement, designed to bring them closer to the enemy barricade. The going was difficult for the troops of both commanders, but particularly for those of McClernand. The regiments of that division not only had to cross open ground under the fire of enemy batteries, but, as time would show, the distance over which they were dispersed was far too great. Spread out in a thin line south and east of Dover along the Wynn's Ferry road, past the intersecting Forge road, and with no reserves, they presented an inviting target for an enemy attack. McClernand immediately realized the possibilities which the situation presented, and made them known to Grant. Lew Wallace, with the Third Division, was then moved into the center of the Union line on February 14, thus allowing McClernand to move farther to the right. Furthermore, in order to protect an especially vulnerable place on the far right, Colonel John McArthur's command was placed on the right of McClernand on February 14. This brigade, consisting of three tough Illinois regiments, was a most fortunate choice. Beyond these, however, there were still no reserves; nothing to seal a break in the Union line, if such a development should occur.[16]

The night of February 13 brought an abrupt change in the weather. Snow, drifting in lightly from the west in the afternoon,

[15] *Fort Donelson National Military Park Pamphlet* (Washington, D.C., 1961).

[16] Wallace, "Capture of Fort Donelson," 67–68. George Hunt, "The Fort Donelson Campaign," in *Military Essays and Recollections,* IV (1907), 70.

now turned to a blizzard, and the temperature plunged well below freezing. On the right, where most of the Illinois troops were bivouacked, McClernand ordered that fires not burn during the night, an order which other generals along the line also issued. The blankets and overcoats lying useless along the Dover road were now sorely missed. Oglesby's men huddled together, nearly "torpid from the intense cold of the night." "All night long," that officer reported later, "we could hear them [the enemy] felling trees and using picks and shovels to strengthen their defences." Cold or not, Oglesby told his men: "We came here to take that fort, and we will take it." Down the line in Smith's division, men of the 7th Illinois found their ponchos so covered with ice that they could stand them on end. There could be no sleep for them either, so they ran and scuffled about the whole night. It now occurred to some that war "would not be a picnic."[17]

The cold was especially hard upon the wounded. Fighting along the line had been vicious that day, particularly in Morrison's brigade of McClernand's division. During the advance through the undergrowth the brigade ran head on into rifle pits which were manned by troops recently evacuated from Fort Henry. Spotting an enemy battery in an exposed position, Colonel William R. Morrison decided to take it. His own regiment, the 49th, along with Colonel Isham N. Haynie's 48th Illinois, led the attack. Racing to within 40 yards of the Confederate abatis, the Illinois soldiers met the concentrated fire of five enemy regiments. For 15 minutes they held on. Morrison fell wounded, and then the underbrush caught on fire. "It was not possible for brave men to endure more," Lew Wallace wrote later. They were not the only Illinois soldiers who met misfortune during the assaults on Donelson. Three unfortunate infantrymen of Oglesby's regiment, the 8th, confused by the fallen trees and underbrush before the rifle pits, rushed right through an embrasure and were killed.[18]

[17] *Official Records,* Ser. I, Vol. VII, 174. McClernand to Oglesby, Feb. 14, 1862, Richard J. Oglesby Papers, ISHL. Other sources indicate that no campfires were allowed. Oglesby Report, Feb. 20, 1862, Oglesby Papers. Givler, 13.

[18] Wallace, "Capture of Fort Donelson," 70–71. Junius H. Browne, *Four Years in Secessia: Adventures Within and Beyond the Union Lines* (Hartford, Conn., 1865), 74.

On February 14 Foote's gunboats appeared on the Cumberland below the fort. After discharging reinforcements for Grant's army in the morning, the boats moved upriver in order to engage the heavy batteries of the stronghold; they hoped to achieve the same kind of victory which had been accomplished earlier at Fort Henry. The *St. Louis*, the *Louisville*, the *Carondelet*, and the *Pittsburg*, all ironclads, quickly closed the distance to the enemy Columbiads. This time, however, the results were not so fortunate. Staying tenaciously at their guns, the Confederates blew away the pilot house of the *St. Louis*, and wrecked the steering mechanism of the *Louisville*. The *Pittsburg* and the *Carondelet* took a frightful beating. The Cumberland swept the boats downstream and helped prevent further damage to the Union fleet.[19]

The night of February 14 was bitter cold, and Union troops in the line which stretched in a long arc in front of the enemy rifle pits slept very little. Inside the fort important decisions were being made. Cognizant of the growing strength of the besieging force, the Confederate generals planned a counterattack on the following day. The attack, to be directed by General Gideon Pillow, would strike the Union right held by McClernand's thin line. The plan was to open the road, which ran through the camps of the 8th and the 18th Illinois, for an escape to Charlotte, Tennessee, and the South. Buckner's division, which would support the assault, was to fight the rear-guard action, should the movement be successful.

At exactly 5:45 Colonel William E. Baldwin's brigade of Mississippi troops filed out of the embrasures of the rifle pits in line of battle. The Illinois troops stood up immediately, and reached into their cartridge boxes to load for firing. Pillow's troops continued to pour out of their trenches, moving forward as quickly as they formed. Thus it was that the 26th Mississippi and the 26th Tennessee, aiming directly for the Forge road, came in contact with the 8th and 18th Illinois.[20]

Fighting spread quickly down the line. W. H. L. Wallace's brigade was hit viciously by a Confederate charge, which, when

---

[19] Force, 46. Ulysses S. Grant, *Personal Memoirs* (2 vols., New York, 1885–86), I, 302–303. *Official Records*, Ser. I, Vol. VII, 166.

[20] Oglesby Report, Feb. 20, 1862, Oglesby Papers. Wallace in "Capture of Fort Donelson" calls it the Gorge road. Force, 47–49.

repulsed, was followed quickly by another. This, too, was sent reeling. McArthur, on the far right, gave support to Oglesby and Wallace by throwing his brigade, led by the 9th Illinois, to the forefront. Soon his whole command was "hotly engaged."

The brunt of the Confederate attack fell upon Oglesby's men, who found difficulty in spotting the butternut uniforms in the thick underbrush. Slowly the Federal line began to give way. Buckner increased the pressure by throwing his regiments against Lew Wallace's brigade. By ten o'clock Oglesby's regiments were in a bad way. The cartridge boxes of the 8th and 18th Illinois, both regiments vital to the defense of the Forge road, were empty. Both Lawler, the commanding officer of the 18th, and his replacement were taken off the field wounded. Reluctantly, Oglesby gave the order to retire.[21]

Now it was Logan, with his 31st Illinois, who grimly held the hinge of the Union right near the Forge road. Soon Logan was wounded, however, and the regiment, also out of ammunition, gave way. The burden now fell upon the 11th Illinois, under Ransom. Coolly directing his troops, Ransom threw off the Confederate attacks, but it appeared to be too late. The Forge road was open; Floyd could now move his garrison into open country.

It was hardly possible for the Confederate forces to have picked a better time for their assault upon the Union right. After the failure of the gunboats on the previous day, Grant had left his command to consult with Foote, who had been wounded. On the morning of February 15, Union troops fought without their commander. One may suppose that it was because of the capacity of the western soldier to improvise in such an emergency that a catastrophic defeat was forestalled. McClernand courageously made decisions which carried with them a terrible responsibility. McArthur's early forward movement, done principally of his own volition, gave Oglesby a needed moment to prepare for the storm. Lew Wallace's decision to strip his own command to send reinforcements to the right wing was brave and vital. There was surprisingly little confusion. The 25th Kentucky, sent forward to relieve the staggering 8th Illinois, became flustered and fired into the ranks of the latter regiment, causing some casualties. This

[21] Oglesby Report, Feb. 20, 1862, Oglesby Papers. Wallace, "Capture of Fort Donelson," 73–77.

was understandable, in view of the dense underbrush through which the fighting took place. Even Oglesby, riding up and down his shattered line, became lost. By chance he blundered upon the regiments of McArthur's brigade on the far right. "Excuse me . . .," he shouted with needless courtesy, "I believe I am out of my brigade."[22]

For the first time, Illinois troops came against the real specter of war. Belmont had been child's play. Some of the men were not up to it at all, and fled to the rear claiming injury; others simply disappeared, not to report until days later. One officer of an Illinois regiment rode down the Union line in panic, shouting: "We are cut to pieces." Yet bravery was a commodity commonly found. Logan, fighting hard to hold his 31st in the line, was knocked from his horse by an enemy bullet. Picking himself up, with blood streaming from his left arm and thigh, he rallied his men to continue the fight. T. E. G. Ransom, handling Wallace's 11th Illinois, seemed to be everywhere; he was a man truly in his element. McClernand, who had also come to fight, courageously exposed himself to enemy fire in order to inspire his troops. After the war almost every man in his command remembered that general's role in the battle with great feeling. Lew Wallace recalled later that McClernand's eyes, because of the "snow light," took on a severe squint. Sitting far back in his saddle, wearing an abominable wool hat which was hooked up at one side, he presented a memorable picture.[23]

The ordinary private soldier took the brunt of the fighting, however. To stand in line against a surging enemy rush with an empty cartridge box required great courage. Private William H. Tebbetts of the 45th Illinois, holding the line along the Wynn's Ferry road, was later to describe some of the aspects of that day, writing: "I have seen trees a foot and a half through cut off entirely by the cannon balls and I have had balls strike the trees at full force not more than a foot from my head. . . ." Tebbetts con-

---

[22] *Ibid.* Hunt, "The Fort Donelson Campaign," 71.

[23] Horace Wardner, "Reminiscences of a Surgeon," *in Military Essays and Recollections*, III (1899), 181. Force, 53. Dawson, 22. W. H. L. Wallace to his wife, Feb. 7, 1862, Wallace-Dickey Papers. Wallace, *Autobiography*, I, 411.

cluded that "the Lord still has more work for me to do." Less than a month later, Tebbetts was killed at Shiloh.[24]

The forced retirement of the Union right wing gave the Confederate army its great chance to escape. Ransom's 11th Illinois, its colors tattered shreds on a shattered staff, was beginning to collapse under the weight of Pillow's attack. General Lew Wallace, in answer to urgent messages from McClernand, brought up his last remaining brigade at this point of the fight. That general later recalled meeting W. H. L. Wallace just as he retired with the remnants of his command. The colonel appeared "perfectly cool, and looked like a farmer from a hard day's plowing." Greetings were casually exchanged, after which General Wallace asked: "Are they pursuing you?" His subordinate replied in the affirmative, and indicated the closeness of the pursuit. "You will have about time to form line of battle right here," said the colonel. "Thank you," was the reply. "Good day." One might suspect that an Illinois officer had perfect justification for writing the following concerning Lew Wallace: "I dont think him much of a hand for words or jokes. Think there is blood in him. . . . I like his style except his profanity. He is prompt ready and exact-brief."[25]

Wallace's last brigade, under Colonel John M. Thayer, having, among other regiments, the 32nd and 58th Illinois, moved immediately to the forefront of the fight. Time was of the essence, and time was what Wallace's arrival gave to the hard-pressed Union right. W. H. L. Wallace and Oglesby reformed their men behind Thayer's brigade, replenished their cartridge boxes, and stood at rest awaiting their next command.

At this point, with the outcome still in the balance, General Grant returned to the field. Riding to where McClernand and Wallace were deep in conversation behind Thayer's brigade, he asked both subordinates for their estimates on the condition of the Union line. His face flushed with embarrassment at being absent from his command during a most crucial time, he reached a

[24] "The Story of an Ordinary Man," ed. Paul M. Angle, *Journal*, XXXIII, No. 2 (June, 1940), 232.

[25] Wallace, "Capture of Fort Donelson," 76. W. H. L. Wallace to his wife, Feb. 17, 1862, Wallace-Dickey Papers. Colonel Wallace wrote: "The colors of the 11th are riddled with shot and the staff was struck twice with bullets breaking off the spear at the top." John Wilcox to his wife, Jan. 30 Feb. 4, 1862, Wilcox Papers.

quick decision. "Gentlemen, the position on the right must be retaken," he ordered. If one is to believe both Grant and Wallace in their recollections of the incident, McClernand demurred, claiming that his troops were in no condition for another engagement. Grant insisted, however, and Federal troops moved to the offensive at that end of the line.[26] The Confederates, after some confusion, returned to their defensive position, having failed to break out.

Grant himself carried an order for Smith to make an assault on the Union left. That division, led by their general shouting "This way, boys; come on," hit the enemy hard. The 7th Illinois and 14th Iowa managed to climb over the escarpment and into the outer rim of rifle pits. When they got there, they found the redoubtable Smith already turning a captured cannon upon the retreating Confederates. When the dim winter twilight of the long day faded, the Union line was not only back to where it had been at dawn, but beyond it on the left. With Union troops now inside their barricades, the Confederate situation was desperate.[27]

The night of February 15 was fearful. The wounded lay throughout the battle area, their blood freezing them to the ground in the terrible cold. The Confederate command inside the fort came to some important decisions. It was Buckner's judgment that to continue the fight would be virtual suicide. Though Floyd and Pillow agreed, neither one wished to fall into Union hands. Leaving the command of the army with Buckner, Floyd marched most of his own brigade aboard two steamers which had just arrived and sailed away. Pillow managed to escape upon a flatboat. Forrest led his command through the icy backwater of a nearby creek. Only Buckner and Bushrod Johnson were left.[28]

On the following morning Buckner sent Grant a request for terms of surrender. Grant replied: "No terms except an unconditional surrender can be accepted. I propose to move immediately upon your works." These words thrilled the nation and Grant's name became a household word. For Buckner they offered no

---

[26] Wallace, "Capture of Fort Donelson," 77. Wallace, *Autobiography*, I, 411–412.

[27] Wilbur F. Crummer, *With Grant at Fort Donelson, Shiloh and Vicksburg and an Appreciation of General U. S. Grant* (Oak Park, Ill., 1915), 33.

[28] Wallace, "Capture of Fort Donelson," 80. Kenneth P. Williams, III, 255.

alternative; he surrendered. The Confederate general may have felt Grant's reply to be "ungenerous and unchivalrous," but it certainly was effective.[29]

Shortly after daybreak on February 16, as Union soldiers along the Wynn's Ferry road were beginning to warm their morning coffee, news of the enemy surrender passed along the line. To the left of McClernand's division, where the 45th Illinois was encamped, orderlies from the various headquarters rode pell-mell through the troops "swinging their caps and proclaiming the news. . . ." The North had won a battle. A soldier of the 45th wrote later: "Did we shout? Well, if we didn't use our lungs then we never did. Hip! Hip! Hurrah! from every man in blue." Not long afterward, the triumphant soldiers marched into the fort. "It was a grand sight," wrote an Illinois soldier, "as regiment after regiment poured in with their flags floating gayly in the wind, and the brass bands playing . . . in such style as the gazing captives had never heard in the palmy days of peace."

The defeated, numbering between 12,000 and 15,000 troops, did not seem to impress the victors as much now as they had in the previous days. "If they are the 'flower of the youth' of Miss.," wrote an Illinois officer, "I can hardly conjecture what the *leaves* must be. . . ." So overcome were the winners that they failed to notice Bushrod Johnson, who would later tear the lines of Illinois regiments to shreds at Chickamauga, calmly walking off the battlefield without so much as a salute from a sentry. The feat must have been as much a shock to Johnson as it was to the Federal forces.[30]

Besides the prisoners taken in the fort, Grant was able to report to Halleck that he had taken "20,000 stand of arms, 48 pieces of artillery, 17 heavy guns, from 2,000 to 4,000 horses, and large quantities of commissary stores." In exchange, the price had been high. The 11th Illinois, a northern Illinois regiment, lost 339 in killed, wounded, and missing. Oglesby's 8th, from eastern Illinois, lost 242. Lawler's 18th tabulated 228 casualties; the 9th, from southwestern Illinois, reported 210; and Logan's 31st had 176. An

---

[29] Grant to Buckner, Feb. 16, 1862, *Official Records*, Ser. I, Vol. VII, 161. Buckner to Grant, Feb. 16, 1862, quoted in Grant, I, 312.

[30] Crummer, 42–43. John Wilcox to his wife, Feb. 18, 1862, Wilcox Papers. Kenneth P. Williams, III, 258.

Iowa regiment suffered 197 casualties, the highest reported by a non-Illinois regiment.[31]

Sights about the battlefield on the day following the battle were grisly. Many of the wounded had to be chopped from the frozen ground. Mary Bickerdyke made five trips to the field in order to find wounded men. One night, shortly after the battle, an Illinois officer observed a flickering light moving about the field of conflict. An orderly, sent out to ascertain the cause of it, found Mrs. Bickerdyke, lantern in hand, moving slowly among the dead. "Stooping down, and turning their cold faces towards her," Mary Livermore was later to write, "she scrutinized them searchingly, uneasy lest some might be left to die uncared for."[32]

Mrs. Bickerdyke's experience must have been frightful. A month after the battle, James A. Connolly of Charleston, Illinois, visited the scene and described it as follows:

> A great many horses were lying on the field, just where they fell, scattered all over the field, singly, by twos, threes and fours. Frozen pools of blood were visible on every hand, and I picked up over twenty hats with bullet holes in them and pieces of skull, hair and blood sticking to them inside.
>
> The ground was strewn with hats, caps, coats, pants, canteens, cartridge boxes, bayonet scabbards, knapsacks, rebel haversacks, filled with biscuits of their own making . . . pieces of exploded shells, six and twelve-pound balls, and indeed all sorts of things that are found in the army. . . . You can form no conception of what a battlefield looks like. No pen and ink description can give you anything like a true idea of it. The dead were buried from two to two and a half feet deep; the rebels didn't bury that deep and some had their feet protruding from the graves.[33]

The Union victory at Donelson had an electrifying effect on the North. In Chicago, the bells were rung incessantly and cannon were fired until the city itself sounded like a battleground. Flags flew from almost every window, and men clapped each other on the back, embraced, wept, and shouted. Public schools displayed

[31] Grant's Report, *Official Records,* Ser. I, Vol. VII, 625. Also see *ibid.,* 171, 190–191. Fox, 509, 427. In *ibid.,* 36–37, it is claimed that the 11th Illinois suffered 50.1 per cent losses in killed, wounded, and missing in the battle of Fort Donelson.

[32] Crummer, 39. Mary Livermore, 484–487.

[33] James A. Connolly, "Major James Austin Connolly's Letters to His Wife, 1862–1865," *Transactions, 1928,* No. 35 (1928), 223.

new flags, and students were allowed to give patriotic speeches and to sing national airs. Bonfires burned late that night.[34]

News of the victory was received in the General Assembly at Springfield with great enthusiasm; the *Illinois State Journal* recorded: "Illinois prowess has broken the backbone of the rebellion." "Light is breaking," proclaimed the *Macomb Journal*. "God speed the right." Illinois troops, added that paper, "are entitled to the chief share of the glory." From New York City, the *New York Tribune* conceded that "Western men fight like heroes. . . . No long period of preparation is required to make them fit to fight for their country." General McClernand, once again, shared the laurels of victory with Grant, and rightfully so. The *Illinois State Journal*, commending the former upon his courage, wrote: "General McClernand was continually with his command, exposing his person day and night to shell, shot, and even the enemy's rifles." [35]

In his battle report McClernand's pen once again ran away with him. He wrote of a contest fought with "obstinacy and protracted duration" in which "my division sustained much the greater loss." The spoils of victory were, as he put it, "our trophies." To his troops he wrote: "The battle field testifies to your valor and constancy. Even the magnanimity of the enemy accord to you an unsurpassed heroism, and an enviable and brilliant share of the hardest fought battle and the most decisive victory ever fought and won on the American continent." That last phrase, so splendidly written, was quoted and requoted by the ordinary soldier in his letters home to Illinois. Oglesby, however — one of McClernand's own brigade commanders — placed the report in his files with the sarcastic notation that it was another of McClernand's missiles.[36]

Grant's reaction to McClernand's battle report was immediate. He forwarded his subordinate's account of the battle, but attached the following comment to it: "I transmit herewith the report of the action of the First Division at the battle of Fort Don-

---

[34] Mary Livermore, 177–178.

[35] *Chicago Tribune*, Feb. 18, 1862. *Macomb Journal*, Feb. 21, 1862. *New York Daily Tribune*, quoted in *Macomb Journal*, March 28, 1862. *Illinois State Journal*, Feb. 27, 1862.

[36] McClernand's Report, *Official Records*, Ser. I, Vol. VII, 180. Also in Oglesby Papers.

elson. I have no comments to make on it, further than that the report is a little highly colored as to the conduct of the First Division, and I failed to hear the suggestion spoken of about the propriety of attacking the enemy all around the lines on Saturday."[37]

Grant's concern was proper. Though McClernand had taken the brunt of the initial attack, Smith's division suffered heavy casualties in its afternoon attack upon the Confederate right wing. Furthermore, as Grant implied in his statement on McClernand's report, McClernand's obvious claim that he had urged the full assault upon the enemy was overdrawn.[38]

Two days after the battle McClernand sent a copy of his commendatory order to his troops directly to the President, and two weeks later he followed with a copy of his battle report. This, tragically for the man, was the flaw in his character, and no amount of bravery would eliminate the enemies it made for him. The country thanked both him and Grant for the victory on the Cumberland by awarding Grant another star in February, and by giving a promotion to McClernand a month later.[39]

While Grant's troops were consolidating their positions around Fort Donelson and preparing for a move farther up the Tennessee to Pittsburg Landing, events were building to a climax west of the Mississippi. Brigadier General Samuel Ryan Curtis, a former army officer and Iowa congressman commanding the Army of the Southwest, began to move against "Pap" Price's Missouri Confederates.

Price had left Springfield, Missouri, and retired into northwest Arkansas. He had been joined by a force under Brigadier General Benjamin McCulloch. Major General Earl Van Dorn, commanding the Confederate Trans-Mississippi District, took over command of all the Confederate forces on March 3. Pulling in other troops, including a force of Indians, Van Dorn decided to attack

---

[37] *Official Records*, Ser. I, Vol. VII, 170.

[38] According to Force, 63, McClernand suffered 1,445 in killed and wounded, with 74 missing. Smith suffered 1,351 in killed and wounded, with 167 missing.

[39] McClernand to Lincoln, Feb. 17, Feb. 28, 1862, Lincoln Papers. Note that the date on which the commendatory order was sent to the President was just two days after the battle.

Curtis in the Sugar Creek–Pea Ridge area before the Federals could advance farther into Arkansas.

On March 5 Curtis was informed of the Confederate movement by scouts and fugitive citizens, including Wild Bill Hickok, who came originally from Illinois. After ordering his division commanders, Eugene A. Carr and Jefferson C. Davis, to stand fast, Curtis sent couriers racing into northwestern Arkansas to bring up the divisions of A. S. Asboth and Peter J. Osterhaus, both under the command of General Franz Sigel. By the night of March 6, the four Union divisions were united and in line of battle on the bluffs above Little Sugar Creek southwest of Elkhorn Tavern.

The morning of March 7 dawned clear enough to show that Van Dorn's men had slipped away from their campfires during the night. Under the cover of darkness, the Confederates had marched in two columns around Pea Ridge to strike the Federals from the rear. Fortunately for Curtis they did not move fast enough. The coming daylight exposed the deception in time for Curtis to turn his army northward to face the enemy.[40]

The Confederate wing under Price appeared in front of Carr's division about ten o'clock, driving the Union pickets ahead of them. Outnumbered three to one, Carr's division, which included Colonel Gustavus A. Smith's 35th Illinois, held the line near Elkhorn Tavern. After Smith and Carr both were wounded, and the Federal batteries were put out of commission, Carr backed off and called for reinforcements. There were none to be had, however, for fighting had also broken out at the other end of the line. A wave of Indians, led by their chieftain Stand Watie, and McCulloch's Texans broke out of the underbrush, overrunning the lines of Osterhaus' division. The 59th Illinois, which had been moving cannon about all morning in preparation for such an attack, was surprised by the enemy onslaught. "Turn back! Turn back!" the officers of the 59th were told. Colonel Philip S. Post, in command of that regiment, rallied his men, however, and conducted a fighting retreat through the small village of Leetown.[41]

Despite the suddenness of the enemy assault upon the 59th, there was little confusion in the ranks. Organized originally as the

[40] *Official Records*, Ser. I, Vol. VIII, 195–197, 283. Monaghan, 231–241.

[41] David Lathrop, *The History of the Fifty-ninth Regiment Illinois Volunteers* (Indianapolis, 1865), 92–93, 96. Herr, 72–74.

9th Missouri, the regiment had more experience than most, and gave way before the screaming Choctaws and Texans in an orderly fashion. Nevertheless, one might suppose that this was not a moment of tranquility and repose. One private in the line, overcome with the zest of battle, hit his ramrod so hard that the point was driven through his hand. An officer of the regiment, Lieutenant Beach, was wounded in the foot and unable to keep up with the retreat. As the triumphant Indians stripped him of his shoes and money, Beach played dead in spite of the intense pain and managed to rejoin his regiment later.[42]

McCulloch attempted to smash Osterhaus' division completely. He doubletimed an Arkansas regiment into his battle line. Waiting behind a rail fence directly in front of the new assault was a reinforcing regiment, the 36th Illinois, commanded by an obstinate and tough officer, Colonel Nicholas Greusel. As the Confederates advanced, a private of the 36th, Peter Pelican, picked out a tall enemy officer in sky-blue pantaloons, and knocked him off his horse with a perfect shot. When the Confederate advance paled before their accurate fire, the 36th counterattacked, retaking most of the field. There, lying in the grass, was the officer with the blue pantaloons, Ben McCulloch.

The advancing 36th Illinois also found something else. On the initial battleground, where the 59th Illinois had been surprised by Stand Watie's Indians, lay the allegedly scalped dead of that regiment. One Illinois soldier, finding the body of his brother, swore vengeance upon the enemy, a vow fulfilled in the Union victory the following day.[43]

At the opposite end of the Union line, Carr tenaciously held on. Later to be described by a newspaper correspondent as being brave enough but lacking energy and initiative, he gave sufficient evidence of the first of those characteristics. Wounded three times, Carr refused to leave the field, ordering his wounds bandaged while he remained upon his horse. This courage was to win for him a promotion in rank, as well as the Medal of Honor.[44]

---

[42] *Warfare Along the Mississippi*, 24–28, 34.

[43] Herr, 72–74. Monaghan, 242. Although there are a number of stories of alleged scalping, the extent of it is in dispute.

[44] Charles A. Dana, *Recollections of the Civil War with the Leaders at Washington and in the Field in the Sixties* (New York, 1898), 65. *Civil War Medal of Honor Winners from Illinois* (Springfield, 1962), 6.

When the day ended, the soldiers of Curtis' army had much to discuss. Besides Colonel Carr, Colonel Philip S. Post of the 59th Illinois and Colonel Gustavus Smith of the 35th had been wounded. An officer of the 59th Illinois, Lieutenant Colonel Calvin Frederick, was still staggering about after having been knocked unconscious by a cannonball during McCulloch's morning attack. Much was said about Captain William Black of the 37th Illinois, who had refused to give ground in front of the Confederate rush. The 37th also expressed satisfaction with the weapons they had been given.[45] As good fortune had effected the turn of events, the flanking companies of the 37th had been armed with repeating rifles which they had acquired earlier through the personal intervention of the wife of General Frémont.[46]

There was much talk of the Cherokees and Choctaws, who had reportedly scalped Illinois soldiers, as well as of the Texans, who were said to have smashed heads of wounded Union soldiers with their bowie knives. Others, more introspective, reviewed their own actions during the battle. "I was so sure that I should lose my life," wrote a member of the 36th Illinois later, "that I really felt no concern about it." Others in the same regiment gleefully examined the gold watch which Private Pelican had taken from the body of Ben McCulloch; some laughed at the story told by another soldier of the 36th, who had recently purchased a book of ribald songs. Not wishing to lose it during the battle, he placed it in the band of his hat. The book was just thick enough to stop a musket ball from entering his skull. A good many soldiers huddled by their fires with thoughts such as those expressed by a member of the 59th Illinois who came from Tennessee, Illinois. "Every soldier seemed to know we had been defeated," he recalled later, "and the gloom of a final attack, which could only bring us capture or death, pressed heavily upon us and shut out hope."[47]

---

[45] Carr's Report, *Official Records*, Ser. I, Vol. VIII, 259. Smith had part of his scalp torn off. He never again was physically fit to command. Lathrop, 96. Frederick was not touched by the cannonball, but it went so close to his head that he lost his sense of balance. *Civil War Medal of Honor Winners*, 5.

[46] Edward A. Blodgett, "The Army of the Southwest and the Battle of Pea Ridge," in *Military Essays and Recollections*, II (1894), 305–306.

[47] Mary Livermore, 649. L. G. Bennett and William M. Haigh, *History of the Thirty-sixth Regiment Illinois Volunteers* . . . (Aurora, Ill., 1876), 148. Browne, 104. *Warfare Along the Mississippi*, 24–28.

On the night of March 7 Curtis realigned his troops, knowing the battle was not over. Van Dorn, meanwhile, was having his difficulties. Two of his subordinates, McCulloch and James McIntosh, had been killed; and many of the Indians who had done so well in the initial attack refused to continue to fight. While the Confederate general attempted to deal with these problems from a sickbed, his opponent was busy. By the time the first light of morning showed itself upon Pea Ridge, the two Union divisions of Sigel were in line of battle, ready to resume the fight.

Franz Sigel was a strange paradox of inepitude and ability. His handling of troops later in the war gave sufficient evidence of the first of those contradictions. Nevertheless, he inspired a strange loyalty not only among the Germans in his regiments, who proudly proclaimed, "I fights mit Sigel," but also in other troops in his command. "Where he leads," wrote one Illinois soldier, "the Thirty-sixth Illinois will follow." Now, in the early dawn of March 8, Sigel rode among his cannon, personally instructing the men how to aim them.[48]

The Union artillery barrage was furious. Up the slopes of the hill charged the 3rd and 17th Missouri, Greusel's 36th Illinois, and Colonel Charles Knobelsdorff's 44th Illinois. Carr's and Davis' divisions followed with attacks upon their own fronts. When the 36th Illinois reached the top of the ridge they found the tremendous damage which Sigel's artillery had created. "Great God!" wrote a member of that regiment later, "what a scene was there presented!" The bodies of decapitated and dismembered Confederates lay all about, and Union soldiers had to tread carefully to avoid stepping upon the remains. Farther along the line, where the Illinois boys of the 59th had smashed through the woods east of Elkhorn Tavern, they met a happy General Curtis, who cavorted about on his horse shouting "Victory, Victory!"[49]

Curtis was experienced enough to know what his soldiers had done. The Confederates, streaming off Pea Ridge in three different

[48] Monaghan, 245–247. Mark Mayo Boatner, III, *The Civil War Dictionary* (New York, 1959), 761. See W. H. Marsh to his father, March 21, 1862, William Henry Marsh Papers, ISHL, for more interesting comments on Sigel's popularity.

[49] Davidson and Stuvé, 755. Brief reference is made here to Day Elmore, the drummer boy of the 36th, who took up a musket and fought the battle with distinction. Bennett and Haigh, 168. *Warfare Along the Mississippi*, 32.

directions, had been thoroughly whipped. But the Union army had lost 1,384 in killed, wounded, and missing. The 9th Iowa suffered the heaviest regimental losses — 218; Colonel Julius White's 37th Illinois led the regiments of his own state with losses of 144.[50]

Thus, by the evening of March 8, the Union armies of the West could claim two important victories in the past month — Fort Donelson and Pea Ridge. But the year was 1862, and in another month such Illinois regiments in Grant's army as the 9th, 11th, 28th, 43rd, 50th, and 55th would meet the true test of patriotism in the woods near Shiloh Church in western Tennessee. For many of the Illinois regiments serving in Missouri, major fighting there was almost finished. By June the 35th Illinois would be at Holly Springs, Mississippi. By May Greusel's 36th would be at Corinth in the same state, and the Forty-fourth Brigade, under Greusel, would go with it. Colonel Post's hard-fighting 59th Illinois would soon follow. For these regiments, whether in the Army of the Tennessee, the Army of the Ohio, or the Army of the Mississippi, the battles won in February and March of 1862 were to seem like child's play by comparison to what was to come.

Donelson and Pea Ridge, however, were preparation for the horrors ahead. The terrible nights at Fort Donelson, the morning attack by the Confederates on February 15, the fighting in the dense underbrush, mingled with the proved resiliency of the western soldier, were all a part of the victory at Shiloh. The stand which the 59th Illinois took against the savage charge of McCulloch's Texans and Stand Watie's Indians at Pea Ridge, and the behavior of the 35th and 36th Illinois on the following day, helped to create a pride of achievement in those regiments which stood the tests of Perryville and Stone's River.

[50] Fox, 427. *Official Records*, Ser. I, Vol. VIII, 204–205, 218.

CHAPTER III

The Battle of Shiloh

The 30-day period following the capture of Fort Henry in 1862 was indeed eventful for the Union cause in the West. Vital victories were won by Grant at Donelson and by Curtis at Pea Ridge; and John Pope, an Illinois general, began what was to be the successful investment of the Confederate post at Island No. 10 on the Mississippi. Furthermore, important changes were made in the western command. Halleck, whose promotion to the control of the Department of Missouri in 1861 was followed with a string of successes, was rewarded with a larger command. He was placed in charge of the new Department of the Mississippi, which not only included his old department but that which had been the Department of the Ohio. This significant change added a whole new list of players to the increasingly climactic drama in that theater of war. Don Carlos Buell and William T. Sherman, among others, now joined a cast which already included such persons as Grant, McClernand, Lew Wallace, and W. H. L. Wallace. All were to play substantial roles in the master plan for the move up the Tennessee River to capture the major Confederate rail center at Corinth, Mississippi.

In a way, however, the days following the Union victory at Fort Donelson had a strange character. After the capture of Nashville by Buell, which probably could not have been done without the accomplishment at Donelson, Grant traveled to the Tennessee capital to confer with that commander. McClernand and W. H. L.

Wallace went with him, paying a visit to the widow of President Polk.[1]

The trip was a mistake for Grant. Halleck, who had been firing a series of messages from St. Louis to Fort Henry without receiving answers, was piqued. Complaining to George B. McClellan, the general-in-chief of the army, that he had been unable to receive any reports from Grant, he asked permission to remove the latter from his command. Given a vote of confidence from McClellan, Halleck acted, wiring Grant: "You will place Maj. Gen. C. F. Smith in command of the expedition and remain yourself at Fort Henry." Thus Smith headed the Union army at the opening stages of the movement up the Tennessee, while Grant was virtually confined to Fort Henry.[2]

McClernand, who could not comprehend the developments, added to the general confusion by complaining that Smith had been given command of the expedition rather than himself. Writing to Grant, who was now powerless to do anything but wait, he charged: "I rank him [Smith] as a brigadier and cannot recognize his superiority without self-degradation, which no human power can constrain me to do." The atmosphere along the Tennessee must have been sulfuric. Grant, in puzzlement, waited out the frustrating days at Fort Henry. Smith, a modest man whose surprise at the turn of events must have been as great as Grant's, reluctantly began the movement of the army to Savannah, a small village up the Tennessee River. And McClernand, like a new Achilles, sulked in his headquarters, continuing to fire his letters in broadsides. Even the innocent Smith was the recipient of one of his blasts. "While entertaining the highest respect for you both as an officer and as a man," he wrote to his new commander, "yet as I understand my relation to Maj. Gen. Grant, I only receive orders from him."[3]

The misunderstanding between Grant and Halleck eventually cleared, and by March 17 the former was able to rejoin the army, already well established up the Tennessee. The unfortunate

[1] Isabel Wallace, *The Life and Letters of General W. H. L. Wallace* (Chicago, 1909), 166.

[2] *Official Records*, Ser. I, Vol. VII, 679–680.

[3] McClernand to Grant, March 6, 1862, McClernand to Smith, March 26, 1862, McClernand Collection.

Smith, suffering from a leg injury which was to bring him death within a month, was forced to give up not only his division command but also that of the army. Colonel W. H. L. Wallace, that most promising officer from Ottawa, was given command of Smith's troops.

Before leaving command Smith surveyed points along the Tennessee which might serve as adequate bases for operations by Union forces. Stationing Lew Wallace's division at Crump's Landing, upstream from Savannah, he concentrated the remaining forces at Pittsburg Landing, still farther upstream and on the western bank of the river. As new regiments arrived, they were quickly forwarded to the latter location. Twelve were given to General Sherman, who placed them in the direction from which an enemy attack might come. Other new regiments were organized into a new division under Ben Prentiss, a general officer from Quincy. Prentiss' new troops were also placed on the outer rim of the Union concentration at Pittsburg Landing.[4]

Thus was the army gathered. McClernand's First Division, camped near Tilghman Creek, included ten regiments of Illinois infantry (eight of which had seen violent fighting at Fort Donelson), Thomas H. Carmichael's and Stewart's Illinois cavalry, and elements of the 1st and 2nd Illinois Light Artillery. W. H. L. Wallace's Second Division, in reserve near Pittsburg Landing, also had a number of Illinois troops in it, including eight infantry regiments together with units of artillery and cavalry. Of these infantry regiments, only three, the 7th, 9th, and 12th, had fought at Donelson. The Third Division, commanded by Lew Wallace and stationed at Crump's Landing, consisted mainly of Indiana and Ohio troops; the only Illinois contingent attached to that command was part of the 11th Illinois Cavalry. General Stephen Hurlbut's Fourth Division, located near the East Corinth road, included six regiments from Illinois. Hurlbut, who came from Belvidere, in Boone County, Illinois, was to play an important role in the coming event. Sherman's Fifth Division was camped near Shiloh Church. It contained but two Illinois regiments, the 40th and the 55th. The latter, with Stuart's Second Brigade, was camped near Lick Creek and the Hamburg road, while the 40th Illinois, in Colonel J. A. McDowell's brigade, was camped with

[4] Kenneth P. Williams, III, 310. Boatner, 752–753.

the main body of Sherman's division. The Sixth Division, under Prentiss, had among its several untried regiments the new 61st Illinois, the rest of the 11th Illinois Cavalry, and units of Illinois light artillery. Prentiss, as it turned out, had a most vital spot at the Shiloh encampment – a location which ran at right angles across the East Corinth road.

The creation of the Department of the Mississippi brought Buell's Army of the Ohio under Halleck's command. This army, which included only one Illinois regiment, the 34th, was ordered by the department commander to reinforce Grant at Savannah. Events were to prove that Buell's movement was most important.[5]

As spring broke in west Tennessee, Pittsburg Landing assumed an entirely new appearance. There was a businesslike air about the place. Sherman and McClernand held reviews of their divisions in the sparkling sunlight, and troops of all divisions struggled to make their encampments more pleasant. One Illinois officer, serving in Thomas W. Sweeny's Third Brigade of Wallace's Second Division, wrote to his wife in late March, portraying the scene at Pittsburg Landing:

> The ground is well timbered and rolling between each rise unnumberable springs of excellent water. No words of mine can give you any idea of the scene that presents itself in riding through the camp – the soil is a heavy clay and the heavy government wagons have cut it into huge ruts through which four and six mule teams are floundering and struggling in every direction their drivers cursing shouting whipping pounding at every step – here a wagon is stuck fast and abandoned in the mud – there one is broken against a stump or tree. Yonder lies a dead horse or mule and then staggers along a sick soldier while on every side blue coats some mounted some on foot are wading through the mud. Axes are pounding drums resounding – fifes screaming – mules braying horses neighing – trees falling at one and the same time on every side. . . .[6]

For most soldiers, the coming of spring provided a pleasant contrast to the hard days of winter. Sergeant Payson Shumway, serving in the 14th Illinois of Hurlbut's division, wrote his wife back in Taylorville, Illinois, that the weather was so warm and delightful, the birds were singing so prettily, and the flowers were

---

[5] S. M. Howard, *The Illustrated Comprehensive History of the Great Battle of Shiloh* (Gettysburg, S.D., 1921), 40–46. Kenneth P. Williams, III, 326–327.

[6] John Wilcox to his wife, March 22, 1862, Wilcox Papers.

so beautiful that life in camp was almost bearable. "Now Hattie," he concluded, "you may think that I am getting almost childish in my ideas . . . but no for it is all these *small* things which compose the whole of life's happenings. . . ." At night, the reflective Shumway strolled about camps "lighted up . . . with . . . fires and lights of different kinds." He wrote that the sight gave the impression of a "vast city at night," all of which was enlivened by regimental bands "trying to see which can make the best music." "No doubt," he philosophized, "a 'looker-on' would be led to think war a 'glorious thing.'"[7]

In the 61st Illinois, Private Leander Stillwell spent most of his days wandering through a nearby peach orchard hunting for wild peas and onions. It all seemed wonderful to this young boy from Carrollton, arising in the cool and fragrant mornings to hot coffee, pancakes, and bacon, then strolling through grounds strewn with fallen peach blossoms.[8]

To the rear, in the camp of the Second Division, W. H. L. Wallace proudly tried on the uniform of a brigadier general, having received his promotion on March 21. Yet military life was not attractive to this 41-year-old lawyer from northern Illinois. Making preparations for a coming visit from his wife, he wrote the latter of his wishes to return home with her: "Dear wife, when will our Good God in his providence permit a return to those happy times?"[9] Within three weeks Wallace would be dead.

There were some who had a premonition of events to come. A lieutenant colonel of the 52nd Illinois, struck by the mood, wrote his wife on March 26 that the entire regiment felt the nearness of battle; both the men and the officers were writing last letters to their wives. In the same regiment, Private Edwin C. Sackett wrote his family on March 21: "We expect a battle near here and soon it is reported that there is a large rebel force concentrating back a few miles from the river. . . ." In the 53rd Illinois, stationed downriver at Savannah, Sergeant Major Charles Brush wrote his father at Ottawa: "They are undoubtedly preparing for a great battle somewhere between Pittsburg Landing and Corrinth."

[7] Shumway to his wife, April 1, March 19, 1862, Shumway Papers.

[8] Leander Stillwell, "In the Ranks at Shiloh," *Journal*, XV, Nos. 1–2 (April-July, 1923), 463.

[9] Wallace to his wife, March 25, 1862, Wallace-Dickey Papers.

Brush gave Grant's headquarters a good deal more credit for prescience than it was entitled to, however. Writing to his wife on March 29, Grant gave little indication that he was a commander about to face the supreme test, claiming that the only problem facing his army at the moment was too much "dioreah." Six days later, on April 5, Grant wrote Halleck: "I have scarcely the faintest idea of an attack (general one) being made upon us. . . ." At that very moment, almost within the sound of Union bugles, General Albert Sidney Johnston, with 40,000 Confederate soldiers, was preparing for a morning assault upon the Union regiments camped near Shiloh Church.[10]

Johnston's force consisted of four brigades under General Leonidas Polk, the fighting bishop, six brigades under General Braxton Bragg, three brigades under General W. J. Hardee, and three brigades under General John C. Breckinridge. The Confederate plan was to strike a surprise blow at Grant before he could be reinforced by the arrival of Buell. The attempt would be made to force the Union left flank in order to separate the body of Grant's army from the river landing. Thus, it was hoped, the Federal commander would be compelled to surrender. Implicit in all of these plans was not only the mere defeat of the Union army, but its destruction.[11]

Strangely enough, the battle of Shiloh began April 6 with a Federal attack upon a detachment of southern soldiers. Colonel Everett Peabody, in command of the First Brigade in Prentiss' division, fearing that enemy forces might be gathering in the woods on the road from Corinth, ordered an early-morning reconnaissance. Between five and six o'clock, as the sun rose to reveal a bright and clear day, the patrol, comprising three companies from the 25th Missouri, ran head on into the advance pickets of the 3rd Mississippi Infantry. After an hour of savage fighting, the Union soldiers retired before the steadily growing weight of enemy force. By this time the fighting had spread to advance units

[10] John Wilcox to his wife, March 26, 1862, Wilcox Papers. Sackett to his family, March 21, 1862, Edwin C. Sackett Papers, ISHL. Brush to his father, March 30, 1862, Brush Family Papers, ISHL. Grant to his wife, March 29, 1862, Ulysses S. Grant Papers, ISHL. Grant to Halleck, *Official Records*, Ser. I, Vol. X, Pt. 1, 89.

[11] *Ibid.*, 382–384. Force, 109–112.

of the 21st Missouri, a Federal regiment led by Colonel David Moore. Thus began the battle of Shiloh.[12]

Soon it was Sherman's division upon which the full force of the Confederate attack fell. Brigades headed by colonels J. Hildebrand, R. P. Buckland, and J. A. McDowell fell back stubbornly before an assault led by Patrick Cleburne's Confederate brigade. The lines of troops seemed like a sea; the "flux and reflux of ocean breakers dashing themselves with tireless repetition against a yielding, crumbling shore." Union regiments, fighting an uncoordinated battle, found themselves constantly outflanked as companion regiments withdrew without warning. The Federal line could not stabilize itself. The 40th Illinois, for example, fighting a heroic defense in McDowell's brigade near Shiloh Church, found itself almost surrounded by enemy troops which had unhinged the Union regiments right and left of it. Faced by an enemy battery which fired directly at the regiment's position, the commander ordered a bayonet assault. The attack failed and the regiment retired, cartridge boxes empty, with losses of over half its effective force.[13]

The behavior of Hildebrand's brigade, which was located to the left of Sherman's division, offers insight into the tragedy in the early hours at Shiloh. Consisting of almost entirely raw recruits, it virtually exploded before the Confederate assault. In particular, the 53rd Ohio, led by a colonel whose major contribution to the fight were the immortal words "Fall back and save yourselves," it panicked and fled. Thus veteran regiments, attempting to stand their ground, found themselves dangerously outflanked and forced to withdraw. Some untried soldiers ran so precipitously that they stopped only upon reaching Pittsburg Landing. One Illinois surgeon recalled, years later, that a young recruit ran headlong into his hospital, pointed at his own foot, and cried: "Take it off, it will have to go." Examination revealed a minor puncture of the skin. The soldier had been so unnerved by the fighting that he was ready to escape by any means.[14]

On the Union left, the green regiments of Prentiss' division had

[12] Kenneth P. Williams, III, 356–358. Force, 123–124.

[13] Nicolay and Hay, V, 325. Eddy, I, 320–321.

[14] Bruce Catton, *Grant Moves South* (Boston, 1960), 228. Joseph Rich, *The Battle of Shiloh* (Iowa City, Iowa, 1911), 58–59. Force, 131–132. Wardner, "Reminiscences of a Surgeon," 187.

been up since dawn. Men of the 61st Illinois, camped on a tributary of Lick Creek, had eaten breakfast and were busily polishing muskets when the sounds of cannon and musket were heard. Soon the regimental drummer called the troops to formation. Companies dressed on the colors and waited at parade rest. In due time their colonel, Jacob Fry, appeared before them and in a loud voice shouted: "Gentlemen, remember your state and do your duty today like brave men." The regiment was so new that their commander's brief speech did not seem the least unusual. It was only after Shiloh that the troops realized an experienced officer would have addressed his men as "soldiers."

Soon a line of Confederate soldiers appeared before the 61st, bearing a flag which Private Leander Stillwell later described as one he had never seen before. Decades afterward he recalled the appearance of the enemy at that moment: "A long brown line, with muskets at a right shoulder shift, in excellent order, right through the woods they came." Paralyzed by the thought of shooting human beings, the bewildered soldiers of the 61st watched the approaching Confederates. "Shoot! shoot! shoot!" cried a company lieutenant. "Why don't you shoot?" One Illinois soldier, three months off the farm, frantically replied that he couldn't see anything at which to shoot but smoke. "Shoot, shoot, anyhow!" the officer shouted in his ear.[15]

The 61st, like many new regiments at Shiloh, was simply too inexperienced to withstand the shock of such a frontal attack. Soon it was running through the woods to the comparative safety of Hurlbut's line, located to the rear near the Peach Orchard. Here the 61st, along with a companion regiment, was placed in Hurlbut's reserve, where, as it lay upon the ground, it could hear the dreadful sounds of cannister and shell whirling through the air. The remaining regiments of Prentiss' division, also driven to the rear by the enemy flood, rallied near an old wagon trail which had been washed into a deep rut by repeated rains. There, in the Sunken Road, they waited for the next onslaught, their commander having been informed by Grant that the position must be held "at all hazards."[16]

[15] Stillwell, "In the Ranks at Shiloh," 465–470. Stillwell, *Story of a Common Soldier,* 42–45, 55.

[16] *Official Records,* Ser. I, Vol. X, Pt. 1, 277–280.

In McClernand's First Division, to the left and rear of Sherman's command, some of the regiments had arisen early to engage in firing practice. Colonel Julius Raith, the commanding officer of the 43rd Illinois, a regiment raised mainly in Saint Clair County, had rousted his men early every morning for the previous week. They had made so much noise in the days prior to attack that other divisions had sent objections to McClernand. Now the 43rd and the other regiments in Raith's brigade were already in line, probably better prepared for the coming assault than most troops in other divisions. Indeed, the same could be said of most of McClernand's command. This may have been due to that division commander's high-strung personality, or his normally suspicious nature. Sensing a surprise attack, he had written to Grant on March 27, warning him of a probable assault by the enemy. Four days later he sent the same kind of warning to Sherman. Both were ignored. In the case of the First Division, McClernand's men were quickly prepared to fight. That division commander merely addressed "a few brief, but burning words" to each brigade before he sent it forward into the woods to engage the foe.[17]

As McClernand's Illinois regiments moved into the battle line, they were met by Hildebrand's fleeing Ohio troops, who stopped only to shout: "We're whipped, we're all cut to pieces. . . ." The veterans of Fort Donelson moved forward, however, their officers striding up and down the skirmish line shouting, "Stand up to it boys, I'll shoot the first man that falters." Nevertheless, as the hours of conflict crept by, McClernand's command was forced to give up ground, "refusing first one flank, then the other, shifting slowly back from one position to another. . . ." The wounded were hauled back to the bluffs along the landing, where the surgeons worked in an old log house which reminded a battle-hardened veteran of the 20th Illinois of a "butcher shop when the trade was good." "If the sight along the line of battle was terrible, this along the landing was simply *horrible*," he concluded.[18]

---

[17] McClernand to Grant, May 27, 1862, McClernand Collection. In Grant to McClernand, April 9, 1862, McClernand Collection, there was a warning from Grant concerning firing practice by the First Division. McClernand to Sherman, March 31, 1862, McClernand Collection. Grant to Halleck, April 5, 1862, *Official Records*, Ser. I, Vol. X, Pt. 1, 89. "Biography of General John A. McClernand" (2 vols., unpublished manuscript, ISHL), I, 91.

[18] Blanchard, 40–44. Force, 134–140.

Too little has been written about McClernand's stand along the Union right at Shiloh, perhaps of the character of that division commander. Historians, favoring Grant as the great soldier of the war, have deprecated McClernand because of the personality conflict which existed between the two men. At any rate, one cannot deny that McClernand's regiments fought savagely at Donelson and Shiloh.

The 18th Illinois, the roughneck regiment from southern Illinois, once again was in the midst of the conflict. It went into the fight with few officers available for combat, including its commander, and came out of it with even fewer. One captain, William Dillon from Hardin, wounded at Donelson, returned just ten minutes before the battle commenced, presumably upon the same steamer which carried Mrs. W. H. L. Wallace to a visit with her husband. Dillon barely managed to get his company into battle before he was killed. Mrs. Wallace, who was also to witness tragedy, narrowly missed meeting her husband, who had gone to organize the Second Division for the fight. She saw him the next day—unconscious and mortally wounded.

The 18th Illinois came upon hard times during the day. Three color bearers fell in rapid succession. The regiment was outflanked and almost captured, an occasion colorfully described by one soldier: "We found ourselves nearly surrounded and then we had to run to save No. 1 . . . we got out but it was done by some of the tallest running that we ever done." Nevertheless, the 18th was composed of tough men. When the situation really became most desperate, even its regimental surgeon joined the fight, exclaiming that he would not feel happy until he had fired "45 rounds, by God."[19]

This southern Illinois regiment was not the only one in McClernand's command which found itself in desperate straits during the day. In Colonel Carrol Marsh's brigade, the 45th Illinois also had a bitter experience. Outflanked, and completely out of ammunition, the regiment had to flee to avoid capture.

One member of the 15th Illinois regiment, of Colonel James

[19] Diary of Lieut. W. D. Harland, Company H, 18th Regiment, Illinois Volunteers and Thos. C. Watkins, Orderly Sergeant, Company H, 18th Regiment, Illinois Volunteers . . . ," comp. Mrs. Clyde A. Hornbuckle, in *State of Illinois: Daughters of the American Revolution Genealogical Records 1940–41* (3 vols., ISHL), III, 282.

Veatch's Second Brigade of Hurlbut's division, remembered later that musket balls fell upon his outflanked companions like hailstones. Most of its officers down, the regiment fell back upon the reinforcing 14th Illinois. The latter regiment, a strong battery placed in the forefront of its ranks, cut a huge swath in the enemy attackers. A week later, a sergeant of the 14th wrote admiringly of the brave foe: "Yet still on they came and as I watched them I could not but admire their courage." Again outflanked, the Illinois troops gave way, and again the Confederates came on at the double quick. This time the 14th held, pouring "volley after volley into the rebel ranks until they recoiled and fell back." [20]

At three o'clock in the afternoon, following orders from Grant, McClernand launched an attack designed to clear the approach to the battle area by which Lew Wallace's expected reinforcements would arrive. As Sherman wrote in his battle report, the First Division made "a fine charge on the enemy and drove him back into the ravines. . . ." During the brisk fighting here, McClernand himself could be seen, "bravely rallying and pushing forward an Ohio regiment . . . apparently destitute of field officers." Thus did the position on the Union right become stabilized.[21]

While McClernand was holding his eighth and last position of the day, the fighting raged unabatedly on the left. On the far end of the Union line, the conflict had spread to Colonel David Stuart's brigade, separated from Sherman's division, which consisted of the 54th and 71st Ohio and the 55th Illinois. Stuart, originally a Chicago lawyer, held a most vital position, running between the Peach Orchard and the Tennessee River. If the Confederate army was to push Stuart far enough, it would unhinge the entire Union army from its landing at the river bank. About noon James R. Chalmers' and William H. Jackson's Confederate brigades descended upon Stuart's brigade; the ensuing battle was vicious. The 71st Ohio, a new regiment, quickly disintegrated and fled in terror,

[20] Force, 134–140. Lucius W. Barber, *Army Memoirs of Lucius W. Barber, Company "D," 15th Illinois Volunteer Infantry* . . . (Chicago, 1894), 52–54. P. Z. Shumway to his wife, April 13, 1862, Shumway Papers. Shumway and Barber both agree upon the fact of the retreat of the Ohio regiment, the former writing that the regiment on the right gave way.

[21] *Official Records*, Ser. I, Vol. X, Pt. 1, 250. According to Richardson, 238, McClernand took his staff exceedingly close to the line of battle.

leaving the outflanked 55th Illinois and 54th Ohio to fight it out. As the men of the 71st broke, Stuart, a brave though pompous man, flailed them with his sword, shouting "Halt! Men, halt!" Holding his other two regiments in line, he gradually withdrew before an overwhelming Confederate advance. By two o'clock Stuart was in dire trouble. Outflanked, and trapped in a ravine with the 9th Mississippi pouring fire into his troops, he called for help.[22]

During the early stages of the battle, Grant's only reserve force was W. H. L. Wallace's Second Division. Gradually, and in piecemeal fashion, the various brigades and regiments were peeled off and forwarded to critical areas of conflict. Often they were simply ordered forward to where the sound of musketry was the loudest. The 7th and 58th Illinois were sent in response to one of McClernand's requests for reinforcements. Colonel John McArthur's Second Brigade, which included the 9th and 12th Illinois, was sent along with Colonel Moses Bane's 50th Illinois to aid the beleaguered Stuart. Bane's men were in line only a few minutes when the enemy was upon them – almost before they knew it, as one soldier wrote. Within 15 minutes and with 79 men down, the regiment retreated, firing from behind trees.[23]

Thus the bulk of fighting in Stuart's brigade fell upon the 55th, a northern Illinois regiment raised by Stuart himself. It was a most peculiar collection of men, hard-headed and tough. Fighting where they stood, sometimes so long that individual soldiers were outflanked and captured by the enemy, they held together until their cartridge boxes gave out. Taking ammunition from their dead, they eventually backtracked to the last defense line near the bluffs of Pittsburg Landing. There their unusual chaplain Milton Haney, worn by the ardors of the day, took a healthy swig of brandy and, thus revived, rallied the regiment for a last stand.[24]

[22] *Official Records*, Ser. I, Vol. X, Pt. 1, 119. Rich, 61. Edwin L. Hobart, *The Truth About the Battle of Shiloh* (Springfield, 1909), 90–91. In [Crooker *et al.*] Stuart is portrayed as a ludicrous figure. See *ibid.*, 111–114, for the account of the fight with the 9th Mississippi. According to Hobart, the 55th fought for some time in the outmoded hollow-square formation.

[23] C. H. Floyd to his friend Mr. Turner, July 6, 1862, Charles H. Floyd Papers, ISHL. Hobart, 92–97.

[24] Alvan Q. Bacon, *Thrilling Adventures of a Pioneer Boy, While a Prisoner of War* (n.p., n.d.), 4. [Crooker *et al.*], 444–448.

By mid-morning most of W. H. L. Wallace's division had been called to the aid of the hard-pressed Prentiss, who, faithful to his orders to hold, grimly threw back repeated Confederate attacks upon the Sunken Road. The First Brigade of the Second Division and Colonel Thomas Sweeny's Third Brigade (all Illinois troops) were sent to occupy the position to Prentiss' right. Wallace himself went along to aid in the placement of his men.

Sweeny, who came from Ireland by way of Illinois, was a hard-tempered, irascible, one-armed veteran of the Mexican War. He was so aggressive that during the Atlanta campaign, in 1864, he got into a fist fight with his superior, General Grenville M. Dodge. Now, at the Sunken Road, temperament almost precluded any further role in the war for him. Spotting troops which he could not identify, he tested them the hard way by riding within musket range of their colors. They turned out to be Confederate soldiers who, as good fortune would have it, were so flustered at Sweeny's seemingly erratic behavior that they forgot to fire. But the Irishman's luck later failed: within an hour he was painfully wounded in the foot. Handicapped as he was with one arm and with blood dripping from his boot, he still remained with his command for the entire day.[25]

As Stuart's brigade fell back on the left, and McClernand's division was pushed back on the right, the Union center, held by Wallace, Prentiss, and Hurlbut (from right to left), was gradually outflanked. Holding at the Sunken Road, rapidly becoming the "Hornets' Nest" of Civil War memory, Union soldiers faced the supreme test – holding an untenable position against overwhelming odds. One officer, fighting with the 52nd Illinois, which was anchored along the right of the Sunken Road, later wrote that the "balls flew around and among us like hail and it seemed as though we could not escape." The firing was so heavy that men who were there remembered as long as they lived a sound akin to that made by hundreds of insects – hence the "Hornets' Nest." An Illinois soldier later recorded that five-sixths of the shots fired in his direction "struck higher than a man's head," flicking leaves from the trees in a constant rain. Another man from the same regiment recalled two weeks later that he fought so close to "an elegant Regt the 'Louisana Guards'" that he could read the in-

[25] Richardson, 239.

scription on their regimental colors. Sergeant Edward Spalding of Rockford, also in the 52nd, was struck in the spine by a musket ball. Though he was to be crippled for life, this day he stayed at his task, firing and reloading his gun until his ammunition gave out.[26]

On the left of Prentiss, where the Federal line hooked back to the Peach Orchard and Bloody Pond, Hurlbut's division was fighting for survival. The breakup of Stuart's brigade had left Hurlbut in a most dangerous situation. Surmising a Confederate attempt to exploit Stuart's collapse, Hurlbut ordered his First Brigade to the edge of the Peach Orchard, instructing it to wait quietly in the underbrush. The First Brigade, an experienced fighting unit, had in it three battle-tested Illinois regiments. These were the 28th Illinois, commanded by Colonel Amory Johnson; the 32nd Illinois, commanded by Colonel John Logan from Carlinville (not to be confused with John A. Logan from Carbondale); and the 41st Illinois, under the command of Colonel Isaac Pugh. The 41st had fought with distinction on the Union right at Donelson.

About 2:30 a contingent of enemy troops headed by a high-ranking Confederate officer advanced on the concealed brigade. The 28th Illinois fired first, driving the enemy officer and his men back into the underbrush; the men of the Illinois regiment could not have known that they had shot the highest-ranking Confederate officer on the field, Albert Sidney Johnston. Having received an arterial wound in the leg, Johnston foolishly elected to stay in the fight, literally bleeding to death. As events would prove, that blindly thrown volley had a most profound effect upon the outcome of the battle.[27]

Despite Johnston's mortal wound, the Confederate attack upon Hurlbut's left developed with savage intensity. The First Brigade was quickly swept from its position near the Peach Orchard by the oncoming tide of enemy soldiers. The 32nd Illinois, going into the fight with 546 effectives, lost 224 men within a few minutes. Virtually all of the officers of this Macoupin County regiment were either killed or wounded. So rapidly did the assault

[26] William Wilcox to John Wilcox, April 9, 1862, John Wilcox to his wife, May 12, 1862, E. S. Wilcox to John Wilcox, April 25, 1862, Wilcox Papers. *Civil War Medal of Honor Winners*, 5.

[27] S. M. Howard, 84–85.

develop that the 28th Illinois was swept away from its ammunition container. Private Ellwood Williams of Havana ran through the opposing lines of fire to retrieve it. For this display of courage he was awarded the Medal of Honor.[28]

To the right of Prentiss' division, the Confederates, thwarted by the stubborn defense of W. H. L. Wallace's men, gathered a giant battery of 62 guns under the command of General Daniel Ruggles. As these massed cannon fired point blank into the Federal line, it became absolutely impossible to hold Prentiss' right. When it was also reported to General Wallace that the last road to the rear was being closed off, he decided to take his division out of the fighting. With Sweeny's brigade leading the withdrawal from the "Hornets' Nest," most of the Illinois soldiers made it to safety. Wallace, bringing up the rear, did not. Attempting to run the gauntlet of Confederate fire, he was severely wounded, the musket ball penetrating his skull and coming out through one eye. Struggling mightily, his brother-in-law Cyrus Dickey attempted to drag the general from the field, but advancing rebels forced Dickey to run for his own safety.

Wallace did not die immediately. When the Union surge of the following day cleared the Confederate troops from the battle area, he was found alive. He had lain all night in the falling rain, covered only by a blanket placed upon him by a kindly Confederate soldier. He was carried unconscious to the landing and to his waiting wife. He never regained consciousness, and died a few days later.[29]

The withdrawal of Hurlbut on the left and Wallace on the right left Prentiss alone and surrounded. Bringing Ruggles' huge battery to bear upon the remaining Federal troops, the Confederates poured a savage fire into the area of the Sunken Road. Finally, at approximately 5:30, "having lost everything but honor," Prentiss surrendered his little band of about 2,200 men.[30]

As Prentiss played his vital role in the great drama at Shiloh, Grant ordered Hurlbut to form a last line of defense stretching

[28] J. F. Drish to his wife, April 10, 1862, James F. Drish Papers, ISHL. *Civil War Medal of Honor Winners*, 10.

[29] Force, 143–148. Cyrus Dickey to his brother, April 10, 1862, Wallace-Dickey Papers.

[30] Force, 146. *Official Records*, Ser. I, Vol. X, Pt. 1, 274.

from the landing around to McClernand's detachments, which were still maintaining desultory exchanges with the enemy. Using as a core Colonel James Veatch's brigade, whose men of the 15th and 46th Illinois had fought so hard alongside McClernand's division that they actually wept when they were withdrawn from battle, Hurlbut built a line from remnants of regiments which were shattered in the day's fighting. Stuart's brigade, which included the 55th Illinois, the 61st Illinois from Hurlbut's own division, and the 9th and 12th Illinois of McArthur's brigade, both of which had been badly mauled in the fight on the Union left, were gathered together for the last fight of the day.[31]

Soon Chalmers' and Jackson's Confederate brigades appeared in line of battle. Surging so close to the landing that the patter of bullets could be heard on the vessels at the landing and at the field hospital nearby, the enemy troops almost engulfed Hurlbut's defenses. The scene was frightening. In the hospital, a wounded soldier of the 12th Illinois whose leg had been amputated began to push himself toward the river on his back, his bandaged stump held in the air. The surgeon of the same regiment vividly recalled that a cavalryman became so frightened that he rode his horse into the river, only to fall off when the animal got into deep water. The horse swam to safety with his master clutching his tail, while the troops on shore roared with laughter.[32]

It is difficult to know, even today, just how close the Confederate army came to complete victory on April 6. As the two Confederate brigades moved on Hurlbut's waiting line, three determinants of this conclusive battle were being revealed. First, the southern troops were running out of steam. Facing resolute Union soldiers on a last line of defense was different from fighting outflanked or isolated Union regiments. Furthermore, concentrated fire from the Union batteries and the naval guns on the boats at the landing presented an obstacle which even fresh troops might not overcome. Colonel Lyle Dickey, the Illinois cavalry leader, graphically described the action of these guns: "Boom — boom —

[31] Diary of Colonel William Camm," 846–852. Stillwell, "In the Ranks at Shiloh," 474–475. Both Camm and Stillwell write of stopping to drink in the Bloody Pond.

[32] Wardner, "Reminiscences of a Surgeon," 186.

went the big guns — faster and faster until so many were brought to work — that you could not distinguish between each boom and the noise was converted into a continuous howl of cannon."[33]

Finally the arrival of Colonel Jacob Ammen's brigade of the Army of the Ohio, part of General William "Bull" Nelson's division, which had been marching at top speed all day, helped stem the Confederate drive. Their appearance had, to say the least, a tremendous effect upon the soldiers in Hurlbut's line. Private Leander Stillwell, waiting in the ranks of the 61st Illinois, later wrote that he first noticed the fresh troops as they came out of the darkness at the rear, led by Ammen's band playing "Dixie." As the soldiers came within talking distance, Stillwell shouted to them, asking the number of the regiment. When told, Stillwell had what must have been the reaction of an entire army: "I gave one big, gasping swallow and stood still, but the blood thumped in the veins of my throat. . . ."[34]

These were the first Union troops to arrive in the evening. Lew Wallace, who had been floundering about the roads of Tennessee all day within sound of the battle, appeared with his Third Division about 7:15. Other elements of Buell's army disembarked at the landing around five o'clock Monday morning, April 7.

Few veterans of Shiloh ever forgot that horrible night of April 6. Officers and men, detached from their regiments by the day's fighting, attempted to find their commands. Opposite the 14th Illinois, in Hurlbut's division, the cries of the wounded who still lay in the woods were soul-stirring. Private Will Crummer of the 45th Illinois, a regiment which had fought with McClernand all day, later told of wounded soldiers hobbling through the lines using their ramrods as crutches. "Twice during the night I awoke and could hear the groans and cries of the wounded lying out there on that bloody field," he wrote. "Some cried for water, others for some one to come and help them. . . . God heard them, for the heavens were opened and rain came." Even the cries of the wounded could not keep some soldiers awake. The 34th Illinois, having marched all day with Nelson's division, was ex-

---

[33] Kenneth P. Williams, III, 373–375. Dickey to Mrs. W. H. L. Wallace, May 17, 1862, Wallace-Dickey Papers.

[34] Stillwell, "In the Ranks at Shiloh," 474–475.

hausted. Many of its sentries fell asleep at their posts, one of them even toppling across a campfire.[35]

Rain and the cries of the wounded were only part of the ghastly scene, however. All night long, as Sergeant Shumway of the 14th Illinois later wrote to his wife, the guns of the boats went "boom, boom," firing shells up a long ravine into the enemy lines. The firing was so incessant that hundreds of soldiers, thinking the landing to be the safest refuge from the Confederates, gathered around fires near the boats. Henry Villard, a reporter who arrived with Nelson's division, later wrote of "skulkers" lining the river bank, and of officers attempting with little success to "re-form the disorganized and demoralized throng." Talking with the same officers Villard found that their recollections of the day generally began with such phrases as: "We were surprised at breakfast by rebels four times as strong as ourselves"; "My regiment was cut all to pieces"; or "We were ordered to retreat."

It is difficult to disbelieve Villard's account of the demoralization of the troops on the night of April 6. David Givler, a bugler of the 7th Illinois, made similar observations in a letter written two weeks later to his friends in Naperville. Recalling his feelings at the end of that crucial day, he described an atmosphere in which most of the soldiers in his regiment thought that "Grant's army was past redemption." The truth in Villard's portrayal of the sights and sounds at Pittsburg Landing was to be found in the rumors which passed about the army concerning the nature of the surprise attack. Soldier after soldier reported stories telling of unready troops bayoneted in their sleep. Private Edwin W. Payne of the 34th Illinois wrote his family that he had been told by numerous privates that many men were killed in that fashion, and that several sick men had their throats cut, "the surprise being so complete that they could not be removed."[36]

---

[35] Boatner, 756. Crummer, 70. Payne, 22. An amusing aspect of the retreat at Shiloh was that most sutlers in the camp lost their supplies to Grant's hungry soldiers. Augustine Vieira to Mrs. Harriet Stoddard, May 10, 1862, Augustine Vieira Papers, ISHL.

[36] Shumway to his wife, April 13, 1862, Shumway Papers. Charles Brush to his father, April 6, 1862, Brush Family Papers. "Diary of Colonel William Camm," 854. Henry Villard, *Memoirs of Henry Villard: Journalist and Financier, 1835–1900* (2 vols., Boston, 1904), I, 244–246. Givler, 86. Payne to his parents, May 18, 1863, Edwin W. Payne Papers, ISHL.

Considerable evidence has been collected showing that the atrocity stories of the battle of Shiloh were only the products of the minds of demoralized troops. Albert D. Richardson, the war correspondent, devoted a good deal of time investigating the rumors and found none which were true. Modern historians have given further proof of the falsity of the stories. Nevertheless, despite the earnest efforts of apologists for Grant, few can deny that the army was unprepared for an attack of this nature. The most overwhelming proof of this is in the course of the battle. Though all regiments were up and about, some having hours to prepare for the assault, they did not prepare. The character of the attack, the disposition of Union divisions, and Grant's own correspondence indicate that the commander of the Union army at Shiloh was caught unready.[37]

As the sun rose on April 7, the Union troops at Pittsburg Landing began organizing for a counterattack. Nelson's division, including the 34th Illinois, dined on raw ham and hardtack before forming a battle line. "No sooner had we begun to advance," wrote the regimental historian, "than the swish of cannister and the droning of musket balls began to give us a new experience . . . and we begun to realize that we were earning our thirteen dollars a month." Private Edwin Payne, writing home a week after the fight, described a hard and bitter exchange of fire with the rebels, after which Illinois soldiers had the pleasure of seeing the enemy run like "quarter horses."[38]

Not all fighting on April 7 was so quickly concluded. McClernand's and Sherman's divisions got into some fierce fighting on the right wing, where defeat was eventually inflicted upon the Confederate army. Veatch's brigade, consisting of the 14th, 15th, and 46th Illinois, plus the 25th Indiana, stormed the center of the enemy line, finally turning the tide of battle. By noon, the Sunken Road and the Peach Orchard had been regained, and Shiloh Church would be taken shortly. By late afternoon, General Peter

[37] Richardson, 236–237. Catton, *Grant Moves South*, 256. Grant's comment to the *New York Herald*, May 3, 1862, is an interesting one: "If the enemy had sent word when and how they would attack we could not have been better prepared." His words hardly stand up before the facts.

[38] Payne to his parents, April 13, 1863, Edwin W. Payne Papers. Payne, 20. According to [Crooker *et al.*], 118, the 34th Illinois fought brilliantly on the second day at Shiloh.

G. T. Beauregard, who replaced Johnston, was retreating with his defeated divisions toward Corinth. The battle of Shiloh, which one historian has called the first great battle of the war, was over.[39]

The Union soldiers were then confronted with the sad scenes which are the inevitable aftermath of battle. A member of Taylor's Illinois Light Artillery, wandering about the area which his cannon had helped to defend the day before, found a Confederate officer propped against a tree, a Bible clutched in his lifeless hands. The bugler of B Company, 55th Illinois, was found leaning against a tree, rigid in death. In his hand was the last letter he had received from his wife. Corporal George Smith of the 17th Illinois, returning to the camp from which he had been driven on the previous day, found a dead Confederate soldier in his bed. Albert Richardson, the reporter, was later to write that wounded men were still being found eight days after the battle; Villard, the correspondent, detailed at length his impressions upon seeing the dead.

> Neither the one side nor the other had removed its dead, and there they were, blue and gray, in their starkness, lying here singly and there literally in rows and heaps. . . . There was a little frame church . . . known as Shiloh meeting-house (it gave its name to the battle), whose interior presented the most woeful scene in all this sadness. The seats for the worshipers had been removed, and on the floor were extended in two rows, on the bare planks and without any cover over them, twenty-seven dead and dying rebels, officers and men.[40]

In the weeks following the fight, Shiloh was visited by a number of governors and other prominent people in the West. Governor Yates of Illinois went down and, along with General McClernand, made a speech to the troops from his state in which the latter were praised for "their patriotic devotion, the luster which they had shed upon Illinois, and their soldierly appearance and expertness." The governor visited Colonel Lawler, in whose company five months earlier, according to one Illinois soldier, Yates would have "blushed had he been caught." There were other visitors to the field. Three days after the shooting was over, Mrs. Bickerdyke showed up wearing the old gray coat of a Confederate

[39] Kenneth P. Williams, III, 385. Jonathan Daniels, *Prince of Carpetbaggers* (Philadelphia, 1958), 53.

[40] *Reunions of Taylor's Battery B, First Ill. Artillery* (Chicago, 1890), 41. Villard, I, 251–252.

officer and a slouch hat replacing her lost Shaker bonnet. Within hours she had her portable laundry going, and was dispensing tea and crackers to the men.[41]

Much has been written about the tremendous cost of the battle at Shiloh Church, and the share which Illinois contributed. Of the total loss of 13,047 in killed, wounded, and missing, Illinois contributed over one third. The 9th Illinois, fighting with McArthur's brigade on the left, had 366 casualties, the greatest loss suffered by any infantry regiment in the battle. Only five of that number were missing, which was testimony to the courage and tenacity of the regiment in withdrawing in good order. The 55th Illinois, in Stuart's brigade on the far left, lost over half of its numbers with 275 casualties. The 28th Illinois, fighting near the Peach Orchard and Bloody Pond, suffered 245 casualties; the 40th Illinois with Sherman had 216; and the 45th Illinois with McClernand lost 213. Twenty-six Illinois regiments were present at the opening of the fight on April 6. Later in the day, the 53rd Illinois was brought from Savannah and added to Lauman's brigade in Hurlbut's division, and the 34th Illinois made its appearance with Nelson's division. Thus, out of the 65 regiments engaged in the Shiloh battle, 28 came from Illinois.[42]

The South, which disputed the Union claims of victory, had much to be sad about. Despite total losses of 10,699, the Confederacy had not achieved its great goal, the destruction of Grant's army. Furthermore it had lost an able general in Albert Sidney Johnston. It is little wonder that the southern author George Washington Cable wrote a generation later that the South "never smiled after Shiloh." Not even the capture of the Illinois general Ben Prentiss gave the Confederacy much satisfaction. That individual, who had fought as noble a battle as any in the entire war, was placed upon a train and taken to a southern prison. Undaunted, Prentiss, who was essentially a politician, called to bystanders at

---

[41] *Official Records*, Ser. I, Vol. X, Pt. 1, 755. Mary Livermore, 490. [Crooker *et al.*], 124. George O. Smith, "Brief History of the 17th Regiment of the Illinois Volunteer Infantry, U.S.A." (unpublished mimeographed transcript, ISHL), 3. Richardson, 246.

[42] See Chapter I on the formation of the 9th Illinois. Fox, 354, 428. John Moses, *Illinois: Historical and Statistical* (2 vols., Chicago, 1889), II, 737–740. Moses lists 27 Illinois regiments at Shiloh, though he probably does not include the 53rd Illinois, which came later into the fighting.

each train stop and "indulged in oratory to his heart's content." Even while in prison, as Albert Richardson wrote, "the Illinois general continued to harangue the people, and his men to sing the 'Star-Spangled Banner,' until at last the Rebels were glad to exchange them."[43]

Despite the disorganized retreat of Confederate forces on April 7, the North found little to cheer about. Grant, particularly, was criticized. The *St. Louis Democrat*, which carried out a personal vendetta against that commander, demanded that the administration place the responsibility for the Shiloh losses squarely upon Grant's shoulders. Failure to follow his successful attack of April 7 with an effective pursuit of the Confederate army also brought Grant much criticism. Of all the major Union generals at Shiloh, only McClernand received a good press. Sherman, who reacted to any praise of McClernand or criticism of himself, particularly noticed this, complaining to his father-in-law that Missouri and Illinois newspapers were "making their little heroes big fools." Even so, McClernand had done well on the field.[44]

McClernand himself delayed little in writing Lincoln an account of the battle and in forwarding his official report of the conflict. "We have just passed through a terrible battle lasting two days," he told the chief executive. The First Division had "borne, or shared in bearing the brunt" of the fight, he claimed, and had lost the greater number of men (a statement which doesn't hold up under a study of figures). Criticizing Grant, he wrote: "It was a great mistake that we did not pursue him, the Confederate Army, Monday night and Tuesday."

Grant might have disagreed with McClernand's claims, noting that they were faulty in "particulars," but it soon became obvious that the latter's activities were having a cumulative effect. Not only did McClernand receive a most favorable press after Shiloh,

---

[43] Ephraim Allen Otis, "Recollections of the Kentucky Campaign of 1862," in *Military Essays and Recollections*, IV (1907), 126. Richardson, 237.

[44] Douglas Putnam, "Reminiscences of the Battle of Shiloh," in *Sketches of War History, 1861–1865: Papers Read Before the Ohio Commandery of the Military Order of the Loyal Legion of the United States*, ed. R. Hunter (5 vols., Cincinnati, 1888–1903), III, 100. Putnam quotes a St. Louis paper. *Home Letters of General Sherman*, ed. M. A. DeWolfe Howe (New York, 1909), 228. James H. Wilson, *The Life of John A. Rawlins . . .* (New York, 1916), 88.

but the President is reported to have said in regard to McClernand: "Why, he saved the battle of Shiloh, when the case seemed hopeless . . . he is a natural-born general."[45]

With all of the charges and countercharges, the claims of victory and defeat, and implications concerning dereliction of duty and irresponsibility, the common soldier from Illinois now knew the full horror of war. He may have realized it as did Corporal George Smith of the 17th Illinois on the night of April 6, when he lay with McClernand's troops and listened to the moaning of the wounded. Some of the unfortunate men who remained between the battle lines called for their wives or mothers; others prayed so loudly that they could be heard by the men of the Illinois regiments. What citizen back home, quick to criticize, would know the impact of hearing one such wounded soldier sing the first line of "Jesus, Lover of My Soul," with successive lines taken up by one dying soldier after another! Or what citizen back home, certain of the vulnerability of the southern soldier, would understand the revelation experienced by Private Edwin Payne? "I have a much different opinion of the secesh from what I formerly had," he wrote; "although they are not uniformed, they have as a general thing very good arms and fight with a kind of bravery that is no disgrace to an American."[46]

[45] *Official Records*, Ser. I, Vol. X, Pt. 1, 113–114. David D. Porter, *Incidents and Anecdotes of the Civil War* (New York, 1885), 122–123.

[46] Smith, 4. Payne to his parents, April 25, 1862, Edwin W. Payne Papers.

CHAPTER IV

The Aftermath of Shiloh

The dubious victory at Shiloh, almost simultaneous with a more certain one at Island No. 10 on the Mississippi, had a tremendous impact upon the Union military effort in the West. At the end of April, Halleck reorganized his entire command. Grant's Army of the Tennessee, Pope's Army of the Mississippi, and Buell's Army of the Ohio were amalgamated into one grand army to continue the drive upon Corinth, a major Confederate rail center in the West, and Confederate base. Since Halleck decided to assume command of the army himself, Grant, under a cloud as a result of the unfavorable aspects of Shiloh, was relegated to second in command.[1]

The change was, for the Galena general, a bitter disappointment. A commander without the power of command, he was responsible to a degree without having responsibility, a "mere dummy upon a stage," as Villard, the reporter, was to describe him. Quite naturally, he quickly became disgusted with his position, and considered for a time resigning from the army. Yet it was no worse for Grant than it was for his fellow Illinois general, McClernand, to whom Halleck gave the innocuous command of the reserve corps for the movement upon Corinth. It seemed, for the moment at least, that Halleck had little sympathy for any general officers from Illinois except Pope, who was in command of the left wing.[2]

---

[1] Bruce Catton, *This Hallowed Ground* (Garden City, N.Y., 1956), 124.

[2] Villard, I, 270. *Official Records*, Ser. I, Vol. X, Pt. 1, 754. McClernand's

The first days of Halleck's movement toward Corinth appeared successful. There was a sharp skirmish near Farmington, Tennessee, on May 3 involving elements of Pope's Army of the Mississippi. Here the 16th Illinois, leading the advance, clashed with Confederate forces. Reinforcing regiments, the 8th, 10th, 22nd, and 27th Illinois moved up quickly and drove the Confederates back. Again, on May 9, Pope was engaged by the rebels. The 22nd, 26th, 27th, 42nd, 47th, and 51st Illinois were involved.[3]

Though both General Eleazer Paine and General John Palmer were involved in the fighting around Farmington, it was the latter who was most prominently mentioned in dispatches from the field. Palmer, from Carlinville, Illinois, was a solid, conservative man. Though he was inclined to be mildly phlegmatic, he could rouse his men for a battle as well as any general officer. In the attack at Farmington, one Illinois sergeant was so charged with spirit that he took personal control of a captured enemy captain, and offered to fight him bare-handed on the spot. The captain, however, refused.[4]

As the campaign moved toward Corinth it bogged down. Halleck, who was a naturally cautious man, entrenched his lines at the end of each day. He was determined to have no Shiloh. Illinois soldiers did little else but dig with spades, and fight ticks and lizards, which made their lives miserable. Despite the occasional deserters who came into the lines of the Illinois regiments complaining about food shortages inside Corinth, the Confederate army under Beauregard made a skillful retreat, forcing Halleck to pay for his advances with time. So anxious did the common soldier of the advancing army become for fight that he occasionally attempted to provoke one. A lieutenant of the 32nd Illinois wrote home on May 16 that in a skirmish on the previous day, a picket of his regiment had climbed out on the parapet of the trench and shouted to the enemy that it was firing too high. The response from the Confederate lines was immediate; one of the defenders cried out, "Listen at the d—–d sons of bitches – they say

---

role in the Corinth campaign was printed in the *Missouri Democrat* (St. Louis) and the *Illinois State Journal*; see the latter newspaper, Aug. 1, 1865.

[3] "Diary of Colonel William Camm," 865–866. See also Richardson, 251, who describes Pope's army as being "perfectly drilled and disciplined. . . ."

[4] *Army Life of an Illinois Soldier*, 86.

we are shooting too high." The crowning insult came when the aforesaid picket of the 32nd ran out to within 80 yards of the enemy trenches and sang the "Star-Spangled Banner" to the accompaniment of his own shooting. It was truly a young army, one which was too little inspired by the kind of campaign which Halleck was carrying out. As one despairing Illinois officer wrote to his wife: "I think – Darling – I shall enjoy a battle if we have one – I do indeed."[5]

By May 24 Halleck was ready to begin bombarding Corinth. The tempo of fighting speeded up: short but violent infantry clashes occurred as the Federal lines were adjusted. "These skirmishes amount almost to battles," wrote the lieutenant colonel of the 52nd Illinois. "I should think our side had fully one thousand men engaged yesterday." Five days later, on the night of May 29, the 10th Illinois, located on the Federal left wing, heard loud cheering from the Confederate lines. The next day Corinth was found evacuated, and the Union army marched in.[6]

Briefly pursuing Beauregard's forces, Halleck now turned his attention toward consolidating his gains in western Tennessee. The northern press, meanwhile, severely attacked the Union commander's strategy of digging his way into Corinth. "I do not know how the matter strikes abler military men," wrote the correspondent for the *Cincinnati Commercial*, "but I think we have been fooled." Other northern newspapers followed suit. Fortunately for Halleck, he was relieved from the necessity of further field command by the administration, which, on July 11, ordered him to assume command of the "whole land forces of the United States as general-in-chief." Grant assumed the over-all control of his old Army of the Tennessee, plus the Army of the Mississippi. The latter force was now under the immediate charge of General William S. Rosecrans, Pope having departed in late June in order to take command of the Army of Virginia. Buell, whose army had taken part in the investment of Corinth, had regained the independent

[5] Henry Harrison Eby, *Observations of an Illinois Boy in Battle, Camp and Prisons*, 1861–65 (Mendota, Ill., 1910), 51–52. E. W. Payne to his parents, May 18, 1862, Edwin W. Payne Papers. Payne reported that rebels were deserting in droves, and that they stated that there was little food inside Corinth. Lt. W. T. Burnett to his parents, May 16, 1862, Crum Collection, ISHL. John Wilcox to his wife, May 22, 1862, Wilcox Papers.

[6] Wilcox to his wife, May 24, 1862, Wilcox Papers. Jamison, 185.

command of the Department of the Ohio some days earlier, and therefore was no longer immediately subordinate to Grant.[7]

The summer of 1862 was, for Grant, a most arduous one. Enemy cavalry raids and the threat of direct frontal attacks made life miserable for the Illinois general. For most lower officers and private soldiers who came from Illinois, the hot months of 1862 presented an opportunity for relaxing and seeing an enemy people at first hand. Experiences differed, of course, and were greatly dependent upon the immediate circumstances. Some Illinois soldiers reported surprisingly normal relationships with the southerners in conquered areas; others reported the opposite. An officer of the 21st Illinois, Philip Welshimer, describing the occupation of a southern town in early July, reported that "everybody came out to see the Yankees," and the "front of every house was lined with the finest of ladies, children [*sic*] and Negroes of every shade. . . ." To Welshimer, it was a grand scene, the "silk regimental flag was flying and brass band playing and the boys marching in the best of order with bright bayonets gleaming in the Southern sun. . . ." The town women, Welshimer sarcastically noted, pointedly turned their backs upon the national flag as it passed, causing one soldier from Illinois to call out: "Its just as people are raised whether they will show their —— or their faces." [8]

Welshimer's experience with southern women was not an uncommon one at this stage of the war. On one occasion, when the 7th Illinois Cavalry led units of Buell's army through Pulaski, Tennessee, the northern soldiers were hissed by a group of women working in a cotton mill on the outskirts of the town. When the hissing appeared to have little effect, the women began to cry out: "Run you cowards. . . . They will catch you before you get to Nashville. . . ." At this juncture, General Palmer, who commanded the column, rode forward and shouted: "Ladies, do you know that these soldiers carry matches in their pockets? This building would burn nicely." The catcalling ended.[9]

Though one Illinois soldier was later to write that most of the

---

[7] Halleck was severely attacked by the reporter, Whitelaw Reid. *Official Records*, Ser. I, Vol. X, Pt. 1, 771–773.

[8] Welshimer to his wife, July 6, 1862, Philip Welshimer Papers, ISHL.

[9] Eby, 55–56. John M. Palmer, *Personal Recollections of John M. Palmer* . . . (Cincinnati, 1901), 118, also writes an account of this incident.

opposite sex in the South was mortally afraid of being "ravished and ruined," young soldiers found ways of meeting, or at least observing, southern girls. On a good many occasions, what the Illinois soldier saw he did not like. Rarely were Illinois women known to use tobacco; some southern women did. A Canton, Illinois, officer, attempting to purchase some tallow from farm women in northern Mississippi, was shocked by the sight. "Their ages were from 18 to 24," he wrote. "Each of them had a quid of tobacco in her cheek about the size of my stone inkstand, and if they didn't make the extract fly worse than I ever saw in any country grocery, shoot me. These women here have so disgusted me with the use of tobacco that I have determined to abandon it." The same soldier, commenting upon the use of tobacco and its relationship to courtship, wrote: ". . . sometimes girls ask their beaux to take a dip with them during a spark. I asked one if it didn't interfere with the old fashioned habit of kissing. She assured me that it did not in the least, and I marvelled." An Illinois surgeon, equally amazed at the use of tobacco by women, wrote his wife of an experience in Memphis: "As I walked the streets . . . I met a lady. . . . As I approached her she . . . spit upon the pavement a great stream of *Tobacco Juice*. She then returned the little stick which I saw had a little swab on the end of it. *She* was dipping." It was almost as an Oquawka, Illinois, soldier recalled after the war: ". . . those people had one never-failing resource – they could chew snuff."[10]

An Illinois chaplain, barely literate himself, found time to confide his amazement at the ignorance of the lower classes in the South to his diary: "Many dont or Cant Read or write and Dont know County Town or place, only Dads house, and Uncle Sams Just over yonder." Some simply objected to the looks of southern girls. One Illinois man advised a friend back in the home state never to go South for a wife, for he had not seen a good-looking girl since coming to "dixie." Others objected to the attitude of women in the South. James T. Ayers, the aforementioned chaplain, giving way to un-Christianlike sentiments, wrote on one oc-

[10] Onley Andrus to his wife, May 1, 1865, *Civil War Letters of Serqeant Onley Andrus*, 130. *Army Life of an Illinois Soldier*, 215, 99–101. H. H. Hood to his wife, Dec. 20, 1862, Humphrey Hughes Hood Papers, ISHL. Jamison, 206–207.

casion: "Why sir the Haughty Stinking heiffers here in Huntsville [Alabama] will go and Draw there grub of us and with there mouth filled with our bread treat us with utter Scorn and Contempt. . . . Lets Clean them out; give them Pills Boys instead of Bread, and kicks instead of huggin and kissing. . . ."[11]

Even Ayers changed his mind at times, however. Fresh from a conversational exchange with an attractive southern lady, he confided to his diary: "God bless the Little widow, them Blue Eyes that Little plump Rosy Cheek them Delicate Lilly white hands that Lady Like Smile that well Seasoned Christian Like spirit. Man would be A monster Could he Deny such an Angel as this." The Canton, Illinois, officer who had found the tobacco habit so disgusting eventually met a southern girl who so entranced him that he wrote to friends back home: "I found the sweetest girl here that ever man looked at. . . . I swear I was never bewitched before." In the 44th Illinois, Lieutenant Peter Weyhrich of Pekin found time to write a warning concerning women to a friend in the 8th Illinois: "I see you are as great a woman's man as ever. Instead of soldiering having altered the tendency of your mind from women I see you are still prone to go in raptures about the beauty of the feminine sex."[12]

In some areas, and at certain times, the fraternization between northern officers and southern women was quite extensive (to the great disgust of some soldiers). One western Illinois officer could not help but compare the situation in western Tennessee with what he thought might happen in his own home town, should the situation be reversed. "How'd you like to see a 'Captain St. Clair de Monstachir' with C.S.A. on his buttons, making calls in Canton?" he wrote. "I'll bet ten to one he could enjoy himself in that burg."[13]

During the period immediately after Shiloh and Corinth, most Union officers made a serious attempt to keep foraging by their

---

[11] *The Diary of James T. Ayers, Civil War Recruiter*, ed. John Hope Franklin (Springfield, 1947), 13, 36. *The Civil War Letters of Henry C. Bear: A Soldier in the 116th Illinois Volunteer Infantry*, ed. Wayne C. Temple (Harrogate, Tenn., 1961), 9.

[12] *Diary of James T. Ayers*, 24. Civil War Diary of Charles W. Wills, Jan. 9–March 23, 1865, ISHL, 4–5. Peter Weyhrich to D. C. Smith, Jan. 30, 1863, D. C. Smith Papers, ISHL.

[13] *Army Life of an Illinois Soldier*, 76.

soldiers down to a respectable level. As with other portions of the army, this was also true of Illinois regiments. In March, a member of the 19th Illinois informed his family that an Illinois colonel in his area had been placed under arrest because one of his men had stolen six cabbage heads. "We are not permitted to take anything but even a fence rail from any one secesh," he complained. As late as August, 1862, there was, in some Illinois regiments, strict enforcement of regulations against foraging. It was commonly reported in the Corinth area, for example, that Colonel Nicholas Greusel, the officer who had performed so well at Pea Ridge, had ordered a soldier in his brigade to be hung by the thumbs for six hours as a penalty for stealing two ears of corn.[14]

During the summer months, however, two factors impinged upon the outlook of Union soldiers in the South. First of all, there were a number of incidents, and countless rumors of incidents, involving the mutilation of northern soldiers caught foraging by guerrillas. It was reported, for instance, that when a member of the 20th Illinois was so captured, his ears and nose were cut off, he was "otherwise mutilated," and then released. A soldier of the 7th Illinois reported to friends at home that mutilation of foragers was common, his conclusion being: "A great many of our soldiers do not like the idea of our generals feeding the families of the secesh while the sons, and maybe also the father, is in the rebel army or in some Guerilla [*sic*] party trying their best to injure us all they can."[15] A lieutenant colonel of the 52nd Illinois, John Wilcox of Elgin, Illinois, wrote his wife in July protesting the protection given to the "property and homes of men who if not actively engaged . . . in open warfare against us are still either secretly our enemies or entirely indifferent." Wilcox, whose hardening attitude toward southerners was typical of Illinois soldiers in 1862, proposed a different treatment for the South: "I begin to think the better way would be to *utterly desolate wherever we went and then it would not be necessary to leave a guard behind. . . .* I am heartily sick of seeing a constant detail of eight or ten men kept night and day around the dwelling of a man who is but 50

[14] Alexander Raffen to his parents, March 20, 1862, Raffen Papers. J. H. Sackett to his brother, Aug. 17, 1862, Sackett Papers.

[15] Blanchard, 115. Mary Livermore, 379. David Givler to a friend, Aug. 6, 1862, Givler, 90.

or 100 miles distant openly laboring for our destruction . . . if I had control when this army had marched through the Gulf states no land marks would be left to show the boundaries of towns counties or states. . . . ."[16]

A second reason for the breakdown of regulations against foraging was the actual shortage of supplies for the Union army in west Tennessee and northern Mississippi. Guerrilla raids by Forrest, the movement of Van Dorn upon Holly Springs, and a series of misfortunes in late 1862 sometimes caused a shortage of rations. A Carrollton, Illinois, soldier informed his parents in December of 1862 that his company was on half-rations of coffee, and quarter-rations of bacon and hardtack. A northern Illinois sergeant wrote his wife in November: "If we could have a little Butter O golly, but I dont expect to have any such thing till I get home again." Furthermore, the food supplies remaining on hand left much to be desired. A soldier of the 61st Illinois, commenting on the meat ration for his regiment, wrote his parents: "But it's awful poor beef, lean, slimy, skinny and stringy. The boys say that one can throw a piece up against a tree, and it will just stick there and quiver and twitch for all the world like one of those blue bellied lizards. . . . ." By late December many Union regiments were having a "serious time" finding rations at all.[17] The Christmas allowance for some Illinois regiments was exceedingly small, as one soldier from the state noted: "I have seen boys this morning that have been on ¼ Rations for 3 days, & they said all they had for breakfast was 1 hard Bread for 2 of them, & I have seen them reduced to corn, nothing but corn, to eat as they were a mind to. . . . But it is a Galorious cause. It would pay a man of *ordinary* means to starve for the sake of meddling with other peoples affairs."[18]

Foraging did not begin in 1862; it had existed from the beginning of the war. In the late summer and fall of 1862, however, it

[16] Wilcox to his wife, July 11, 1862, Wilcox Papers.

[17] Stillwell, *Story of a Common Soldier*, 124. Onley Andrus to his wife, Nov. 27, 1862, *Civil War Letters of Sergeant Onley Andrus*, 30. Stillwell, *Story of a Common Soldier*, 124. Givler, 98.

[18] Onley Andrus to his wife, Dec. 25, 1862, *Civil War Letters of Sergeant Onley Andrus*, 44.

was as if the whole Union army had not only been turned loose, but encouraged to take what it wished. Sheep, cattle, and even watermelon fell to the troops, according to the historian of the 55th Illinois. A member of the 7th Illinois wrote home in autumn that foraging put a "new zeal into the soldiers for they think they have protected rebel property about long enough now, they intend to help themselves to anything that will add to their comfort!" Another Illinois soldier wrote in October: "I think it perfectly right to take the hog and leave them none and then if they ain't Satisfied I am fore banish ever Rebel and rebel simpathiser from the U.S." [19]

Though the earlier regiments raised in Illinois were restricted to some extent by a natural discipline in respect to foraging, the units which were raised and sent to the front in 1862 seemed to operate under no restrictions, personal or otherwise. A member of the 111th Illinois, sent into Kentucky in November, illustrated the typical rationalization of these more undisciplined troops when he wrote: "Some of the boys will go out in the woods. They accidentally come across a hog. They order it to halt. It never lets on it hears them. Their gun go off accidentally *hits* him in the head, all of course done accidentally. He is then striped of his *hide-head*, etc. He is then caried to camp and named a *bear*." [20]

The 124th Illinois, raised by Colonel Thomas J. Sloan in Henry, Kane, Jersey, McDonough, Mercer, and Sangamon counties, arrived in Bolivar, Tennessee, in 1862. The shine still upon their uniforms, the troops were so new that they could not form a "straight line in an hour . . . !" Their first attempts at foraging were revealing — at least to them. When they brought their forage to camp, soldiers from the nearby veteran regiments cornered them, held mock trials, and fined them. The fines were collected from the forage gathered by the rookie regiment, of course. It was gleefully recounted from camp to camp, and even by Grant himself, how the tents, blankets, and overcoats were stolen from

[19] [Crooker *et al.*], 150–160. David Givler to a friend, Aug. 6, 1862, Givler, 91. Joshua R. Barney to his brother, Oct. 24, 1862, John C. Dinsmore Papers, ISHL.

[20] James McGee to his cousin Robert, Nov. 9, 1862, "Civil War Letters of Robert G. Ardrey, 111th Illinois Infantry," comp. Joseph L. Eisendrath, Jr. (unpublished typed transcript, ISHL).

over the sleeping soldiers on the first night the new regiment bedded down.[21]

Within weeks, however, the 124th could match its foraging practices with any veteran regiment. Marching through Tennessee in late October, troops of a rear company noticed six calves in a nearby meadow. Covering them with coats, they marched the cattle with them until that evening, when the animals were slaughtered. Shortly thereafter, the regiment arrived at La Grange, Tennessee, where it was quartered on the campus of a local college. Within the hour, the soldiers had butchered a cow and a hog, and were well on their way toward being a plague to the military command of the town. "Hang all the officers who won't let us steal from the rebel property. . . ," wrote Private John Given of the 124th. "I will steal it whenever I get a chance." Given was able to write his family a few weeks later that the regiment had added a few more dubious laurels to its crown, having "stole lots of niggers," killed six cattle, and burned the fence around the college — all in one night. It was, Given was moved to write, "one of the most jovial nights I ever experienced." [22]

Before long, the antics of the regiment brought censure upon the troops. After breaking into the commissary, as well as the sutler's stores, it was generally recognized by the military authorities that the regiment was a "bad lot." Charging the 124th with a "great deal of stealing," a provost guard was placed in control of the regiment, and it was confined to quarters. After suitable discipline, however, the regiment quickly developed into a fine fighting unit. It not only participated in the Vicksburg campaign, but in January, 1864, it was awarded the "Excelsior" banner for being the best-drilled regiment in its division.[23]

La Grange, the little town so terribly mistreated by the 124th, must have taken some time to recover. A member of the 7th Illinois Cavalry wrote his family in late 1862 that the once pretty town was now a "vulgar desolation. . . . The fences are all burned, the gardens trampled. . . . ." A Canton, Illinois, officer

---

[21] *Three Years with Grant as Recalled by War Correspondent Sylvanus Cadwallader*, ed. Benjamin P. Thomas (New York, 1955), 17–18.

[22] Richard L. Howard, 30. Given to his aunt, Oct. 11, 1862, Given to his parents, Nov. 5, 1862, Given Papers.

[23] Richard L. Howard, 34–35, 39. Given to his parents, Nov. 13, 1862, Given Papers.

who visited the town after the "Vandal Yankees" had occupied it for some time, wrote that the fences of the town had all disappeared after having fulfilled their mission of "boiling Yankee coffee, and frying Yankee bacon." Not content with wrecking the town, the soldiers had also desecrated a nearby cemetery by adding their own names to all the grave markers.[24]

The Illinois soldier, like his companions in service from other states, developed a fine sense of the dramatic with respect to foraging, as well as appropriate knowledge of the regulations under which he operated. When he was told by his commanding officer that he could take only the top rail of a nearby fence for firewood, he quickly understood that as long as there was any rail at all, it was the top rail. When fences disappeared, as they eventually did, the cattle roamed unrestrained — and usually into the camps of Union regiments, where they were slaughtered.

In time, foraging developed the aspects of an art marked by subtlety and cleverness. On one occasion, the 13th Illinois, termed the "Stealing Regiment," stole a regimental surgeon's stove, fire and all, while his back was turned. It was left to the 36th Illinois to prove the artistic facets of foraging, however. During a march in Tennessee, this regiment, which was composed of troops from Warren, Kendall, and McHenry counties, stole the uniforms of the 24th Wisconsin. Then, wearing the clothing of the latter regiment, the troops of the 36th conducted large-scale forays into nearby farming areas. The Wisconsin regiment quite naturally received the blame. Not content with this feat of skill, the 36th then stole 30 sheep belonging to a Tennessee farmer, and threw the pelts into the tents of the 73rd Illinois, the "Preacher's Regiment." When Colonel James Jaquess of the 73rd could not explain the presence of the pelts, he was ordered to march at the rear of his regiment. Truly the men of the 36th, as well as those of other Illinois regiments, could have been well described by the comment of a Carlinville, Illinois, soldier in November, 1862: "The men seem to have adapted the Lycurgian law of morals — no wrong to steal if you don't get caught at it." [25]

---

[24] Letter of Henry Forbes, 7th Illinois Cavalry, quoted in D. Alexander Brown, *Grierson's Raid* (Urbana, Ill., 1954), 6–7. *Army Life of an Illinois Soldier*, 162.

[25] Eby, 60. Mary Livermore, 332–333. Bennett and Haigh, 298. "Diary of Col. William Camm," 918.

Just as the summer of 1862 marked a turning point in the attitudes of Illinois soldiers in the lower ranks, it also saw a definite turning point in the relationships of the general officers who commanded them. Most of the latter individuals, including Grant, had reached a kind of frustration in their dealings with each other. Both Buell and Rosecrans developed a dislike of Grant, and the Illinois general reciprocated. Sherman disliked McClernand almost irrationally, though the latter, more confident of his political connections and therefore less envious of the Ohio general, did not return such intense sentiments. By May McClernand had reached a point of irreconcilability with Halleck which was almost at the level of that between himself and Grant. All of this hurt McClernand's career, not only in the field where such relations affected decisions, but also back in Illinois, where supporters of Grant began to work actively against the southern Illinois general in 1862. Governor Yates, who in his way was a supporter of McClernand, called this turn of events to the attention of the latter in March, when he advised him that there were some jealous partisans working against him, though the bulk of the politicians of the state had the "warmest feeling" for the general. "The conspicuous and pre-eminent services you rendered at Fort Donelson is well understood and highly appreciated," Yates wrote. "Let me assure you that I miss no occasion to do you justice, and that it affords me pleasure to do it." Included in this strange March letter to McClernand is a statement from the governor that he had certain "requests" to make of McClernand. By way of reminder, it may be added that Yates paid a visit to McClernand's headquarters in May, and one suspects that the "requests" were put to the general at that time.[26]

The key word at the conclusion of Yates's March letter offers a variety of possibilities for conjecture. Was Yates so worried about the level of recruiting in Illinois that he felt McClernand, with his great public influence, should add his efforts toward filling the quotas laid upon the state? Had the Copperhead movement, strong in southern Illinois from the beginning, become so powerful that the governor wanted McClernand's political power to be used against it?

[26] Yates to McClernand, March 26, 1862, McClernand Collection.

If these concerns were involved in Yates's May visit to McClernand, the latter did not immediately offer any assistance. Chafing under Halleck, restive under Grant, McClernand seemed to feel that his future really lay outside of the West. When Grant regained command of the Army of the Tennessee, the change was almost too much for the southern Illinoisan and he quickly wrote to Senator Orville H. Browning of Illinois, including a request for a command on the James River. A part of the appeal was the strange notion that Illinois troops be allowed to go with him. Browning, mindful of McClernand's contribution to the war effort, carried the petition to the War Department, but Secretary Stanton cleverly played off the senator by stating that, according to military protocol, he could not even hear McClernand's request. The interview between Stanton and Browning must have been an interesting one, with the secretary concluding that Halleck was in "command of the army of the west, and he [McClernand] must consult with him, and not civilians as to the proper disposition of the army under his command." The rebuked Browning then carried McClernand's request to the White House, where the President, likewise, gave him an inconclusive answer. Lincoln may have been forewarned, however, for in late March he had received a previous plea from McClernand for an independent command. "I will try and reward your confidence with success," McClernand had written.[27]

With the failure of the July request, McClernand seemed to become desperate to escape from Grant's command. On August 12 he again wrote to Lincoln, informing the President that he wished a leave of absence. The action, once again, was an illustration of McClernand's inability to understand the line of command. Lincoln merely sent the letter to Halleck, the person to whom it should have been sent in the first place. The general-in-chief, who disliked McClernand intensely, blasted the application for a leave, stating: "Permit me, Genl, to call your attention to the fact that in sending this application directly to the President, instead of transmitting it through prescribed channels, you have violated the

[27] *Diary of Orville Hickman Browning*, I, 560. McClernand to Lincoln, March 31, 1862, Lincoln Papers. The request was included with McClernand's battle report of Fort Donelson.

Army Regulations. This is not the first instance of this kind, for I remember to have reminded you . . . some months ago. . . ."[28]

Besides being a determined man, McClernand was basically a politician. The very same day on which he had sent his request for a leave of absence to the President, he had covered himself with a similar request to Governor Yates. Now he was willing to deal with the governor concerning Yates's May "requests," writing: "I think I could offer some information and assistance in regard to the refilling of our old regiments. Ask the Secretary of War to order me to visit you at Springfield for that purpose." Yates quickly responded, instructing his own secretary to write "Sec. of War earnestly & write McClernand have written – write be glad if can come."[29]

Though Halleck had torn McClernand apart for going through the wrong channels with his original application for leave, one must suspect that the general-in-chief realized that the Yates matter had to be handled differently. Here was the governor of an important western state – and this governor wanted McClernand to return to Illinois, and in a hurry. There were no lectures to McClernand on army regulations this time; only a hurriedly written order: "General J. A. McClernand will repair to Springfield, Ill., and assist the Governor in organizing volunteers." Halleck's note must have been written with some chagrin. Still, the general-in-chief had lost but a skirmish – the major battle was yet to come.[30]

The return to Illinois was, for McClernand, in the way of a triumph. The reception in Springfield, with the great gathering of people about the capitol building, was magnificent. The turnout at Jacksonville, headed by the faculty of Illinois College, was just as great. In early September McClernand traveled to Chicago, where he again addressed large crowds. What long-range purpose did McClernand have in mind when he stated in that city: "Any commander who relies wholly upon STRATEGY must fail. We want the right man to lead us; a man who will appoint a subordi-

[28] Halleck to McClernand, Aug. 20, 1862, McClernand Collection.

[29] McClernand to Yates, Aug. 12, 1862, Yates Papers. See the same collection for Memorandum to Secretary, Aug. 12, 1862.

[30] Halleck to Grant, Aug. 25, 1862, *Official Records*, Ser. I, Vol. XVII, Pt. 2, 187.

nate officer on account of his merits, and not because he is a graduate of West Point. Neither Ceasar [*sic*] nor Cromwell were graduates of West Point." Was he really striking at Grant or Halleck here, or did he have in mind some greater project?[31]

The return of McClernand to Illinois, and its consequent results, was connected not only to that general's personal problems with his commanders, but also to national difficulties, which, by their very nature, had to involve such a man. Beyond the simple fact that Grant and McClernand were antipathetic were the great problems of the war effort – the repeated failures in the East, the growing strength of the Copperhead movement in the West, and the startling comeback of the Democratic Party in Illinois in 1862.[32]

Though it is doubtful that McClernand had elaborated upon a plan to solve his personal difficulties during his return to Springfield, one may suppose that he soon saw within the national difficulties an outlet for his ambitions. He had a clever and facile mind: he could read the signs. When Governor Yates of Illinois and Governor Morton of Indiana indicated that success in the Mississippi valley would answer a great many questions in the West concerning the war, and when McClernand received letters from such practical politicians as Samuel S. Cox of Ohio urging the "practical and complete rescue of the Mississippi from our *treacherous* and *treasonable* foes," he soon realized the direction he should head himself in. The conclusion was obvious. The West wanted a free Mississippi valley; he wanted an independent command; therefore, he would go to Washington with a plan to achieve both.[33]

The story of McClernand, the Illinois general in Washington, may be told principally in relation to three men: Salmon P. Chase, the Secretary of the Treasury; Admiral D. D. Porter of the U.S.

---

[31] *Chicago Tribune*, Sept. 3, 1862. *Illinois State Journal*, Sept. 6, 1862. *Chicago Tribune*, Sept. 8, 1862.

[32] There was also the matter of the Democratic state convention, held on Sept. 16, 1862. McClernand had hoped to influence this gathering, but the convention drew up a strong critique of the war effort. Davidson and Stuvé, 877–878.

[33] Wood Gray, *The Hidden Civil War: The Story of the Copperheads* (New York, 1942), 216. Cox to McClernand, Dec. 9, 1861, McClernand Collection.

Navy; and James H. Wilson, a young and ambitious man from southern Illinois. The tale which the three tell in their diaries and memoirs, mingled with the comments of such casual observers as Gideon Welles, Secretary of the Navy, is essentially one of a promoter swimming in a sea of promoters.

Shortly after his arrival in Washington, McClernand managed an introduction to Chase, himself a man with vast ambitions. The Illinois general quickly introduced his scheme to the secretary—one must remember that the latter came from Ohio. The impact of the men upon each other must have been interesting; Chase was to inform his diary later that McClernand made a "very favorable impression" upon him. One must suppose that McClernand did an exceptional job of selling both himself and his plan, for 24 hours later Chase sent the general a short note in which he indicated that he would "have an interview with the President in relation to your wishes." Soon afterward, on September 27, Chase again met McClernand, and, as he informed his diary, the "favorable impression of the last evening was strengthened." "Many things in a plan of campaign which he urged seemed admirable," Chase wrote, "especially the Eastern movement from the Mississippi River." On the very same day, the secretary had introduced the subject of McClernand to the President during a cabinet session. Lincoln's response indicated that he knew McClernand well; the general was a brave man, but "too desirous to be independent of everybody else."[34]

McClernand's next step was to bring his Mississippi project before Lincoln himself. On the day following the cabinet meeting of September 27, he presented the grand design of the Mississippi plan to the President. Deferring to his friend's "superior intelligence and judgment upon the subject" of capturing the valley of the Mississippi, McClernand argued that the movement should have several phases to it. First the Mississippi should be opened, then the army should move to Mobile. Supplied from the sea at this point, it would then strike for the East Coast. An important

---

[34] "Diary and Correspondence of Salmon P. Chase," *Annual Report of the American Historical Association for the Year 1902*, II (Washington, D.C., 1903), 96, 97. See also John Cowan to McClernand, Sept. 25, 1862, McClernand Collection. McClernand carried with him a glowing letter of introduction from Governor Yates.

corollary of the whole plan was the destruction of all southern railroads as the army moved from west to east. One needs but little imagination here to see that McClernand's scheme as presented in Washington, although far from original, was not too different from the plan which was eventually followed in 1864 and 1865.[35]

In Washington at this time was a young army officer by the name of James H. Wilson. From southern Illinois, Shawneetown to be exact, he was a West Point graduate, and a kind of protégé of McClernand. Before the war ended he became one of the foremost cavalry leaders in the conflict; before the end of his life he, like Lew Wallace, became a fine writer. Decades later, he recalled meeting McClernand in Washington in 1862. The general confided deeply in Wilson, relating the story of his problem with Grant, and his desire to obtain an "augmented command" or a "department of his own." If one is to believe Wilson's remembrance of things past, McClernand seemed to be positive that in view of his own bargaining power, that is, his political strength in Illinois, the President could hardly turn him down.[36]

Lincoln played it cautiously, however, according to McClernand's recollections years later, "pretending to be otherwise engaged." This is the way it had to be, for the President's judgment was, in the end, a compromise of conflicting opinions. First of all, there were those such as Yates and Chase who wanted a Mississippi campaign, and wanted McClernand to head it. And then there were those who wished for a Mississippi campaign, but desired its control to be in other hands. These included West Pointers such as Halleck, who distrusted McClernand's lack of professional military training. During Chase's travels around Washington in September, he had sounded out the general-in-chief concerning the Illinois general. The response which the Ohioan added to his diary is an interesting one: "He said he is brave and able but no disciplinarian; that his camp was always full of disorder; that at Corinth he pitched his tents where his men had been

[35] McClernand to Lincoln, Sept. 28, 1862, Lincoln Papers.

[36] James H. Wilson, *Under the Old Flag . . .* (2 vols., New York, 1912), I, 120. Wilson was in Washington hoping to get an assignment to the West. Through McClernand's help he did, but soon after his arrival at Grant's headquarters he became an ardent supporter of the Galena general.

buried just below ground, and with dead horses lying all around. The cause of the evil was that his officers and men were his constituents." [37]

On September 30 McClernand made another trip to the White House, the only result being that the President asked the Illinois general to accompany him on a trip to the battlefield at Antietam. There, while Brady, the noted photographer, took plate after plate, and while McClernand and McClellan put their heads together and compared notes, Lincoln made up his mind. On the return to Washington, the President informed Chase of his decision; he was planning to send McClernand out west to head the Mississippi campaign. This may not have been news to Chase, however, for even before Lincoln's return from Sharpsburg, the *Philadelphia Press* had indicated that McClernand was about to receive an important assignment. Two weeks later, James H. Wilson again saw McClernand, and the latter was unable to contain himself with joy. It was now certain that he would obtain the command of the Mississippi expedition.[38]

By this time another important visitor had come to Washington. He was David Dixon Porter, an admiral of the U.S. Navy. Years later Porter claimed that he saw both Lincoln and McClernand in this period. If one is to believe Porter, and there are discrepancies in his story, Lincoln asserted great confidence in his "old and intimate friend" McClernand, claiming that he was a "natural-born general." Porter's visit to McClernand uncovered the same kind of optimism. According to the admiral, the sanguine Illinoisan spoke of "taking Vicksburg in a week!" [39]

There is little doubt that McClernand obtained the prize assignment of the Mississippi campaign not so much because Lincoln wished to help a friend, but because of what the general could do for the administration. Channing, the great portrayer of American history, described the appointment as a bargain in which McClernand offered the President troops and loyalty in return for the

[37] Biography of John A. McClernand, I, 139. "Diary of Salmon P. Chase," 98.

[38] *Illinois State Journal*, Oct. 2, 1861. *Chicago Tribune*, Oct. 2, 1862. According to Wilson, McClernand and McClellan, both Democrats, spent much time with each other. Wilson, *Under the Old Flag*, I, 123–127. "Diary of Salmon P. Chase," 103.

[39] Porter, 122–123.

Mississippi command. Charnwood, the British historian, claimed that McClernand's proposal to recruit troops in Illinois in return for the assignment was a perfect exchange—"it would have been folly to slight this offer." Both were right. The West was filled with discontent over the conduct of the war, and western governors were making it known. More than anything else, they wanted the Mississippi valley rescued for the Union. Empowered to show his orders to the governors of Iowa, Indiana, and Illinois, McClernand was to forward troops from those states to designated points in the South. Unwritten, but there all the same, was the implication that McClernand, as the leader of northwestern Democrats, would throw his full weight behind recruitment for the army. When a sufficient number of troops had been raised, McClernand was to open the campaign against Vicksburg.

As clever as McClernand was, he did not understand at this stage that he was operating against three of the subtlest minds in the nation—those of the President, Stanton, and Halleck. Written into McClernand's orders was a sentence so cleverly worded that McClernand may well have missed its alternate meaning. The Mississippi campaign, said the orders, could only be independent provided the troops involved were "not required by the operations of General Grant's command." As time would prove, these may have been the most important words of McClernand's entire life. They gave Halleck, Stanton, and most of all Grant the safety valve for depriving McClernand of his power should he prove too troublesome.[40]

The crispness of fall was in the air when McClernand arrived back in Springfield with his great prize. The news of his achievement being commonly known, he was once again welcomed in triumph. Lithographic pictures of the general were hawked about the streets of the capital, and even Governor Yates was on hand to greet him when he stepped from the train. By the end of the month, McClernand had seen the governors of Iowa and Indiana, and almost every day brought new evidences of a successful future. "Every confidence is reposed in your zeal and skill," wrote the Secretary of War, "and I long to see you in the field striking vig-

[40] Edward Channing, *A History of the United States* (6 vols., New York, 1912–25), VI, 547. Godfrey R. B. Charnwood, *Abraham Lincoln* (3rd ed., New York, 1917), 351. *Official Records*, Ser. I, Vol. XVII, Pt. 2, 502.

orous blows against the rebellion in its most vital point." Two days later, another message arrived from Stanton, urging the general to fulfill his end of the bargain, that is, to raise the necessary troops, and to develop "local interest and feeling in favor of the Mississippi operations. . . ."[41]

McClernand was not lacking in intelligence, however. Having been in politics a good many years, he had vague notions about the men with whom he was dealing. By November 9 he sensed that something was not quite right in respect to Stanton and Halleck. To Governor Yates, who had gone to Washington, he telegraphed: "Please see the Secretary of War and learn the status of the enterprise." After he reported to Stanton in mid-November that 20 regiments had been forwarded to the front, his normally suspicious nature told him that something was vitally wrong. Besides, he was not a man without sources of counsel. Back in Washington in September, he had been warned by Wilson that Halleck preferred Grant over himself. By mid-November, certain "influences" had convinced him that he should be on guard. By December 1 he seemed fully aware that his Mississippi command was in great danger, writing Stanton a peculiar little note in which he hoped that the secretary would not desert him now that the troops had been raised. This was coupled with a telegram to Browning in which he urged the senator to look into the matter. Browning's reply, at least, was encouraging: "Go ahead," it read, "you are in no danger."[42]

Looking back from the vantage point of a hundred years, it is not difficult to understand McClernand's concern. The news of the Mississippi venture had spread throughout the entire West. Even General Benjamin Butler had heard of it in New Orleans, being informed by his own sources that McClernand would be down his way "near the last of December. . . ." The papers were

---

[41] *Illinois State Journal*, Nov. 25, 1862. Stanton to McClernand, Oct. 29, 1862, *Official Records*, Ser. I, Vol. XVII, Pt. 2, 302, 308.

[42] McClernand to Yates, Nov. 20, 1862 (copy), McClernand Collection. According to Wilson, it had "evidently not occurred" to McClernand that Halleck would prefer Grant over himself. Wilson, *Under the Old Flag*, I, 138. McClernand was in close correspondence with an officer in the War Department by the name of Robert Halsey. See McClernand to Halsey, Oct. 28, 1862 (copy), McClernand Collection. Browning to McClernand, Dec. 2, 1862, McClernand Collection.

full of the news; the *Illinois State Journal* reported on November 20 that the "Mississippi expedition is assuming definite proportions." Three days before, the same newspaper had urged young men to "join the expedition to Vicksburg and Texas under that popular and fighting commander, Gen. McClernand." The *Louisville Journal* guessed that McClernand would lead an expedition against Vicksburg on December 10. In Memphis, Sherman heard the news and was mildly disquieted. Informed by James H. Wilson and Admiral Porter, both of whom had gone to the West after a September in Washington, Grant also knew that McClernand had been given an important command.[43]

One does not have to conjecture to realize that the man most concerned with McClernand's activities was the man from Galena. He was wise enough, politically and militarily speaking, to know what might happen to himself and to McClernand should the latter gain the laurels for the capture of Vicksburg. It must be admitted, even by the most ardent of Grant's biographers, that their hero did a little plotting of his own at this point. The obvious solution to the whole situation would be to take Vicksburg before McClernand arrived on the scene. Sensing support from Halleck and Stanton in such a plan, Grant had sent Sherman to Memphis with instructions to gather a force for a quick strike at the Mississippi fortress. As Grant was to write later: "I doubted McClernand's fitness, and I had good reason to believe that in forestalling him I was by no means giving offense to those whose authority to command was above both him and me." Whether Grant was really being fair when he wrote this statement two decades later is questionable. Halleck thought McClernand to be "brave and able. . . ." Was the southern Illinois general really as unfit as Grant felt he was, or was Grant searching for an excuse for his own actions in 1862 when he wrote in retrospect 20 years afterward?[44]

As the news of McClernand's project was seeping down to Grant and Sherman in the South, information concerning Sherman's

[43] Gustavus V. Fox to Butler, Nov. 17, 1862, quoted in *Private and Official Correspondence of Gen. Benjamin F. Butler . . .* (Norwood, Mass., 1917), 349. *Illinois State Journal*, Nov. 20, 1862. *Louisville* (Ky.) *Journal*, quoted in *Illinois State Journal*, Nov. 22, 1862. Wilson, *Life of John A. Rawlins*, 103. Porter, 125.

[44] Grant, I, 430–431.

movement upon Vicksburg was being brought upriver to Illinois. Both Grant and McClernand, separated by many miles, knew who was encouraging the venture. Halleck, by delaying orders which would forward McClernand to the front, gave Sherman time to gather his forces. On December 16 McClernand again reminded Halleck of the fact that he had done his duty in Illinois, and was waiting for orders which would send him to his command. On the same day a letter went out to Browning which stated: "I think I understand the Genl in Chief as well as any man living. I think he designs to give the command of the Expedition to Sherman, whom he unjustly gave the credit of the victory at Shiloh." On the following day, he sent wires to both Lincoln and Stanton asking if he had been "superseded."[45]

Within days, the wave of the future for McClernand was made known. A return wire from Stanton indicated that the secretary had assumed from the beginning that McClernand was to be "under the general supervision of the general commanding the department. . . ." On the following day, December 18, Grant received orders from Halleck which divided his command into four corps, with McClernand in command of one. Cleverly, as if he was attempting to spell out the intent of the message slowly, Halleck added the phrase: "It is the wish of the President that General McClernand's corps shall constitute a part of the river expedition, and that he shall have the immediate command, under your direction."[46]

Whatever McClernand's faults, it is clear from this space of time that he was being cleverly handled by the men who opposed him. Even Gideon Welles, the Secretary of the Navy, confided to his diary back in Washington that he suspected that McClernand, not being of the "Regular Army," was "no favorite . . . with Halleck." Postmaster General Montgomery Blair also spoke of "a combination" which was attempting to keep McClernand from his

[45] McClernand to Halleck, Dec. 16, 1862, *Official Records*, Ser. I, Vol. XVII, Pt. 2, 415. The letter to Browning is a pitiable one. In it, McClernand points to Halleck as his personal enemy, "and senselessly so." McClernand to Browning, Dec. 16, 1862 (copy), McClernand Collection. McClernand to Lincoln, McClernand to Stanton, Dec. 17, 1862, *Official Records*, Ser. I, Vol. XVII, Pt. 2, 420.

[46] Stanton to McClernand, Dec. 17, 1862, *ibid.* Halleck to Grant, Dec. 18, 1862, *ibid.*, Pt. 1, 476.

command. On the December 18 that Grant received Halleck's orders to divide his command into corps, he immediately sent orders in turn to McClernand. However, McClernand did not receive Grant's communication until December 29 in Memphis. The same orders sent to Sherman, which would have superseded that general, did not arrive, the excuse being that the wires to Memphis had been cut by guerrilla activities. However, McClernand did receive, on December 22, a dispatch from Halleck dated December 21 which was a copy of the December 18 orders to Grant. McClernand wired Stanton December 23 asking to be allowed to go forward from Springfield, and received approval the same day. Then he found no transportation available for his passage. Angered and frustrated, McClernand wired the President from Memphis December 29: "Left here by myself, I shall have to run the gauntlet of the Mississippi in a command steamer in order to reach my command. . . . Either accident or intention has conspired to thwart the authority of yourself and the Secretary of War and to betray me. . . ."[47]

Sherman's army, which had slipped away from Memphis before McClernand's arrival, reached Milliken's Bend by Christmas day. On the following day that general moved up the Yazoo River, landing his forces opposite Steele's Bayou. By December 27 the army was in line of battle and ready to move.

The story of the attack at Chickasaw Bayou is a sad one, indeed, and one for which there was little excuse. Hurriedly planned and carried out in a disorganized fashion, the three-day movement ended in defeat. Of the Union regiments involved, the 13th Illinois achieved the most distinguished record in the fighting. Heavily involved almost from the time of the landing on the Yazoo, the 13th Illinois, led by General John B. Wyman, took part in a brilliant charge on December 27. Wyman, "a very profane man" as described by one of the privates of the regiment, had shown the gift for military leadership in the Missouri campaigns of 1861. On the following day the 13th and 16th Illinois, again led by Wyman, took the forefront in the assault. This time Wyman, who had moved the attack to within a few yards of an important

[47] *Diary of Gideon Welles* (3 vols., Boston, 1911), I, 217. *Official Records*, Ser. I, Vol. XVII, Pt. 2, 425, 461–462, 534. McClernand to Lincoln, Dec. 29, 1862, Lincoln Papers.

enemy battery, was knocked from his horse by a musket ball. After ordering his men to continue the attack, he was taken to the rear, where he died.[48]

On December 29, before Chickasaw Bayou, the day was filled with error and tragedy. The attack was poorly timed and uncoordinated, regiments lost their brigade commanders, and there was poor artillery support. The 13th and 55th Illinois, both regiments singing "The Battle Cry of Freedom" as they moved to the attack, were in the center of the fray. Other Illinois regiments involved on that dreadful day were the 77th, 97th, 108th, and 131st. Nothing was gained, and the Federal losses for the three-day affair were 1,776 in killed, wounded, and missing. The 13th Illinois led all other regiments with total casualties of 134.[49]

By January 2 Sherman had withdrawn his army to the mouth of the Yazoo, where McClernand was waiting to assume command. Grant had not succeeded in his attempt to take Vicksburg before his opponent's arrival. Furthermore, as the *Chicago Tribune* was to imply two weeks later, he had sacrificed a thousand men in a senseless campaign. The whole matter, concluded the newspaper, was worth an investigation. One may little doubt that McClernand found an army in a "most demoralized state," needful of a victory no matter how small.[50]

The year of 1862 had been both good and bad for the Illinois soldiers serving in the Army of the Tennessee and the Army of the Mississippi. Fort Henry and Fort Donelson had been taken, Pea Ridge had been won, and they had helped to throw back the desperate Confederate assaults at Shiloh. The pleasure of success had been tempered by hard-won victories at Iuka and Corinth, Mississippi. At the very end had come the debacle at Chickasaw Bayou.

These 12 months had also been marked by a series of squabbles among general officers. There was Halleck against Grant, Grant

---

[48] *Military History and Reminiscenses of the Thirteenth Regiment of Illinois Volunteer Infantry . . .* , prepared by a regimental committee (Chicago, 1892), 241. W. H. Marsh states that Wyman was very popular with his troops. Marsh to his mother, Aug. 14, 1862, William Henry Marsh Papers, ISHL.

[49] [Crooker *et al.*], 189. Boatner, 154. Fox, 434. Eddy, I, 441–443.

[50] *Chicago Tribune*, Jan. 13, 1863. Porter, 130–131.

against McClernand, and McClernand against Halleck. On and on it had gone, until it appeared even to the common soldier that, for the good of the nation, the great national hero must soon emerge. The year 1863 would not bring complete victory, but it would serve to solve some problems. By the time the next Christmastide came around, many of the early heroes would have faded, and fate would be on the way toward awarding the laurels of success to the chosen ones.

CHAPTER V

Death Under the Cedars

John Alexander McClernand was not the only person who made news in September of 1862. While this mercurial individual was engaged in the pursuit of the Vicksburg command, important events were building to a climax in other theaters of war. Strangely enough, they involved two men who, like McClernand, were victims of their own enlarged personality defects. The first, Don Carlos Buell, commanding general of the Department of the Ohio, was a ramrod-stiff professional soldier, a man whose icy personality elicited little inspiration from his subordinates. Regaining command of the Department of the Ohio in July, he began a long-awaited invasion of eastern Tennessee, the purpose of which was to take and hold the important railroad center of Chattanooga.

The second performer in the forthcoming drama was Braxton Bragg, the commanding general of the Confederate Army of Tennessee. Like Buell, he was a cold and uninspiring man who carried within his character an added fault: he had an almost unequaled capacity for offending those to whom he gave orders. Vague in language as well as personality, he could never forgive those who questioned his meaning or intent. Nevertheless, he did have some concept of grand strategy. While his opposite, Buell, moved into southern Tennessee and northern Alabama with such a lack of speed that it appeared as if the war had a century to run, Bragg undertook a maneuver which was to affect profoundly the course of history for the remainder of the year. In late August he neatly sidestepped the ponderously moving Buell and headed northward for an invasion of Kentucky. Thus, for a moment, the war assumed the aspects of a giant chessboard, one general threatening Chattanooga, the other checkmating him with a strike at Kentucky and, if the signs were right, the Ohio River.

It was a great game of bluff involving many factors. As McClernand had found in his timely visit to Illinois in September, the position of the Northwest was shaky. Copperheads, emboldened by the course of events, were openly soliciting and getting support in Illinois[1] and Indiana; the bitterly anti-war Democrats were gaining increasing public backing. Foremost among these was Clement L. Vallandigham, the Ohio politician, who was both a Copperhead and a Democrat. Since he already had strong support in Ohio, it would not do to allow Bragg's invasion of Kentucky to continue unhampered. Buell was ordered to check his opponent's northward maneuver.

Buell and Bragg confronted each other for three days south of Munfordville, Kentucky. Then, on September 21, Bragg veered off east to Bardstown. Buell continued his forced march straight northward, concentrating in Louisville on September 29. There he found a considerable force of new and untried troops which had been hurriedly assembled for the defense of the city by General William Nelson, the same officer who had marched a division ashore at Pittsburg Landing that crucial night of April 6. This multitude of raw soldiery had been raised in the great fall recruitment campaign in Illinois, Indiana, and Ohio. The governors of those states had been so frightened by Bragg's march north that they had rushed the new regiments into Kentucky with almost no training. One Illinois regiment, the 123rd, raised in the Charleston and Mattoon area, had been comfortably encamped in the latter town just a few weeks before. Only its commanding officer, Colonel James Monroe, had seen a gun fired in anger. The 123rd was forwarded to the front so quickly that it had never had the privilege of battalion drill; in fact, rarely had its troops drilled as companies.[2]

---

[1] Cole, 301–303.

[2] Henry M. Cist, *The Army of the Cumberland*, Vol. VII of *The Army in the Civil War* (New York, 1885), 57–60. *Report of the Adjutant General*, VI, 416. *Official Records*, Ser. I, Vol. XVI, Pt. 1, 1023–24.

The difference between the raw and tested troops in Buell's partially new army was not missed by the officers and men in it. By some quirk of command, and with good fortune, Buell had been given Jefferson C. Davis' veteran division of the Army of the Mississippi. It was one of those units which had worn away the patina of inexperience upon the hills of Missouri, and at Pea Ridge in Arkansas. Conspicuous in Davis' division was the 35th Illinois, a regiment which had been raised principally in Vermilion and Fayette counties. The 35th, now commanded by Colonel William P. Chandler of Decatur, was "tough and tanned," and carried "as little load as possible," according to an admiring recruit of a newer Illinois regiment. Furthermore, the untried soldiers could not keep up with the rangy veterans – the 35th "passed down the road and out of sight in a short time, no straggling, no falling out of line, all in step." [3]

Upon reaching Louisville, Buell was faced with two immediate problems. The first, the appropriate disposition of the new troops, was handled in the only manner possible. The commanding general of the Army of the Ohio simply brigaded his rookie regiments with those which had heard the sound of gunfire at Pea Ridge or Shiloh, and hoped for the best. The second problem, unequivocally tied to the first, was what to do with Bragg. Again, Buell's solution was the obvious one; in the early days of October he moved to the attack. On October 7 the Army of the Ohio, consisting of three corps, approached the central Kentucky town of Perryville from the direction of Springfield. There, with the partially dry Doctor's Creek running at right angles through the encamped troops, the Army of the Ohio came face to face with the Confederate Army of Tennessee.

Fighting began on the outskirts of Perryville October 8, not so much because either side wished to engage the other at that moment, but because of the want of water in the Union command. The fall dry spell had cut the flow of water in Doctor's Creek into a string of pools. General Charles Gilbert, commanding the Federal III Corps, felt that access to these pools (puddles) was necessary to the army, and ordered one of his division commanders, Philip Sheridan, to take them. Sheridan passed the order on to one of his brigade leaders, Colonel Dan McCook, who com-

[3] "Memoirs of Lemuel Adams," 86.

manded the 85th, 86th, and 125th Illinois, as well as the 52nd Ohio. McCook was never a popular officer with the Illinois regiments he commanded; one Illinois captain wrote that if his own company got the opportunity, it would shoot the brigade commander during a battle. McCook was "held in utter contempt" by all who knew him, concluded the officer of the 86th Illinois.[4]

Nevertheless, on the morning of October 8 McCook pushed his four regiments to the water holes, the 86th Illinois taking the lead. The resistance was stubborn, however, and McCook was forced to bring the 125th Illinois, plus Wallace Barrett's Illinois battery, into position before the Confederates were driven back. In support of the brigade operation Sheridan launched a division assault upon high ground near the creek, with the veterans of the 36th Illinois, a Pea Ridge regiment, leading the attack. Led by Nicholas Greusel, now wearing a brigadier's star, the regiment dug in along the high ridge and waited for an enemy counterattack. It soon came, for Hardee, commanding the Confederate corps opposing Gilbert, needed the water holes as much as the latter. Fighting alongside three other veteran regiments, the 36th held its fire, according to Greusel's instructions, until the troops could see the whites of the eyes of the advancing enemy. Opening fire at close range, and with the Parrott guns which Sheridan had brought up, the regiment dispersed the attacking force. Firing their guns so rapidly that the weapons became overheated, the 36th finally ran out of ammunition and was relieved by the 88th Illinois, a Cook County regiment commanded by Colonel Francis T. Sherman.[5]

In this comparatively brief flurry of fighting there were some incidents to remember. Private William Galloway, an ebullient little Irishman from Morris, Illinois, complained bitterly during these morning hours about having to fight on an empty stomach, for the regiment had been sent into the attack before having an opportunity to build fires. He complained for so long that a fellow soldier, hoping to shut Galloway up, pointed out that the Irishman would soon get enough to eat in the way of enemy

[4] Bennett and Haigh, 268. L. A. Ross to his father, Sept. 16, 1862, Ross Papers.

[5] J. H. Sackett to his brother, Oct. 16, 1862, Sackett Papers. Bennett and Haigh, 267–268.

musket balls. As Galloway opened his mouth to reply, a Minie ball entered his mouth and tore out ten teeth. But of all the sights remembered from this small prelude to the battle of Perryville, one which intrigued the historian of the 36th Illinois involved a fellow officer of the regiment. It was one of those incidents in a great play in which the spotlight flickers upon a minor player. The lieutenant, standing in front of his company and exhorting it on, was hit by a musket ball in the leg. Grotesquely, like a puppet on the end of a string, the officer danced off the field on one leg, clutching the injured knee in his hands.[6]

Neither commander, least of all Buell, had wished to start a general engagement on the morning of October 8. Yet the little attack by Sheridan's division was just enough to bring one on. Also, brisk skirmishing between General A. M. McCook's I Corps and Polk's Confederate corps, beginning in the early-morning hours, flared into hard fighting by the afternoon. McCook managed to get two divisions into line on the Union left; the first, under General James S. Jackson, included the 34th, 80th, 89th, and 123rd Illinois; and the second, under General L. H. Rousseau, included the 19th, 24th, and 39th Illinois. At approximately two o'clock, Benjamin F. Cheatham's veteran Confederate division hit the north flank of the Union army precisely at a spot occupied by the 123rd Illinois. This regiment, raised in Clark and Coles counties, was scarcely ready for combat, and the division commander knew it. Jackson was one of those men who felt that a general's mere presence was enough to strengthen the backbone of a new soldier. He had hardly arrived on the line, however, when before the startled eyes of the soldiers of the 123rd, he fell dead. That was not the only such sight which the regiment was to see that day. After Jackson's death, General William R. Terrill, the brigade commander of the 123rd, came forward to steady the faltering regiment. Terrill, likewise, was killed, his body being torn away by a neatly placed artillery shell. All of this was too much for the untried troops. The 123rd, along with the other raw regiments of Terrill's men, broke and fled to the rear, leaving 154 of its men behind.[7]

---

[6] *Ibid.*, 278–281.

[7] *Three Years in the Army of the Cumberland: The Letters and Diary of Major James A. Connolly*, ed. Paul M. Angle (Bloomington, Ind., 1959), 22.

As Terrill's troops made for the rear, they passed through the waiting ranks of John C. Starkweather's brigade of Rousseau's division, a veteran unit which, by good fortune, was placed behind the very spot at which the Union line broke. This brigade, consisting principally of Ohio troops, did have one Illinois regiment in it – the veteran 24th, raised mainly in Cook County and led temporarily by two captains. With two of the Ohio regiments anchored to the right and left of it, the 24th made its way forward in order to repair the breach in the Union line. Unfortunately, however, the Ohio regiments broke, leaving the Illinois regiment outflanked on both sides. The 24th was ordered to charge bayonets, which it did. The shock of the attack, with the 24th clubbing its muskets, was too much for Cheatham's men. The Confederates broke and retreated.[8]

The pressure was still on the remaining brigades of McCook's corps. L. A. Harris' and William H. Lytle's brigades were forced in, and for a brief moment it appeared that one of those preludes to disaster had been reached. McCook, who, as it turned out, fought all day without Buell even knowing that a battle was taking place, sent an urgent request for help to General Robert B. Mitchell's division. The latter quickly forwarded Michael Gooding's brigade, which consisted of the 59th Illinois and 22nd Indiana, both veteran regiments, and the 74th and 75th Illinois, both untried regiments. Doubletimed into a breach on the right of McCook's corps, Gooding's troops were the heroes of the day. The two new Illinois regiments, the 74th and 75th, raised principally in Winnebago and Whiteside counties respectively, fought like professional soldiers. The 59th, Post's veteran regiment which had fought Stand Watie at Pea Ridge, did the major share of the work. At no time backing ground before the determined attackers, the regiment suffered horrendous losses.[9]

The fighting continued into mid-afternoon. General Mitchell's division, which included the 21st, 25th, 35th, 38th, 42nd, and 58th

---

Eddy, I, 345. Kenneth P. Williams, IV, 130. *Report of the Adjutant General*, VI, 416.

[8] *Chicago Tribune*, Oct. 15, 1862. Villard, I, 318–322. *Report of the Adjutant General*, II, 325.

[9] Lathrop, 164–166. Sumner Dodge, *The Waif of the War; or The History of the Seventy-fifth Illinois Infantry* . . . (Chicago, 1866), 45–47.

Illinois, plus the Illinois regiments of Gooding's brigade, moved to the support of Sheridan at the center of the Union line. The hero of this maneuver was Colonel William P. Carlin of Carrollton, Illinois. Described by a fellow Illinois officer as being "careful, painstaking," and as having "two o'clock courage," Carlin led his brigade, which included the 38th Illinois, in a smashing attack upon the Confederate line. So sharp was the assault that Hardee's divisions broke and fled to Perryville itself, leaving behind a large ammunition train for the 38th to capture.[10]

Carlin's dash into the Confederate rear was, in a sense, the last act of the battle of Perryville. With darkness coming on, Buell, who was completely unaware that a battle was being fought until about four o'clock in the afternoon, called a halt to the proceedings. It had been one of those days in history when the elements of nature effected the course of events. Though he was only a few miles away, the vagaries of sound and wind had carried the noise of battle away from the commander of the Army of the Ohio. This freak of nature, plus Buell's caution after becoming aware of the fight, deprived his army of a brilliant victory.[11]

Considering the number of men engaged in the actual fighting, the losses were considerable. Out of the 36,940 effectives which Buell had in the fight, the Union casualties totaled 4,211, which, when broken down, amounted to 845 killed, 2,851 wounded, and 515 missing. Among the Illinois regiments involved, the 75th Illinois, commanded by Colonel John E. Bennett of Morrison, suffered the greatest. Its loss of 213 in killed and wounded, and 12 men missing, a total of 225, was exceeded only by two Ohio regiments, each having 229 casualties. The 123rd, from eastern Illinois, received a sorry introduction to battle with 189 casualties; the 59th Illinois, still undersized because of losses at Pea Ridge, lost 113 men out of 361 effectives. Truly, Perryville presented a quick and brutal initiation of new Illinois regiments to warfare. For some soldiers, just weeks away from home, it had all happened too suddenly. "I was not shocked, surprised or startled," wrote one Illinois officer, "but I suppose I was too green

[10] Eddy, I, 347. *Three Years in the Army of the Cumberland*, 143.

[11] Villard, I, 320–321. The phenomenon, known as "acoustic shadow," also occurred in the battles of Seven Pines, Gaines's Mill, and Chancellorsville.

to appreciate my danger." The battle did serve one purpose, however. It taught all of the new troops, including those of the 73rd Illinois (the "Preacher's Regiment"), that war had a startling definition all its own – it meant killing.[12]

The battle of Perryville had its own meaning for Don Carlos Buell. Never popular in the ranks of his army, his maneuvers during the fight brought him into further disrepute. It was darkly hinted by some Illinois regiments, for example, that Buell had tried to destroy his army at Perryville. Veterans of Pea Ridge, accustomed to more forceful command, were most apt to criticize. Private J. H. Sackett of Hebron, Illinois, later to die of wounds inflicted in the battle of Nashville, expressed the sentiments of his regiment, the 36th, when he wrote home that Buell was a "traitor" and a "scamp."[13] Sentiment against its commander grew rapidly within the Army of the Ohio, and when the governors of the western states also began to bay for his removal, Buell's tenure in command was limited. In the last week in October, the administration gave way and the unfortunate general was removed in favor of Rosecrans.

William Starke Rosecrans was one of the great enigmas of the war. A marvelous organizer, he gave his troops in the newly created Department of the Cumberland a real feeling that here was a soldier's general. Indeed, one might doubt that there ever was a general more popular during a given period than was Rosecrans in the first year of his command. Extremely religious (a Roman Catholic), choleric, and sentimental by nature, he was a happy contrast to the departed Buell. To the men of the 21st Illinois, the men who had also known Grant's immediate command, Rosecrans was a "noble and brave" man, a better commander than any they had ever known. "No better soldier ever drew the sword than our brave Chieftain," wrote Captain Levi Ross of the 86th Illinois. "As a scholar he hardly has any superiors, as a professor of Christianity he is faithful, devoted,

---

[12] Fox, 544, 433. Thomas L. Livermore, *Numbers and Losses in the Civil War in America, 1861–1865* (Bloomington, Ind., 1957), 76. Livermore places the Perryville casualties at 100 for every 1,000 Union soldiers engaged. The *Chicago Tribune*, Oct. 23, 1862, points out that casualties at Perryville were more disastrous because the ambulances had to travel over 60 miles of rough roads. *Three Years in the Army of the Cumberland*, 22.

[13] Lathrop, 164–166. Sackett to his brother, Nov. 19, 1862, Sackett Papers.

zealous, as a commander he is cool, self-reliant, enthusiastic. . . ." Everywhere in the Army of the Cumberland, the men sensed that he was for them. The food seemed to improve; the mail and pay, both important to a soldier's life, came more on time. A member of Greusel's 36th Illinois wrote in November, 1862, that for the first time in months certain embellishments—pickles, pepper, and "Irish Murphys" (potatoes)—were beginning to appear in the diet. One would have to miss pepper for a while before knowing how to appreciate it. "We in the Army of the Cumberland think him almost as big a man as 'Old United States' [General Grant] or 'Tecumseh' [General Sherman]," the private wrote of Rosecrans. One could add that there would be a time when the Army of the Cumberland would place their commander behind no one.[14]

Reality was sometimes at odds with what the ordinary soldier thought he saw during the war, however. There were times when the very organization for which he was famous became too much for Rosecrans. There were times when he became flustered and overcome by responsibility, and when he could not quite pull the trigger of command. These were serious failings which the common private, concerned with the mere amenities of military life, could not see. These faults, coupled with the unfortunate accident of being saddled with some fairly incompetent corps commanders, were to bring both Rosecrans and his men to disaster.

That tragedy was to be nearly a year in coming. In November of 1862, Rosecrans, at Nashville by now, undertook the reorganization of the Army of the Cumberland. Dividing his army into three corps, he spent the first weeks of his new command organizing supplies and refurbishing equipment. By December 24 his army was ready to move.[15] Christmas day was spent by the troops in last-minute preparations and in the time-honored ritual of a soldier, the last letter home. For a few it was a time for thought. As Sergeant Henry Freeman of the 74th Illinois wrote

[14] Philip Welshimer to his wife, Jan. 4, 1863, Welshimer Papers. Note that the letter was written immediately after the battle of Stone's River. Ross to his father, June 26, 1863, Ross Papers. Mary Livermore, 669.

[15] Alexander F. Stevenson, *The Battle of Stone's River . . .* (Boston, 1884), 1–16.

in his diary: "Last night . . . was Christmas Eve. It brought to my mind a thousand recollections of the past. The contrast is great. I sat up late in the evening at the (camp) fire, after attending to drawing rations, for we were under marching orders for this morning at five o'clock. A grand movement seems to be at hand. . . . Where will the next Christmas Eve find me?"[16]

The day of December 26 broke sullen and gray. While the fife and drum corps played "inspiring music," the troops, seemingly lighthearted and gay, fell into line of march. For some it was a special moment, the first great campaign, and they took their places in the assembling columns, each loaded with as much as any human being could possibly carry. Years later, in attempting to remember just what he strapped upon his body that December day, a veteran soldier of the 7th Illinois Cavalry listed his gun, canteen, knapsack, haversack, cartridge box, blanket, and various odds and ends which any young trooper might carry. But the rain fell in steady torrents, the cavalryman recalled, and some of the equally loaded infantrymen, hitting particularly soft spots in the road, sank to their knees. "Fairly poured," a sergeant of the 74th Illinois wrote in his diary; "worst mud I ever walked in." When Rosecrans finally ordered the day's march ended, the soldiers had to spread their rubberized ponchos upon the ground in order to keep dry.[17]

Rosecrans was leading his army southeast in the general direction of the Nashville and Chattanooga Railway and the Murfreesboro pike. General Thomas L. Crittenden's corps advanced along the railroad proper, with the two other corps, led by General George H. Thomas and General A. M. McCook respectively, flanked to the right. By the night of December 30, Crittenden's divisions were camped on the banks of Stone's River. From this location, where the river took a broad loop to the north, the remainder of the Army of the Cumberland stretched out to the south at nearly right angles to both the Nashville and Wilkinson's pikes. In the center were elements of Thomas' command; on the right, with its flank resting upon the Franklin road, was McCook's corps. The position in which the army was thus arranged

---

[16] Henry Freeman, "Some Battle Recollections of Stone's River," in *Military Essays and Recollections*, III (1899), 229.

[17] Eby, 65–68. Freeman, "Battle Recollections," 230.

had been in part determined earlier in the day by a sharp engagement between the 21st Illinois in Colonel William P. Carlin's brigade of McCook's wing, and an enemy battery defended by infantry. As fires burned along the line of encampment that night, it was obvious to officers and men of the Army of the Cumberland that both they and the enemy were "in readiness for battle." [18]

The disposition of the Illinois regiments along the line of battle was significant in terms of the coming fight. On the right wing of the Union army, in August Willich's brigade of McCook's corps, was the 89th Illinois (the "Railroad Regiment") under the command of Lieutenant Colonel Charles T. Hotchkiss of Chicago. In the same division, that of General Richard W. Johnson, and in the brigade of General Edward N. Kirk, who came from Sterling, Illinois, were the 79th and 34th Illinois (the "Rock River Rifles"). The first-named regiment was under the command of Colonel Sheridan P. Read of Paris, Illinois, whose promotion in rank had just arrived, and whose death would come before the new year. The latter regiment was under the command of Colonel Alexander Dysart of China, Illinois.

In Jefferson C. Davis' division, in the center of McCook's corps, were a number of Illinois regiments. In the First Brigade, commanded by Colonel Philip S. Post of Galesburg, Illinois, were the 59th, under strength from Pea Ridge and Perryville, and the 74th and 75th Illinois. The 21st Illinois, from Macon, Piatt, and assorted eastern counties, and the 38th, from central Illinois, were in Carlin's brigade. In W. E. Woodruff's Third Brigade of Davis' division were the 25th Illinois, whose commander, Colonel Thomas D. Williams of Chebanse, would not live past the old year, and the 35th, commanded by Colonel William P. Chandler from Decatur.

In Sheridan's division, on McCook's left flank, were seven Illinois regiments. The 36th of Pea Ridge fame and the 88th (the "Second Board of Trade Regiment") were in J. W. Sill's First

[18] Thomas Van Horne, *History of the Army of the Cumberland: Its Organization, Campaigns, and Battles, Written at the Request of Major-General George N. Thomas Chiefly from His Private Military Journal and Official and Other Documents Furnished by Him* (2 vols., Cincinnati, 1875), I, 224–225.

Brigade. The 73rd (the "Persimmon Regiment" or "Preacher's Regiment"), commanded by Major William Presson, held a place in the Second Brigade; in the Third Brigade of Colonel George W. Roberts, which was to play an important role in the day's events, were the 22nd, 27th, 42nd, and 51st Illinois.

There were still other Illinois regiments which were to play important roles in the activities of December 31. In General James S. Negley's division of Thomas' corps was the sturdy 19th Illinois, the "Chicago Zouaves," as experienced a unit as any on the field. Its original commander, General John Basil Turchin, was now gone, however, having been assigned to another duty. The leadership of the regiment was presently in the hands of a capable and popular Chicagoan, Colonel Joseph R. Scott. Down the line from the 19th Illinois, in Palmer's division of Crittenden's corps, were two other Illinois regiments, the 84th and 110th. The 110th was a new regiment, a southern Illinois unit which had been raised by Colonel Thomas S. Casey. As fate would have it, the 110th got itself into some of the severest battles of the war. In every case it seemed to be where the battle waxed the heaviest; today would be no exception. The 84th was likewise destined to effect the course of history. Commanded by Colonel Louis H. Waters of Macomb and assigned to William Grose's brigade, it took part in savage fighting during the day.[19]

It hardly seems that the battle of Stone's River was avoidable. Rosecrans intended to fight that day, though as events developed he was too slow at getting in the first punch. The Union regiments along the line were rousted up at varying times, and none seemed anxious to meet any deadlines. The 36th Illinois, for instance, in J. W. Sill's brigade, was up and building fires between four and five o'clock. Having finished a solid breakfast of hoecake and fat pork, its soldiers were ready to move early.

On the far right, however, everything moved at a slower pace. The troops of Willich's and Kirk's brigades were slow in rising, and had just built their fires a few minutes before six o'clock. It was then that disaster struck. The men in the 89th Illinois,

---

[19] *Ibid.*, I, 281–285. The information in Van Horne was supplemented by further study in the complete *Report of the Adjutant General* and *Illinois Military Units in the Civil War* (Springfield, 1962).

Lieutenant Colonel Charles T. Hotchkiss commanding, were completely surprised when, out of the morning mists, the battle line of John P. McCown's Confederate division appeared. The whole regiment fell back in panic, save a solitary sergeant, a Scot named John M. Farquhar, who calmly rallied a few frightened troops and briefly formed a line. The 89th was not the only regiment taken unaware. Indeed, the whole of Willich's brigade was quickly swept back, offering little or no resistance.

Kirk's brigade was less surprised. Hearing the roll of musketry resulting from the assault upon Willich, that commander quickly ordered the 34th Illinois to be thrown out in advance of the brigade. This regiment, as unprepared as it was, fought a bitter battle with the onrushing troops of the 10th Texas. The fight almost amounted to a personal duel. Five color bearers of the 34th fell, one of them after a hand-to-hand struggle with his opposite in the enemy regiment. The colors were temporarily rescued by a private of the regiment, who placed them atop a nearby battery. The colors again fell, however, when the Confederate line surged past the artillerymen who had died at their guns. Kirk himself seemed to be doomed from the beginning. Two horses were killed beneath him before he fell wounded in the thigh. He died some seven months later.[20]

Disaster was now at hand. Before being carried to the rear, Kirk ordered the 79th Illinois forward and into the fight. No sooner had this regiment formed in line before its colonel, Sheridan Read, was struck frontally in the head by a musket ball. With Kirk wounded, four other officers of the 34th down, Willich of the neighboring brigade captured, and Read and some of his subordinates killed, the leadership of the two right-flank brigades disappeared. Furthermore, there was little artillery support for the hard-pressed troops. At dawn many of the horses for the supporting batteries had been sent to the banks of the river for water, so the guns were maneuverable only by hand. Moreover, the casualties in Kirk's brigade were horrendous: over 500 men were killed or wounded in the first stage of the fight. The 34th, which "never wavered" in its initial contact with the enemy, suffered particularly. Of the 354 men who were present and ac-

[20] Stevenson, 38–39. *Civil War Medal of Honor Winners*, 11. Payne, 44–45. Van Horne, I, 228–232. *Chicago Tribune*, July 23, 1863.

counted for before the beginning of the battle, 128 were killed or wounded, and 74 taken prisoner.[21]

The pressure upon Kirk's brigade continued to grow. The 34th Illinois now broke, and fell back through the ranks of the 79th, its companion regiment. The panic was infectious, and whole companies disappeared to the rear, some of the men shouting: "We are sold again! We are sold again!" As a soldier of the 34th, Private Lon Payne, was to inform his brother Ira three weeks later, it had become "too warm for them." The fight continued to spread down the line. Davis, whose division was in line to the left of Kirk's brigade, sought to halt the rapidly enveloping assault of Cleburne's and Cheatham's Confederate troops by wheeling Philip S. Post's brigade around to face the oncoming line. Years later, Sergeant Henry Freeman of the 74th Illinois, one of the three regiments from his state in the brigade, remembered that small interlude before contact with the enemy. As the brigade filed through the cedar woods, Freeman heard his own name called. Turning, he saw a young sergeant from an Illinois regiment, an old friend, lying on the ground with his leg terribly mangled. There, as the sunlight filtered pleasantly through the trees and the birds flitted nervously from branch to branch, the two men exchanged confident thoughts concerning the battle. An hour or two later, when Freeman returned through the same woods, his friend was dead.[22]

Now the attack fell upon Post. The brigade had taken a position in the cedar woods behind a stone fence. Suddenly, as Freeman was later to write, the advancing line of Confederates seemed to burst through the thicket just in front of the 74th and 75th Illinois. The two Illinois regiments poured a devastating fire into the ranks of the attacking Texas troops. "Men were dropping here and there, and others filled the vacant places," wrote the Illinois soldier. "The rebel flag, seen dimly through the smoke and trees, wavered, started forward, and then surged back. Yes, there was no mistake about it, it was going back!" For the moment, the surprised Confederate line broke, and in the sun and shadow of the midwinter forest, the Winnebago

[21] Stevenson, 44–50. Van Horne, I, 265–266. Payne, 58.

[22] Stevenson, 44–50. Lon Payne to Ira Payne, Jan. 31, 1863, Ira A. Payne Papers, ISHL. Freeman, "Battle Recollections," 236–238.

County men of the 74th could see the officers and file closers of the enemy regiments striking at their men with swords in order to bring them back to the assault. "We realized then what war really was," concluded the sergeant of the 74th.[23]

Now the attack spread beyond Post, and began to hit the regiments in Carlin's and Woodruff's brigades. The former, the Illinois officer whose "two o'clock courage" had stood up well at Perryville, was presently to face a bigger test. Post's brigade, which had held temporarily, was being forced back upon the right of Davis' division, bringing the enemy with them. McCown's Tennessee regiments poured down upon a comparatively new regiment, the 101st Ohio, and the 21st and 38th Illinois. Despite occasional skulking by some of the officers of the 21st, Grant's old regiment, the three units held rather handsomely. In fact, had they not been outflanked on the right, it might have been possible to have held at that point all day. Carlin, his courage apparently in proper operating order, even managed to get the Ohio regiment and the 38th into a counterattack. The brief assault was brilliantly supported by elements of the 21st Illinois, headed by Lieutenant Nineveh S. McKeen of Marshall, Illinois. McKeen's bravery despite the handicap of three wounds was to win for him the Medal of Honor. It did not win the day, however, for Carlin's attack gained only time for the hard-pressed Union right. Outflanked, Carlin was forced to pull back with Post still anchored to him — unbroken, but badly bent. Here, the 59th Illinois, which was rapidly becoming the workhorse of the Army of the Cumberland, again performed yeoman duty, covering the withdrawal by using each tree as protection, and by occasionally striking back at the oncoming enemy with bayonet charges.[24]

As Johnson's division disintegrated in the early hours of the attack, and as Davis bent under the weight of three Confederate divisions, one must suspect that the scene to the rear was one of utter confusion. A member of the 7th Illinois Cavalry, stationed to the rear right of Rosecran's army on that fateful day, wrote later of wagon teams rushing back at a furious rate. Early in the fight, a six-mule-team army wagon careened violently through

[23] *Ibid.*, 235–236, 245.

[24] *Civil War Medal of Honor Winners*, 4. Van Horne, I, 228–232. Lathrop, 195–200.

the waiting ranks of Post's brigade and vanished to the rear. Decades later a sergeant of the 74th Illinois recalled a vivid picture of men attempting to drag cannon by hand, soldiers, with and without guns, retiring from the fighting, troops carrying wounded comrades, and the peculiar sight of riderless horses dashing through the line to the rear, where, halting in the comparative calm of a meadow, they turned and curiously watched humanity in conflict. Over all was the dreadful noise which settled like a pall over the fighting troops. The musketry was so incessant and loud that soldiers stuffed pieces of raw cotton into their ears. There was another sound which men who fought there never forgot. It was like the sound of steam escaping from a kettle – the strange, high-pitched whine of men shouting, mingled with the curious Confederate "cheer of defiance."

By the time some regiments reached the line of battle, or it reached them, a kind of hypnotic influence had settled upon some of the men. Soldiers were affected in different ways: some, who had never cursed before, now did so violently and constantly; others ran to the rear weeping. One man was afflicted by the delusion, common to the war, that his regiment had been wiped out, and that he was mortally wounded. Examination proved that he had only a small puncture on one hand, and investigation showed that his regiment was intact and still in the line. These phenomena particularly affected the men of the 74th Illinois – at least one of them was willing to admit, years afterward, that such happened. It is little wonder that, in the days following the end of the battle, two of the dead of the 74th were found rigidly half-risen from the ground, as if, even in the throes of death, they were reacting to the violence of the day.[25]

With the gradual erosion of Davis' regiments, Cheatham's and Jones M. Withers' divisions of Confederate troops began to exert considerable pressure upon Sheridan's division, now holding the angle at the bending of the Union right wing. Sill's brigade, which included the tried and true 36th Illinois as well as the newer 88th from the same state, threw back the first enemy onslaught upon the division, inflicting enormous casualties on the attackers

[25] Freeman, "Battle Recollections," 223–240. Payne, 44. In almost every source concerning the battle of Stone's River, one finds concurring evidence of both the noise and the curious position of the dead.

in so doing. Sill then took his brigade to the attack with disastrous results. Sill was killed, four officers of the 88th went down, and over 230 men were killed or wounded in the vicious fighting. The brigade was finished as an effective fighting unit, and was thus led to the rear by General Greusel. The burden of battle was now taken up by Roberts' Third Brigade of Sheridan's division.[26]

Colonel George W. Roberts, a Pennsylvanian by birth, was a fine specimen of a man. Physically large, "almost herculean" according to a contemporary writer, he had a flair and temperament which might have taken him to the pinnacle of success, had fortune been kind. He was one of those hardened graduates of fighting in Missouri, and had performed excellently in the battles of Island No. 10 and Farmington. On this day, with Cheatham's division washing away all opposition on the right, Roberts was called upon to exert all of his talents of leadership. There, in the "slaughter pen," as history called this place where death flourished in the cedars, he formed his brigade, which included the 22nd, 27th, 42nd, and 51st Illinois. The first named was a fine old regiment which had fought heroically at Belmont, and in scattered places from there to Corinth. The 27th had been at Belmont too, and is best remembered as Napoleon B. Buford's regiment which took the wrong trail. Now, near the Murfreesboro pike, Buford was gone; his command was in the hands of Colonel Fazillo A. Harrington of Erie, Illinois. The 42nd and 51st had both been formerly in the Army of the Mississippi and had considerable experience behind them.

Roberts was the kind of citizen-warrior who had a good deal of common sense about him. Determined not to fritter away his men in senseless attacks, he ordered them to "lie low and not fire till he gave the order." Soon the enemy came on — Withers', Cheatham's, and Arthur M. Manigault's divisions. Three times the advancing lines were thrown back with horrible losses. In the second of the assaults, the Confederates came within rock-throwing distance of the Illinois regiments before the latter opened fire.

Whether Roberts realized it or not, the only prize of any value

[26] Stevenson, 57. Van Horne, I, 228–232.

won by his efforts was time – and precious little of that. Cheatham soon brought up two batteries and began to pulverize the cedar grove which sheltered the men of the Third Brigade. Roberts was killed, and the commanding officer of the 27th, Harrington, fell dead when an artillery shell tore his jaws away. The brigade went through three different commanders in one hour. Over half the horses in the supporting Illinois battery were killed, and half of the artillerymen were slumped over their guns. The ranking officer of the 22nd was wounded, and over half of its men were down in the cedars. In the same space of time, the entire brigade, all Illinois regiments, lost over 400 men in killed and wounded. Still it held, inflicting heavy casualties upon the enemy all the while. Only when the ammunition boxes fell empty did the thought of retreat occur to the men. In what may have been one of the most welcomed orders of the day, Major William A. Schmitt, a German from Quincy, gave the order to retreat. "Boys, we must get out of this!" he shouted. "To the rear, march."[27]

The fighting was not yet done for Roberts' brigade, however. Just as they emerged from the cedars, unbroken but completely out of ammunition, they were met by McCook, the right-wing corps commander, who turned them about and ordered a bayonet charge. These were tough men, just about as rugged a set of regiments as were ever clustered in one brigade. They fixed their bayonets, and with a most unearthly yell drove the Confederates away from the Murfreesboro pike and recaptured two guns as well.[28]

The story of the battle of Stone's River on December 31, 1862, is not difficult to understand. The great Union line, which had stretched unbroken like a straight iron bar from Stone's River to the east-running Franklin road, was now being hammered into a semi-horseshoe shape with its right running along the Murfreesboro pike. The Confederate attacks, which had begun on the Federal far right, moved inward toward the center of the Union line, peeling off each regiment, each brigade, and each division as each was outflanked. There was no comparison be-

[27] Eddy, I, 383. Stevenson, 72–73. See also *Report of the Adjutant General*, II, 414. Van Horne, I, 271.

[28] Stevenson, 57, 69–72. Van Horne, I, 270–271. *Report of the Adjutant General*, II, 414.

tween this and Shiloh. The latter conflict was an oncoming flood washing away scattered barriers set up to impede its advance. Stone's River was the iron bar, one end set into the river itself, and the other being bent around by the repetitive Confederate assaults. There was another difference, too. Veterans of Shiloh rarely recalled the sounds of the battle fought in the dense thicket near the Corinth road. At Stone's River, the cedar woods and the little hollows which ran between them seemed to amplify the sound to an inhuman pitch.

With the retreat of Roberts' brigade, the defense of the Union angle now devolved upon Negley's division of Thomas' corps. Quickly enveloped by the rapidly advancing enemy line, this division, which included the 19th Illinois, soon found itself in difficulty. In attempting to form a juncture with the withdrawing regiments of Sheridan's Third Brigade, part of the division was cut off. Only a bayonet charge by the 19th, which regiment was called the "bravest of the brave" by the *Chicago Tribune*, saved the day for Negley and allowed his escape to the rear.[29]

The retreat of Negley's division of Thomas' corps with so little in the way of a vigorous fight left the fate of the Union army in the hands of the men of the Second Division and their sturdy commander, John McAuley Palmer of Crittenden's corps. This Carlinville, Illinois, officer had earned a promotion to general rank through tough service in Missouri and had secured his reputation with a vigorous performance in the campaign against Corinth. Palmer gave orders in a most informal way, even in times of severe stress. "Fight where you can do the most good," he told a battery commander along the Murfreesboro pike. Were his orders to his brigade commanders, W. B. Hazen, Charles Cruft, and William Grose, that simple? History will never really know. It does know what Palmer himself knew at noon on this crucial day, however. His division, already bending under the weight of two Confederate divisions, was fighting not only for its own survival, but also for that of every Union command on the field. If Palmer failed, the Army of the Cumberland would possibly never fight again.

The pressure quickly developed on Palmer's right. Grose, whose

[29] *Chicago Tribune*, Jan. 9, 1863.

brigade was supposedly in reserve, soon found himself fighting a perilous rear-flank battle for survival. Palmer hadn't intended it this way, for his Third Brigade was to be used only in emergencies. Now the emergency existed in the Third Brigade itself. Among the regiments under Grose's command was the 84th Illinois, Colonel Louis Waters commanding. As the fighting grew heavy along the front held by the 84th, an officer of the regiment, Captain Moses Davis of Mount Sterling, took time out to draw up a battlefield will. Wrapping it around a plug of chewing tobacco, he gave it to a subordinate and left to lead his company into battle, where he was subsequently killed.[30]

The battle of Stone's River, like all conflicts in the war, had a turning point. It occurred along the Murfreesboro pike in the angle formed by the intersection of the Nashville and Chattanooga Railway with the road itself. Here, Hazen's brigade, which included among others the brand-new 110th Illinois, held a position in a cedar woods atop a knoll. It would only be fair to write that other regiments, including the 100th Illinois, were sent to Hazen's support during that commander's stubborn defense of "Hell's Half Acre," or the "Round Forest." Three grand Confederate assaults were thrown back, the first two by Chalmers' and Daniel Donelson's brigades, the last, a magnificent and daring attempt, by Breckinridge's four brigades.[31]

The last attack, at four o'clock in the afternoon, was the final major Confederate effort of the day. Hazen's regiments, including the 110th Illinois, which was perched uppermost on the slight knoll, had saved the day for the Army of the Cumberland. In a qualified way, the battle was over for the day. Rosecrans, his uniform splattered by the blood of his aide, Colonel Julius P. Garesché, who was killed in the last fight of the afternoon, spent the night adjusting his lines. For the soldiers themselves, the eve of the new year was not one which they could easily celebrate. Having eaten only hardtack all day, some regiments, such as the 73rd Illinois, had to wait until midnight for warmed side meat and coffee. The smoke from the fires curled into a cool crisp night lightened by a full bright moon. Frost lay heavily

---

[30] *Official Records*, Ser. I, Vol. XX, Pt. 1, 515–519, 559–561. *Macomb Journal*, Jan. 30, 1863.

[31] Van Horne, I, 242–243.

upon the sleepless armies, and upon those who lay dead between them. And soldiers who would never forget the sounds of that day would remember always the sounds of the night – the constant rumbling of ambulance wagons back and forth into the fields nearby.[32]

For the next three "weary long" days, as Lieutenant Peter Weyhrich of the 44th Illinois wrote, the two armies faced each other – cold and "shivering wet to the bone." There was considerable fighting, particularly on January 2, 1863, when Federal batteries tore a Confederate attack to shreds. It was a rather amazing show of power. Years later, Illinois soldiers who were there remembered the brilliant work of the "Illinois Board of Trade Battery," and how the men handled the large guns like playthings. With all of the display, however, there was nothing similar to that first day. All which followed had to be anticlimactic. Finally, on the night of January 3, Bragg decided he had had enough, and began the withdrawal of his army. When dawn broke on the following morning, Rosecrans could see a front cleared of the enemy. The battlefield of Stone's River or Murfreesboro, for what glory there was in it, was his.[33]

The losses on both sides had been tremendous; the gains had been few. Bragg claimed the taking of 28 Union cannon and more than 3,000 prisoners, but the cost was too much, about 11,700 casualties out of the 38,000 troops engaged. Rosecrans could claim very few captured cannon and almost no prisoners, but having held the field he proclaimed himself the victor. For this the price had been great – 13,249 out of the 45,000 men involved, slightly more than the losses at Shiloh. Within these figures is evidence of one of the most terrible battles of the war from the Union point of view. One authority, in calculating the casualties for each 1,000 Union troops engaged, places the number for the battle of Stone's River at 223. With Gettysburg showing a comparable figure of 212, Shiloh rating at 162, and Antietam at 155, Stone's River stands beyond all others.[34]

---

[32] *Ibid.* Palmer, 147, states that Rosecrans was covered with the brains and blood of Garesché, but that he "never blanched." W. H. Newlin, *A History of the Seventy-third Regiment* (n.p., 1888), 127–135. Eby, 76.

[33] Weyhrich to friends, Jan. 30, 1863, Smith Papers. Freeman, "Battle Recollections," 235.

[34] Fox, 544. Thomas L. Livermore, 76, 97–98.

Illinois regiments suffered their share of casualties in the battle. The 21st Illinois, now commanded by Colonel John W. Alexander of Paris, Illinois, counted 57 killed and 187 wounded. The 36th, as one of its privates reported in a letter home, was "cut up very bad," losing 46 killed and 151 wounded. The 84th, fighting in that strange rear-flank action involving Grose, suffered 159 casualties in killed and wounded. The 38th, Carlin's regiment from central Illinois, was hard hit with losses of 143; the 44th of Sheridan's division lost 138; the 22nd Illinois, raised principally in Bond, Randolph, and Saint Clair counties, had 137 casualties in killed and wounded. None of these figures represented the largest loss by any single regiment. That dubious honor was won by the 39th Indiana, which counted 31 killed, 118 wounded, and 231 missing. The largest number of deaths alone was suffered by the 18th U. S. Regulars.[35]

The list of losses of Illinois regiments is revealing indeed. The six units from the state which suffered the greatest came from Davis', Sheridan's, and Palmer's divisions. None were in Johnson's division, located on the far right flank. Indicative of what went on in that command is the number of casualties listed above for the 39th Indiana. The 231 missing men serve to illustrate the nature of the catastrophe which struck the Union right near the Franklin road. Nevertheless, some credit should be given to the 34th Illinois, which fought in Kirk's doomed brigade. Its losses of 21 killed, 93 wounded, and only 36 missing would indicate that the regiment was able to pull back in some kind of order, despite the fact that for some time it fought a solitary battle against overwhelming odds. The failure of Johnson's division to be prepared for the enemy onslaught did not pass over the heads of soldiers of other divisions, however. "*Oh God* my company and my regiment," wrote an officer of the 21st Illinois, "we went into the fight with over seven hundred men and now have about 300 . . . may God save our army from all such insignificant Generals [Johnson] and may Heaven pardon his weak and treacherous soul." [36]

The list of heroes at Stone's River who came from Illinois is a

---

[35] Fox, 434–435. J. H. Sackett to his brother, Jan. 10, 1863, Sackett Papers.

[36] *Report of the Adjutant General,* II, 688. Philip Welshimer to his wife, Jan. 4, 1863, Welshimer Papers.

long one. General Kirk, who had received his second serious wound in nine months, lingered for over six months after the battle, dying in Chicago. Colonels Read and Roberts were killed in leading their regiments or brigades into the heaviest action along the line. Colonel Scott was severely wounded in this assault, dying a few months later. Colonel Thomas Casey of the 110th Illinois and Colonel Fred A. Bartleson of the 100th earned reputations which were to spread beyond the battlefield itself. Besides the ranking officers, however, were the thousands of enlisted men from the state who had fought it out in the line. It was a battle which required a special kind of courage. One may suppose that it was in recognition of that fact that some of the towns of Illinois, Oquawka for instance, buried their veterans of Stone's River together, something which never occurred in respect to Shiloh or other serious conflicts.[37]

Stone's River most certainly had its effect upon the commanders and soldiers of the Army of the Cumberland. Coming as it did, when the spirits of the North were low from Ambrose E. Burnside's terrible defeat at Fredericksburg in mid-December, and Sherman's repulse at Chickasaw Bayou, the battle served to inspire a lagging cause. A great deal of confidence was established in Rosecrans' army; it now appeared "invincible" to a soldier of the 44th Illinois. After such a battle, the officer wrote, "who wouldn't be a soldier?" For Rosecrans, however, the impact of the fight took on a different tone. Following Iuka and Corinth, Stone's River was his third savage battle in four months; his troops had suffered close to 17,000 casualties in all. One could not go on like this without it's having some effect upon one's capacity to dare. It may have been, as Henry Villard, the reporter, claimed; Rosecrans, he wrote, was never the same after Stone's River.[38]

---

[37] Kirk had just recovered from wounds inflicted at Shiloh. *Chicago Tribune*, Jan. 9, July 16, 1863. *Quincy* (Ill.) *Daily Whig and Republican*, Jan. 19, 1863. Both papers lauded the brilliant bayonet charge of the 19th Illinois on January 2.

[38] Peter Weyhrich to friends, Jan. 30, 1863, Smith Papers. Not all of the army was invincible; for evidence of skulking during the battle, see Philip Welshimer to his wife, Jan. 7, 1863, Welshimer Papers. This officer of the 21st Illinois states that several officers in his regiment were not as brave as they ought to have been.

In a way there grew to be a kind of mystique within the Army of the Cumberland concerning Stone's River. This was where it had been put to the test and not found wanting. This was where it had stood face to face with death and not flinched. The army itself would go through many trials – Chickamauga, Missionary Ridge, the drive to Atlanta, Franklin, and Nashville. But beyond all these, there remained the battle of Stone's River. Feeling as they did about the fight, some of those who had taken part returned to the battlefield early in 1863 and attempted to make sure that generations to come would know the role they had played. Right on the spot where Casey's southern Illinois boys of the 110th Illinois had fought with Hazen's brigade, a solid block monument was laid. Today most of the names originally cut into it have been washed away, but two words are still legible: "deathless heritage."

If one had to pick major times at which doubt most assailed the supporters of the Union cause, and when it appeared that the North was least able to carry the war to a successful conclusion, one would be that period between the beginning of fall in 1862 and the end of spring in 1863. It was a nine-month winter of discontent and despair in which the army, frustrated at the seeming lack of ability in its leaders and undecided about the principles for which the remainder of the war was to be fought, suffered a rapid and dreadful decline in morale.

Nor was the doubt and indecision concentrated in any single part of the nation. The bruised and battered Federal forces in Virginia could most certainly raise questions concerning the conduct of the war. Saddled with the incompetent Illinois general Pope, commanding the Army of Virginia, it had received a terrible beating at Second Bull Run or Manassas. This was followed by George B. McClellan's disappointing Antietam campaign with the Army of the Potomac. In November the administration had given the command of the same army to Burnside, with the same ghastly results – this time at Fredericksburg.

It was a season of reverses mingled with hard-won victories. The retreat of Buell from southern Tennessee and northern Alabama, after what had appeared to be an auspicious beginning, was most disappointing to the soldiers who fought in his command. The battle of Iuka, which could be called a victory in

Mississippi, brought 782 casualties to the cause; Corinth, in early October and involving primarily Rosecrans, bought success at the price of 2,520 men. Perryville was a savagely fought affair, little by comparison to the battles and campaigns to come, but nevertheless an expensive fight. The generalship of the Army of the Ohio, it seemed to the common soldier, left much to be desired in that brisk encounter. Grant's December venture, wrecked by Van Dorn's raid upon the Federal supply base at Holly Springs, and Sherman's repulse at Chickasaw Bayou were stunning blows to the North. In the first of those engagements, most of the defending force were caught in their beds, and Confederates were able to capture over $1,500,000 worth of supplies. The second, the attack on the Yazoo, was equally catastrophic, and gave ample evidence of hurried and incomplete planning. The only light that shone during the dark months which ended the year was the terrible fight at Stone's River, but whatever existed of cheer and warmth in that was diminished by the long casualty lists, and by the fact that it was largely a defensive victory.[39]

This list of major battles does not tell the complete story of the last six months of the year, however. The effect of the raids of Forrest and John H. Morgan upon Union supply bases must also be recounted. In July, 1862, Forrest's raids brought down the Federal garrison at Murfreesboro. The feat was done rather handily and in typical Forrest fashion; he threatened to put the Michigan and Minnesota troops who guarded the place to the sword if they did not surrender. They did—and Forrest rode off with supplies valued at close to a million dollars. At almost the same moment, Morgan moved into Kentucky, managing to destroy several depots of supplies as well as to capture 1,200 prisoners. Both of these July raids cut severely into Union morale.

In December, Forrest went at it again and moved rapidly into Tennessee with a force of 2,500 men. He was able to destroy a good deal of property and to disrupt Grant's communications considerably before returning to his base. Morgan, likewise, raided in Tennessee. Under orders from Bragg to "harass" the Union forces in every conceivable manner, he struck sharply at Federal bases in that state. His greatest triumph was to come

[39] Boatner, 429, 177, 405–406.

with the attack upon the Union garrison which guarded the railroad town of Hartsville.

The defenders at Hartsville were not inconsiderable in terms of size. The garrison was of brigade proportions, totaling around 1,200 effective soldiers, and was commanded by Colonel Absalom Moore of Ottawa, Illinois. There were four full regiments in all, the 106th and 108th Ohio, the 104th Illinois, the 2nd Indiana Cavalry, part of the 11th Kentucky Cavalry, and some artillery. The Illinois outfit was under the immediate command of Lieutenant Colonel Douglas Hapeman, who also came from Ottawa.

The 104th was one of those regiments which had been raised in the tremendous recruitment drive of midsummer in Illinois. With the appropriate determination of a winner, Morgan got his force across the Cumberland River on the night of December 6 and moved upon Moore's brigade at the break of dawn.[40]

Morgan attacked in due time, sending his forces frontally at the Union line and to the right, where they had an immediate success. It soon appeared that the 108th Ohio was unable to return an adequate fire upon the attacking troops due to the outmoded and dangerous Austrian muskets which had been issued to it. Within a short time that unfortunate regiment retreated, along with the 106th Ohio, which was stampeded, leaving the 104th Illinois under Moore and Hapeman to fight it out alone heroically. The 104th was soon surrounded, but managed to hold out for another hour before finally surrendering to the overjoyed enemy.[41]

Moore was bitterly censured by the northern press for surrendering with what it claimed was so little fight. Rosecrans, likewise, condemned the Illinois colonel, claiming that he had allowed himself to be caught unprepared. One finds little need to add that Moore was never again allowed to command. He was sent home, and allowed to resign his command in 1863 for reasons of disability. In all fairness, however, it should be pointed out that the 104th Illinois, which was originally raised by Moore, did fight sturdily. Before the war's end the regiment became a crack

[40] William W. Calkins, *The History of the One Hundred and Fourth Regiment of Illinois Volunteer Infantry . . .* (Chicago, 1895), 61–66.

[41] Van Horne, I, 213–215. *Report of the Adjutant General*, V, 667. Van Horne claims that the Confederates got into the camps of Moore's brigade before being discovered.

one, and its commander, Colonel Hapeman, eventually was to win the Medal of Honor. Never, however—no matter how fine the reputation of the regiment became—did the soldiers of the 104th ever blame Moore for the affair at Hartsville.[42]

The capture of the 104th Illinois, plus the failure of the accompanying Ohio regiments, was simply one of those unaccountable tragedies of the war. Seemingly insignificant today, it was an event which received widespread notice at the time of its occurrence. It was part of that season of defeat, however, and served to contribute to the rapid and steady deterioration of morale within the Union army. But even so, Hartsville was only part of a pattern. Were one to study the comments put to paper by the Illinois soldier in late 1862 and early 1863, he would note that the decline did not occur overnight. In the summer of the second year of the war there seemed to be a frustration over inaction. The notion existed throughout the army that it didn't really matter about the kind of movement carried out, just so long as there was action. "Armies—American armies at least," commented the *Chicago Tribune*, "are not enlisted to rest. They are sent forth to fight against traitors and put down rebellion." Illinois politicians who were unable to understand the character which the war had assumed began to place pressure upon Governor Yates to use his influence to speed up the war. There was a "criminal lack of energy, and a settled policy in regard to the conduct of this war," wrote one such party leader. The total weight of many such complaints could not be resisted, and by late fall of 1862 Yates had joined Morton of Indiana in actively campaigning against the retention of such slow-moving commanders as Buell.[43]

The unrest spread through the ranks of Illinois soldiery both in the Army of the Ohio and the Army of the Tennessee, particularly and strangely among the higher-numbered regiments. It would be difficult to reason why this happened, unless it be that it took more genuine patriotism to volunteer in 1861 under no pressure at all than it did to volunteer later when the draft was imminent. Nor was the decline in morale to be found only among southern

[42] *Ibid.* Henry Tipton to John Marsh, Dec. 16, 1862, Marsh Papers.

[43] *Chicago Tribune*, Sept. 3, 1862. John B. Messland to E. Moore, Aug. 9, 1862, Yates Papers.

Illinois regiments, or among Democrats who served in the army. It was to be found everywhere, and among northern Illinois Republican soldiers as well. Most illustrative of the attitude which many soldiers developed in the late months of 1862 was the comment by Sergeant Onley Andrus of the 95th Illinois in a letter to the folks back home: "I wish the war & its leaders were all in the bottomless pit with the Devil on top of them. They say that the war will be wound up in 3 months! That is the kind of gammon the nation has been fed on for the last year. . . ."[44]

After the turn of the year, Grant put his army to digging canals and passages which he and some of his general officers felt would facilitate the operations about Vicksburg. The projects just didn't turn out to be effective, but a great many soldiers died in the effort to make them so. These failures, plus the high death rate which accompanied them, pushed morale even lower. "The soldiers dies their so fast," wrote a western Illinois soldier, "that they cant hardly find dry ground to burry them." Five days later the same private took time to congratulate his brother upon his decision to stay home rather than to join the army. "Thank your God that you stayed with your mama for if you had been down here this winter you may have been stuck in some mud hole somewhere in Mississippi," he wrote. This last was written just one month before the author, Private Collin Cordell from Macomb, Illinois, died from dysentery contracted while working upon a canal.

There were many who would have agreed with young Cordell, especially among those regiments assigned to the canal digging. One Illinois soldier, later to die in the charge up Missionary Ridge, wrote his parents that he hadn't had a good meal for months, just hardtack, sowbelly, and sand from the canal operations. And in the year which followed the war, when each regiment attempted to recall its past with a published regimental history, those units which had spent the early months of 1863 in the bayous remembered the time with reluctance.[45]

The fact that it was so obvious to many Illinois soldiers that

---

[44] *Civil War Letters of Sergeant Onley Andrus*, 25.

[45] Private Collin Cordell to his parents, March 7, 12, 1863, in possession of Mr. Howard Cordell, Tampa, Florida. Ira Payne to his parents, March 17, 1863, Ira A. Payne Papers. See also [Crooker *et al.*], 212.

their own welfare could be better handled, and that the war could be more ably prosecuted, profoundly affected their estimates of Union leadership. The common soldier of a century ago was not any more likely to be mislead by flamboyancy in his general officers than the warrior of a more modern age. The true test of ability lay eventually in the results achieved. In time the common soldier learned to respect Grant because of that general's unswerving determination to win. By 1864 he came to admire Sherman because the innate genius in the Ohio general was uncovered by the success of his army. There was that period in late 1862 and early 1863, however, when it seemed to many Illinois soldiers that, for some reason, nature had seen fit to deprive all northern generals of competence. To the doomed Private Cordell, the entire Army of the Tennessee was being led by "card players" who were interested in "money and whiskey." It did not seem possible to some of the men that with most of the resources, most of the human support, and virtually all of the money, the Union cause was doing so badly. One Illinois soldier, in contemplating this contradiction, concluded that "we are entirely dificient in *great Military leaders. . . .*" Another, a soldier in the 116th Illinois, wrote the people back home that the attack upon Chickasaw Bayou would very likely be called "a great stragatic movement" by the leaders of the army. One suspects that he was being effectively, if illiterately, sarcastic.[46]

When general after general was given extended leave after military failures in 1862 and 1863, some of them never again to command, Illinois soldiers had their own private reactions. An officer from Charleston, Illinois, wrote that he wished that he had received a general officer's commission. Then, he concluded, "I could make a blunder, sacrifice two or three thousand men, be relieved of my command, be ordered to report to Cincinnati, Columbus or Washington, go there and draw my pay regularly and spend a season in fashionable society." One could hardly blame the soldiers for such thoughts. There were times when, long before the War Department or the administration, they could see that certain generals were unfit for important com-

[46] Cordell to his parents, March 7, 1863. Oliver Look to W. C. Flagg, May, 1863, Oliver Look Papers, ISHL. *Civil War Letters of Henry C. Bear*, 25.

mands. When Pope was appointed as the commanding general of the Army of Virginia by President Lincoln, one Illinois soldier was moved to write to friends back home explaining that it was a horrible mistake. Pope, he asserted, had "no judgment to command more than a brigade or Division." It took so little time to prove him to be correct.[47]

For most soldiers the war and the army did not quite measure up to what they had expected. The romanticism of an age filled with grandiose prints of national heroes atop prancing white steeds was not to be found in the half-dug canals and bayous of Mississippi, or among the frost-covered dead at Stone's River. No general officers seemed to fit the public conception of the noble Washington or the unbeatable Napoleon, even though some of them desperately struck the appropriate poses or wrote the appropriate words. Somehow, Pope's address to the Army of Virginia only sounded ridiculous despite its faint Corsican flavor. A hand inserted in a half-buttoned coat, also in the mode of Napoleon, did not necessarily bring victories. War just didn't turn out to be filled with nobility and wisdom, but rather with a good deal of waiting around punctuated by moments of wholesale death. "*War war war Oh this Horrible War,*" wrote a young Illinois private who had been shocked by the death and desolation he had seen in southwest Tennessee in 1862. As for the waiting, an adequate description was written by the bugler of the 7th Illinois Infantry in February of 1863: "Soldiering is a drudge unless there is some excitement to feed upon as bacon and beans are not sufficient stimulants to keep the spirits up, although some would gladly 'keep spirits up' by pouring spirits down."[48]

The saving grace about it all was that the first to recognize the rapid decline in army morale and one of its causes was the soldier himself. Naturally, there were those who were ready to place the blame upon the people back home, the "rich" of the North who "should sacrifice more in suppressing this infernal Rebellion and in restoring the Union. . . ." Others simply extended the blame to the entire nation. "The great trouble is our whole

[47] *Three Years in the Army of the Cumberland*, 131. C. H. Floyd to Mrs. Turner, Sept. 13, 1862, Floyd Papers.

[48] Harvey Bruce to his mother, Nov. 25, 1862, Bruce Family Papers, ISHL. David Givler to a friend, Feb. 14, 1863, Givler, 100.

people are too wicked, too little patriotism, too much selfish dishonesty—too much hate and prejudice—too little love and forbearance," asserted Colonel Lyle Dickey to his widowed daughter, Mrs. Anne Wallace. Some were considerably less delicate in assessing the change in the outlook of the army, particularly the young soldiers who had swarmed to the recruiting booths in the great surge of 1862. There was no difficulty in divining the problem of the army, wrote Private John Given of the 124th Illinois, the regiment which had stolen its way across southwest Tennessee. "As regards patriotism," he explained, "it is about played out among the soldiers generally." [49]

In a way, however, it would have to be left to a young soldier of the 86th Illinois to summarize the emotions and frustrations of the entire army. As Corporal Levi Ross of Princeville wrote:

> The troops are becoming very much disheartened in consequence of recent disasters in the field and the bad management of the War Department. When we enthusiastically rushed into the ranks at our Country's call, we all expected to witness the last dying struggles of treason and Rebellion ere this. . . . But in these expectations we have been disappointed. Over 200,000 of our noble soldiers sleep in the silent grave. Almost countless millions of treasure has been expended in the unsuccessful effort of the Government to put down this Rebellion. But after all this great sacrifice of valuable life and money, we are no nearer the goal.[50]

Almost equal to the effects of military failures as a factor in the decline of army morale in the winter of 1862 and 1863 was the promulgation of the Emancipation Proclamation. One would find it impossible to estimate just how few men joined the army from Illinois in the first two years of the war in order to free the slave. It would be infinitely safer to write that most did so simply to save the Union. When emancipation finally went into effect in January of 1863, many young soldiers were shocked, particularly those who had enlisted from western and southern Illinois. These areas of the state had been settled by immigrants who streamed northward out of the Carolinas, Tennessee, and Kentucky. Their attitudes toward slavery and the Negro were strangely contra-

---

[49] L. A. Ross to his father, March 25, 1863, Ross Papers. Dickey to his daughter, Jan. 22, 1863, Wallace-Dickey Papers. Given to his brother, Jan. 4, 1863, Given Papers.

[50] Ross to his father, Feb. 3, 1863, Ross Papers.

dictory; they disliked the former, and yet were conservative in respect to concepts of equality. Their reaction to the proclamation was, in many cases, positively explosive. To their sons and relatives serving in the army they wrote letters. "Richard take a fools advice and come home if you have to desert," was the advice given by a citizen of McDonough County to his nephew in the 16th Illinois; "you will be protected—the people are so enraged that you need not be alarmed if you hear of the whole of the Northwest killing off the abolitionists." Such sentiments spread like a contagion over parts of Illinois, and soon there were pockets of opposition to the proclamation in such areas as Coles County and northwestern Illinois. Since it was really impossible to separate the sentiments of the civilian back home from the soldier in the army, the attitudes of one would most certainly affect those of the other.[51]

It would be improper and incorrect to designate entire regiments as being in opposition to emancipation, with the exception of rare instances. Each regiment was made up of companies from different counties, or companies from particular parts of certain counties. Persons living within a few miles of each other might have different backgrounds and thus different attitudes toward emancipation. There was, for instance, a good deal of Copperhead activity in McDonough County during the latter half of the war, yet Warren County, directly north of it, had comparatively little. Even within McDonough County itself, however, attitudes corresponded to the particular location or township. Near the little hamlet of Tennessee, close to the southern border of the county, the sentiment was strongly against emancipation, while along the northern line, where people of a New England background had settled, feelings were directly opposite. Understanding this, it is easy to realize that Illinois regiments in 1863 rarely had a single opinion regarding the proclamation. Many troops of the 34th Illinois (the "Rock River Rifles") were strongly anti-Lincoln, for example. Yet one suspects that these soldiers came from a company in the unit which had been recruited in Randolph County in southern Illinois. Other companies in the 34th were equally strong in favor of the President and his policy with regard to the Negro. "I go in for it with

[51] *Macomb Journal*, April 3, 1863.

my whole heart and hand," fervently wrote a young soldier of the regiment. "I do not believe in stopping short of attaining the object for which the war has been carried out on the part of the government."[52]

Though one can generalize about individual companies or individual soldiers and their probable reaction to emancipation, it is not possible to be truly accurate. Factors other than background played upon the judgment of the ordinary soldier from Illinois – his educational level, how he had been conditioned in respect to the Negro, and a hundred others. Those who came from Pike County, for instance, were most often against the President's policy. The comments of Private Joshua R. Barney of the 99th Illinois, recruited mainly in that county, probably reflect the attitudes of most of his fellows. "I am not in favor of freeing the negroes and leaving them to run free and mingle among us nether is sutch the intention of old Abe but we will send them off and Colonize them," he wrote. The government, he concluded, was "already making preparations for the Same and you may be assured it will be carried into effect!"[53]

Still, there were contradictions. One Illinois officer reported that his regiment, recruited mainly in the Canton area, was definitely against the freeing of Negroes. One would have suspected a different reaction from that section of the state. A lieutenant of another regiment, the 86th Illinois, made a survey of his own company shortly after the proclamation went into effect, and was shocked with the results. As he wrote to his father: "You can judge how we feel here in the 86th when I tell you that only 8 men in Co. K approve the policy and proclamation of Mr. Lincoln." The entire company came from Princeville, which was in the center of an area having abolition sentiments. Then there was a private of the 13th Illinois, a regiment recruited in northwestern Illinois. This soldier minced no words about his own ideas as he wrote: "I do despise and hate an Abolitionist almost as bad as a secess." A sergeant of the 95th Illinois, Onley Andrus, who

[52] E. W. Payne to Miss Kim Hudson, March 18, 1863, Edwin W. Payne Papers. Payne, 14–15. Payne, in *ibid.*, claimed that when the troops were forced to return escaped slaves to their masters, there was indignation in his regiment.

[53] Barney to his brother, Oct. 24, 1862, Dinsmore Papers. The most important general officer to oppose emancipation was McClernand.

came from the northern part of the state, wrote a steady stream of anti-abolition sentiments to his wife. "I certainly hope that they may lay down their arms before the first of Jan in order to keep the Niggers where they belong," he asserted in a letter written in November, 1862. His attitude was no different two years later. "I think I see myself reenlisting to help make the Nigger my superior," he wrote. "I expect to stay my time out and not one minute longer." What Andrus apparently did not know was that one of his comrades-in-arms, one Ford Douglass of Chicago, was actually a Negro.[54]

There was the other side of the coin, quite naturally; large numbers of Illinois soldiers saw the Emancipation Proclamation as a major step in the war. An Illinois soldier stationed at Memphis wrote early in 1863 that he felt that at last the war was identified with some important cause. Parts of many regiments seemed to be enthusiastically in favor of the abolition of Negro servitude. When Owen Lovejoy spoke to the state Republican convention in late 1862, he was most warmly greeted by an audience including soldiers. "Every mention of old Abes name in connection with his late proclamation drew forth tremendous applause," wrote Private Sam Gordon of the 118th to his wife. "I think the President has struck the blow in the right time."[55]

In a great many instances, however, the Illinois soldier took a stand for emancipation which was not so much based upon his own altruism in respect to the Negro, but upon the desire to see the war brought speedily to a close. To a great many it seemed to mean a step closer to home. This approach was ably expressed by a member of the well-worn 7th Illinois when he wrote: "Among the soldiers, the proclamation is just the thing because it is the only remedy, and all know it will have a tendency to terminate the war shortly and permit us to return to better and more desirable vocations." Nor was this attitude expressed only by those in the lower ranks. Feeling that the war would be fought out on the issue of slavery "*from absolute necessity,*" the Illinois officer Wil-

[54] *Army Life of an Illinois Soldier*, 125–126. L. A. Ross to his father, Feb. 3, 1863, Ross Papers. W. H. Marsh to his mother, Aug. 14, 1862, Marsh Papers. *Civil War Letters of Sergeant Onley Andrus*, 28, 75. Dudley Taylor Cornish, *The Sable Arm: Negro Troops in the Union Army, 1861–1865* (New York, 1956), 215–216.

[55] Gordon to his wife, Sept. 26, 1862, Gordon Papers.

liam Ward Orme wrote in October, 1862: "I have not met a soldier but that is in favor of closing the war as speedily as possible; and they all believe that the institution of slavery once out of the way, the war would be closed."[56]

It can truly be said that emancipation as a policy in the war drew greater and greater acceptance by the army as the war progressed. Whether this development was part of the intensification of emotion against the South because of the prolongation of the war, or for other reasons, it did seem to occur among troops from Illinois. Some soldiers from the state retained their original opinions at the end of the war, of course, but for many there was a great change of opinion in respect to the problem of the Negro. One Illinois officer wrote at the end of January, 1863, that the attitude of his regiment had changed since they had entered the army. Soldiers who had been against emancipation at the turn of the year were now persuaded that it was a good thing, and were planning to vote for "Old Abe" should he run for the presidency again. But the most succinct comment along this line was made by a member of the 59th Illinois, that sturdy bulwark of the Army of the Cumberland. "I am well but turning black," the soldier informed his commanding officer, Philip S. Post; "abolition sentiments probably."[57]

Part of the growing popularity of emancipation must have been due to the actual association of the army with large numbers of contraband slaves of the South. As the Union troops moved into southern Tennessee, northern Alabama, and northern Mississippi, they began to encounter the "institution" at its solid root. There is little question that, in the beginning, the invading soldiers took almost as great an advantage of the unknowing Negro as did the former masters. A member of the 99th Illinois, for instance, wrote his wife that several men in his regiment had a Negro helper or cook. There were so many of them in the camp, he concluded, that even some of the "Negro lovers" were "geting anough of them." In other cases, the actions of certain soldiers

[56] David Givler to a friend, Oct. 13, 1862, Givler, 96. Orme to a friend, Oct. 1, 1862, Orme Papers.

[57] A. W. Hostetter to Mr. and Mrs. O. P. Miles, Jan. 29, 1863, Amos W. Hostetter Papers, ISHL. Hostetter was in the 34th Illinois. Samuel West to Post, May 17, 1862, Post Papers. The phrase "turning black" was a popular reference to changing sentiments on abolition.

with respect to contraband Negroes offended even the most hardened commanding officers. The surgeon of one Illinois cavalry regiment was court-martialed on charges that he had mustered a Negro woman, one Mary Francis, as a private soldier, and was paying her out of army funds. Would one need to conjecture long about the officer's use of the girl? How much worse was it for some regiments to make cruel sport of contraband Negroes? On one occasion, near the Big Black River in Mississippi, a Negro was blown over 20 feet into the air when a group of soldiers set off powder under a box on which they had the Negro dancing. The division commander, William Sooey Smith, was so angry over the incident that the 40th Illinois was detailed to guard the camp in which it had occurred.[58]

In time, however, such happenings diminished in number; particularly when it began to occur to many Illinois soldiers that their only true friends in the South were the Negroes themselves. Furthermore, the occasional escape of Union soldiers from such southern prison camps as Andersonville in Georgia were often managed with Negro help. More than one Illinois soldier was converted to pro-abolition sentiments by his own experience in this respect, or by the stories of such incidents which passed through the army.

The real test of Union determination to win the war did not come with the emancipation of the Negro, however, despite its specific effect upon the morale of certain troops in the army. The ultimate trial of the ordinary soldier came when the freed Negro was actually allowed to become a soldier, and to bear arms against a white foe. If emancipated Negroes were offensive to some Illinois soldiers, armed Negroes were infinitely more so, and as in the case of the proclamation, their effect upon army morale was deleterious in the beginning.

It would be next to impossible to arrive at the exact time and spot at which an American Negro became the first colored soldier in the Union army. The reason for this is twofold. First of all, as the various northern armies moved into Tennessee, Virginia, or other states in which there were large concentrations of Negroes,

[58] J. C. Dinsmore to his wife, Nov. 5, 1863, Dinsmore Papers. "Charges and Specifications Against L. Spofford Hunt," Oct. 1, 1863 (document in James Monroe Ruggles Papers, ISHL). *Army Life of an Illinois Soldier*, 192.

it was common for Union regiments to allow escaping Negro slaves to accompany them in their movements against the enemy. At the very beginning, these men were employed in menial tasks about the camps, cooking, building roads, and erecting buildings. Then there were occasions when they actually performed feats of combat. The 20th Illinois kept a Negro boy by the name of Ben whose courage won much affection for him in the regiment. The 47th Illinois, likewise, carried with it a "contraband of war," a Ned, who went to the Peoria area after the war. Were these men to be considered soldiers? If not, who was the first Negro to wear the blue of the Union army? As it has been pointed out previously in the case of Ford Douglass of the 95th Illinois, there were Negroes who volunteered and served as whites with or without the knowledge of their commanding officers. Yet how many of these instances remain undisclosed?[59]

In September of 1862, just days after President Lincoln announced his intention to emancipate some slaves, steps were taken in certain areas to form regiments of troops which would be principally Negro. In the New Orleans district, General Benjamin Butler had already begun the organization of a unit which he called the 1st Louisiana Native Guards, and in May of 1862 General David Hunter had begun the creation of a South Carolina Negro regiment. Though both of these efforts were opposed by the President, they were never completely stopped, and the organization of colored regiments continued. By the end of the year Negro soldiers had fought in such far-flung places as Florida and Missouri, and had fought well.

After the Emancipation Proclamation went into effect in 1863, President Lincoln placed executive force behind the attempt to bring the Negro into the war as a soldier by calling for the formation of four Negro regiments, and certain of these units were quick to gain reputations for valor and courage. Remarkable among these was the 54th Massachusetts Infantry, whose soldiers not only came from the state which authorized its organization, but also from such other places as Illinois and Indiana.

On March 1, 1863, General Halleck, acting under instructions from the Secretary of War, ordered General Grant to begin the conscription and training of Negro regiments in the Mississippi

[59] Bryner, 72. Blanchard, 50.

valley. In order to facilitate this action, General Lorenzo Thomas, the Adjutant General of the U.S. Army and a great advocate of the recruitment of colored regiments, was sent to confer with certain western governors, and to make speeches to the troops upon the subject. Soon Grant's troops made grand sweeps into the southern countryside in order to pick up contraband slaves and conscript them into the army. In July of 1863, for instance, the 92nd Illinois Mounted Infantry left its base in Mississippi and scoured through a hostile area for four days. The raid was a considerable success: some 8,000 Negroes returned with the regiment.[60]

By the fall of 1863, Negro regiments had been involved in military combat throughout the battle area. None were conflicts of major importance, but all were bitter and hard-fought. At the fight at Milliken's Bend on June 7, 1863, for example, a fragment of William H. T. Walker's division of Confederate troops attacked an equal number of Union troops consisting of two Louisiana Negro regiments brigaded with some white soldiers. The contest was a brisk one and involved a bayonet exchange and some rough hand-to-hand fighting. The colored regiments fought extremely well. Colonel John C. Black of the 37th Illinois, who watched a review of the same soldiers a few weeks later, expressed the feelings of a good many western soldiers when he wrote: "How humiliating [to the South] and how convincing a proof of the wisdom of the administration." The *Quincy Herald*, commenting upon the same fight, added its own interpretation, stating: "Colored soldiers do not fight better than white men, but they fight better than Rebellious Texans."[61]

[60] Joseph T. Wilson, *The Black Phalanx: A History of the Negro Soldiers of the United States* . . . (Hartford, Conn., 1888), 176–180. Mary Livermore, 599–600. Sergeant Onley Andrus had this to say about the raid of the 92nd: "Part of Sherman's great expedition has returned bringing, they say, 8,000 Niggers. Some of the boys was in Town when they come in and they say that they didnt see an able bodied nigger in the whole gang that was 2 hours in passing a given point." See *Civil War Letters of Sergeant Onley Andrus*, 75.

[61] Black to his parents, June 11, 1863, Black Papers. *Quincy Herald*, Sept. 12, 1863. The *Chicago Tribune*, Aug. 6, 1863, commented: "The question is no longer debatable. . . . The negro will fight — for his liberty, for his place among men, for his right to develop himself in whatever direction he chooses. . . ."

The evolution of the Negro in relation to Illinois followed the pattern which existed elsewhere in the country. As many Illinois regiments moved into the South they picked up Negro contraband slaves and attached them to the army. Before emancipation, it was often a matter of fortune as to which might keep the slave in question – the regiment or the master. "Niggers what they will fetch," wrote Sergeant Charles Brush of the 53rd Illinois, "the princapal *fetch* is to *fetch* them with us on the road for cooks and to be *fetched* back by Massa when he can find them. . . ." Sometimes the newly freed Negroes would become so attached to certain Illinois regiments, with the sentiment reciprocated, that regimental officers would openly add their names to the muster rolls. The 12th Illinois, for example, carried with it a number of "Unassigned Recruits of African Descent." The 11th Illinois listed upon its muster rolls a large number of so-called "under-cooks." Though not designated as such, these were obviously Negroes whom the regiment had picked up during its wanderings.[62]

Most authorities credit the state of Illinois with supplying 1,811 colored soldiers to the Union army during the war. As one might gather from a study of the facts, however, this number may be far from correct. Scores of Negroes passed as white soldiers, and, as indicated above, others served in various capacities but were simply not listed as soldiers. The figure of 1,811 comes from a tabulation of all those Illinois Negroes who were organized into U.S. infantry, cavalry, or artillery units, and who were eventually credited to Illinois. The most important organization of this type was the 29th U.S. Colored Infantry, whose muster rolls listed all of its Negroes as coming from Illinois.[63]

The background of the 29th U.S. Colored Infantry is an interesting but not unusual one. On September 24, 1863, shortly after General Lorenzo Thomas' visit with the western governors, the War Department authorized Governor Yates to raise "one regiment infantry" to consist solely of Negroes from Illinois. Entirely sympathetic to the cause of the Negro, and one of the first to advocate his emancipation and use as a soldier, Yates moved

[62] Brush to his father, June 17, 1862, Brush Family Papers. *Report of the Adjutant General*, I, 573, 530.

[63] Fox, 532.

slowly to act upon the authorization mainly because of bitter Copperhead opposition within the state to the free colored soldier. Finally, on October 26, he issued General Order No. 44, which laid out the principles upon which the regiment would be organized. Soon after, recruiting agents began the task of persuading Illinois Negroes to join the colors.[64]

The pressure to fill the 29th U.S. to capacity, as well as to add Illinois Negroes to other regiments, grew in intensity throughout the fall of 1863 and in the early months of 1864. Such newspapers as the *Quincy Herald* printed eloquently written articles upon the necessity of raising Negro troops and of sending the 29th to the front. Not all of the desire to do this came from noble motives, however, for draft quotas were beginning to press down upon the state and many people, including the governor, saw the Negro recruit as a way by which the indignity of the draft might be avoided. The *Chicago Tribune*, in January of 1864, urged all "benevolent patriotic citizens" of Chicago to raise money for bonuses in order to spur recruiting of the 29th, and thereby avoid the onus of the draft. Earlier in the same month, the *Tribune* had written that the regiment ought to be filled before the end of January, lest the "impending draft" be allowed to take place.[65]

The coming of the Negro into the ranks of soldiers serving Illinois was accepted in time as a good thing by most white troops. "What do you think of the 'Negro Regiment Bill?'" inquired a soldier of the 7th Illinois. "Some of the soldiers make some few trivial objections but as a general rule most all say that if a negro can stop an enemy's ball, why let him go and do it." One southern Illinois regiment, the 81st, at first bitterly opposed the use of Negroes in any form, but soon became convinced of the "propriety" of using them in certain capacities. An officer of the 123rd Illinois, hearing of opposition back home to the recruitment of Negroes, bitterly proclaimed: "Can't they [the citizens of Illinois] see, without conventions or proclamations, that it is an abolition war?" An Illinois soldier, attempting to explain the changing attitudes of his regiment to his parents, wrote: "For my part I would like to see all the negroes we could raise armed

[64] George W. Williams, 133.

[65] *Quincy Herald*, Dec. 8, 1863, Jan. 28, 1864. *Chicago Tribune*, Jan. 13, 3, 1864.

and put under military discipline although there are a great many of the soldiers who are so foolish as to say that they would not fight if the negroes were armed. But I think if a negro could save their lives by sacrificing theirs they would be willing."[66]

It would be wrong to write, however, that there was no opposition at all. There was, indeed, a substantial amount, which, added to emancipation and the military reserves, gave fuel to the Copperhead cause. The anti-war press in Illinois had a field day with the issue of the Negro soldier, and local Copperheads went all the way in attempting to exploit it. A white citizen of Saint Albans, Illinois, wrote to members of the 10th Illinois Cavalry that he hoped that the soldiers were now proud of their "black uncle Abe." "I hope you and the rest of the whole damned Black army will go to Hell the short way" was his benediction to the regiment. Widely printed among Copperhead newspapers in the state was the comment of the *New York Independent* upon the issue of arming the Negro. "We must advance to that inevitable goal," stated that paper, "when we shall meet him [the Negro] as an officer, a general, a ruler. . . ." An Illinois newspaper, bemoaning the rush of white soldiers to volunteer for commands in colored regiments, proclaimed: "Colonel Chetlain of Illinois will have command of a negro brigade. Oh shame! that Illinois has a son so degenerate."[67]

One of the standard techniques of the Copperhead newspapers was to focus attention upon the unwillingness of white soldiers to serve with colored troops. One paper claimed that white members of an Illinois cavalry unit had been threatened with whippings if they continued to object to being brigaded with a colored regiment. Another approach was to play upon rumors that Negro troops were mistreated by Confederate armies whenever they were captured. On one occasion, an obviously untrue report that an entire colored regiment had been hung by the Confederate General Marmaduke received wide circulation. A third technique was a standard one. There were scores of stories about the killing of whites by Negroes, or the raping of white women by

[66] David Givler to a friend, Feb. 14, 1863, Givler, 101. Newsome, 11. Ira Payne to his parents, Feb. 27, 1863, Ira A. Payne Papers. *Three Years in the Army of the Cumberland*, 146.

[67] *Macomb Journal*, March 20, 1863. *Macomb Eagle*, May 28, Jan. 2, 1864.

the same. Few of these tales had foundation, of course. As General Clinton B. Fisk, later a member of the Freedmen's Bureau, pointed out after investigation of a number of these stories: ". . . a colored man hunting squirrels was magnified into a thousand vicious negroes marching upon their old masters with bloody intent."[68]

There is no question that the lack of military success against the enemy, the ending of Negro servitude, and the arming of the freed Negro had an impact upon the effectiveness of Illinois regiments in the Union army, as well as upon the willingness of young men to volunteer. Enlistments declined rapidly after the August rush of 1862, and only the fact that Illinois was credited with those enlistments in the regiments of other states saved it from the application of the draft.[69]

Worst of all, however, was the rapid increase in the number of desertions during and following the winters of 1862 and 1863. Once again this development seems to have occurred mainly, though not only, in the higher-numbered regiments. Desertions for the entire war totaled 13,046 for the state of Illinois, but the largest number for any one period is to be found in the months following emancipation, the arming of Negroes, and the military reverses of 1862. On January 24, not even a month beyond the moment when emancipation went into effect, a sergeant of the 95th Illinois reported to his friends back in Illinois that desertions in his and other regiments nearby were "not unfrequent." A Canton, Illinois, officer wrote home three months later that his regiment, the 103rd, was suffering from heavy desertion; 23 had disappeared within several weeks, 17 of these coming from a Lewistown company. By April it had become so bad that the *Illinois State Journal* was able to report that "Democratic Boys . . . are coming home every day."[70]

In all of this, there were two extreme examples of regiments being affected by developments in 1862 and 1863. The first of these

[68] *Macomb Eagle*, July 18, June 6, Sept. 12, 1863. John Sappington Marmaduke, educated at Harvard, Yale, and West Point, had a tendency toward duels and violence. J. T. Trowbridge, *The South: A Tour of Its Battlefields and Ruined Cities* (Hartford, Conn., 1866), 375.

[69] *Report of the Adjutant General*, I, 36–37.

[70] Cole, 306. *Civil War Letters of Sergeant Onley Andrus*, 46. *Army Life of an Illinois Soldier*, 163. *Illinois State Journal*, April 14, 1863.

was the 109th Illinois, a regiment which had been raised in Union, Johnson, Pulaski, Jackson, and Alexander counties. After the turn of the year the 109th seems to have gone into a state of mutiny. The regiment stacked its arms and refused to obey further orders; its commanding officers quit and went home. Grant was forced to place the entire regiment under arrest for reason of "disloyalty." Eventually the unit was disbanded, and the troops were amalgamated with the 11th Illinois.[71]

An equally bad case was the 128th Illinois, a regiment raised principally in Williamson County. The regiment virtually disintegrated. At one time it was reported that only 35 men reported for morning muster. Eventually the unit was disbanded by special order of General Lorenzo Thomas, the Adjutant General, due to "an utter want of discipline" in the organization. Like the 109th, it seemed to be another instance when the troops simply could not accept the changing policies of the war. The sentiment was not only to be found in southern Illinois or among regiments from that area, but also among the citizens and soldiers from other sections. A member of the 86th Illinois, a northern Illinois regiment, informed his father in Illinois that a considerable number of his regiment had deserted, and that many of those remaining hoped for the recognition of the Confederacy by the Union government. "Alas! for our beloved Republic!" wrote the soldier.[72]

There was nothing really wrong with the army, however, that several fine victories could not cure. The capture of Vicksburg, the repulse at Gettysburg, and Rosecrans' successful invasion of east Tennessee were to palliate the discontent and drive away the aura of despair. In the end it was the soldier who regained the sense of victory long before the people went back home. The long sad letters from wives and sweethearts who bemoaned the

[71] H. H. Hood to his wife, March 26, 1863, Hood Papers. J. C. Cottle to a friend, Jan. 8, 1863, John C. Cottle Papers, ISHL. *Army Life of an Illinois Soldier*, 52.

[72] *Illinois State Journal*, Jan. 12, 13, 15, 28, 29, Feb. 3, 1863. This paper occasionally confused the 128th Illinois with the 129th, which had a good record of combat. *Report of the Adjutant General*, VI, 532. L. A. Ross to his father, Feb. 3, 1863, Ross Papers. It was stated in the *Chicago Tribune*, Sept. 3, 1863, that deserters roamed the streets of Vandalia and Danville attacking Union men.

continuation of the war were soon to be answered by their recipients in a different spirit. "Remember, *we are suppressing the rebellion*," a Canton soldier advised his wife back home, "and you agree with me that it must be done at all hazards; you are doing your part of it, quite as well as I, in bearing with bitter disappointment and almost neglect." [73]

As for the Copperheads, the Illinois soldier developed his own thoughts on the matter. "I am sorry to hear that there are copperheads in Newton but let em wait," wrote a soldier in the 34th Illinois; "they will *dry up* when the sojer boys get home or else they will fare badly." A soldier of the 95th Illinois had equal sentiments, and hoped that the rebel raider Morgan could get up into Illinois and do "a little of their stealing & burning" there. Nor were such feelings only to be found among officers and men of the lower ranks. The lieutenant colonel of the 33rd Illinois, writing to a high public official of the state of Illinois, indicated that the "crack of the guns" near Vicksburg reminded him of Copperheads. "And, talking about hell," he concluded, "our Soldiers would like to kindle one for some people in Illinois and may one day do something towards it." But of all the expressions of loyalty put to paper by Illinois troops in that period following the winter of discontent, the most forceful was a succinct comment by Private Henry C. Bear of Oakley, Illinois, a member of the 116th Illinois. "You may tell evry man of Doubtful Loyalty for me, up ther in the north," he wrote, "that he is meaner than any son of a bitch in hell." Out of such an attitude was victory to be fashioned.[74]

[73] *Three Years in the Army of the Cumberland*, 126.

[74] E. W. Payne to Miss Kim Hudson, March 22, 1863, Edwin W. Payne Papers. *Civil War Letters of Sergeant Onley Andrus*, 65. C. E. Lippincott to Newton Bateman, June 15, 1863, Bateman Papers. *Civil War Letters of Henry C. Bear*, 9.

CHAPTER VI

The Capture of Vicksburg

The Union army at Milliken's Bend on the Mississippi north of Vicksburg had a new commander. John Alexander McClernand was now in charge, having superseded Sherman, the unsuccessful invader of Chickasaw Bayou. The new commanding general had come a long way since the early days of the war. He was at the high point of his career, where success and victory might eventually bring to him the highest office of the land, where failure might bring oblivion.

There is little question that the arrival of McClernand upon the scene was a difficult blow for both Grant and Sherman, and for all of those professional military men for whom the army had been a career. There was a natural disposition on the part of these officers to oppose such men as McClernand, whom they considered as political and ambitious interlopers, and to throw the weight of their support to the West Pointer who seemed most likely to succeed. It is difficult to understand the opposition to McClernand by these men upon any other basis than that, for, after all, this self-taught general officer had done well in every conflict in which he had previously been engaged. His troops had fought as well as if not better than those of Sherman at Shiloh, and his contributions to the Union cause up to the end of 1862 had been more important. Nevertheless, bitter feelings were to meet McClernand upon his arrival. Sherman, whose handling of the troops at Chickasaw Bayou left something to be desired, was quick to express his displeasure. To his brother John Sherman, the Ohio politician, he wrote: "Mr. Lincoln intended to insult me and the military profession by putting McClernand over me. . . ." It was a sentence which clearly implied the sentiment of the professionals concerning McClernand. And to his wife he wrote a petulant little note: "It was simply absurd to supersede me by McClernand, but Mr. Lincoln knows I am not anxious to command, and he knows McClernand is, and must gratify him. He will get his fill before he is done." It would be difficult to accept Sherman's portrayal of the modesty of his own character. Common sense and the course of subsequent events would show that Sherman was as anxious to command as any other man in the army.[1]

Sherman was not the only one who felt strongly about the new commander of the Union army on the Mississippi. Admiral Porter, who had developed a closeness to Sherman during the previous weeks of campaigning, kept his lines to Washington hot with deprecations of McClernand's military ability. Writing to no less than Gustavus V. Fox, Assistant Secretary of the Navy, Porter claimed that Sherman was "every inch a soldier" and that McClernand, who did not fit those specifications, had "the confidence of no one, unless it may be two or three of his staff." "This is a great enterprise," he concluded; "no personal considerations should keep a man at the head of this Army who is incompetent to direct it. . . ."[2]

The major opposition to McClernand came from the higher officers of the army, however. In this category was General Thomas K. Smith, an Ohioan whose pre-war associations with Grant and Sherman cemented his loyalty to those generals. Smith wrote of his opposition to "political generals" of any kind. Several of them had come down with McClernand, he asserted; only "two or three of them" were "educated" military men. Now, Smith continued,

---

[1] William T. Sherman to John Sherman, Jan. 17, 1863, *The Sherman Letters: Correspondence Between General and Senator Sherman from 1837 to 1891*, ed. Rachel Sherman Thorndike (New York, 1894), 181. William T. Sherman to his wife, Jan. 24, 1863, *Home Letters of General Sherman*, 235.

[2] Porter to Fox, Jan. 16, 1863, *Confidential Correspondence of Gustavus Vasa Fox, Assistant Secretary of the Navy, 1861–1865*, ed. Robert M. Thompson and Richard Wainwright (2 vols., New York, 1920), II, 154.

there was a serious attempt to place these men in control of the army. "The advent of McClernand is deprecated," he concluded.[3]

Was there any evidence of collusion in the opposition to McClernand? If not, there was considerable coincidence. Smith's letter to his family back in Ohio has much of the phraseology of Porter's letter to Fox in the implication that it was unsuitable to put a so-called political general over a professional, and in the use of the words "two or three" in relation to McClernand's staff. Collusion or not, the opposition to the new commanding general seemed to be a cold and abiding one. It was a situation most appropriately described by General Clinton B. Fisk, an old friend of Grant's: "General McClernand is to command the down stream force. This arrangement causes much bitterness among us generals, who are all ambitious of doing brave deeds in opening the Mississippi."[4]

There is no doubt that McClernand could feel the coolness of his military subordinates after his arrival at Milliken's Bend. He was a man of infinite confidence, however, and one who had the added tendency to gamble. It is also entirely probable that he realized that his time as the immediate commander of the instrument of his own creation, the Army of the Mississippi, was limited by such an opposition; therefore he should strike for a victory, and strike fast. By January 3 he had conceived a plan. A summons went out to Sherman: "Please come down tonight, or in the morning, as you prefer, and we will decide the question in the light of mutual suggestion." The problem under consideration by the two generals was the taking of the Confederate bastion on the Arkansas River called Arkansas Post or Fort Hindman.

Arkansas Post, about 50 miles up the Arkansas from the Mississippi, was no inconsiderable military fortification. It was a square solid establishment, somewhat on the order of Fort Donelson, and stood at the bend of the river. High enough to command the surrounding countryside, it dominated the river with two nine-inch guns and an eight-inch gun plus eight smaller guns. Trenches, more than a mile in length, defended the landward

[3] Smith to his mother, Jan. 7, 1863, *Life and Letters of Thomas Kilby Smith . . .* , ed. Walter G. Smith (New York, 1898), 256–257.

[4] *Official Records*, Ser. I, Vol. XXII, Pt. 2, 31.

side. Inside of the fort were a substantial number of defenders and a large collection of supplies.

According to the recollections of Porter, whose memory was not always reliable, the planning session of January 5 between Sherman, McClernand, and himself was an interesting and revealing one. The admiral and the Ohio general had seen each other before the meeting, and had then discussed the character and plans of the opposition – McClernand. The commanding general, both agreed, seemed to be vague in his notions as to what should be done with the army. Sherman relayed the information that McClernand's solution to the war was to cut "his way to the sea." Both concluded that McClernand had to be relieved in some way for the good of the army. Armed with such sentiments, the admiral and the general proceeded to their meeting with McClernand, who met them with the comment that the army was in a "most demoralized state," and that something must be done to "raise their spirits." Porter's reply, which most certainly must have been a sullen one, was that if such was the case, McClernand should do something about it. "Certainly," was the Illinois general's reply. "And if you will let me have some of your gun-boats, I propose to proceed immediately and capture Arkansas Post." [5]

If Porter's recollections about the meeting aboard the *Tigress* were correct, McClernand's plan of action was much more positive than it was vague. As McClernand later wrote to Grant, the move up the Arkansas would serve to raise Union morale, it would erase an important enemy post to the rear, and it would give the army some profitable exercise. Sherman's comment about McClernand cutting "his way to the sea" was probably a reference to the plan for victory which the latter had presented to Lincoln in the previous September. It had called for a grand movement to Mobile and then to the Atlantic coast.

Much has been made by Grant biographers of what they consider to have been McClernand's flighty nature, his rashness and impetuosity, and his lack of planning. One writer, overcome by his admiration for Grant and his dislike of McClernand, implies that the latter had little else in view for 1863 but a series of minor

---

[5] William T. Sherman, *Memoirs of Gen. W. T. Sherman* (4th ed., New York, 1891), 324–325. Porter, 130–131. *Official Records*, Ser. I, Vol. XVII, Pt. 1, 705.

strikes against secondary enemy posts. In all fairness, however, if such were the case, then McClernand was only one among many. As has been pointed out, Grant's initial attempts to take Vicksburg met with disaster. He would attempt several solutions before applying the right key to the lock of the Mississippi. Yet McClernand would scarcely be allowed the privilege of a minor success. Furthermore, if planning was not McClernand's forte, the handicap failed to show in the little campaign up the Arkansas. As Nicolay and Hay, the Lincoln biographers, wrote: "The expedition once resolved was carried through with the greatest dispatch." By January 8 the Union gunboats reached the mouth of the White River, a short distance from the fort. By January 10 the army was ashore and within three miles of the Confederate fortification at Arkansas Post.[6]

On the following day, McClernand informed Porter that the army was ready for the assault, whereupon the Navy ironclads moved in to engage the guns of the fort, as they had late on January 10. Union artillery joined the cannonade with a brilliantly aimed barrage, and Sherman, who commanded the ground forces, moved the infantry to within 100 yards of the enemy works. The coordination of the entire movement was extremely smooth, which should have been of some credit to the commanding general, and the results were expeditiously achieved. Success was gained "swiftly and decisively," even in the view of Grant's greatest military biographer, Kenneth P. Williams. In a relatively short time, the white flag of surrender floated above the defenders of the Confederate bastion.[7]

Illinois troops played a prominent part in the reduction of Arkansas Post. The ubiquitous 13th Illinois was there, as were the 55th, 77th, 97th, 113th, 116th, 118th, and 131st regiments from the state. It was the 97th Illinois which achieved the greatest credit in the assault, however. This regiment, raised in Macoupin, Calhoun, and Cumberland counties, was rapidly coming to the forefront as one of the most daring of the newer units. During

---

[6] Nicolay and Hay, VII, 139. The move was so out of line with what the Confederates expected that it was reported that the Union army had been stricken with plague. *Official Records,* Ser. I, Vol. XVII, Pt. 1, 702.

[7] Kenneth P. Williams, IV, 295–298. *Official Records,* Ser. I, Vol. XVII, Pt. 1, 702–708.

the expedition up the Arkansas, it was part of William J. Landram's brigade of the XIII Corps, as were also the 77th, 108th, and 131st Illinois.

The casualties incurred in the taking of Arkansas Post totaled 1,061, of which some 900 were wounded. The greatest number of these came among Iowa, Missouri, and Ohio regiments making the assault. In return, the Army of the Mississippi took close to 5,000 prisoners, plus a considerable number of cannon and small arms. One of the larger guns was immediately dispatched by McClernand to Governor Yates of Illinois as a "testimonial of the esteem and admiration of the brave men whose valor wrested it as a trophy." [8]

The response of various general officers in the army to the capture of Arkansas Post could make an interesting and, in some cases, amusing study. Grant's response was a vigorous one. "General McClernand has fallen back to White River, and gone on a wild-goose chase to the Post of Arkansas," read his telegram to Halleck. Nor would Grant's mind be changed about the maneuver until he received Sherman's assurance that it had been a good one. Other general officers who might have criticized McClernand endlessly had he failed in the assault now gave the credit for conception of the idea to Sherman; though it would be just as fair to believe McClernand's own explanation that the thought of taking the Confederate fort had occurred to him as early as December 20 in the previous year.[9]

Though McClernand received no benefit of the doubt at Grant's headquarters, he most certainly gained considerable credit on the home front. The victory was an illumination, small and strategically minor as it was, in an otherwise dreary scene. As McClernand had predicted at the moment of leaving Milliken's Bend, it lifted the morale of both those in the army and the people back home. The *Illinois State Journal* was moved to describe it as "one of the most complete successes of the war. . . ." The *New York Herald* gave McClernand full credit for the achievement, stat-

---

[8] William H. Bentley, *History of the 77th Illinois Volunteer Infantry . . .* (Peoria, Ill., 1883), 116–118, 122–123. Fox, 435. *Illinois State Journal*, April 3, 1863.

[9] Grant to Halleck, Jan. 11, 1863, *Official Records*, Ser. I, Vol. XVII, Pt. 2, 553–554, 701.

ing that the Illinois general "laid his plans to make his victory not only sure, but decisive." Governor Yates, back in Springfield, was delighted, writing: "You cannot imagine with what delight I heard of your brilliant success at Arkansas Post and everybody speaks of it as a brilliant affair." McClernand's battle report, though unnecessarily overdrawn and florid as befitted the nature of the man, naturally gained a wide publication. The character of its writer shone through with unmistakable clarity as he wrote: "Soldiers! Let this triumph be the precurser of still more important achievements. Win for the Army of the Mississippi imperishable renown. Surmount all obstacles, and relying on the God of battles, wrest from destiny and danger, the still more expressive acknowledgments of your unconquerable constancy and valor."[10]

Despite the color of his prose, McClernand was gifted with an ability to make a realistic estimate of his own position. He must have known that he was fighting a battle for his army career with his fellow Illinoisan, Grant. He most certainly was aware that his competitor was backed by the solid authority and prestige of Halleck in Washington, and that the general-in-chief was encouraging Grant to take the active command of the army. On January 7, just before the success at Arkansas Post, McClernand wrote a curious but revealing letter to Lincoln in which he gave full vent to his frustration in dealing with Halleck. Writing that he had "no concealments in regard to this letter," he charged his superior with a "wilful contempt of superior authority," and with an actual subversion of presidential authority. Halleck's only claim to fame, he wrote, was the publication of a book on military practice, but he had handled the army around Corinth in a most disgraceful manner. "How can the country be saved in its dire extremity, with such a Chief at the head of our armies!" McClernand concluded.[11]

Too late, McClernand was to realize that the Arkansas Post campaign, though resulting in victory, was a trap for his own ensnarement. The manner in which the movement had been hurriedly executed gave Grant the leverage for which he had been seeking. In order to understand the action which Grant took fol-

[10] *Illinois State Journal*, Jan. 19, 1863. *New York Herald*, Jan. 21, 1863. Yates to McClernand, Jan. 20, 1863, McClernand Collection. Bentley, 121.

[11] McClernand to Lincoln, Jan. 7, 1863, Lincoln Papers.

lowing the success upon the Arkansas, it is necessary to refer to an interesting note written on December 20, 1862, by General James B. McPherson, and directed to the commanding general of the Army of the Tennessee. It appealed to Grant to read Halleck's order concerning the Mississippi expedition very carefully. The phraseology gave Grant the outlet he needed, McPherson stated; McClernand could become an ineffectual subordinate to Grant's actual command of the army. In conclusion, McPherson wrote: "I have merely suggested these remarks in consequence of the note at the bottom of your letter; and I will also add that in consequence of orders from Washington placing General McClernand in charge of the expedition under you I would, if in your place, proceed to Memphis and take command of it myself. It is the great feature of the campaign, and its execution rightfully belongs to you."[12]

Grant's move to follow McPherson's suggestion began on January 11, just after McClernand's success at Arkansas Post. "Unless absolutely necessary for the object of your expedition you will abstain from all moves not connected with it," he telegraphed the commanding general of the Army of the Mississippi. On the following day, Halleck followed through by reminding Grant of the next step which could be taken. "You are hereby authorized to relieve General McClernand from command of the expedition against Vicksburg, giving it to the next in rank or taking it yourself," he informed Grant.[13]

Though it can properly be supposed that McClernand did not know of the second message, that of Halleck to Grant, he had some kind of insight into what might be transpiring. Using the only real weapon he had, he sent a continuous stream of messages and appeals to his political connections. The politician in him could not allow anything but an attack upon a broad front plus the necessary backfilling. A note to Governor Yates asking for help elicited a prompt reply which assured McClernand that he would be "sustained" in his views. There was a revealing letter to the Illinois educator Jonathan Baldwin Turner in which

[12] McPherson to Grant, Dec. 20, 1862, *Official Records*, Ser. I, Vol. XVII, Pt. 2, 446.

[13] Grant to McClernand, Jan. 11, 1863, Halleck to Grant, Jan. 12, 1863, *ibid.*, 553–554, 555.

McClernand advised the professor that it was obvious that the victory at Arkansas Post was outside of the "contemplation of the Genl. in Chief." "Whether he will undertake to dismiss me for it, I cannot predict," he added, "though I believe he will regret my success, personally, as much as the enemy will repine their disaster." Why the letter to Turner? Yates and the eccentric Jacksonville, Illinois, teacher were close personal friends; McClernand was merely making sure that Yates would have a little help in any decision to support himself against Halleck or Grant.[14]

On January 16 he wrote a long and wordy letter to Lincoln in which he carefully explained his move upon Arkansas Post. He would have "felt guilty" if he had remained inactive, he wrote. "Do not let me be clandestinely destroyed . . . without a hearing," he appealed. The desperation of the man was obvious; he could feel the strings of military authority tightening around him. Lashing out at his tormentors, he concluded:

> I believe my success here is gall and wormwood to the clique of West Pointers who have been persecuting me for months.
>
> How can you expect success, when men controlling the military destinies of the country are more chagrined at the success of your volunteer officers than the very enemy beaten by the latter in battle?
>
> Something must be done to take the hand of oppression off citizen soldiers, whose zeal for their country, has prompted them to take up arms, or all will be lost.[15]

The stream of notes and communications continued. The day following the letter to the President, he sent a strange message to Senator Browning in Washington. It included "unsealed" information which McClernand wished the senator to deliver to the President. Added was a small message for Browning, a reiteration of what McClernand had written to Lincoln. "I have acted wisely and well," he claimed, "and do not let Halleck destroy me without giving me a hearing." [16]

McClernand's sorties into the world of politics brought quick

---

[14] Yates to McClernand, Jan. 17, 1863, McClernand Collection. McClernand to Turner, Jan. 11, 1863, Jonathan Baldwin Turner Papers, ISHL.

[15] McClernand to Lincoln, Jan. 16, 1863, Lincoln Papers.

[16] McClernand to Browning, Jan. 17, 1863, Orville Hickman Browning Transcripts, Illinois Historical Survey, Urbana. McClernand apparently spent all of January 16 writing letters. He also found time to write a vigorous defense of his actions for Grant: *Official Records*, Ser. I, Vol. XVII, Pt. 2, 567.

repercussions. Stanton sent word that it was the "sincere desire" of the President and himself to "oblige" McClernand in every manner "consistent with the general interest of the service. . . ." Lincoln himself answered with a long and beautifully written letter of advice:

> I have too many family controversies, so to speak, already on my hands to voluntarily, or so long as I can avoid it, take up another. You are doing well – well for the country, and well for yourself – much better than you could possibly be if engaged in open war with G Halleck. Allow me to beg that, for your sake, for my sake, for the country's sake, you give your whole attention to the better work.
>
> Your success upon the Arkansas was both brilliant and valuable, and is fully appreciated by the country and the government.[17]

Thus did McClernand's military career reach its zenith during the early days of January, 1863. The ten days between January 20 and January 30 marked the beginning of the outgoing tide for the general from Springfield and southern Illinois; from then on, the flow of events against him would become stronger and stronger. Arkansas Post was both a turning point and the high mark. That single victory illustrates what might have happened if McClernand had retained control of the Mississippi expedition. As Robert R. McCormick wrote in his biography of Grant: "The expedition up the Arkansas River, which showed his bent to seek the road of least resistance so momentously demonstrated two and a half years later, suggests that under McClernand's command and Sherman's planning the campaign might have assumed a totally different complexion. . . ."[18]

This was not to happen, however. As a consequence of Arkansas Post, many of Grant's supporters were alerted to the possibility of another military stroke by McClernand. Sherman, for instance, wrote to Grant on January 17 that there was considerable bustle around the commanding general's headquarters which suggested that he might "attempt impossibilities." It was necessary for Grant to come down now and assume personal direction of the campaign, Sherman warned. Grant's aide, Rawlins, was also placing much pressure upon his superior to act. It was pos-

[17] Stanton to McClernand, Jan. 24, 1863, *ibid.*, 579. Lincoln to McClernand, Jan. 22, 1863, Nicolay and Hay, II, 304–305.

[18] McCormick, 70. McCormick's treatment of McClernand is one of the few sympathetic attempts to understand that general's character.

sible, that Galena officer claimed, for McClernand to cement his position with the administration with a victory elsewhere. For the moment, it seemed, Grant's supporters were more afraid of success than failure.

There is some evidence to suggest that McClernand did have further plans in mind. A study of the papers of Colonel Lewis B. Parsons, officer in charge of military transportation on the Mississippi at this time, indicates that boat movements increased in number after January 24. On January 26, for example, McClernand placed an urgent request for all available vessels in Parsons' area of control. Two days later the ax fell. Parsons received a note from Grant indicating that McClernand was to see the commanding general of the Army of the Tennessee on January 29. Shortly thereafter, McClernand received General Order No. 13 from Grant's headquarters. It seems strange that the message which indicated that Grant was taking immediate command of the army, and that McClernand would be given control of the XIII Corps, was to have such a number.[19]

Thus was the gauntlet thrown down to McClernand. He reacted quickly, of course, sending out a flood of messages in his usual fashion. He rather petulantly asked Grant for an explanation and received a calm reply. After that he sent Grant a bitter little note in which he indicated deference to the general order for "the purpose of avoiding a conflict of authority in the presence of the enemy," but asked that a statement of his position be sent to Stanton and Lincoln. He seemed to be anxious to give Grant no obvious cause for dismissal on the grounds of disregarding the line of command. Not so obvious to Grant would be another letter to the President which, in effect, reminded him what was going on in the high command of the Army of the Tennessee.[20]

Much has been made of McClernand's faults of character by Grant's biographers in the years since the war. It has been alto-

---

[19] Sherman to Grant, Jan. 17, 1863, *Official Records*, Ser. I, Vol. XVII, Pt. 2, 570–571. Wilson, *Life of John A. Rawlins*, 134. It was freely admitted in Grant's headquarters that McClernand's corps was the best in the West. Parsons to McClernand, Jan. 26, 1863, Parsons to Walter B. Scates, Jan. 28, 1863, Lewis B. Parsons Papers, ISHL. *Official Records*, Ser. I, Vol. XXIV, Pt. 1, 11.

[20] *Ibid.*, 12–14. McClernand to Lincoln, Feb. 2, 1863, Lincoln Papers.

gether too easy to place that general in the role of villain in the story of Grant's part in the war, which was undoubtedly a heroic one. Few have attempted to understand the nature of the man whom they are so quick to label a political general. Yet there was another side, one which presents an impulsive, overly ambitious, and genuinely patriotic man who was frustrated at every turn by men who knew the ritual of the military profession better than himself. One might even guess that McClernand would not have had a more brilliant success than that of Grant in the taking of Vicksburg. It may be added, however, that he never had the chance. As one Grant biographer described McClernand's position after the issuance of General Order No. 13: "It is plain that faith was not kept with him and that his indignation was just."[21]

While the struggle between Grant and McClernand persisted to its inevitable conclusion, the campaign against Vicksburg reverted to the pattern of failure. The army continued its work on the canals, even though the first such attempt was known to be a disappointment by the beginning of February. As McClernand, who despised such efforts, advised the President, not only was the canal a fiasco, but further, the troops who had worked on it were beset by a variety of illnesses including smallpox. The "Ditch," as a member of the 3rd Illinois Cavalry put it, was "a humbug." Nor were the other attempts to be any more successful. The Steele's Bayou expedition conducted by Porter was one of the near tragedies of the war. As the *Chicago Tribune* had written in mid-January, Vicksburg was stronger than anyone had supposed. There was clearly but one alternative left to Grant, and that was to bring the army across the river to the south of Vicksburg.[22]

In late March, with the coming of spring, Grant readied his army for the effort after keeping it busy and diverting the enemy's attention by various schemes. McClernand's XIII Corps was ordered to clear the roads from Milliken's Bend to Perkin's Plan-

[21] McCormick, 72–73, 95. McCormick writes: "All the history of McClernand was written by his enemies. Its virulence is evidence of his capacity. Successful generals do not storm at the memory of insignificant rivals they have combined to overcome."

[22] McClernand to Lincoln, Feb. 2, 1863, Lincoln Papers. Col. J. M. Ruggles to his family, Feb. 9, 1863, Ruggles Papers. *Chicago Tribune*, Jan. 16, 1863.

tation, and from there to Hard Times, on the west bank of the river to the south of Vicksburg. Some difficulty was experienced in getting McClernand to move quickly, however. On March 24 he held a needless review of his troops for Governor Yates, who had come down in response to McClernand's January pleas for help against Grant. There were further delays. Whether these delays were due to the fact that McClernand was newly married and had his bride with him, as his opponents later claimed, or whether they were the result of difficulties with the passage around Bayou Vidal, it would be difficult to determine. But high water and bad roads certainly played a part. At any rate, it was a march which many Illinois troops later remembered with pleasure. The surrounding areas were foraged bare by the advancing regiments, and many an Illinois soldier obtained his first look at a genuine southern plantation. Almost every one of them was to come home with stories concerning the daily menu on that long march—veal, mutton, poultry and beef,—and of the beautiful little family cemetery in the center of Perkin's Plantation.[23]

History had no time for sentiment, however; events were in the making. On the night of April 16 Porter managed to get 11 of his boats past the enemy batteries and below to Grant's new base at Hard Times. Within the week more transports made it past the Confederate guns. At almost the same time, Colonel Benjamin H. Grierson was leading a column of three cavalry regiments, the 6th and 7th Illinois and the 2nd Iowa, out of the Tennessee city of La Grange. The purpose of the raid was to cut a swath through Confederate communications and to draw troops from the defense of Vicksburg. The entire force totaled 1,700 troopers and a six-gun battery. The grand attempt upon Vicksburg was under way.

The notion of conducting a cavalry raid into Mississippi was not a new one. Just how Grierson was picked to lead the expedition is a story in itself. He had been a music teacher in Jacksonville, Illinois, with limited success. Like Lincoln, he had made a brief attempt at merchandising. Opening a store in Meredosia, an Illinois river town, he stayed on in that small and unpromising place for several years. There is a sense of poignancy and regret

[23] *Official Records*, Ser. I, Vol. XXIV, Pt. 1, 46–47, 139–141. Dana, 40. *Reunions of Taylor's Battery B*, 62. Way, 37.

in a statement he was reputed to have made later: "I've often wondered since why I spent five years of my life in Meredosia." Furthermore, Grierson disliked horses due to a childhood accident.

He was saved from his unpromising career in the produce business by the war. Obtaining a commission early in the conflict, his rise was rapid, and he soon became recognized as a solid, dependable, and enterprising commander. It is strange that the characteristics which brought him such great success had never emerged earlier in his life. Still, war acts as a strange catalyst in human affairs. Grierson's was not the only example of its kind during the conflict. "How profoundly surprised Mrs. Grant must have been," once wrote a reporter, "when she woke up and learned that her husband was a great man!"[24]

In April of 1863, Grierson was leading one of the most important expeditions in the entire conflict, a raid deep into enemy territory. News that the Illinois cavalry commander was making an impression upon Confederate communications was not long in coming. Telegraph wires went down in a succession of places, the railroad line to Meridian was damaged, and a train was captured. The heart of Mississippi felt the sting of the raider. Finally, after a narrow escape at Wall's Bridge near the Louisiana line, Grierson made it into Baton Rouge and to safety. As one most admirable authority on the war has judged, the Grierson raid could well be studied even today "when there are no columns of men on horseback with booted carbines and awesome sabers."[25]

While Grierson was making his historic ride through Mississippi, the grand movement upon Vicksburg was well under way. At dawn on April 30, McClernand's XIII Corps was loaded aboard gunboats and transports near Hard Times and taken to Bruinsburg, on the eastern bank, where it was landed. There is little question as to why Grant gave the lead to McClernand's men. The XIII Corps consisted of old and tested regiments from Illinois and other western states. Its division and regimental commanders were among the most courageous men in the Army of the Tennessee, and had proven the fact upon the field of battle.

---

[24] Brown, 8–9, 24–25. *Official Records*, Ser. I, Vol. XXXVI, Pt. 1, 38, 49–50, 58. McCormick, 100. Richardson, 244.

[25] Kenneth P. Williams, IV, 345.

One division leader was General Alvin P. Hovey, who had been awarded his rank for reason of gallantry at Shiloh. Before the Vicksburg campaign ended he earned greater laurels. Osterhaus and Carr, both of whom were present at Pea Ridge, also were divisional commanders for McClernand's corps, as was General Andrew Jackson Smith, a small waspish man whom the corps commander did not like but nevertheless respected. McClernand's last blessing was in good brigadiers, among whom was Michael Lawler, the rollicking Irishman from Shawneetown, Illinois.[26]

Early on the morning of May 1, McClernand met his first major opposition near the river city of Port Gibson. There was heavy fighting involving the 20th, 33rd, 45th, and 99th Illinois, and the Confederate force was eventually pushed back in confusion. The next day, when McClernand and McPherson moved their respective corps forward, they found that Port Gibson had been evacuated by the enemy. The first clash of arms in the southward movement had been a hard one, and in it the XIII Corps, aided by Logan's division of McPherson's corps, had done particularly well, a fact which was recognized even at Grant's headquarters. At the height of the struggle near the river town, one of Grant's aides witnessed a telling illustration of McClernand's peculiar inspirational power over his subordinates. At the moment of success, McClernand took the hand of one of his hard-pressed brigadiers to congratulate him on the success of his troops. "Gen. Benton's bosom heaved with emotions of joy," the onlooker later wrote.[27]

Success or not, there was still a shock in battle, particularly among those regiments which had not previously seen much action. The battlefield near Port Gibson was an impressive one—Confederate blankets and knapsacks littered the ground as far as the eye could see. And there was death. A private of the 93rd

---

[26] Dana, 63–65. Alvin P. Hovey is not to be confused with C. E. Hovey, who raised the 33rd Illinois.

[27] Wilson, *Under the Old Flag*, I, 174. Wilson tried to get Grant to congratulate McClernand upon "his good conduct and brilliant success," but he refused. Grant does praise McClernand in his report, *Official Records*, Ser. I, Vol. XXIV, Pt. 1, 48–49. "With Grant at Vicksburg: From the Civil War Diary of Captain Charles E. Wilcox," ed. Edgar Erickson, *Journal*, XXX, No. 4 (January, 1938), 473. Blanchard, 77.

Illinois was moved to write, after the battle, that he found it "rather hard to see the poor fellows laying there stretched upon the ground," even if they were the bodies of the enemy. Yet this was only the beginning of the campaign.[28]

On May 12 McPherson's corps reached a point near Raymond, a town to the northeast of Port Gibson, where it ran into stern resistance from a brigade commanded by the Confederate general John Gregg. Since McPherson's leading divisional commander in the march was John A. Logan, the fight amounted to a struggle between Gregg and Logan. The latter was now coming into his own as a troop commander. One may find any number of word portraits of the man as he appeared in this campaign. Charles A. Dana, whose mission in the Vicksburg movement was a secretive one, described him as a "peculiar character." He was, Dana reported, "sometimes unsteady," and a "man of instinct and not of reflection." There was one characteristic in Logan upon which everyone agreed, however; he was the bravest man ever—a person who saw no danger, and who went right on fighting until the battle was over. Then, wrote Dana, there was always a period of remorse and regret in which Logan assumed the battle had been lost.

There was still another side to this strange and complex man. Sylvanus Cadwallader, a reporter, saw Logan often during the Vicksburg campaign. On one occasion he saw the general sitting with nothing on but a hat, shirt, and boots. Logan was playing a violin for some dancing Negroes. The moment at which either the dancing or the music lagged, one or all would stop to take another drink from a nearby supply of whiskey.[29]

Logan, like many western officers, was a reckless fighter with an instinct for the jugular—no West Pointer, of course, a fact which was to handicap him severely throughout the conflict. At Raymond, however, he was a man in his element—a tough western general officer in command of some equally tough western regiments. Among them were the 8th, the 20th, the 45th, and the 81st Illinois, the last named from Logan's stamping grounds in southern Illinois. Years later Logan loved to recount how the battle of Raymond was won. Just at the moment when the Fed-

---

[28] Ira Payne to his parents, May 4, 1863, Ira A. Payne Papers.

[29] Dana, 67–68, 54. *Three Years with Grant*, 67.

eral attack was lagging, a tall, careless-looking soldier from the 81st shambled up to his division commander and said: "Gineral, I hev been over on the rise yonder, and it's my idea that if you'll put a rigiment or two over thar, you'll git on their flank and lick 'em easy." Logan took the suggestion, and soon the enemy was in retreat. That night, when the victorious troops went into bivouac, one of the southern Illinois soldiers called out to his division commander, who was standing nearby. "Flank 'em General," he shouted. "That's the way to do it boys, flank 'em," was Logan's reply.[30]

After the sharp exchange at Raymond, McPherson's and Sherman's corps moved eastward toward Jackson, sealing off Confederate reinforcements to Vicksburg from the east. On May 14 Jackson fell, and the doom of the river fortress seemed to be sealed. McClernand's corps now moved northwestward from Raymond toward the railroad between Jackson and Vicksburg. Osterhaus' division, backed and flanked by Carr, moved along the middle road from Raymond; A. J. Smith's division, backed and flanked by that of Francis P. Blair of Sherman's corps, moved along the southern route from that town. On the right and to the north moved Hovey's troops in the direction of a place called Champion's Hill. Early on May 16, McClernand's left began to meet heavy skirmishing on the two southern roads. Shortly thereafter Hovey ran into a heavy concentration of Confederate troops on his end of the advancing XIII Corps. Grant immediately ordered Logan's division (McPherson's corps), consisting mainly of Illinois troops, to a position on Hovey's right. Thus did the battle of Champion's Hill begin.

Champion's Hill was in a good position, with enough height and protection to control the approach to Vicksburg from the east. By eleven o'clock the hill was being severely contested, with Logan attempting to work his way westward and to the rear of the defending force, while John S. Bowen's Confederate force was making a solid attempt to crack what amounted to the Federal left. Once again Logan was in his element, and so were his troops. The latter, described by one young Illinois soldier as the "hardest set of men I ever saw . . . all the time quarreling with each other," and as the "hardest" swearers in the army, were

[30] Way, 39. Newsome, 45.

given an appropriate pre-attack message by their division commander. Giving some of his men the impression of an alcoholic redness in his face, Logan shouted: "Boys, we have got work in front of us. . . . Now all we want to do is get at them to make them 'git.' We always make them 'git' when we get at them. You won't have to go alone, I'm going down with you. Now forward; double quick!" Down into a ravine and to the attack dashed a brigade of troops, led by the 20th Illinois.[31]

Hovey's position on the Union right was not so easily won. The hill in front of the Union troops changed hands several times, the fighting was terrible, and the casualties were high. Finally, with the appearance of M. M. Crocker's division of McPherson's XVII Corps, which contained a number of Illinois regiments including the 56th and 93rd Illinois, the battle turned definitely in favor of the Union troops. A smashing attack drove Bowen's men off the hill for good, and soon Lawler's brigade came up in the center to the south of Crocker to help clinch the victory.

The battle of Champion's Hill or Baker's Creek was one of the most severe in the war, considering the length of the clash and the number of troops involved. Of the 29,373 effectives which Grant had in the fight, there were 2,441 casualties. Confederate losses totaled 3,851 of the 20,000 men which that army had in the battle. The largest number of casualties in any Union regiment was that suffered by the 24th Indiana in the XIII Corps. The largest Illinois regimental loss was that of the 93rd, a regiment from Bureau and Stephenson counties and commanded by Colonel Holden Putnam of Neponset. In those last charges up Champion's Hill it lost 162 men – 38 of them killed, 113 wounded, and 11 counted as missing. If possible, the battle seemed worse than the figures indicated, due to the narrow area over which it was fought. A member of the 33rd Illinois who visited the scene of the fight shortly afterward recalled years later that it was almost impossible to walk over certain spots on the hill without stepping upon a body. It was reminiscent of Pea Ridge.[32]

[31] *Official Records*, Ser. I, Vol. XXIV, Pt. 1, 146–152, 51–53. J. G. Given to his family, Nov. 14, 1862, Given Papers. Blanchard, 84–85.

[32] *Official Records*, Ser. I, Vol. XXIV, Pt. 1, 150–151. Way, 40. Fox, 437, 544. Thomas L. Livermore, 99–100. Osborn H. Oldroyd, *A Soldier's Story of the Siege of Vicksburg* (Springfield, 1885), 23. Oldroyd confirms the admiration of other corps for the XIII.

On May 17, McClernand's XIII Corps continued to press the retreating Confederates westward along the roads to Vicksburg. It was not until the army reached the Big Black River that the initial resistance of the day was met. Here the Confederate John C. Pemberton had entrenched himself across the path of the Union advance, and had fortified high positions near the battle line. McClernand moved Carr's division to the right of the main road, and Osterhaus' to the left. Lawler's Second Brigade of Carr's division was on the far right of Carr's men, and touching upon the banks of the Big Black. Lawler's regiments included three from Iowa and one from Wisconsin — an odd combination to be commanded by an Irishman from Shawneetown, Illinois.

Descriptions of Lawler abound in the literature of the Vicksburg campaign. He had carried into this stage of the war a good-sized reputation as a peculiar character, based mainly upon a hanging incident in which his original regiment, the 18th Illinois, had been involved. Now, as the investment of the Confederate fortress continued, the tradition surrounding the man grew by leaps and bounds. During the battle of Champion's Hill, according to the recollection of one southern Illinois veteran, Lawler rode exceedingly close to the line of fire. The flying bullets assumed that peculiar drone of nearness to Lawler and to one of his aides, who could not resist the temptation to duck his head. "You dam little fool!" Lawler shouted. "Don't dodge! Don't you know when you hear the bullets they have already passed." In later years the historian of the 77th Illinois, itself a fine regiment in A. J. Smith's division, recalled that Lawler was easily distinguishable during the entire Vicksburg campaign; he wore a blue checkered shirt, loose gray pantaloons, and a battered hat beneath which protruded a flaming red nose. The last, his brigade was to conclude, had been helped into existence by Lawler's adherence to an Irish custom — whiskey. All in all, he was, concluded the chronicler of the 77th, "a man of some consequence in his own estimation, if not in ours." [33]

Like Logan, Lawler could match color with courage. Charles A. Dana, observing for the War Department, was later to describe him as one who was "as brave as a lion, and has about as much

[33] Bluford Wilson, "Southern Illinois and the Civil War," 101. Bentley, 201–202.

brains . . . his purpose is always honest, and his sense is always good." The "High Dominie Dudgeon," as Dana was inclined to call him, was a good disciplinarian whom Grant was forced to "reprimand" gently from time to time. The most catching description of the man was written by reporter Sylvanus Cadwallader, however. "General Lawler was a large and excessively fat man . . . ," that reporter recalled. "His cherished maxim was a Tipperary one: 'If you see a head, hit it.'" On this day, May 17, on the Big Black, Lawler did see a head, and he hit it hard.[34]

Late in the afternoon, when it appeared that the Union advance had been halted for the day, Grant, who had been moving troops into the line, heard cheering far to the right. There was Lawler, wearing his checkered shirt with sleeves rolled up to the elbow, leading a charge of his brigade through mud up to the armpits. It was one of the indisputable great moments of the war, once again illustrating the western instinct for the jugular. As Cadwallader later wrote, "nothing could check them for an instant." "It was at the same time the most perilous and ludicrous charge that I witnessed during the war," that reporter concluded. Over on the left, the 33rd Illinois, fighting a hot skirmish in a nearby cornfield, witnessed Lawler's grand effort with unchecked emotion, hence the cheers which Grant heard. "It was a serious business," later wrote the historian of the 33rd, "but at the same time the fun of it was indescribable." Before the day came to an end, Lawler had captured 1,120 prisoners, more than the total of his own brigade, 1,460 muskets, and four stands of colors. More than this, however, was the fact that the Confederate line upon the Big Black was broken. It is little wonder that, at the end of the day when it was all over, Grant made a special trip to Lawler's camp in order to thank the hero of the day. The commanding general of the Army of the Tennessee found his relaxed subordinate seated before a fire with some of his soldiers, dressed in the same checkered shirt, waiting for his coffee to boil.[35]

---

[34] Dana, 65. Wilson, *Under the Old Flag*, I, 177. *Three Years with Grant*, 83.

[35] Grant, I, 524–527. According to Grant, he had just received a message from Halleck ordering the recall of the expedition when he heard the cheers on the right. *Three Years with Grant*, 83. Way, 41. Jonathan T. Dorris, "Michael Kelly Lawler: Mexican and Civil War Officer," *Journal*, XLVIII, No. 4 (Winter, 1955), 393. Dana, 55.

Lawler's smashing and somewhat surprising assault at the Big Black left no further defensive line for Pemberton's forces but the hills and ravines surrounding Vicksburg itself. McClernand's XIII Corps, coming straight ahead on the Jackson railroad, moved to the Union left on a line stretching near Durden's Creek. McPherson's XVII held the center, and Sherman's XV Corps streamed in to occupy the line stretching around to the right. Completing the investment of Vicksburg on May 19, Grant made a hurried attack upon the new Confederate line just outside the city, but was thrown back. In this aborted attempt to follow the defenders into the city itself, it was a West Virginia regiment which suffered the greatest losses, a total of 137. Among Illinois regiments participating on that day, the 116th not only lost its lieutenant colonel but 70 others, and the 95th, charging near the celebrated little "White house," had 62 casualties.[36]

While the Union army moved with increasing confidence and success in its investment of Vicksburg, relations between Grant and McClernand, beginning with the January assumption of field command by the former, deteriorated from bad to worse. By the time of the battle of Port Gibson, Grant's distaste for his subordinate had grown so great that he refused to congratulate McClernand upon his fine performance in that fight. By the end of May there was a bitterness between the two which would last all of their lives.

Looking back, it is easy to see that the personalities of the two men clashed like oil and water. McClernand was irascible, energetic, overtly ambitious, flamboyantly patriotic, and polemic. Grant was taciturn, phlegmatic, quietly ambitious, and studied in nature. The conflict between the two was therefore a natural one, and it was gradually intensified because one could never be subordinate to the other, no matter which arrangement existed. Nor could it be a discreet quarrel between the two, beneath public view, and solitary unto themselves. Rather, it was to develop an openness which even the least important could see. As one minor Illinois politician was to report following a visit to the Army of the Tennessee: "There is a strong feeling of jealousy between Grant and McClernand. . . . They are together again and

[36] Fox, 437.

of course will quarrel – privately if not openly. They are both democrats and both trying to be great men. . . ."[37]

Grant's decision to take active charge of the great attempt upon Vicksburg did not have the impact on McClernand which one might otherwise expect. It did not, one may assume, because it was not unexpected. "I may be standing on the brink of official ruin," McClernand had written Jonathan Baldwin Turner. When the moment came for Grant to throw out his challenge to McClernand's political power, the reaction of the latter was strong but only sporadic. "I have the immediate command of all the forces operating on the Miss. river," he pointed out to Grant in an almost pleading manner, "but in fact you exercise immediate as well as general command over all. . . ."[38]

It was almost a month before McClernand struck in his usual manner, on the ides of March, to be exact. Why he began to direct a new stream of letters concerning his position at this time is difficult to determine. On March 15 he wrote a letter of introduction to President Lincoln for a Captain W. J. Kountz, who had obviously reported two facts to McClernand: first, that he had heard certain rumors concerning heavy drinking on the part of Grant, and second, that he, Kountz, was going to Washington. "Permit me to present to you Capt. Kountz an honest and reliable gentleman," McClernand scribbled. "I would add more but he must embark." Kountz's message to the President, added later on the train going east, was that Grant had been "gloriously drunk" on March 13, and was "in bed sick all next day." "If you are averse to drunken Genl's," Kountz offered, "I can furnish the names of officers of high standing to substantiate the above."

It would be impossible to prove the mendacity in Kountz's claim, as many of Grant's biographers have attempted to do. Was this part of an incident which Sylvanus Cadwallader tried to describe several years later, or the one to which James H. Wilson alluded in his biography of John Rawlins which was published in 1916? Or was it nothing at all – one of Grant's migraine headaches, or an enlargement of a really insignificant occurrence?

[37] S. Noble to Lyman Trumbull, Feb. 24, 1863, Lyman Trumbull Transcripts, Illinois Historical Survey, Urbana.

[38] McClernand to Turner, Jan. 16, 1863, Turner Papers. McClernand to Grant, March 19, 1863, McClernand Collection.

After all, liquor was to be commonly found in the headquarters of general officers at the time. When Yates visited the army in April, he brought a large barrel of whiskey with him. When Adjutant General Lorenzo Thomas visited McClernand's headquarters, he was entertained royally—the rumor was that Thomas had complained because there was "no ice for his champagne."[39]

Whatever the truth of the story concerning Grant's drinking, McClernand vigorously seized upon it in order to pass it on. To his friend Turner up in Jacksonville he wrote that his position under Grant had become "mentally excruciating," and hinted that "incapacity and drunkenness" were to be found in the headquarters of the army. One may suspect that McClernand hoped that Turner would pass these impressions on to Yates, but the general was taking no chances upon that not occurring. On the same day that he wrote the brief attachment to Captain Kountz's introduction and the interesting letter to Turner, he composed a long but important letter to the governor. "Time is passing & the Republic is dying of *inertia*," he warned Yates. The months had passed with few favorable results for the nation. "Can't you prevail upon the President to send some competent commander?" he pleaded. "For our country's sake, do." Then, in a summation which was to affect his military career more than he could ever know, he concluded:

> My success upon the Arkansas has drawn upon me the malevolence and persecution of petty minds in this quarter. My situation is intolerable. I would have resigned or asked to be transferred before now, but I have waited to hear from you. What have you done? or what can you do? If, as you & other loyal governors recommended, the government would give me an independent command . . . I could do something for the Country.
>
> Come down and see us. Bring Gov. Morton & Kirkwood if you can —at all events, come yourself.[40]

Nor was McClernand through with his string pulling. One of his closest friends was Murat Halstead, an influential reporter

[39] Correspondence carried to Washington by Kountz and endorsed by McClernand, March 15, 1863, Lincoln Papers. *Three Years with Grant*, 103–104. Wilson, *Life of John A. Rawlins*, 128. Porter, 182.

[40] McClernand to Turner, March 15, 1863, Turner Papers. McClernand to Yates, March 15, 1863, Logan U. Reavis Papers, Chicago Historical Society.

for western newspapers. Not only did Halstead have connections in his own field of enterprise, but he knew people in Washington. By April 1, he was not only sending a number of strongly written anti-Grant articles to his papers, but was forwarding vicious attacks upon that commander to Secretary of the Treasury Chase. McClernand followed Halstead's notes with a personal letter to the President. He carried the burden of the campaign, he wrote. His men, loaded with 80 to 100 rounds of ammunition apiece, plus provisions, had kept up a blistering pace over the Mississippi hills. There was another complaint about Halleck, followed by the marked-out phrase "Such personalities are too small." Not crossed out was a parting shot at the general-in-chief: "I can see nothing to justify such invidiousness." [41]

McClernand's desperate intriguing was to bring results. The letters which he had sent to the President in January, February, and March, the secret communications forwarded to Washington through Browning and Kountz, and the pressure placed upon Yates, brought an eventual reaction from the governor of Illinois and the national administration. Yates went down to Smith's Plantation in late April on the pretext of visiting Illinois troops in the Army of the Tennessee. The aforementioned Lorenzo Thomas made an appearance in the West on the pretext of raising Negro regiments for the army. The most important visitor, however, was Charles A. Dana, the former managing editor of the *New York Tribune*. Ostensibly sent by the War Department in order to investigate pay conditions for western troops, the real purpose of his mission was to look into McClernand's complaints about Grant's drinking, and to give the administration a clear picture of the Grant-McClernand controversy and other army matters. The impressions which this 34-year-old former reporter relayed to Washington were to affect profoundly the course of the war.

When Dana arrived at Grant's headquarters in April, he immediately came into contact with the solid anti-McClernand clique which existed in the Army of the Tennessee. Sherman, for example, had reached a point of no return in his relations with the commander of the XIII Corps, a fact which he pointed out to his wife a week and a half after Dana's appearance in the

[41] Halstead to Chase, April 1, 1863, McClernand to Lincoln, May 6, 1863, Lincoln Papers.

Vicksburg theater of war. "Indeed, I am on the best of terms with everybody," he wrote, "but I avoid McClernand because I know he is envious and jealous of everybody who stands in his way." Again, a few days later, he warned his wife to prepare for newspaper reports about McClernand's ability as a military leader. "Should, as the papers now intimate, Grant be relieved and McClernand left in command," he warned, "you may expect to hear of me at St. Louis, for I will not serve under McClernand."[42]

There were still others who, for some reason, had come to dislike McClernand. One may presume that Dana, because of his age, came into close association with the younger men attached to the staffs of both Sherman and McPherson, and that he could not avoid the influence of their attitudes toward the remaining corps commander. One of the stories commonly passed about by these men concerned a speech McClernand reputedly made in Illinois during the recruiting campaign of 1862. "Some men were born to one walk of life, and some to another," he was reported to have said. "Thank God, I . . . was born a warrior insensible to fear." Other stories concerned McClernand's "theatrical" behavior at Arkansas Post, and his violent temper. For example, James H. Wilson, then an engineering officer attached to Grant's staff, quickly became Dana's closest associate during the campaign. He had been roundly cursed out by McClernand just before Dana's arrival, and had not forgiven his former Shawneetown neighbor for the episode.[43]

Another incident which must have affected Dana's attitude toward McClernand was an informal meeting of general officers, minus the commanding general of the XIII Corps, which Dana had occasion to attend. Grant maintained his stand to have McClernand's troops lead the advance in the forthcoming campaign. The reaction to this announcement was an explosive one. According to Sherman's later recollections of the discussion, the conversation soon turned to "what was notorious, that General McClernand was still intriguing against General Grant, in hopes

[42] "With Grant at Vicksburg," 465. Dana, 256–257, tells the story of his visit to the Vicksburg theater of war at length.

[43] William Jenney, "Personal Recollections of Vicksburg," in *Military Essays and Recollections*, III (1899), 251, 264. Jenney was attached to Sherman's staff. Wilson, *Life of John A. Rawlins*, 121, admits that Dana was catered to by the younger officers for "obvious reasons."

to regain the command of the whole expedition." Virtually every officer agreed, once again according to Sherman, that if the campaign failed, Grant's career would be finished and McClernand would take his place. In order to forestall this possibility, Sherman urged Grant to ask all corps commanders to put their ideas concerning the campaign into writing. This, he felt, would pin McClernand to the failures as well as the successes which might follow. Dana, whose presence at the session seems not to have been questioned, agreed with this strategy.[44]

There are a number of questions which one might raise in relation to Dana and his immediate commitment to the Grant side of the controversy with McClernand. Was his mission a well-kept secret, or had information as to the purpose of his journey been leaked to Grant by a friendly Halleck? Why was Dana, who was only supposed to be investigating pay conditions in the western armies, present at an unofficial staff meeting obviously programmed to castigate McClernand? Why was McClernand not present to defend himself? One could easily reach a conclusion that the gathering was neatly arranged to sway the sentiments of an important representative of the War Department whose mission was not as secretive as originally intended.

In any case, Dana became a strong Grant supporter, and an even stronger McClernand antagonist. In that brief period in 1863 he became one of the strongest influences in the army. Impressions of virtually every brigadier, divisional commander, and staff officer flew from his pen; he made or unmade their careers. Wilson, for example, who had such a tremendous impact upon Dana after the latter's arrival, was reported to be a "brilliant man intellectually, highly educated, and thoroughly companionable." Those last two words tell a story in themselves. Rawlins, another Illinoisan with whom Dana had a sociable moment or two, was adjudged to have a "very able mind." And it most certainly affected the course of another career when he wrote: "My own judgment is that McClernand has not the qualities necessary for a good commander, even of a regiment."[45]

How dependable were Dana's estimates of people? It does seem that his concise and harsh opinion of McClernand was re-

[44] Sherman, 343. Dana, 31–33.

[45] *Ibid.*, 62. *Official Records*, Ser. I, Vol. XXIV, Pt. 1, 86–87.

flective of considerable personal bias. Whether McClernand could have commanded an army is a matter of conjecture, and could never be proven one way or the other. He did command a division at Donelson and Shiloh, however, and his record in both places was equal to or better than others holding comparable positions, including Sherman, who fought in the latter conflict. He took Arkansas Post with what amounted to a corps, and he commanded an equal number of troops, the XIII Corps, in the investment of Vicksburg. There are some who write that his handling of his divisions in that campaign could have been better, but one must remember that the XIII Corps did a good deal of the fighting.

McClernand was not the only Illinois general who would feel the effects of Dana's reports. The statement concerning Logan was written in such a qualified manner that the Carbondale officer may have suffered in being considered for high command. For this reason it would be well to recall another man's estimate of Dana himself. Henry Villard, a newspaperman who had some knowledge of the man's character, was moved to describe him as follows: "Justice calls for the statement that he was entirely wrong in some of his animadversions upon those corps commanders, and showed strong, bordering on malignant, bias against them. He received and conveyed impressions like the professional journalist that he was, hastily, flippantly, and recklessly . . . his zeal often degenerated into officiousness, and he fell at times into the role of the informer, without perhaps being conscious of it. . . ."[46]

Following the unsuccessful attack upon the Confederate line at Vicksburg on May 19, Grant passed the next 48 hours in bringing the remainder of his army forward and in consolidating his positions. On May 21 he felt that the army was now strong enough to make another frontal attack upon the enemy lines, and so ordered one to begin at ten o'clock the following day. There were a number of considerations in Grant's decision to move so soon following the investment of Vicksburg. First, he had a Confederate force under General Joseph E. Johnston operating to his rear and there was some fear of an assault from that quarter. Second, there was a feeling in Grant's headquarters

[46] Dana, 67–68. Villard, II, 189.

that the Confederate defenses would become stronger day by day, while the Union army would gradually lose its initiative and confidence. An attack also might well avoid a costly siege.

It is possible that the men of the Army of the Tennessee were anxious to get on with the assault, but it is also true that they knew the nature of the defenses about the city. The deep cuts and irregular hills behind which the enemy had constructed trenches and artillery emplacements looked immensely formidable, even to the most professional eyes—and the Army of the Tennessee was as professional as it would ever become. The tough 17th Illinois, in McPherson's corps, spent the night before the attack writing the usual last letters home. The technique was a well-used one. After these men, who came from central and western Illinois, had written their notes, the envelopes were gathered and kept by a soldier not scheduled to make the charge. All along the line, as one Illinois soldier remembered it, men took rings from their fingers and pictures from their knapsacks and gave them to the cooks, who would send them home if the owners failed to return. Over in the First Division of the XIII Corps, Private Edward H. Ingraham of the 33rd Illinois, unaware of the losses which his regiment would suffer on the following day, wrote and mailed a letter to his aunt back in Illinois. "If Gen. Grant resorts to storming the works with infantry there will be bloody work . . . ," he wrote, "but if he relies mainly upon cannon shooting . . . he will save many lives." In any case, Ingraham concluded: "We are ready for it."[47]

The assault went off at ten o'clock on May 22. One Illinois soldier, years later, described that last moment before the order to charge was given: "We lay there about eight minutes and yet it seemed an age to me, for showers of bullets and grape were passing over me. . . . Oh, how my heart palpitated! It seemed to thump the ground (I lay on my face) as hard as the enemy's bullets. The sweat from off my face run in a stream from the tip ends of my whiskers. . . . Twice I exclaimed aloud . . . "*My God, why don't they order us to charge!*"[48]

Sylvanus Cadwallader, who watched the attack develop from a position near the XIII Corps, saw McClernand's men as they

[47] Smith, 5. Ingraham to his aunt, May 21, 1863, Ingraham Papers.

[48] "With Grant at Vicksburg," 479–480.

were "mercilessly torn to pieces by Confederate shot and shell. . . ." By the time that the line was halfway across the battleground, it had lost all semblance of alignment and formation. Over in the front of other corps, the result was the same. In the XVII Corps, Ransom's brigade of McArthur's division, which included the 11th, 72nd, 95th, and 116th Illinois, got off a sharp attack. Midway across the field, however, most of its officers went down, and the assault faltered. Three regimental colonels were killed or wounded, and Ransom himself was forced to pick up the colors and lead the attack. The brigade went no farther than the base of a Confederate fort, from which it was quickly driven. Ransom's order to retreat was typical of this promising Illinois general. "Move slowly," he was reported to have said. "The first man who runs or goes beyond the ravine shall be shot on the spot." [49]

On Sherman's end of the line, the hard-fighting 55th Illinois of Blair's division, last described in the battle of Shiloh, managed to carry its colors close to the parapet of another enemy fort which was held by Louis Hebert's Louisiana brigade, but a rifled cannon placed on a nearby hill tore its line apart. Nevertheless, the regimental flag bearer, Corporal Robert Cox, planted the regimental banner of the 55th on the top of an enemy trench, and fought a hand-to-hand battle with a young Confederate soldier who reached over and attempted to pull it in. In the same corps, the XV, Joseph A. Mower's "Eagle Brigade," which included the 47th and 26th Illinois among others, got its line out in good formation in front of the Confederate redans before being hit hard by Confederate fire. Nevertheless, with its mascot "Old Abe," the famous eagle, rising and screaming above it, the brigade reached halfway to the enemy parapet before the attack was stalled.[50]

Another major part of the assault also fell once again upon the XIII Corps. W. P. Benton's brigade, which had done good work at Port Gibson, and which included the 8th and 18th Indiana and the 33rd and 99th Illinois, mounted a fine attack near the right of McClernand's line, at the point where the Jackson to Vicksburg railroad cut ran transverse through the Union line. As

---

[49] *Three Years with Grant*, 194. Eddy, I, 468–470.

[50] [Crooker *et al.*], 241–246. *Civil War Medal of Honor Winners*, 6. Bryner, 86.

the charge progressed, however, the men of the 33rd, leading the assault, were slowed by fallen strands of telegraph wire which lay in the deep grass. The momentum of the forward movement was slowed, and the brigade only managed to reach the ditches below the Confederate forts, from which it could go no farther. Most of the men of the 33rd were forced to stay in the ditches all day—from ten o'clock in the morning until seven or eight o'clock at night—while Confederate troops above them threw lighted shells down the escarpment. The Union soldiers were virtually unable to return the fire except by raising their rifles above the ditch and shooting blindly.

It would be difficult to find a worse predicament than that in which the 33rd Illinois found itself on the morning of May 22. Among the 32 men of E Company who made the initial charge, only one was able to return at the end of the day unmarked. In that company, recruited in western Illinois, bravery was a common characteristic, however. Private Parmenas Hill of La Moille, for example, though fatally wounded in the leg, joked pluckily to his stretcher bearers, "Now I can go home and make stump speeches."[51]

In the same brigade, the 99th Illinois, a tough regiment recruited almost totally in Pike County, suffered horribly in attempting to hold its position near the enemy escarpment. The regimental colors had been carried to the top of the Confederate trench by Sergeant Thomas Higgins, a little Canadian from Barry; once planted, they were to wave most of the day. In sustaining its line in the face of enemy rifles, the list of casualties in the regiment was horrendous. Out of 300 men, 103 were killed or wounded.[52]

As the assault developed, it was W. J. Landram's brigade of the XIII Corps which came closest to achieving the success necessary to break the Confederate line. In A. J. Smith's division, Landram's unit consisted in part of four Illinois regiments: the 77th, from Peoria and Knox counties, commanded by Colonel David Grier; the 97th, a superb organization from Macoupin and Madison counties, commanded by Colonel Friend Rutherford; the

[51] Way, 44–45, 7.

[52] *Civil War Medal of Honor Winners*, 11. *Report of the Adjutant General*, V, 543.

108th, from Tazewell and Peoria counties, led by Colonel Charles Turner; and the 130th, from central Illinois, commanded by Colonel Nathaniel Niles.

Before the attack, the brigade waited behind the brow of a hill until the signal gun was sounded. Then, in one vast wave, it stormed over the ridge, down into a ravine, through brambles, and up the enemy escarpment. It was, as the historian of the 77th later pointed out, a "half hour which may God grant we shall not be called upon to experience its like again." The 77th got its flag planted upon the parapet of the opposing fort; the substitute flag bearer of the 130th, Frank Dunn, also carried the colors of his regiment to the top of the escarpment, waved them in the face of the enemy, and planted the shattered stump of the staff in the ground. Men of the 77th and 97th, particularly the Gillespie, Illinois, company of the latter, managed to carry their attack into the defiles of the Confederate bastion just east of the railroad cut. One of them, a private of the 97th, so the tradition of the regiment later held, actually charged through the enemy fort and made it into Vicksburg proper.[53]

The fighting here was worse than at any spot along the entire line. Having no artillery support, some of the men of the 77th carried a small cannon forward by hand, and fired it through the embrasure into the enemy works. By noontime some of the hard-pressed attackers were into enemy forts and defending the colors of the 77th and 130th still planted there. Farther down the line, the indomitable Lawler had pushed his brigade into the enemy defiles and was defending the bright flag of the 48th Ohio, which waved defiantly from the top of an enemy trench.[54]

One of the great disputes of the study of Civil War history has concerned the high point of the attack of May 22. How far did the men of Landram's and Lawler's brigades get in the assault? Did they actually make it into the main sections of several enemy fortifications, and if so, how many achieved that success? Cadwallader, whose errors in his recollections of the Vicksburg cam-

[53] Jacob W. Wilkin, "Vicksburg," in *Military Essays and Recollections*, IV (1907), 232. Bentley, 150–160. The 97th won a disproportionate number of Medals of Honor during this campaign: see *Civil War Medal of Honor Winners*, 3–13.

[54] *Ibid.*, 9. McClernand's Report, McClernand Collection. Bentley, 153–158.

paign are numerous, wrote that he saw "one stand of our colors," presumably of Landram's troops, planted halfway up the embankment of the Confederate forts, but that McClernand's men "never gained a footing" inside the works. Kenneth P. Williams, whose study of Grant's military achievements is undeniably the best in that respect, states that the flags of several regiments were "placed upon the parapets in several points. . . ." In judging the case of McClernand's XIII Corps, however, it would seem best to accept the opinion of the men who actually took part in the attack. The historian of the 77th Illinois, for instance, claimed later that men of both the 130th Illinois and his own regiment carried their charge inside an enemy fortification, but were not numerous enough to carry the place completely. To substantiate his assertion, he quoted Confederate sources which admitted that some 60 of the attackers had breached a Confederate redoubt. Some years later a reliable veteran of the 130th made an even stronger claim, stating: "The men who fought under McClernand and many others, have believed and will probably continue to believe, that they were once within the rebel lines and could have held their position if they had been promptly and sufficiently supported." After the war it was commonly accepted that one of Lawler's men, an Iowa sergeant by the name of Griffith, had led a number of men into the enemy defiles and held them there until recalled. Even James H. Wilson, who was never inclined to give McClernand the benefit of any doubt, was never positive that the men of the XIII Corps had not made it in the charge of May 22. Admitting that improper support had been given to the men of Landram's and Lawler's brigades, he accepted the principle that the large number of casualties in the entire assault were due to the lack of preparation for the "contingency of success." General Pemberton reported that a few Federals got into exterior ditches and even reached the parapets but were thrown back.[55]

The fact of the matter was that McClernand thought his men

[55] *Three Years with Grant*, 90–92. Cadwallader tells a story which has a "Col. Jo. Mower" being killed in leading a doomed charge which was designed to help McClernand. The writer most certainly was terribly mixed up; General Joseph A. Mower was in the Vicksburg campaign, but he lived until 1870. Bentley, 153–158. Wilson, *Under the Old Flag*, I, 181. The quote concerning the 130th Illinois comes from Wilkin, "Vicksburg," 229. *Official Records*, Ser. I, Vol. XXIV, Pt. 1, 275–276.

had breached the enemy line and so informed Grant, pleading for support from other troops in Sherman's and McPherson's corps. Upon receiving McClernand's note, Grant reputedly turned to Sherman standing alongside and said: "If I could only believe it." Sherman's reply was that a corps commander could not possibly be wrong about such an important matter. With some hesitancy in the matter, Grant finally sent I. F. Quinby's division of McPherson's corps to Landram's and Lawler's section of the line, and ordered a full assault by the XV and XVII corps in order to provide the necessary diversion for the attack upon the left.[56]

Either because the attack was doomed to failure by the staunchness of the Confederate defense or because of the delay in ordering reinforcements to McClernand, the second assault was a terrible failure. The attacking regiments were torn apart and hurled back upon the Union line. Still, those staunch Illinois and Iowa soldiers of Landram and Lawler maintained their slender hold upon the enemy forts until late in the day, when a spirited charge by Thomas N. Waul's Texas Legion overwhelmed their diminishing numbers.[57]

The losses of the Army of the Tennessee were considerable: 3,199 killed, wounded, and missing out of the 45,000 committed to the attack. The largest single loss — killed, wounded, and missing — of any regiment was that of the 22nd Iowa of Lawler's brigade, which had a total of 164. Among the Illinois troops, the 77th in Landram's division led all the rest with 130; the 95th, a regiment raised in Brown and McHenry counties, had 109; and the 99th of Benton's brigade suffered 102 casualties.[58]

The enormous losses of the day brought both regret and recrimination to the officers and men of the Union regiments now wrapped in a tight noose around Vicksburg. Private Edward H. Ingraham, whose letter to his aunt on the night of May 21 was not his last, reported to the family back home that the night of May 22 was a bitter one; most of his regiment, the 33rd, looked upon the attack as a "sad mistake," and one for which Grant could not be faulted. Over at Grant's headquarters, sentiments

[56] Jenney, "Personal Recollections of Vicksburg," 261. *Official Records*, Ser. I, Vol. XXIV, Pt. 1, 56.

[57] Bentley, 153–158. *Official Records*, Ser. I, Vol. XXIV, Pt. 1, 275–276.

[58] Fox, 437. Thomas L. Livermore, 100.

were of a different nature. John Rawlins, whose dislike of McClernand was now at white heat, pinned the entire blame upon the commander of the XIII Corps. Charging into the command tent, he angrily ordered a subordinate to "open the record book and charge a thousand lives to that —— McClernand." Grant, likewise, was inclined to place much of the blame upon that general. On May 24, two days later, he wrote to Halleck: "General McClernand's dispatches misled me as to the real state of facts, and caused much of this loss. He is entirely unfit. . . . Looking after his corps gives me much more labor and infinitely more uneasiness than all the remainder of my department." Dana also found his way into the general attack upon McClernand, and a steady stream of reports from him began to arrive upon the desk of Secretary of War Stanton. McClernand, Dana wrote, was to blame for the losses of the 22nd; furthermore, his trenches were "mere rifle-pits, three or four feet wide," allowing neither the "passage of artillery" or the "assemblage of any considerable number of troops." As for McClernand's staff, he added, not one of them is "worth having." [59]

It was not long before McClernand heard rumors of the bitterness directed toward himself in Grant's headquarters. As one would suspect, he turned once again to the one weapon at his command, his political association with Yates and Lincoln. To the governor went a letter in which he attempted to absolve himself of any blame for the attack on May 22. The rumors of the "responsibility of the failure of the assault on the 22nd instant . . . must be the spawn of petty prejudicial partisans . . . ," he charged. "It is foreign to my purpose to complain . . . let there be an investigation of the whole campaign." On the same day he wrote a letter to the President. In it was a report of the Vicksburg campaign, with an outright charge that the leadership and planning of the campaign had been impractical. "Failure having resulted," he continued, "indications of a disposition to shirk responsibility are becoming manifest. Among other *dodges* it is whispered, that I urged that other corps should attack as well as mine." In conclusion he added: "These pretexts are too

[59] Ingraham to his aunt, May 29, 1863, Ingraham Papers. Jenny, "Personal Recollections of Vicksburg," 261–262. *Official Records*, Ser. I, Vol. XXIV, Pt. 1, 37. Dana, 75, 89–90.

silly and contemptible to be dwelt upon. My apology for noticing them at all, is honest and irrepressible indignation."

There is no real proof that Lincoln read McClernand's latest letter with something less than sympathy. It would be hard to believe that the President was not tiring of the monthly complaints from that quarter, however. At any rate, someone, either Nicolay or Hay, the two presidential secretaries, added a small notation to the letter for the purpose of filing it. It read, simply: "claims the glory of the Vicksburg campaign thus far and denounces those, as he says, who are trying to injure him. . . ."[60]

Having written to Yates and Lincoln, it was likely that McClernand now felt either that a proper base had been set for what he was about to do next, or that the time had come for throwing down the gauntlet to the commanding general of the Army of the Tennessee. Once again he placed his pen to paper and began a long and floridly written congratulatory order to his own XIII Corps. This body of troops, McClernand claimed, was made up only of brave men. Had they not almost accomplished the impossible by driving the enemy back into Vicksburg proper? The corps, he wrote, should not now have to defend itself against the petty rumors that the failure of May 22 was a result of its own inadequacies. McClernand gave them the reason:

> How and why the general assault failed, it would be useless now to explain. The Thirteenth Army Corps, acknowledging the good intentions of all, would scorn indulgence in weak regrets and idle criminations. According justice to all, it would only defend itself. If, while the enemy was massing to crush it, assistance was asked for by a diversion at other points, or by re-enforcement, it only asked what in one case Major-General Grant had specifically and peremptorily ordered, namely, simultaneous and persistent attack all along our lines until the enemy's outer works should be carried, and what, in the other, by massing a strong force in time upon a weakened point, would have probably insured success.[61]

These were strong words by a corps commander about the commanding general of the army, and Grant could never have passed upon them had they been submitted to him. But McClernand's error was in not submitting them at all. The entire con-

[60] McClernand to Yates, May 28, 1863, McClernand Collection. McClernand to Lincoln, May 29, 1863, Lincoln Papers.

[61] *Official Records*, Ser. I, Vol. XXIV, Pt. 1, 159–161.

gratulatory order, when finished, was forwarded by McClernand's adjutant to various western newspapers without Grant's knowledge. Actually, other than those who were directly within McClernand's command, Sherman was the first to read McClernand's congratulatory order. Over three weeks after the assault of May 22, his attention was called to a copy of the *Memphis Evening Bulletin*. There, for all to see, were the inflammatory phrases of the leader of the XIII Corps.

The next day, June 17, Sherman wrote to Rawlins. McClernand's order, he claimed, was a colossal misrepresentation of the facts – "a catalogue of nonsense . . . an effusion of vain-glory and hypocrisy." A note from McPherson quickly followed. "I cannot help arriving at the conclusion," wrote that brilliant young officer, "that it was written to . . . impress the public mind with the magnificent strategy, superior tactics, and brilliant deeds of the major-general commanding. . . ." Thus was Grant forced to act. The newspaper clipping was forwarded to McClernand with an accompanying note which asked if it was a "true copy." The answer, returned on the following day, was concisely framed: "The newspaper slip is a correct copy of my congratulatory order No. 72. I am prepared to maintain its statements." [62]

The conclave of officers which gathered in Grant's quarters to discuss the problem of McClernand were now of one mind – how to rid the army of that general. Most felt that Grant had an appropriate reason; McClernand, they claimed, had violated military regulations by not passing his order through proper channels. Furthermore, it was an error for which he had been warned on previous occasions. James H. Wilson, the Shawneetown acquaintance of McClernand, stood in the background, watching and listening to the discussion. Grant slowly reached his decision, and ordered Rawlins to write the removal order. It would have to be sent immediately, the generals decided, for it was entirely possible that the XIII Corps, admittedly the best in Grant's army, might bolster McClernand's position with a victory.

Wilson was selected to deliver the message. Though it was almost midnight, the southern Illinois officer walked his horse from campfire to campfire and finally to McClernand's tent. The

[62] Sherman to Rawlins, June 17, 1863, *ibid.*, 162–163. McPherson to Grant, June 18, 1863, *ibid.*, 164. McClernand to Grant, June 18, 1863, *ibid.*, 103.

commanding general of the XIII Corps seemed to know what was coming; before reading the note, he retired in order to dress in full uniform. Wilson, long afterward, described the moments which followed:

> The provost marshal and his squad were within call, and, after saluting him . . . I said: "General, I have an important order for you which I am directed to deliver into your hands and to see that you read it in my presence, that you understand it, and that you signify your immediate obedience to it." I handed him the sealed envelope, watched him adjust his glasses, and then open and read it. When he caught its purport, almost instantly he said: "Well, sir! I am relieved!" And then, as if taking it all in, he added almost in the same breath: "By God, sir, we are both relieved!" [63]

The substitution of General Edward O. C. Ord for McClernand as commanding general of the XIII Corps brought no real difference in the continuing siege of Vicksburg. Slowly but surely the ever extending Union trenches moved closer and closer to the Confederate redans. Great use was made of various ingenious contrivances built by western soldiers in order to give protection to the advancing troops. The 45th Illinois, for example, found that so-called "sap-rollers" offered a great deal of security to advanced diggers and sharpshooters. These were wooden barrels which had been filled with sand or dirt, and which were rolled ahead of the soldiers as they worked. The 81st Illinois, the southern Illinois regiment which had been free with suggestions on strategy to Logan in the battle of Raymond, called their own contraption a "dry land gun-boat." This creation was nothing more than a cotton bale placed on rollers or wheels.[64]

Both devices afforded adequate protection to the men who worked behind them. By the middle of June, some regiments, including the 81st, were so close to the Confederate forts that individual soldiers would occasionally crawl up to the enemy-held trenches at night and pull Confederate rifles from the apertures. Sergeant Payson Shumway of the 14th Illinois, last described as the young man who couldn't sleep at Shiloh because of the noise of the big guns, was able to report to his wife on July 2 that he was so close to the enemy trenches at Vicksburg

[63] Wilson, *Life of John A. Rawlins*, 133. Wilson, *Under the Old Flag*, I, 185–186.

[64] Crummer, 118. Newsome, 57.

he could throw clods of dirt at Confederate soldiers who were behind them.[65]

There was a good deal of unpleasantness about this, of course. The sounds of gunfire were almost continually heard, despite the occasional attempts by individual soldiers to effect battlefield meetings with enemy troops. One had to move carefully in the advanced trenches lest an enemy sharpshooter find the range. "Firing goes on continually along the front," wrote General W. W. Orme of Francis J. Herron's Second Brigade, located far to the left along Stout's Bayou. "I visit the front about twice a day," he informed his wife back in Illinois, "exercising great care however in my movements, as the balls of the enemy whistle through the trees very lively all the time." Still, the troops could become quite casual about the dangers involved in advanced entrenchment. As a member of the 81st Illinois phrased it: "We are accustomed to the sound; and while the cannons are roaring, and shells are screaming over our heads the loudest, some are singing, some reading, writing or cooking; some are even sleeping, unroused by the tumult in the air, and dreaming of loved ones at home. Affairs go on in our camp about as quietly as when we were at Anna or Cairo."[66]

In all of this, the troops remained surprisingly healthy. It was true that at times dysentery made its appearance in various regiments, but soldiers soon learned that boiled water was the best preventative for that type of illness. Furthermore, as the men of the 33rd and 61st Illinois were to discover, there was no better specific for that debilitating sickness than blackberries. It was certainly true then, that with all of the cannonading, the investment of Vicksburg may have been dangerous but it wasn't dull. There was even occasional entertainment for the besieging troops. On one occasion the famous Lombard Brothers, theatrical performers from Chicago, made an appearance near the battle lines in order to regale the men.[67]

The two greatest shows in the period were of a different nature, however. In the middle of June the 45th Illinois, composed par-

[65] *Ibid.*, 63. Shumway to his wife, July 2, 1863, Shumway Papers.

[66] Orme to his wife, June 18, 1863, Orme Papers. Newsome, 55.

[67] Way, 45. Stillwell, *Story of a Common Soldier*, 142. *Three Years with Grant*, 96–97.

tially of lead miners from Galena, Illinois, commenced the digging of a tunnel beneath an important Confederate bastion, a redan occupied by the 3rd Louisiana. On June 25 the mine was exploded and followed by an attack by two regiments of Logan's division, the 45th Illinois and an Indiana regiment. There is no better description of the incident than that written by the young Ottawa, Illinois, soldier Charles Brush, at this time an adjutant in the 53rd Illinois: "I saw and heard the first explosion – a mighty cloud of dust and smoke went hurling high in the air, then another a little to the left of the first blew up and threw the dirt still higher in the air, then the artillery thundered along the whole line, and the simultaneous fire of the Infantry spiced the occasion with the sharp crack and rattle of their pieces."

Into the breach charged the 45th and its companion regiment. Unfortunately, however, the Confederates had provided contingencies for such an event by building a second line of trenches to which they could fall back. The color bearer of the Illinois regiment, Sergeant Henry Taylor of Galena, managed to plant his banner upon the outer works of the fort, notwithstanding, and a number of troops from the Illinois regiment actually obtained the protection of some of the outer defiles. Still, the casualties were heavy. Colonel Jasper A. Maltby, the commanding officer of the 45th, was wounded; his subordinate, Lieutenant Colonel Melancthon Smith, from Rockford, was killed instantly by a musket ball in the head; a large number of minor officers were soon down or killed. The regiment managed to hold its position until relieved by companies of the 20th, 31st, 56th, and 124th Illinois, the last named being the regiment which had virtually foraged La Grange, Tennessee, out of existence. Logan's division held on past dusk, fighting so close to the enemy that rifles were sometimes snatched from their hands by Confederate soldiers on the other side of the trenches, and lighted shells were thrown down the embankment into their midst. During the night, when darkness provided the appropriate protection for retreat, the division was finally withdrawn, and the assault was deemed a failure.[68]

There was a second mine explosion on July 1, but no following

[68] Blanchard, 95–96. Brush to his father, June 27, 1863, Brush Family Papers. Bentley, 175. *Civil War Medal of Honor Winners*, 5. Crummer, 136–137.

attack. Grant seemed to be too sure of victory to waste any more troops. The enemy was still unconvinced, however. On the following day, July 2, the *Vicksburg Daily Citizen*, printed on wallpaper, pointed to the prowess of Confederate soldiers and to the obdurateness of people within the city, and boasted that the river was still controlled by the South: Grant still had to "catch the rabbit [Vicksburg]" before he could eat it.[69]

The boast had a hollow ring to it, however. After the historic meeting of Grant and Pemberton on July 3, the city was surrendered on the following day. The rabbit had indeed been caught. Logan's division, which had moved the closest to the Confederate works, was allowed to lead the Union march into the city. Dressed in full uniform, such regiments as the 8th, 20th, 45th, and 81st Illinois swung down the brick streets to the music of the regimental bands. It was left to the enterprising men of the 45th to get to the famous courthouse first, however; soon the brilliant colors of that sturdy regiment were floating high above that building as well as the river below, which now flowed "unvexed" to the sea.

Grant had proven his possession of a sense of drama, as well, in taking such a victory on July 4. "Oh! What a glorious 4th of July," wrote General W. W. Orme to his wife back in Illinois. "What a proud day for those of us who are so fortunate as to have taken part in this siege." The army was well behaved in its occupation of the town: no taunts, few cheers, and a good deal of fraternizing between the victors and the defeated. In the 8th Illinois, for example, there were many soldiers of German descent. In the Confederate regiment opposite them in the trenches were troops of the same nationality from Texas and Louisiana. Both regiments had witnessed the fateful conference between Grant and Pemberton which had taken place between the lines. Now, with the ending of hostilities, Germans found Germans and, in a way familiar to these people, much beer was exchanged. It was almost like home back in Peoria or Pekin, wrote Lieutenant William Sclag of I Company, 8th Illinois.[70]

If there was any sadness in the day, it was to be found in the

[69] *Vicksburg* (Miss.) *Daily Citizen*, July 2, 1863.

[70] Richard L. Howard, 123. Orme to his wife, July 4, 1863, Orme Papers. William Sclag to D. C. Smith, July 10, 1863, Smith Papers. Newsome, 73.

17th Illinois, where a young man was killed by the explosion of a souvenir shell, or in the regiment where a young private was killed when he pulled a loaded gun from an aperture. Grant could look back upon a highly successful campaign in which the cost of victory had been comparatively small. A total of 9,362 casualties had been suffered by the Union army from its landing at Port Gibson to and including July 4. Of these, 1,514 were killed and 7,395 were wounded. The casualties at Shiloh were just over 13,000, and those at Stone's River were 13,249. It was true that the army was "exhausted," as Grant phrased it in a letter to Halleck, and in no condition for further marching. A sergeant of the 126th Illinois, for example, reported a weight loss from 140 to 108 pounds. All in all, however, it had been the most successful Union campaign of the war thus far.[71]

Illinois had played its part in this momentous turning point of the war. Its generals, Grant, Logan, Ransom, McClernand, and others, had been closely tied in with the success of the campaign. The state had supplied an enormous share of the fighting men of the three corps. One veteran concluded, after the war's end, that Illinois had furnished some 55 of the 194 regiments which had fought their way from Milliken's Bend to the Vicksburg courthouse. Another, arriving at his figures in a different manner, claimed that almost one-third of the troops involved in the victory came from Illinois.

The state had full reason to be grateful and happy over the capture of Vicksburg, then. "Vicksburg is ours!" proclaimed the *Chicago Tribune* on July 16. In an earlier issue the paper had heralded the victory by surmising that the Mississippi would "soon be alive with steamers." Down in Quincy, the *Daily Whig and Republican* of July 9 asked the people of that city to hang out banners in celebration of victory. Belleville held a parade in which the marchers carried 32 variations of Grant's initials, "Undaunted Soldier Grant," "Unabated Siege Grant," and "Universal Sanitive Grant" among them. Indeed, it was true that most citizens of the state would have agreed with the *Chicago Tribune* that the "laurels of Gen. Grant" were "green and flourish-

[71] *Ibid.* James H. Crowder, *Before and After Vicksburg* (Dayton, Ohio, 1924), 68. *Official Records*, Ser. I, Vol. XXIV, Pt. 2, 167.

ing." Illinois had found its hero; for that matter, so had the Union.[72]

If the capture of Vicksburg made Grant into a national hero, the campaign toward that objective brought McClernand's military career to an abrupt halt. There were a number of attempts by the latter to gain reinstatement to his command in the XIII Corps, all without immediate result. "I have been relieved for an omission of my Adjutant," he telegraphed Lincoln. "Hear me," he added. Soon afterward, a letter went out to Washington. Grant, wrote McClernand, had no right or reason to relieve him except that of "personal hostility" resulting from the successes of the XIII Corps. McClernand further claimed that he had done his best. Could he not be restored to his command until after the fall of Vicksburg?[73]

In the end, however, the deposed general made his way back to Springfield; he was, in fact, another general without a command. Nevertheless, to the people back home he was still the hero of Donelson and Shiloh. The *Illinois State Journal* pointed out that the "confidence of the people" in McClernand's personal bravery would be "undiminished." Two days later, on June 27, the same paper argued that "reasons of more than ordinary gravity" would be expected concerning McClernand's removal from command. "It cannot and must not be," the paper stated, "that such a volunteer in the cause of our bleeding country, shall be stricken down by West Point prejudice and narrow-minded jealousy." On July 30 the *Journal* added that McClernand's real enemies were to be found at the top of the military hierarchy. There should be a court-martial in order to clear his name, the paper concluded.

McClernand continued to espouse the Union cause, despite the treatment he had been accorded. He made a series of pro-administration addresses, one of which was in the village of Loami. At a picnic near Chatham on July 18, he introduced himself as a Democrat of the "olden school." In another address in Springfield, he gave a "strong and stirring" oration in which he called

[72] Crowder, 54–55. Way, 6–7. Way makes an interesting summation of Illinois' contributions to the Union cause. *Chicago Tribune*, July 16, 9, 1863. *Quincy Daily Whig and Republican*, July 9, 20, 1863.

[73] McClernand to Lincoln, June 23, 24, 1863, Lincoln Papers.

for the people to bring the war to a successful conclusion. A massive crowd heard this speech, and when he had concluded, the chairman asked the assemblage to give three rousing cheers for McClernand, the President of the United States, and Governor Yates, in that order. One incident marred the day. One Springfield citizen, courageously tipsy, asked for another round of cheers for Grant. This incident may have been the one referred to in an August letter from Yates to Lincoln. "The popular verdict is irreversibly in his [McClernand's] favor as a general, unless by some future act he should himself reverse it," wrote the governor. "Since his return, although taunted by the opponents of the war at his misfortune, he has borne himself with admirable equanimity."[74]

As the days and months rolled by, McClernand's attempts to regain a military command of some sort took a pitiable turn. "You have long known me," he wrote the President. "That I would intentionally fail in anything involving the safety of the country, or the honor of it, you will hardly believe." The deposed general was now learning a lesson which he should have already known: it is difficult to compete with success, and Grant had achieved that. John Hay, the President's secretary, was to note in his diary that McClernand would have little chance to show "his claim that Vicksburg was taken by his plans," and that almost everybody, with the exception of Yates, was keeping out of the Grant-McClernand affair. Then too, Grant had discovered another principle of politics; it was that once started, the ball of success should be kept rolling. In late July, Rawlins showed up in Washington in order to forestall any claim which McClernand might make upon the administration and to remind the administration just which general had commanded the successful expedition against Vicksburg.[75]

McClernand should have seen the pattern of events, yet a natural frustration in the man precluded that. The stream of let-

---

[74] *Illinois State Journal*, June 25, 27, 30, July 1, 9, 20, 21, August 1, 1863. Yates is quoted in Kenneth P. Williams, IV, 436.

[75] McClernand to Lincoln, June 23, 1863, Lincoln Papers. Tyler Dennett, *Lincoln and the Civil War in Diaries and Letters of John Hay* (New York, 1939), 69. *Diary of Gideon Welles*, I, 387.

ters from Springfield to Washington became a continuous one. John Palmer Usher was Secretary of the Interior in Lincoln's administration. In mid-July he received a plea from McClernand as one "western man" to another. Usher simply forwarded the letter to the President. Two days later, on July 18, McClernand sent another letter to Lincoln. Illinois was in ferment, he wrote, and men were openly "hurrahing for Jeff Davis." On August 3, he forwarded another note to Lincoln. He wanted justice, he said; he was being "hawked at by ribald and malicious foes." [76]

Finally, on August 12, Lincoln answered his unhappy friend in Springfield. It was a sad and poignant letter, with hidden shades and meanings. He was grateful for McClernand's patriotism, and for the stand which he had "early taken" in the struggle now going on. But it was impossible for the administration to act. "For me to force you back upon General Grant would be forcing him to resign," Lincoln stated, and he concluded thus: "I am constantly pressed by those who *scold* before they think, or without thinking at all, to give command respectively to Frémont, McClellan, Butler, Sigel, Curtis, Hunter, Hooker, and perhaps others, when, all else out of the way, I have no commands to give them. This is now your case; which, as I have said, pains me not less than it does you." [77]

Lincoln's August refusal to hear McClernand's case did not mean that the story was finished or that the President had judged the issue to be a black and white one in favor of Grant. The fact of the matter was that Lincoln never really believed that his Springfield friend had been fairly treated, and there is a plenitude of evidence of his feelings on the matter. Not only did the President eventually restore McClernand to his command of the XIII Corps early in 1864, but he obviously indicated to the latter in an indirect manner that his feelings were sympathetic to McClernand's point of view. The reinstatement to duty was a

[76] McClernand to Usher, July 16, 1863, McClernand to Lincoln, July 18, Aug. 3, 1863, Lincoln Papers.

[77] *The Collected Works of Abraham Lincoln*, ed. Roy P. Basler, Lloyd A. Dunlap, and Marion Dolores Pratt (8 vols., New Brunswick, N.J., 1953–55), VI, 383. "Biography of John A. McClernand," II, 387, has this comment: "Supposing the loss of Gen Grant's service had been really grievous to the country, what had that to do with Mr. Lincoln's duty, as a dispenser of strick justice between man to man."

short one, however; within a few months McClernand fell very ill with malaria and was forced to resign his commission.

It would be difficult to judge the Grant and McClernand controversy, even today, without becoming involved in probabilities. Grant was undoubtedly the hero of the war, and it is easy to prove his side of the issue by pointing to the results. McClernand, who always believed that time would prove his case, lived until after the turn of the century without seeing that development occur. A feeble old man in 1900, he stayed at the St. Nicholas Hotel in Springfield, whiling away his hours by picking flowers in the wooded area around the new capitol building. Nothing would have pleased him more than if he could have read a comment written some seven years after his death. "While I do not attempt to justify the conduct of General McClernand," the writer stated, "I must be permitted to say that the men of the 13th corps . . . believed religiously in their beloved corps commander, both in his loyalty to the government and in his heroic courage."[78]

[78] Fletcher Pratt, *Stanton, Lincoln's Secretary of War* (New York, 1953), 315. Pratt holds that the President was never really satisfied with Dana's version of the McClernand story. An interesting letter is McClernand to Turner, Jan. 14, 1864, Turner Papers; in it, McClernand states that Lincoln had admitted that there had been injustice done to the general. The story of McClernand's late years comes from an interview the author had in 1953 with Miss Olivia Dunlap, a McClernand relative, who lived in Jacksonville, Illinois. The quote concerning the XIII Corps comes from Jacob M. Wilkin, "Personal Reminiscences of General U. S. Grant," *Transactions, 1907*, No. 12 (1908), 138.

Generals Ulysses S. Grant and John A. McClernand in front of the Cairo, Illinois, post office in 1861. Presumably, they were still friends at this early phase of their stormy relationship.

John Alexander Logan, from southern Illinois, was one of the few politicians to become a successful general officer. In 1861, however, he almost went South.

General John A. McClernand, written up by postwar Grant biographers as a conniver, probably deserves much more credit than given. He fought hard at Donelson, Shiloh, and Vicksburg.

General Michael Lawler, who usually wore a checkered shirt in battle, made an unauthorized crossing of the Big Black River in the Vicksburg campaign in 1863, thus sealing the doom of the Confederate army there. His motto: "If you see a head, hit it!"

Youthful Private George Crane of the 26th Illinois Infantry, armed with the accoutrements of war, including two knives.

Illinois soldiers leaving the Edgar County courthouse with supplies for the troops at Pittsburg Landing (Shiloh) in April, 1862. This is probably after the brutal battle of April 6-7.

A newly formed Illinois infantry company in formation in a Lake County community, probably in 1862.

General John A. Logan's headquarters during the Vicksburg siege. Note the dugouts and rude sheds constructed by common soldiers during that summer of 1863. Some of these troops might have been in the "Miners Regiment," the 45th Illinois Infantry, from the Galena area.

During a lull in the Battle of Atlanta in July, 1864, General John A. Logan, known as "Blackjack," made a daring ride between the lines of opposing troops. It was probably such antics that caused Sherman to deny him the command of a corps, though he thoroughly deserved it. From a painting done by German artists as part of the Cyclorama in Atlanta, Georgia.

Camp Douglas in Chicago and Camp Butler in Springfield were the two main training bases for Illinois soldiers in the Civil War. Butler, shown here, also held a substantial numer of Confederate prisoners.

Lithograph of the Andersonville stockade showing the shooting of a prisoner crossing the "dead line." The prisoner, possibly of the 38th Illinois Infantry, was known as Hubbard and nicknamed "Poll Parrot."

The major method by which wounded western soldiers were brought to hospitals was by steamboat. One such boat was the converted steamer *Nashville*.

A Civil War hospital at Nashville through which many wounded Illinois soldiers passed. Note the number of women at work with laundry.

The fascinating Mary Safford, who nursed Union soldiers at Cairo until her nervous breakdown. After the war, she attended medical school in Germany and became noted for her pioneering surgery. This picture was taken in Dresden.

"Mother" Mary Bickerdyke, who gained a considerable reputation on the western front. With her traveling laundry and her interventions on behalf of ordinary soldiers, she won the hearts of privates and wore the patience of the generals.

Woman Soldier in 95th Ill.

ALBERT D. J. CASHIER
OF
COMPANY G, 95TH ILLINOIS REGIMENT
Photographed November, 1864

ALBERT D. J. CASHIER
OF
COMPANY G, 95TH ILLINOIS REGIMENT
Photographed July, 1913

Private D. J. Cashier (nee Jennie Hodgers) who served in the 95th Illinois Infantry throughout the war. On the left, she is a "boy" soldier. On the right, she is an aging woman at the Quincy Soldiers and Sailors Home.

Ransom Stone, Company 1, 33rd Illinois Infantry, sometimes called the "Teachers Regiment." Stone was fourteen years of age when he enlisted on September 5, 1861. He was barely eighteen when he was discharged on June 9, 1865.

Black corporal, regiment unknown, who probably came from Illinois. The picture was found in a country store near Peterstown, Illinois. One black regiment, the 29th U.S. Colored Infantry Regiment, was raised in Illinois.

Regimental camp of the 52nd Illinois, showing the cookhouse at one end. On the building on the far right is painted the inscription "Fox River Avenue." One of the officers shown, Captain Alphonse Barto, became a governor of Minnesota after the war.

Rifles stacked, soldiers of the 52nd Illinois rest after morning review. The 52nd fought hard at Shiloh in April, 1862.

Wearing a distinctive coat is Chaplain Dunn of the 52nd Illinois. The oldest officer in the regiment (unnamed) is on the right. The site is regimental headquarters.

Company C, 9th Illinois. The picture was possibly taken during Sherman's campaign in Georgia in 1864. The 9th was one of the toughest Illinois regiments and had one of the highest casualty rates in the Union Army.

Officers of the 6th Illinois Cavalry Regiment. The 6th was one of three cavalry regiments participating in Grierson's raid through Mississippi in 1863. Colonel M. H. Starr, second on the upper right, died from wounds while convalescing in Jacksonville, Illinois, in 1864.

Part of Company D, 16th Illinois Infantry, sometimes called the "Stealing Regiment." Note that these veteran soldiers did not wear beards as was customary in the early years of the war.

CHAPTER VII

An American Tragedy

July, 1863, was to bring a change in the pattern of the war. The gloom which had overcast the North during the winter of 1862 and 1863, with the terrible losses at Stone's River and Antietam, was now dispelled with the bright rays of victory at Vicksburg and Gettysburg. In the first of these two victories, the great river had been opened to the sea; by the other, Lee's invading army had been driven from Pennsylvania. By both of them, it seemed to most Union supporters, the corner of the war was turned.

While attention in the North was focused upon the struggle in the East, with its denouement at Gettysburg, and upon Grant's ever extending trenches at Vicksburg, another development of great importance was taking place in respect to the Army of the Cumberland. Rosecrans, whose paper victory at Stone's River had absorbed a great deal of his willingness to dare, holed up at Murfreesboro after that battle, ostensibly reconstituting and rebuilding his army. In May, however, when it was learned in Washington that Grant had successfully crossed the Mississippi below Vicksburg, Halleck became greatly concerned over the possibility that part of Bragg's army opposing Rosecrans might be taken west in an effort to trap the army advancing upon Vicksburg. Rosecrans, then, was urged to take the pressure from Grant's Army of the Tennessee by advancing on his own front and pinning Bragg down in that theater of war.

One fact in Rosecrans' character soon appeared to be obvious both to his superiors and to his own troops. He was most certainly a man who could not be pushed into a hurried campaign. He made his plans in a reflective manner with a good deal of consideration in respect to his lines of supply. Late in June he decided to attempt to turn the Confederate right, north of the Duck River in Tennessee. Dividing his army into five separate columns, he sent Thomas' XIV Corps, which had fought so well at Stone's River, and Crittenden's XXI around Bragg's right flank. McCook's XX Corps, which had suffered so much the previous December, was moved along the Shelbyville pike. Gordon Granger's reserve corps and David S. Stanley's cavalry corps were thrown out against the Confederate left.

Bragg's defense to the south of Murfreesboro was based upon the natural topographical advantages which were held by his army. Any advance in that direction would have to come through one or several of the four gaps in the ridges which lay north of the Duck River. Along the Confederate line from left to right, or from west to north, were Guy's Gap, Bellbuckle Gap, Liberty Gap, and Hoover's Gap. As it happened the last two pathways toward the Tennessee city of Tullahoma were the most important.

As Thomas' XIV Corps moved around to the Manchester pike in the early darkness of June 24, the sky opened up and a steady rain pelted the long blue column of men. The weather, one of the great factors of war, as Napoleon is reputed to have said, slowed the Army of the Cumberland to a crawl. Coincidence neither wins battles nor effects defeat, but in Rosecrans' case it always seemed to be present. The opening of the movement upon Murfreesboro in the previous December was heralded with a day-long cloudburst. Now the moisture-laden clouds hovered low over the long line of ridges to the southeast. To a La Salle County soldier of the 104th Illinois, the cloudburst was no "Presbyterian rain, either, but a genuine Baptist downpour." To a western Illinois soldier of Colonel Louis H. Waters' 84th Illinois, it was "exceedingly muddy and slavish marching.' The wagons of several Illinois regiments bogged down in the Tennessee clay, and the services of eight to ten mules were required to pull them out. For most Illinois soldiers, comparisons were in the making. Which were worse — Illinois roads or Tennessee roads?

A common comment in Illinois regiments on this sullen morning of June 24 was: "Well, this beats our Illinois Roads."[1]

Leading the advance of Thomas' XIV Corps was a unit from Joseph J. Reynolds' Fourth Division, Colonel John Thomas Wilder's First Brigade of Mounted Infantry. Wilder was one of the most interesting figures in the Army of the Cumberland. Independent by nature and a gambler by instinct, he had strained army regulations by purchasing repeating Spencer rifles for his soldiers with money borrowed by a home-town bank in Indiana. The Spencer could fire seven copper rimfire .52 caliber cartridges from one loading. Ten extra magazines could be carried by each soldier, giving him an enormous advantage over his enemy counterpart. The Spencer was not the most accurate or hardest-hitting rifle in the Federal armories, but it was a dependable gun, inspiring to its user and frightening to the enemy.

Wilder's brigade was composed of two Indiana and two Illinois regiments. The Hoosier units were the 17th and 72nd regiments; those from Illinois were the 98th and 123rd. The 123rd regiment had been organized for approximately a year, and was that untried body of men which had fought its first battle at Perryville with somewhat disastrous results — a wholesale and rapid retreat in the face of enemy fire. Now, however, with months of campaigning in Tennessee, and with courage instilled by the repeating Spencers, it was about to prove its right to a place in the Union army. The 98th Illinois, recruited mainly in Crawford, Richland, and Effingham counties, was commanded by Colonel John J. Funkhouser of Effingham, a capable and able leader. Previous experience by this regiment had been confined to a few brisk but unimportant skirmishes on the outskirts of Murfreesboro during the early weeks of June. Wilder's "Lightning Brigade," as it was soon to be called, added a third Illinois regiment at the end of June. This was the 92nd, a sturdy regiment from Ogle and Stephenson counties. Its commanding officer was Colonel Smith D. Atkins of Freeport, who, because of difficulties with General Gordon Granger, asked for a transfer to the XIV Corps. It was a fortunate move for everyone but Granger. The 92nd became, in

[1] John B. Turchin, *Chickamauga* (Chicago, 1888), 215–223. "Diary of James Suiter, Aug. 1863–Sept. 1865," James P. Suiter Papers, ISHL, 2. Calkins, 97. Newlin, 180. Cist, 154–160.

time, one of the best regiments in the west, and Atkins became one of the better field officers in that theater of conflict.[2]

As Wilder moved his men in the rain and pre-dawn darkness of June 24, the advance was led by the 17th Indiana and the 123rd Illinois. At daylight, when the first enemy vedettes were encountered, the two leading regiments broke into a gallop toward Hoover's Gap. As the brigade pushed forward, the Confederate troops withdrew rapidly, apparently suspecting a Union force much larger than that actually making the attack. The Spencers were doing the trick. The 123rd Illinois and its accompanying Indiana regiment quickly reached the narrow part of the gap where breastworks had been built, driving away and taking the colors of the 1st Kentucky Infantry. The time of this success was nine o'clock.

The rapidity of the Federal advance into Hoover's Gap momentarily confounded the Confederate defenders. The latter, retreating before the two forward regiments of Wilder's brigade, piled up in front of the attacking force, so that by the time Hoover's Gap was taken, the swiftly moving westerners were faced by a numerical disadvantage of 20 to 1. Regrouping on the eastern slope of the gap, the Confederates organized a strong attack, headed by the 20th Tennessee, upon the Indiana and Illinois defenders. The assault came too late, however — at two o'clock in the afternoon. The intervening period of five hours had given Wilder the opportunity to bring his four regiments into a good position, particularly the 123rd Illinois, commanded by Colonel James Monroe, which cut the attackers to pieces with their repeating rifles. Increasing support from Robert D. Lilley's Indiana battery inflicted more casualties upon the assaulting troops, and soon Thomas' infantry came up, soaking wet but ready for action. The Federal hold upon Hoover's Gap was clinched.

The rapid advance by mounted infantry armed with repeating rifles had proven a case both for the weapon itself and the men of Wilder's brigade. The risk was a daring one, but the four regiments had been up to it. One of the Illinois officers who was to receive official commendation for the initial success on June

---

[2] *Report of the Adjutant General,* V, 361–363. William B. Edwards, *Civil War Guns: The Complete Story of Federal and Confederate Small Arms . . .* (Harrisburg, Pa., 1962), 144–149.

24 was Major James A. Connolly, serving in the 123rd, who came from Charleston, Illinois. Connolly's comment upon reading his commanding officer's report of the battle was indicative of the nature of Wilder's brisk movement into the gap. "Whew!" wrote the eastern Illinois officer. "He didn't know how badly I was scared or he wouldn't have said all that sure." But to Thomas, who had brought the main body of his corps forward on the afternoon of June 24, the victory was more than frosting on the cake. "You have saved the lives of a thousand men by your gallant conduct today," he told the men of the 123rd. "I didn't expect to get this Gap for three days." [3]

While the 98th and 123rd Illinois were making history at Hoover's Gap, the First Brigade of Richard W. Johnson's division in McCook's XX Corps, under the command of General August Willich, moved rapidly in the direction of Liberty Gap. Willich was that officer whose early capture at Stone's River signaled the collapse of the Union right wing. Having been exchanged, he now had a chance to redeem himself. Supporting Willich was the Second Brigade, which, under Kirk at Stone's River, had also fared badly. Now commanded by Colonel John F. Miller, it followed closely upon the heels of Willich's men.

There were three Illinois regiments in these two leading brigades of the XX Corps. Among Willich's regiments was the 89th Illinois, the "Railroad Regiment," a sturdy unit from the north and northwestern part of the state and commanded by Colonel Charles T. Hotchkiss of Chicago. In the Second Brigade were the 34th and 79th Illinois. The 34th had been cut to pieces at Stone's River, and was now commanded by Lieutenant Colonel Oscar Van Tassell of Grand Detour. The 79th likewise had suffered badly in that battle, losing its commanding officer, Sheridan P. Read. It was now commanded by Colonel Allan Buckner of Arcola.

Willich managed to lodge his brigade in Liberty Gap before nightfall on June 24, but on the following day, late in the afternoon, the Confederates made a strong attempt to retake the position. Willich's brigade was hard pressed, and the 34th Illinois, in Miller's brigade, was forced to fight a sharp duel with

[3] *Three Years in the Army of the Cumberland*, 92–94, 105. *Official Records*, Ser. I, Vol. XXIII, Pt. 1, 457–461.

the 2nd Arkansas at no more than 60 paces. Miller himself was severely wounded. Eventually Carlin's brigade, including the 21st and 38th Illinois, which had performed well at Perryville and Stone's River, was brought forward. Moving by Miller's faltering troops at a brisk pace, Carlin's men drove the attacking force across a plowed field and back down the eastern slope of the gap. Sergeant Nineveh McKean of Marshall, Illinois, fighting with the 21st, singlehandedly took the flag of the 8th Arkansas, and the 34th and the 38th Illinois jointly captured the colors of the 2nd Arkansas. The victory was not without cost. Buckner's 79th Illinois, short of officers since Stone's River, lost more here—three captains and three lieutenants either killed or wounded. The total casualties for the regiment were 47.

Rosecrans' movements through the gaps now became masterful. Troops poured through Guy's Gap and Liberty Gap, and Wilder's brigade led the XIV Corps in a grand sweep toward Manchester. The "Lightning Brigade" was then ordered to move in the direction of Decherd and destroy the railroad bridges near Chattanooga—a venture brilliantly led but only partially successful. Thus did the first phase of the new Chattanooga campaign, known as the Tullahoma campaign, come to a close. By July 2 the Army of the Cumberland was in possession of Tullahoma and most of the region west of the Sequatchie valley. Bragg had been expertly maneuvered back toward Chattanooga and into a position from which he could not possibly aid Johnston in any attempt to drive Grant from the Vicksburg area, although it was too late anyway. So it was that, following the surrender of the great river fortress on July 4, the end of the war seemed nearer than it had for the whole previous year.[4]

Despite his great success at driving Bragg into southeastern Tennessee, Rosecrans held the army at Tullahoma while he argued with Halleck over issues of strategy. It was Rosecrans' contention, and a valid one, that he should keep his army where it was until Grant could support him with an eastward march from Vicksburg. This would pit two armies against Bragg's, creating favorable conditions for an invasion of Georgia. This was basical-

---

[4] *Report of the Adjutant General*, V, 48; II, 688. Dodge, 83–84. Fox, 439. Kenneth P. Williams, V, 234–235. E. W. Payne to his mother, July 7, 1863, Edwin W. Payne Papers.

ly what was done in Sherman's successful campaign against Atlanta. In 1863, however, Halleck could not wait. On August 4 he sent an unequivocal dispatch ordering the reluctant commander of the Army of the Cumberland to move forward, and to report the movement of each corps until he crossed the Tennessee. Halleck was taking no chances that Rosecrans would misunderstand that the object of the campaign was Chattanooga.

Shortly after the mid-point of the month, Rosecrans finally got his army under way toward Chattanooga. Crittenden's XXI Corps was sent to the banks of the Tennessee through the Sequatchie valley; Thomas' XIV Corps was ordered in the direction of Bridgeport, Alabama; McCook's XX Corps struck southward to the west bank of the river opposite Sand Mountain. The idea was to move west and south of Chattanooga to force Bragg out. Wilder's "Lightning Brigade," whose Spencers were recognized to be of special advantage, was given the important task of feinting north of Chattanooga beyond the Tennessee. This task successfully completed, the 92nd Illinois, just added to Wilder's outfit and commanded by Colonel Smith Atkins, was detached and sent to the main body of the XIV Corps. The Illinois regiment joined Thomas' column on September 7, as it reached the foot of Raccoon Mountain.

There was a reason why Thomas needed the 92nd. It had shown itself to be a reasonably solid regiment, ably commanded, and having the added fire power which the Spencer rifles provided. The commanding general of the XIV Corps divided Atkins' men, sending the main body of the regiment to reconnoiter the crest of Lookout Mountain and to occupy Chattanooga if that city was proven to be evacuated. A detachment of the 92nd was given to Crittenden in order to scout for that corps as it moved around Lookout Mountain and into Chattanooga proper. Thus it was that the 92nd Illinois was the first Union regiment to enter that important city on September 9, when Bragg had to evacuate because of Rosecrans' flanking movement. The two portions of Atkins' unit rode into Chattanooga only 45 minutes apart, and when Crittenden's corps swung down the slopes of Lookout, it was met by the sight of the colors of the 92nd floating above Crutchfield House. Later, on the same morning, the remainder of Wilder's brigade, including the 98th and 123rd

Illinois, crossed the river above Chattanooga and entered the city.

Like a river flowing through a three-pronged delta, the great Army of the Cumberland moved through the mountain passes into the valley of Chickamauga Creek. Thomas' XIV Corps marched over Sand Mountain and seized the passes at Steven's Gap. Farther south McCook's XX Corps passed over Raccoon and Lookout mountains and moved in the general direction of Rome, Georgia. Wilder, whose brigade was rapidly becoming the workhorse of the army, was ordered to strike toward Dalton, Georgia. Truly the Union advance, like the great Tennessee River which was now to the west, seemed to be moving in an almost irresistible manner.[5]

The troops felt this to be so, at any rate. The march south through Tennessee to the borders of Alabama and Georgia had been a magnificant one, with the army developing an increasing confidence in itself and its commander. A soldier of the 123rd Illinois was prompted to write that the August and September sun had made him as "red as three very red Indians." To him, crossing the mountains and marching through the broad river plains had seemed more like sport than war. The crops were full and heavy with the results of good summer moisture, and the mountain air was clear and fresh with the hint of fall. To the same eastern Illinois trooper, the view of the plains from the upper ridges was so lovely that he wrote: "I could live a century in that peaceful looking valley."

The Army of the Cumberland was filled with young men whose muscles were hardened by the brisk marching of August, and whose emotions were touched by events of September. Was this not what war was supposed to be? The march to Tullahoma, and from there to the valley of the Chickamauga, had been filled with color, excitement, and victory. There was something exhilarating in seeing the long lines of the various columns stringing their way through the passes and gaps, their banners flapping in the mountain air, almost unhampered by a retreating foe. And there was music — the bands of the various regiments, livened by the

[5] *Official Records*, Ser. I, Vol. XXX, Pt. 1, 47–53; Vol. XXIII, Pt. 1, 592. Villard, II, 86–87. *Report of the Adjutant General*, V, 362. Kenneth P. Williams, V, 244. Turchin, 20–31.

briskness of the mornings, played almost incessantly. The 73rd Illinois, the "Persimmon" or "Preacher's Regiment," marching with Thomas' corps through Steven's Gap, declared itself to have had "a surfeit" of music during the march from Tullahoma. It was for the best, the regimental historian later reported; "all of the instruments and a few of the musicians were captured in the next battle." [6]

The passing of the Army of the Cumberland through the gaps of Lookout Mountain may have been one of the real sights of the war. A soldier of the 104th Illinois later described the view in words of moving reminiscence. "The broad Tennessee below us seemed like a ribbon of silver," he wrote; "beyond rose the Cumberlands, which we had crossed. The valley on both sides was alive with the moving armies of the Union, while almost the entire transportation of the army filled the roads and fields along the Tennessee." Then, as if overcome by the memory of it all, he added: "No one could survey the grand scene on that bright autumn day unmoved, unimpressed with its grandeur and of the meaning conveyed by the presence of that mighty host." Yet the view was even more impressive to a young Oquawka, Illinois, soldier of the 10th Illinois. "Can one name a spot on the round globe so fit for the circumstance and pomp of war?" he later asked.[7]

As for the enemy, the ordinary soldier of the Army of the Cumberland could well wonder what had happened to his spirit. From the moment that Hoover's Gap was pierced by Wilder in late June, the Confederates had been moving back. Time after time deserters from their ranks surrendered to the advanced pickets of Rosecrans' army. "The Rebel army is greatly dispirited and demoralized, and I think in less than a month Braggs army will be almost entirely dispersed," wrote Sergeant Edwin Payne of the 34th Illinois. The same day, Lieutenant Philip Welshimer of the 21st Illinois wrote his wife back in Neoga that the enemy was deserting in large numbers. "We have no fears of the result," added Welshimer. "Rosey [Rosecrans] will whip him when and where ever he meets him." The 21st and 34th Illinois were to

[6] *Three Years in the Army of the Cumberland*, 76, 87–88. Newlin, 190.
[7] Calkins, 111. Jamison, 199.

find out in mid-September that Bragg had a good deal of fight left in him.[8]

Yet, even immediately before the moment when the grand illusion of victory was to vanish, deserters continued to come into the Federal lines. A soldier of the 84th Illinois confided to his diary in early September that one of these Confederate soldiers had come into the camps of the 36th Illinois so frightened and confused that he was unable to talk. Was all of this designed by Bragg in order to inspire overconfidence in the ranks of the Army of the Cumberland? If so, Bragg could have spared himself the effort and the men. The Federal army opposing him had Rosecrans, whose presence alone was enough to create a wealth of confidence. To a campaigner of the 10th Illinois, that "stout-built soldier in fatigue dress and cavalry boots" was everywhere; he seemed to be indefatigable. In a burst of exuberation, an officer of the 123rd Illinois expressed the sentiments of a whole army when he wrote his Ohio-born wife: "Hurrah for Illinois! Her Generals and soldiers are the best in the world, always excepting old 'Rosey' in whom you 'Buckeyes' have a slight interest I believe."[9]

Bragg's Confederate army may have been momentarily down, but it was far from being out of the picture. This commander, whose faults were so few and yet so great that his virtues were overcome by them, gathered his divisions near Lafayette, Georgia, and waited for reinforcements. He missed his great chance to hit Rosecrans hard when the various separated corps of the Union army streamed through the passes to the northwest, at Lookout Mountain. Had he struck then, he might have inflicted a defeat of disastrous proportions upon his opponent. But then, Bragg was like the commanding general of the Army of the Cumberland in that everything, or almost everything, had to be nearly perfect before he felt himself prepared to attack. So he waited for generals Buckner, Hindman, Breckinridge, and Longstreet to arrive with their troops. Some of these had arrived by

[8] Payne to Miss Kim Hudson, July 4, 1863, Edwin W. Payne Papers. Welshimer to his wife, July 4, 1863, Welshimer Papers. Welshimer was captured at Chickamauga two months later.

[9] "Diary of James Suiter," 23. Jamison, 195. *Three Years in the Army of the Cumberland*, 72. Many writers feel that Bragg deliberately sent deserters into the Union lines.

September 18; the last named was bringing two divisions from Lee's Army of Virginia. These veteran soldiers were now not far away, having been seen a few days earlier in Georgia "rolled in their blankets . . . their heads all covered," on a train heading toward Chattanooga.

As Rosecrans struggled to bring the diverse elements of his army together after its passage over the mountains, there was a definite change and diminution in the confidence of some of the Union generals. Coming to Chattanooga from Tullahoma had not seemed very difficult, but now, with the mountains and the river to the rear, the army felt itself to be disembodied. The valley and woods near Chickamauga Creek appeared more like enemy country than anything the army had seen. General John Palmer, the Carlinville, Illinois, officer, wrote his wife of vague fears of an enemy attack, something which the Confederates might have successfully executed back at Lookout Mountain. Palmer seemed to sense that the army was living on borrowed time.[10]

This decline of optimism was hastened when Federal scouts began returning with information that Bragg was concentrating his army at Lafayette and that he had not fled to Rome as first hoped. The Confederacy was not going to retreat ignominiously after all. There would be a fight. "We are close up on the rebels . . . ," Palmer warned his wife on September 17. "When the two armies meet the results of the engagement will be serious if not decisive." There may have been some good in the fact that Palmer was not able to know the correctness of his prediction.[11]

With the exception of a few scattered units, Rosecrans eventually managed to unite much of his army once again. By the evening of September 18 he had maneuvered it into an incomplete line stretching from north to south along Chickamauga Creek. There was a patchwork quality to his troop disposition, and it reflected Rosecrans' tendency to divide his corps and divisions in such a manner that the line of command was often difficult to follow. Illinois regiments were to be found in this defensive position, all the way from Crawfish Springs to the other end of the major line past Kelly's Field. The 89th, Hotchkiss' "Railroad Regiment," held

[10] Mary Boykin Chestnut, *A Diary from Dixie* (Boston, 1949), 308. Palmer to his wife, Sept. 2, 1863, John M. Palmer Papers, ISHL.

[11] Palmer to his wife, Sept. 17, 1863, Palmer Papers.

a spot with part of Johnson's division upon the rear right flank. Forward, near Crawfish Springs, were parts of Sheridan's and Davis' divisions, also of McCook's corps, the former containing the 36th and 88th Illinois in William H. Lytle's brigade, the 44th and 73rd Illinois in Bernard Laiboldt's brigade, and the 22nd, 27th, 42nd, and 51st Illinois in N. H. Walworth's brigade.

Stretching from Gordon's Mill to Cove Spring were the divisions of T. J. Wood, H. P. Van Cleve, and Palmer of Crittenden's corps. These included the 84th, 100th, and 110th Illinois. Carlin's and H. C. Heg's brigades of Davis' division were situated in the middle of the Federal line near Widow Glenn's Vineyard, these units containing the 21st, 25th, 35th, and 38th Illinois. To the left of Heg's brigade were two brigades from Van Cleve's division, and farther down the line were various brigades from J. J. Reynolds' division of Thomas' corps, Johnson's division, and Palmer's division. These included such Illinois regiments as the 80th, 84th, 110th, 79th, 34th, 92nd, 98th, and 123rd, in that order from right to left. Absalom Baird's division on the far left contained the 24th Illinois; J. S. Negley's division, which had not yet assumed its position near the Federal center, included the 104th Illinois. Other brigades, such as Stanley's, which included the 19th Illinois, were also in a state of flux and were not stabilized in the line. Furthermore, Philip S. Post's brigade, which was principally Illinois in character, had been placed at Steven's Gap to guard the supply trains; Granger's reserve corps, which was to play an important role in the coming fight and which also contained many Illinois regiments, was left behind at McAffee Church.

Fixing Rosecrans' line at a certain moment, however, posed considerable danger. Bragg's plan was fairly obvious, even to the Union commanders. He was determined to unhinge the end of the Federal line nearest to Chattanooga and the river. If he could smash the Union left, under the command of Thomas, he would then be able to separate the entire army from its base of supply. Surrender would inevitably follow. For this reason, when fighting flared between the two armies on September 18, Rosecrans did considerable shifting of his forces. Wilder's brigade was a perfect example of this. This unit, which included the 92nd, 98th, and 123rd Illinois, was originally stationed to guard Alexander Bridge, considerably forward of the middle of the

Federal line. On the morning of September 18 Wilder was driven from this position, though not before his repeating Spencers had dealt the attacking Confederates a large number of casualties. At nightfall Wilder was back in the center of the main Federal line. By the morning of September 20th the brigade had been moved to the extreme right, near Sheridan's division at Crawfish Springs. This was the manner in which Rosecrans operated.

Moving his army across the Chickamauga on the Union left at Alexander Bridge, Bragg hurled his troops at Baird's and J. M. Brannan's divisions of Thomas' corps on September 19, driving them back to the region of Kelly's Field. By the afternoon of the same day, the fighting had spread down the line to William Grose's and Charles Cruft's brigades of Palmer's division, near the center of the Federal line. If the battle had ended at this point, it would have been enough in the way of fighting. "Their bullets came over at a fearful rate," wrote a member of the 7th Illinois Cavalry; "at times it seemed as though they came as thick as if one would take a handful of shelled corn and scatter it broadcast."[12]

During this savage fighting on September 19, Illinois regiments were involved in bitter struggles along the line. The 84th, a western Illinois regiment commanded by Colonel Louis Waters, found itself in a perilous position at approximately one o'clock due to strong attacks from Stewart's Confederate division. The 92nd Illinois also participated in the conflict on the left. This hard-fighting regiment, commanded by Colonel Smith Atkins, once again made its presence felt with its repeating rifles. The 21st and 38th Illinois, fighting in Carlin's brigade, got into some hard fighting during the late afternoon. The 110th Illinois, with Hazen's brigade of Stone's River fame, at times found itself hard pressed. But these were not really exceptions. Virtually every unit in the Army of the Cumberland saw action on this day, which, by and large, was a good one for Rosecrans, although neither side had made much progress and the issue was far from decided.[13]

[12] Turchin, 215–223. Turchin's volume contains excellent maps giving the location of each brigade and division in the two days of the battle. Eby, 106.

[13] "Diary of James Suiter," 47–49. Van Horne, I, 334–339. Villard, II, 118. Villard says that the battle on September 19 was not continuous, but "like the rise and fall of the tide."

The night of September 19 was, according to one present-day historian, "unutterably gloomy," filled with troop movements and general activity. In all of this there was considerable confusion, for the regiments of the two armies were scattered over a space of seven miles. Regiments and divisions were moved back and forth by Rosecrans in a hurried effort to fill the chinks and crevices in the Union line. The troops on both sides wrapped themselves in blankets as best they could, and tried to sleep midst the noise of chopping by the pioneer brigades and the countermarching of various divisions. Somehow, the chill which rose in the valley of the "river of death" carried a foreboding to the ordinary soldier: the previous day had been only a beginning; the work of the coming dawn would be infinitely more serious.

Over on the right of the Union line, where the brigade of the doomed General William H. Lytle was encamped, two soldiers of the 36th Illinois made a solemn promise. One of the two men survived the coming day and managed to write a description of that touching little ceremony. "We promised each other that if either fell the other would take charge of his lifeless remains and write home all the particulars," the soldier wrote. "And then," he continued, "I don't mind telling *you* of it – we repeated together the little prayer, 'Now I lay me down to sleep,' and . . . bade each other Good night." And over in the 7th Illinois Cavalry, a lieutenant called his company together in the unbroken black of the Chickamauga woods and solemnly told them with admirable prescience that tomorrow, September 20, would bring the "hardest fought battle" the army would ever see.[14]

During the night, Bragg held to his original notion of hitting at the Federal left, ordering his commanding officer at that end of the Confederate line to commence his assault at dawn. Lieutenant General D. H. Hill, who had just arrived from duty with Lee's army in Virginia, was in no hurry. Delaying his attack to allow breakfast for his troops, he did not get his brigades under way until after nine o'clock. When the Confederates moved forward, they did so with savage intensity. The 104th Illinois, fighting with John Beatty's brigade of Thomas' corps, was one of the

[14] Catton, *This Hallowed Ground*, 281. Mary Livermore, 674. Eby, 99.

first to feel the morning assault. Stationed on the extreme left, these La Salle County soldiers spotted Marcellus A. Stovall's Confederate skirmishers moving through the morning mists, their "light wool hats pulled down over their eyes, like men breasting a storm."

The 104th, by way of reminder, was that unfortunate Illinois regiment which had been captured the previous December back at Hartsville in Tennessee. After its exchange it had been re-equipped and placed under a new commander, Lieutenant Colonel Douglas Hapeman. Now, at ten o'clock on the morning of September 20, the regiment faced another dilemma; it was cut off from the main body of the Federal line by a horde of Confederate attackers. Hapeman was not about to surrender his regiment again. He managed to change the front of his regiment in the heavy undergrowth and work his way to safety, while inflicting heavy casualties upon the Confederates.[15]

It was during this attack that General Daniel Adams led his Alabama and Louisiana troops in such a furious assault that he bypassed Baird's division on the left and ran head on into the 19th Illinois, commanded by Lieutenant Colonel Alexander Raffen. The 19th was a solid and expert Zouave regiment which, up until the battle on the banks of the Chickamauga, was best remembered for its fine charge at Stone's River. The Illinois regiment lashed back at Adams' troops with such fury that, in the resulting melee, Adams himself was captured by Captain James Guthrie of Chicago.

Thus did the fighting begin on the morning of September 20, with the Confederates continuing their pressure upon the far left of the Union line. Down the line, in Grose's brigade of Palmer's division, the men of the 84th Illinois, who had struggled so bitterly the previous day, listened apprehensively as the noise of the battle edged closer and closer to the barricades which they had constructed during the night. Soon these western Illinois soldiers found themselves in the midst of a struggle much worse than that of the day before—musketry which "raged with a fury," as one of the men was to write later, and an attack which became "hotter and hotter." Still farther down the line, on the rel-

[15] Turchin, 105–108. Calkins, 151–152.

atively quiet right flank of the Federal line, the troops waited patiently in battle formation. While standing there, a young private of the 36th Illinois turned to his friend in the ranks and handed him a watch and a number of little keepsakes. "I shall be killed in the first hour of the fight," he warned. Within the hour he was.[16]

Up to this point of the battle, Rosecrans had the upper hand. He had thrown back the best which the Confederates had offered by cleverly manipulating his divisions and brigades. However, he apparently overmanipulated his troops, and somehow became confused as to where certain of his divisions were located. As the fighting on the left grew to a furious pitch, Rosecrans became obsessed with the notion that Thomas' flank was about to become unhinged, and that disaster was in the offing. But it was Rosecrans himself who became unhinged. Brigades were detached from the main Federal line on the right and sent to the left, an odd move in itself, and Wood's division, which had been on reserve, was moved into position to replace them. At slightly after ten o'clock, a report was brought to Rosecrans by an eager young officer who had just returned from a ride up the Federal right that Brannan's division, supposedly in the center of the line, did not seem to be in the appropriate position. Actually Brannan was there; he had wisely withdrawn to a more defensible spot in a nearby woods.

This was the moment when events overwhelmed Rosecrans. His organization became too much for him. Without checking the information concerning Brannan's location, he sent Captain Sanford C. Kellogg, an aide-de-camp, galloping off to Wood with instructions to close up quickly upon Reynold's division. Reynolds was some distance off, on the other side of Brannan, but Wood was a good soldier and chose to obey the orders, and some personal misunderstanding may have entered in as well. Besides, the previous two days had been nothing more than a series of checkerboard moves by the commanding general of the Army of the Cumberland. Who was to question orders now? Wood took

---

[16] Turchin, 108. "Diary of James Suiter," 54–55. Suiter wrote: "Presently the fight, which had begun on our left became hotter and hotter and was now coming down the line to the right like a hurricane and deadly musketry raged with a fury beyond human description." Mary Livermore, 674.

his men out of the line and marched them to the rear of Brannan's division.[17]

On another day in another place, the creation of a hole in the Federal line might have amounted to nothing at all. At this moment, however, as fate would have it, Bragg's attacks were being committed, division by division, down the Union line from left to right. Like a peal of thunder whose sound has been slowed, the roll of musketry had moved from the 104th Illinois on the left to the 100th Illinois just to the right of center. Now James Longstreet's men, who had just joined Bragg's command, hurtled forward in an intense attack upon the Federal right. Elsewhere thrown back, it was Bushrod Johnson's division of the attacking troops which found the hole left by the absent Wood. Johnson, who far back in 1862 had walked unhampered from the Federal sentries at Fort Donelson, was clever enough to realize the significance of his achievement. Directing his troops to the right, he continued to shatter the Union line, followed by other Confederate units.

As Longstreet's divisions continued to exploit the gap in Rosecrans' line, Sheridan, commanding a division on the separated Union right, was the first to realize the calamity. Desperately trying to remedy the situation, he first sent Walworth's brigade, comprising the 22nd, 27th, 42nd, and 51st Illinois, in an attempt to drive the Confederates from their position within the Federal line. Walworth, who came from Oneida, Illinois, made a heroic effort to effect the impossible. Joined by Lytle's brigade, which included the 36th and 88th Illinois, he halted Manigault's brigade, inflicting numerous casualties and capturing the colors of the 24th Alabama. But then the weight of five Confederate brigades pushing to the northwest was too much for the two Union brigades. Lytle was mortally wounded, and the casualties among the Federal regiments were heavy, particularly in the 22nd, 27th, 36th, and 42nd Illinois. The 36th, a veteran Pea Ridge regiment

[17] Dana, 113. During the night of September 19 Rosecrans counseled with his generals. Thomas, who had been on his feet for about 48 hours, kept falling asleep. Every few minutes, however, Rosecrans would awake him with a question as to what should be done to improve the battle line. Thomas' reply each time was: "I would strengthen the left." *Official Records*, Ser. I, Vol. XXX, Pt. 1, 103. Kellogg was the officer who failed to see Brannan's disposition.

ably commanded by Colonel Silas Miller of Aurora, was the last to withdraw. In this comparatively brief period of fighting the 36th lost over 140 of its complement.[18]

Bragg was isolating the Union right, a maneuver which had failed at Stone's River. Federal regiments began to peel off with increasing rapidity in order to escape. Beyond Sheridan's brief attempt at the beginning of the calamity, the only Federal defense on the right was conducted by Wilder's "Lightning Brigade." These men, hidden in the woods near Crawfish Springs, managed to decimate several Confederate regiments with their repeating Spencers until, completely outflanked and pressed by the weight of increasing numbers of Confederate troops, they were also forced to join the Federal regiments fleeing through McFarland's Gap to Rossville.[19]

The brief period between ten o'clock and noon brought tragedy for Rosecrans. His whole line, cleverly manipulated during the previous two days, was falling apart. The ubiquitous Charles A. Dana, last described in connection with Grant's Vicksburg operations, was on the Union right when it began to disintegrate. As he ran to the rear, he noticed Wilder's men waiting in the woods for the oncoming Confederate line. Farther into the woods he met the commanding general of the Army of the Cumberland. Rosecrans, as previously mentioned, was a Roman Catholic. Now Dana's sharp eyes noticed Rosecrans' hand making an almost involuntary gesture at his chest. "Hello!" thought Dana. "If the general is crossing himself, we are in a desperate situation."[20]

While Rosecrans, Crittenden, McCook, and assorted division commanders and their troops fled in confusion toward Rossville and Chattanooga, Thomas, still holding the Federal left, gathered elements of his command and a few others for a last stand. On one end of Thomas' line, in the direction of Kelly's Field, various regiments of Palmer's, Reynolds', and Baird's divisions, and several brigades, were still holding against the Confederate onslaught. Included in these units were the 24th, the 79th, the 84th,

[18] Turchin, 115–117, 118.

[19] Dana, 116. *The Ninety-second Illinois Volunteers*, ed. Committee of the Regiment (Freeport, Ill., 1875), 110–112.

[20] Dana, 115–117.

and the 89th Illinois. Standing firm as they did was not easy. The changing direction of the rolling musketry indicated to them that the Federal right had been turned. Furthermore, confusion was the order of the day. Palmer was to recall some time later that the army at his end of the line was so disarranged that it was difficult to know who was the ranking officer on the field. At one point, Palmer was informed that he held that dubious position and his advisors urged that he order a retreat. Palmer, whose placidity rivaled that of Thomas, refused.

It was approximately two o'clock in the afternoon when Thomas finally became aware of the fact that he alone was bearing the responsibility for the existence of the Army of the Cumberland A member of the 7th Illinois Cavalry, watching the loyal Virginian confer with his remaining generals at this time, saw Thomas shake his head "in a way that indicated trouble." History has credited Thomas with innumerable virtues — stubborness, determination, and patience — but the one least mentioned is that of wisdom. He had an acute military eye, sharp enough to tell him that it was impossible to retreat. Gathering what he could in the way of troops, he took position on the western slope of a long and attenuated hill called Snodgrass Hill and Horseshoe Ridge.[21]

There was now little in the way of military organization among the elements which Thomas grouped on Horseshoe Ridge. Many regiments from Brannan's division were there, mostly Ohio troops. There were some from Stanley's brigade of Negley's division, including the 19th Illinois. To the east of Snodgrass House, toward the middle of the ridge, were Charles G. Harker's "Iron Brigade" of Kentucky, Ohio, and Indiana troops, and Hazen's brigade, which included a battalion of the 110th Illinois. Beyond these were the odds and ends of battalions and companies shattered in the day's fighting, and individual soldiers who just thought they had retreated enough.

It was a patchwork line, and Longstreet seemed to sense it. He also was aware, as was Thomas, that the destruction of the new Union right on Horseshoe Ridge would mean the crushing of Thomas' hope of saving the day. Bushrod Johnson and T. C. Hindman were ordered to send their divisions against Brannan's Ohio and Michigan regiments on the western end of the ridge,

[21] Palmer, 183–184. Eby, 107.

and there was a supporting attack along the whole Federal line. General John Basil Turchin was to write later: "The smoke was so dense that only the rows of flashes from their guns marked the situation of the contending line, but they showed that the enemy was gaining ground, and it looked as though our heroes were going to be swept from the ridge." An Illinois soldier, who had rallied with Brannan's division at about two o'clock, wrote afterward of terrible fighting in mid-afternoon, the shortage of ammunition, and of Federal soldiers robbing the dead of their cartridges. In the midst of all, the young soldier added, was the "noblest Roman," Thomas himself, moving here and there, his placid countenance giving no hint of the crisis at hand.[22]

Nevertheless, there most certainly was a crisis. What Thomas had in mind for the three or four hours of remaining daylight is difficult to ascertain. The ammunition along Horseshoe Ridge was becoming uncomfortably scarce. An Ohio battery which had fired almost continuously with double-shotted cannister during most of the afternoon was now low on both ammunition and water to cool the guns. Moreover, the men were becoming fatigued. Fighting without relief against assaults which one historian was to compare to the "billows of the sea . . . which constantly advanced and withdrew," Brannan's men were in no condition to hold their position until sundown.[23]

All that had gone before was a prelude to what was now to happen. Near Dyer House, on the south slope of Horseshoe Ridge, Confederate commanders could be seen in the woods preparing their men for another assault. Now, however, there was another element to the drama. Off to the north, through the patches of trees which surrounded Mulles Spring, could be seen a moving column of blue. Momentarily there was a question in the mind of Thomas as to whether this was a flanking Confederate movement. Minutes proved it to be something else — two brigades of

[22] See maps in Turchin. Quotation comes from *ibid.*, 138. The comment concerning the "noblest Roman" comes from H. G. Davidson to Mrs. Mary Brown, Feb. 19, 1864, Henry G. Davidson Papers, ISHL.

[23] Archibald Gracie, *The Truth About Chickamauga* (Boston, 1911), 406, 247. Gracie, whose father fought in the battle, makes a case for Thomas' having actually been driven from the field. There is a connection between this family and tthe famous Gracie Mansion in New York City.

Union troops marching at the double quick from the region of Rossville.

After Rosecrans had moved his army across the various gaps toward Chattanooga, and during its consolidation on the banks of the Chickamauga, he had provided for such an emergency as that now occurring on Horseshoe Ridge by establishing a reserve corps to the rear of his lines. It consisted of three brigades, all under the command of an outspoken, profane graduate of the war in Missouri, General Gordon Granger. One of these brigades, that commanded by Colonel Dan McCook, was camped east of Rossville. The next two brigades, headed by General Walter C. Whittaker and Colonel John G. Mitchell respectively, but under the divisional command of General James B. Steedman, were located near Red House Bridge, some five miles distant from Thomas' headquarters.

Whittaker's brigade, which along with Mitchell's was important in the outcome of Chickamauga, consisted of six regiments. Two of these were from Ohio, one from Indiana, one from Michigan, and two from Illinois. Of the latter pair, the 96th Illinois was a regiment raised mainly in Jo Daviess and Lake counties and commanded by Colonel Thomas E. Champion of Warren, Illinois. Its experience prior to September of 1863 had been desultory, consisting of minor skirmishes at Spring Hill, Triune, Liberty Gap, and Shelbyville, all in Tennessee.

The 115th Illinois was a different type of unit. The regiment had been organized in 1862 in Christian and adjacent counties as the "Second Preacher's Regiment." Its commanding officer was a slim, straight-backed Methodist minister by the name of Colonel Jesse Hale Moore, who had also served for a time as the president of Quincy College. Moore and his men took to soldiering as if born to it, despite the religious implication in the regiment's beginnings. One finds a good deal of contradiction in the nature of these fighting men. The 115th was a regiment noted for its hymn singing; Thomas himself would occasionally go down to its camp in order to listen. Yet during the Tullahoma campaign, the unit gained a reputation as one of the best foraging regiments in the entire army. Several of its men had been caught indulging in this practice, and Granger, who disliked this sort of thing, had hung them by their thumbs for several days. A few days later other members of the regiment were again caught foraging, the result being that Granger now proposed to have the guilty parties whipped. At this, Moore blew up—he would not allow this to happen, he argued. Rather, he would take the whipping himself. It was at this stage of its private little duel with Granger that the regiment found itself camped near Rossville.[24]

Mitchell's brigade consisted of four regiments, three from Ohio and the 78th Illinois. The last named was raised in Hancock, Adams, and McDonough counties, and was now commanded by Lieutenant Colonel Carter Van Vleck of Macomb, Illinois. Like the Illinois regiments of Whittaker's brigade, the 78th had a record which was not too imposing. Organized originally by Colonel William H. Bennison of Quincy, its members had quarreled so incessantly with their commanding officer that in the middle of 1863 he had resigned and gone home. The point of the quarrel seems to have been a common one for these years of the war: the regiment was equipped with some of the oldest large-bore muskets ever to be dredged out of the Federal armories. Yet it was not alone in this respect. All three of the Illinois regiments in Steedman's division carried the same cumbersome weapons.[25]

Granger's discipline may have been too rigid for many of the men who served under him; nevertheless there were good qualities to his nature. He had the insight and courage to risk the wrath of his superiors. On the morning of September 20, nine o'clock to be exact, both he and his troops heard booming of cannon to the southwest. Ordering his troops to stand ready, Granger waited another hour. Soon columns of retreating troops began to pass, and ambulances, loaded with wounded, rolled by in the direction of Chattanooga. Still no orders came to Granger from Rosecrans. Finally, somewhere between half past ten and eleven o'clock, Granger's instinct told him he could wait no longer. Without orders, strictly on his own initiative, he ordered Steedman to take his two brigades to Thomas. With the 96th Illinois

[24] *Report of the Adjutant General*, V, 446–472. Isaac Henry Clay Royse, *History of the 115th Regiment Illinois Volunteer Infantry* (Terre Haute, Ind., 1900), 95, 289.

[25] Diary of John Batchelor, 27. Royse, 118–124. Royse claims Illinois regiments were armed with Remington .69 muskets. Batchelor merely describes them as large-bore.

leading his column, the latter marched his division at the double quick. A few scattered Confederate cavalrymen were brushed aside without difficulty, and soon the two brigades wound their way past Mulles Spring. This is where Thomas first saw them — a string of blue winding through the woods. Steedman was a man of action. He moved his column parallel to Horseshoe Ridge until the commanding officer of the lead regiment, the 96th Illinois, reached the end of the Union right flank. The division was then ordered to halt, fix bayonets, and face around to the northwest slope of the ridge. When Steedman's men at last reached the top, there were Longstreet's Confederate regiments coming up the other side.[26]

If there was ever a moment of destiny in the war, when the romanticism and tragedy of it all became so intermingled as to be undistinguishable one from another, this was it. There was no way of describing what happened at the instant of the impact between butternut and blue, though a good many have tried it both from retrospect and research. John Palmer, whose division was fighting farther down the line, would write after the conflict that he had never witnessed "such desperate fighting." "The sound of musketry was so incessant and rapid that it was a continuous roar," he added. Turchin, another Illinois general in the line, wrote later: "The shock was irresistible, and the rebel wave stopped, vacillated, and then rolled back down the steep slope which they had so valiantly and successfully climbed but half an hour before." Bushrod Johnson, whose division was involved in that Confederate effort on the southeast slope of the ridge, concluded afterward that Steedman's charge up the ridge also had a psychological effect upon his own men. It took "every energy and zeal" to keep the Confederate retreat down the slope from becoming a rout.[27]

The charge of Whittaker's and Mitchell's brigades was indeed a brilliant one. Just as the latter officer reached the top of the hill, he was knocked momentarily from his horse. Steedman quickly took his place, moving to the head of the 78th Illinois in order to lead it into the fight. Farther down the ridge, the faltering

[26] Charles A. Partridge, "The Ninety-sixth Illinois at Chickamauga," *Transactions 1910*, No. 15 (1912), 72–81.

[27] *Ibid.* Turchin, 138, 139.

115th Illinois was spurred to greater effort by one of its valiant sergeants, who led his own company to the top of the hill, shouting: "Come on, boys, the day is ours." The noncommissioned officer was cut down just a second later.

The fighting for the next three hours was vicious indeed. A veteran of the 96th Illinois was to write afterward that the "noise was deafening," and that twigs from the trees fell in a continuous shower as musket balls cut them down. Casualties for that regiment in the first 30 minutes of the struggle totaled 100; six out of nine of its regimental first sergeants went down, and eight out of nine of its color bearers were killed or wounded. The commanding officer of the 78th was to report later that there was a "fearful contest" between his own regiment and that which opposed it, and those who were there would write of a continuous musketry duel between the 115th Illinois and Bushrod Johnson's Confederates. On occasion the struggle became a toe-to-toe slugging match. One Confederate soldier charged so close to an Illinois regiment that he was grabbed by the collar and pulled into the Union line. Clubbed muskets and bayonets were used as often as not. And there is the gruesome story of an Illinois captain who became engaged in a personal struggle with a Confederate soldier over a rifle. Reaching for his sword, the officer chopped off the hand of his opponent, put it in his pocket, and ran for the safety of his own skirmish line.[28]

In all of this, if there was any period of respite it was only a temporary one. The historian of the 115th was to write years later of an interlude when that regiment was relieved so that it might retire behind the ridge and eat. It was indeed a strange paradox of war — the "Second Preacher's Regiment" of Illinois, chewing solemnly upon raw fat pork and hardtack, relaxing as best they could within the sights and sounds of bloodshed. But then Johnson and Hindman sent the attackers in again, and the 115th returned to the ridge of the hill once more.

There were two more assaults during the day by Hindman's and Johnson's troops, as well as the Carolinian regiments of Joseph B. Kershaw, which occupied a position in front of Snodgrass House, a log cabin to the left of Whittaker's troops. In the

[28] Gracie, 430–432, 135. Royse, 140. Partridge, "The Ninety-sixth Illinois at Chickamauga," 77–80. *Macomb Journal*, Oct. 9, 1863.

last of these, which took place at approximately four o'clock, all four Illinois regiments played important parts. In this assault, Hindman, whose regiments were directly opposed to those of the 96th and 115th Illinois, later claimed that the "bayonet was used, and men also killed and wounded with clubbed musketry." This was the moment when the Confederates came the closest to attaining their objective of the afternoon, that of throwing the Federal right wing from its lodgment on the crest of the ridge.[29]

At the time of the last Confederate effort of the battle, daylight was rapidly disappearing. As the attack grew in intensity, the condition of the various Illinois regiments fighting to maintain their position worsened. The 78th found itself in serious difficulty. Major William L. Broadus of Macomb, Illinois, was killed by a direct musket shot in the head. Its colonel, Carter Van Vleck, was wounded, and had to be carried to the rear. (He would recover, only to die before Atlanta.) All in all, the western Illinois soldiers of the 78th were just about finished for the day. Backtracking before a triumphant Confederate surge, they were gradually forced off the ridge.

The 115th and the 96th Illinois were having similar difficulties. In the first of these regiments, Lieutenant Colonel William Kinman of Jacksonville, who had fought exceedingly bravely during the battle, was killed. The 96th had not only lost its lieutenant colonel, Isaac Clarke of Waukegan, but five lieutenants, two captains, and 220 of its rank and file. If nothing else denotes the intensity of the fight, then the casualties among the senior officers might serve to illustrate that fact. Sharpshooters on both sides had a field day, as the case of all three Illinois regiments losing their lieutenant colonels tends to show.[30]

With the withdrawal of the 78th came the grudging retreat of the 115th and 96th Illinois, and their companion regiments, the 40th Ohio and 84th Indiana. In front of Snodgrass House, Kershaw's troops from the Army of Virginia also had some success. There the 19th Illinois was engaged in what amounted to a personal duel with the attackers for possession of the crest of the ridge. Eventually, however, the Illinois regiment "sullenly gave way, leaving a box of cartridges, from which the 19th was being

[29] Royse, 130–131. Gracie, 56.

[30] *Report of the Adjutant General*, V, 3, 467–468; VI, 246.

supplied, between the contending forces." Ammunition was in exceedingly short supply; all regiments along the line were robbing the cartridge boxes of the dead. What now was called for was an act of courage. An officer of the 19th ran between the contending lines and dragged the box back to the Federal regiment.

The fighting between the 19th Illinois and the oncoming Carolinians was as vicious as at any place along the line. Several months later, when Lieutenant Colonel Alexander Raffen, commanding officer of the regiment, revisited the place where his men had fought, he found the ground covered with papers from the cartridges, and branches which had been shorn from the trees. To him, it looked as if a tornado had swept over the field, and the trees and stumps were "pluged all over with bullits."

Slowly but surely the 19th was pressed back over the brow of the hill. Suddenly, as the regiment began to cave in, the flag of an Ohio regiment swept quickly by on the right. "For an instant," wrote Captain J. G. Campbell, an Illinois officer, "the flags, Rebel and Union, were close enough to mingle folds. . . ." Then the flag bearer of Kershaw's leading regiment was wounded. As he fell, he flipped his flag, fold over staff, to a nearby soldier, who took the banner down the slope of the ridge. Kershaw's assault in front of Snodgrass House had failed.[31]

Down on the right, the 78th, 96th, and 115th Illinois had not been so fortunate. Driven off the ridge to the downside slope of the other side, the Union troops regrouped under the remaining regimental officers. At this point, Steedman, who was as valiant a soldier as any on the field, made his appearance. Running toward the officers of the 78th, he asked why they had retired from the hill. There were no ammunition or officers left, they replied. Steedman then asked the regiment to fix bayonets, step out 20 paces, and rally upon the colors. As a young Macomb, Illinois, soldier was to confide to his diary almost in amazement—"they did." Steedman then asked if he might carry the regimental colors in one last charge, but the color bearer, whose pride had been touched, replied that if the flag was going anywhere, then by his God he would carry it. Up the hill went the 78th again in one last charge.

[31] Gracie, 445–446. Raffen to his family, March 22, 1864, Raffen Papers.

A few minutes later Steedman made an appearance among the ranks of the 115th Illinois. There was only a slight variation of the story. Why had the regiment retreated, Steedman asked. "We are out of ammunition," replied the commanding officer, Colonel Moore; "give us ammunition and we will hold the hill against all odds." "Give them the bayonet then," Steedman ordered, as he picked up the colors of the regiment and actually carried them in the charge. Confirmation of this gallant story was to come in various ways. Granger, who later claimed that he had ordered the bayonet attack, added his own version of what happened following the successful charge by Steedman. "After an ominous silence of a few minutes," he wrote, "the enemy came rushing upon us again. With fixed bayonets our troops gallantly charged them, and drove them back in confusion. Twice more were those charges repeated, and the enemy driven back before darkness brought an end to the battle." [32]

As twilight darkened, Thomas finally gave the order to withdraw from Horseshoe Ridge. It was not without a sense of pride in their accomplishment that the soldiers left their positions, however. Down near Kelly's Field, John Palmer was emotionally affected as he watched his battered division march off the field and to a road "crowded with wounded men and regiments and fragments of regiments. . . ." But if the Confederates were chagrined at their failure to knock Thomas off Horseshoe Ridge in the late afternoon, they must have been infinitely more upset by the last scene in this day-long drama. As Thomas' men were moving slowly behind the lowering curtain of darkness, the last scattered musket shots of the battle were accompanied by the stirring strains of military music. Far to the left, on the back edge of Kelly's Field, a member of the 104th Illinois had started to sing "The Battle Cry of Freedom." Soon his regiment was following along, and then it seemed as if the whole of the withdrawing army had joined in the melody. Somehow the words, written by an Illinoisan, were more than appropriate for the occasion. The Army of the Cumberland, so the promise implied, would once again "rally round the flag." [33]

---

[32] Gracie, 136–137. Royse, 133–134. Diary of John Batchelor, 35. Gracie quotes Granger's battle report on 133.

[33] Palmer, 185–186. "Diary of James Suiter," 55–61. Calkins, 149.

There was no set pattern in the reaction of Illinois soldiers to the defeat at Chickamauga. If there was any similarity in the thoughts of various individuals, it was in a general thanksgiving that they and the army had escaped death and annihilation. "Well, war is a great thing," wrote an eastern Illinois soldier, "and I tell you that amid the terrible fighting of Saturday and Sunday, whenever I had time to think, I had some very serious thoughts about how I was going to get out of that tornado alive." General Palmer, whose role in the battle had been a courageous one, was equally relieved at his own good fortune. "I have enough of war for life," he wrote his wife back in Carlinville, "though I would like to assist in driving the rascals over the mountains from our front." [34]

Palmer's reflections on revenge were echoed elsewhere in the army. "We are *somewhat* whipped but will get over it," wrote Major James A. Connolly of the 123rd Illinois. Wrapped within this general sentiment were thoughts that the army had been disgraced by the conduct of some of its officers. Palmer, for example, told his wife that he was mildly discouraged by the "self indulgence and an unmanly desire to escape danger" which so many officers had shown. Beyond this, however, was a simple desire to strike back at the Confederacy on the part of most ordinary soldiers. Too many good men had died at the hands of the attackers. "I have never come out from any fight with such a sense of loss," an Illinois private was to write. Truly, the army would have to be revenged.[35]

In a way, however, it was as the *Chicago Tribune* argued: Chickamauga had been a defeat for both sides. On one hand, a Federal army had been driven from the field with losses which totaled over 16,000 casualties. The Confederate army, on the other, had won the day with losses of more than 18,000. These casualties came to about 28 per cent of each side.

The largest total regimental loss in the Union army was that of the 22nd Michigan, which was attached to Steedman's division. In three hours of conflict, the regiment had lost 58 killed, 261 wounded, and 70 missing, a total of 389. Among the Illinois

[34] *Three Years in the Army of the Cumberland*, 124. Palmer to his wife, Oct. 10, 1863, Palmer Papers.

[35] *Three Years in the Army of the Cumberland*, 123. Palmer to his wife, Oct. 2, 1863, Palmer Papers. Mary Livermore, 674.

regiments, there were a number which could count great numbers of vacancies in the ranks. In Steedman's division, the 96th had a total loss of 225, or 56.1 per cent of its effective force; the 115th counted losses of 183; and the 78th suffered 156 casualties, the largest number of any regiment in Mitchell's brigade. In Davis' division, the 25th Illinois, a Champaign and Vermilion counties regiment, lost 205 men, or 54.9 per cent of its total effective force; the 21st Illinois counted 238 missing at its first post-battle muster; and the 35th Illinois, also raised principally in Vermilion County, had losses of 150.[36]

Though the casualties in Davis' division were considerable, it must be remembered that they were stretched over 36 hours of fighting. If intensity of battle were determined by the largest number of casualties suffered in the shortest time, the 22nd Illinois in Walworth's unfortunate brigade would have led all others from the Prairie State in that respect. In fighting on the Federal right flank, this regiment lost 97 men in ten minutes. All in all, however, it was the men of Steedman's division who were involved in the sternest test of the day. In line of battle only three hours, the ten regiments and two batteries of the division lost 1,787 men, about half of the effectives on its muster rolls. This meant that the price which Steedman paid for saving the Army of the Cumberland averaged over 500 men an hour.[37]

Chickamauga had its own special meaning for the ordinary soldiers of both armies, and it came to have further implications for both Rosecrans and Bragg. With all of the possibilities of what might have been for both armies, and with the terrible cost for both sides, Chickamauga was a reaffirmation of the original meaning of the words "river of death." But it was a river flowing with the intermingled blood of almost 28,500 killed and wounded, not to mention the missing. It is little wonder, then, that when the nation went to war with Spain in 1898, one of its first training camps was so located as to symbolize the increasing unity of the nation. Built near Chattanooga to house recruits from all parts of the nation, it was called Camp Chickamauga.

---

[36] *Chicago Tribune*, Sept. 24, 1863. Fox, 441. Turchin, 237–238.

[37] Eddy, I, 313. Royse, 146–147. See Turchin's listing of casualties, 233–240.

CHAPTER VIII

Revenge for Chickamauga

Thomas' daring defense at Horseshoe Ridge served, in time, a dual purpose. Its immediate effect was to lift the morale of the shattered Army of the Cumberland; if the rebels had won a victory, they were made to pay for it. In the long run, Thomas had saved the army. Holding as he did until sundown, he had so battered Bragg's army that it was unable to follow closely its beaten foe. As the days rolled by, Rosecrans regrouped his army and built a defensible line around Chattanooga. The Army of the Cumberland would fight another day.

Chattanooga quickly became a Union Vicksburg, a fortress upon a river. Residences near the outskirts of the city were made into blockhouses, rifle pits were dug in a great arc from river bank to river bank, and long lines of trenches served to create an impregnable establishment. Once this was done, the troops themselves settled to the task of providing for themselves. Huts, called "chebangs," were constructed from notched logs and piled dirt; these were filled with tables, chairs, and benches appropriated from nearby homes, or constructed by ingenious soldiers. In such homes the troops shared their mess, mail, and scraps of gossip which were passed from regiment to regiment. Such a daily routine was interestingly described in the well-kept diary of Captain T. D. Kyger of the 73rd Illinois: "Steadman is now absent; Colonel Sherman, of the 88th Illinois, now commands the brigade. Wrote during the day. Walter Scott came over from the convalescent camp. He reports Sergeant Lewis – color bearer – getting along well. Loud cheering in camp over the news from the election in Ohio; Vallandigham is said to be seventy thousand votes behind Brough. News good from Pennsylvania and Iowa."[1]

If Rosecrans had built a defense sufficient to keep the enemy out of Chattanooga, the Confederates had only to take advantage of natural circumstances in order to keep the Union army in. To the northeast was nothing – only another Union army under the command of A. E. Burnside, besieged at Knoxville. To the north was a river and many miles of mountains which could be passed by individuals but not by an army. To the south and southwest were more mountains, Raccoon and Lookout, and on the east a long attenuated slope called Missionary Ridge. And to the south also was the place from which the Federal army had fled in late September – Chickamauga.

As October came, Bragg began to develop the notion that he could destroy the Army of the Cumberland by merely holding it in Chattanooga and allowing it to fall of its own weight. By his positions on Lookout Mountain and Missionary Ridge, and with the geographical barriers which lay to the north and west, Rosecrans' men were stranded. Little in the way of food and supplies could be brought in, not nearly enough to feed and equip the number of men listed on the muster rolls of the Army of the Cumberland. Furthermore, winter was coming on, which would compound the situation Rosecrans was facing.

It was a perilous time, and the ordinary soldier of the besieged army could sense it. The string of lights flickering on the mountains to the southwest, like jewels according to the later recollections of a member of the 34th Illinois, gave indication of the continued presence of a determined enemy. And, as the days rolled by, the decreasing daily rations which were handed out to him gave notice of the inability of the commanding general to solve the supply situation created by the siege. From a three-quarter ration the allowance fell to a half and then to a quarter. Much of the food which was handed out was spoiled or of poor quality. Members of the 36th Illinois, for example, were given a daily allowance of poor-quality coffee, and bread which was

[1] Newlin, 260.

hard and green with mold. Only the coffee had any value. It could be boiled once, and then sold to more inexperienced troopers.[2]

By the middle of October, the business of survival became a touchy one. There was an implication in the diminishing rations that each soldier would have to forage and make do for himself. The men of several Illinois regiments could be seen searching along the roads for stray kernels of corn or moldy pieces of hardtack. Another Illinois soldier reported later that he had been reduced to two meals a day, each one a solitary hard cracker. Other Illinois regiments, particularly the 19th Illinois, devised their own methods of supplementing this sparse diet. Camped near a grove of oak trees, the soldiers of this Chicago regiment gathered acorns every day, and roasted them until edible. The 104th Illinois was not quite so fortunate. The nearest oak trees were a mile or so into the woods, and behind the Confederate pickets. Every night one of the members of the regiment would crawl into the dark, past the enemy sentries, and to the grove of trees. There he would fill his pockets with acorns and return the way he had come.

For the individual soldier, the amount of food he was able to consume during the siege depended greatly upon his own luck or that of his regiment. The 59th Illinois, a veteran regiment which learned the art of foraging in the Missouri hills, seems to have survived comparatively well. As with other Illinois regiments, the ration in the 59th fell to two or three hard crackers a day, but always with some meat, the latter attained by the superb food-gathering ability of forage details. Other regiments, because of their dislike of the product in easier days, had laid by an ample supply of dessicated vegetables. Now these compressed bricks of vegetable leaves found large numbers of takers. And there were occasional windfalls for certain regiments. A captain of the 104th Illinois was able to write a month later, and with a humor mellowed by recollection, that there was a time during the siege when his regiment had come into possession of an ox. The whole animal, as he described it, was eaten. The heart was skinned and boiled, and made a "splendid feast for the lucky mess that could get hold of it. . . ." But, he concluded, there were parts of that

[2] Payne, 79. Bennett and Haigh, 509.

unfortunate beast which he could not eat, particularly that "liberal slice of ox-lung cooked after the most approved fashion."[3]

Past the middle of October, affairs moved from bad to worse. Guards were placed near the horses and mules so that troops could not steal from the feed bags of the animals, and it was reported that some soldiers were skinning and eating rats. Yet in all of this there remained a surprising degree of humor among the men of the Army of the Cumberland. Captain William Strawn of the 104th Illinois, communicating with a friend back in Illinois, wrote how a fatigue party in his regiment had been broken out early on one rainy morning without anything to eat. The purpose of the detail was to throw earthworks up before the regimental encampment. It was a sullen line of soldiers who stood in line, their ponchos dripping with moisture. The young officer in charge of the detachment, sensing the discontent of the men, began to make a speech "with all the star and stripe flourishes." The troops patiently waited this out, but at the conclusion of the remarks one of them shouted: "Damn your patriotism, give us some hard-tack." The lieutenant, somewhat abashed by the emotionalism in the outburst, stepped back and into a deep rifle pit filled with water. There was a "universal roar of laughter in the party," and the men set to work "cheerily."[4]

Bragg's optimism, born first from the hope that Rosecrans would surrender, and kept alive by the belief that the Union commander would at least evacuate Chattanooga, was doomed to disappointment. The Federal grasp upon the city, achieved through such hard campaigning, was not going to be relinquished so easily. The administration, anxious to save Rosecrans, took immediate steps to help the Army of the Cumberland. Sherman moved toward Chattanooga from the Mississippi with four divisions. Parts of the XI and XII corps of the Army of the Potomac were detached from Virginia in the days following the debacle at Chickamauga and sent westward under General Joe Hooker, who had been in virtual retirement since his defeat at Chancellorsville. In mid-October, Grant, met by Secretary of War Stanton in

---

[3] Benjamin Taylor, *Pictures of Life in Camp and Field* (2nd ed., Chicago, 1875), 147. Calkins, 159–160. Herr, 177. *Three Years with Grant*, 138. Capt. William Strawn to Newton Bateman, Nov. 12, 1863, Bateman Papers.

[4] *Ibid.*

Indianapolis, was given command of all Union operations west of the Alleghenies, with the exception of Nathaniel P. Banks's department in Louisiana. The response of the great Illinois general was twofold: first, he headed straight for Chattanooga in order to see firsthand the condition of the army there; second, he sent a telegram ahead, relieving Rosecrans from his command. The place of that unfortunate general was given to Thomas, now and forever to be called the "Rock of Chickamauga."[5]

The removal of Rosecrans, the appointment of Thomas, and the succession of Grant all received their particular attentions from the soldiers of Illinois serving in the Army of the Cumberland. For Rosecrans, an extraordinarily popular man with the common private, there was a great deal of sympathy. The soldier from Illinois, for instance, still had the "utmost confidence" in the man even if the administration didn't, but then he could understand that too. If Rosecrans had to go, the soldier could think of no better commanders than Grant and Thomas. "If we cant have Rosey, Grant is our next choice," wrote a veteran campaigner of the 34th Illinois.[6]

Among officers of high rank, the appointment of Thomas was well received. That general had steadily gained a universal affection in the army by reason of his gentle stolidity and sincerity of purpose. Henry Villard, who saw a great deal of Thomas during the war, described his character as being greatly different from those of other general officers. "He never made the least effort for personal preferment," wrote Villard, "and rather shunned than sought higher command, from modest doubts of his competency and consequent shrinking from great responsibilities." It was General John Palmer who, in his own reaction to Thomas, summarized the thoughts of an army, however. "I did not as you know admire Rosecrans," he wrote to his wife in Carlinville, Illinois, "but . . . in his fall he had my sincere sympathies. . . . General Thomas his successor is an upright honorable man. So honest that if he were to censure me I should know he thought it deserving. He is not brilliant but I think his judgment sound."[7]

[5] Grant, II, 26.

[6] Newlin, 256. E. W. Payne to Miss Kim Hudson, Oct. 22, 1863, Edwin W. Payne Papers.

[7] Villard, II, 214. Palmer to his wife, Oct. 20, 1863, Palmer Papers.

On October 20 Grant reached Nashville on his way to Chattanooga. There he was met by Andrew Johnson, the military governor of Tennessee. To the assembled throng Johnson gave a speech of welcome which, as Grant pointed out later, "was by no means his maiden effort." "It was long," added the general in his memoirs," and I was in torture while he was delivering it, fearing something would be expected from me in response." Escaping Johnson, Grant arrived in Stevenson, Alabama, on the following day. There he met Rosecrans, and discussed the situation of the army under siege at Chattanooga. The departing general, according to Grant, offered some very good suggestions. "My only wonder," concluded the latter, "was that he had not carried them out."

By October 23 Grant was in Chattanooga. A man of action, he rode out the following day on a tour of the Union line with Thomas and General W. F. "Baldy" Smith, the latter the chief engineer of the newly created Military Division of the Mississippi. Crossing the Tennessee, the trio rode to the edge of the Federal line near Brown's Ferry. Here Thomas had reconnoitered the enemy line well. During the previous week, Captain James T. McNeil of the 85th Illinois, operating on detached duty, had crossed the river on four successive nights and examined the Confederate position in detail. That he was captured on his fifth attempt was of some importance to McNeil, of course; but by that time he had completed the duty assigned to him. The information which his excursions provided, plus all of the intelligence provided by Thomas and Smith, allowed Grant to reach a decision that very night. He ordered that an attempt be prepared to open a new route of supply to Chattanooga.[8]

Two days later, troops of Hooker's relieving force, O. O. Howard's XI Corps, which were located downriver at Bridgeport, moved secretly across the Tennessee. There they were joined by Cruft's division of the Army of the Cumberland. While this force was marching upstream, early on October 27 a brigade of picked soldiers under the command of General W. B. Hazen drifted by the watching eyes of the 34th Illinois camped at Moccasin Point,

[8] Grant, II, 27–28, 31–32. Henry J. Aten, *History of the Eighty-fifth Regiment,* comp. and pub. under the auspices of the Regimental Association (Hiawatha, Kan., 1901), 123–124. McNeil came from Astoria, Illinois.

and made a landing just below Brown's Ferry. Turchin, that redoubtable Russian from Illinois, then led a brigade across the river at Brown's Ford. Hooker, meanwhile, had reached Wauhatchie and the south bank of the river. There a pontoon bridge was put over, and a new supply route for the Army of the Cumberland was now in existence. On October 30 the steamboat *Chattanooga*, which had been built by Smith's engineers, arrived at Kelly's Ford loaded with 40,000 rations and tons of forage. By nightfall the welcomed food was on its way by wagon over the completed "cracker" line, as the soldiers were ready to call the method by which their supply of hardtack was increased.

The continued buildup of Federal forces in the Chattanooga area eventually gave Grant a grand army of considerable proportions. It consisted of Thomas' of the Cumberland, which had been reorganized since Chickamauga into two corps: the IV Corps (formerly the XX and XXI corps), commanded by General Gordon Granger, and the XIV Corps, commanded by General John Palmer. Portions of Sherman's Army of the Tennessee were also brought near to Chattanooga; these included three divisions of the XV Corps, commanded by Osterhaus, Hugh B. Ewing, and Morgan L. Smith, and a division of the XVII Corps, commanded by John E. Smith. The two latter officers both came from Illinois, the former from Bloomington and the latter from Galena. John E. Smith, the son of an officer in the Napoleonic wars, was a jeweler in Galena when the war broke out. Organizing the 45th Illinois, that tough regiment whose banner was the first to fly from the Vicksburg courthouse, he had risen rapidly in the Army of the Tennessee.[9]

From the Army of the Potomac had come two divisions of the XI Corps, under the command of O. O. Howard, and a division of the XII Corps, under the command of a six-and-a-half-foot tough Pennsylvanian by the name of John W. Geary. The over-all command of the eastern troops was in the hands of the aforementioned Hooker.

Illinois troops, as one would suppose, made up a substantial part of this grand army. The IV and XIV corps of the Army of the Cumberland contained no fewer than 40 regiments of infantry

[9] Grant, II, 34–48. *Historical Encyclopedia of Illinois*, ed. Newton Bateman and Paul Selby (Chicago, 1900), 487.

from that state, plus a significant number of artillery and cavalry units. Sherman, likewise, brought with him a number of Illinois infantry regiments from the Vicksburg area, including such familiar organizations as the 13th, of Chickasaw Bayou fame; the 55th, which had fought so well as Shiloh; and the 93rd, which saw hard service at Champion's Hill. Also included among Sherman's men were those of the 56th Illinois, a luckless southern Illinois regiment which, two years later, would lose over 200 of its members in a shipwreck off Cape Hatteras. Now, however, it was only one of the more than 75 Illinois regiments under Grant's command at Chattanooga. Even General Carl Schurz's Third Division of the XI Corps, under Hooker, included an Illinois regiment. It was the 82nd Illinois, raised originally by Colonel Fred Hecker in Cook County, which had taken part in the battle of Gettysburg only a few months before.[10]

Grant's problems in raising the siege of Chattanooga were compounded by the unfortunate situation which existed at Knoxville. There, where a smaller Federal army under Burnside was also under siege, conditions were not really serious, but they could become so. Burnside was to have an effect far out of proportion to his importance upon the strategy of both Bragg and Grant. The latter was naturally influenced by Burnside's condition. And Bragg, thinking too much of the situation in east Tennessee, was to make a mortal mistake by detaching Longstreet's veterans from the besieging army at Chattanooga and sending them to assist in the siege at Knoxville. As he was to discover in due time, he would have found use for those sturdy fighters.

The first difficulty which faced Grant, however, was that of overcoming the Confederate grasp on Chattanooga. It was, without a doubt, a firm one. Missionary Ridge, a sloping formation some 300 to 400 feet high and covered with brush and fallen trees, offered a natural fortification to the east and south. Bragg had complemented its natural resources for defense by a series of trenches at regular intervals, interspersed with many rifle pits. At the top of the ridge were a considerable number of cannon, many of which had been captured at Chickamauga. Bragg's main forces manned these positions.

To the west of Missionary Ridge was Lookout Mountain. About

[10] Taylor, 57–58. Turchin, 215–234.

1,000 feet above the valley floor, Lookout dropped almost straight down to the level of the river below. Not every side was that precipitous, however, and it was up the gentler slopes which any attack would have to come. Because of the natural defensibility of the place, and the departure of Longstreet from other positions, Bragg had cut the Confederate garrison there, leaving Major General Carter Y. Stevenson in command of six brigades. Still, the taking of Lookout Mountain would not necessarily be easy. Federal troops would have to climb a steep mountainside against some of the best sharpshooters who had ever borne arms on American soil.[11]

It was on November 23 that Grant made his first move to break the Confederate hold on Chattanooga after hearing reports of Confederate withdrawals. East of the city, where the river swung back and forth in an S-shaped loop, was a solitary rise of ground called Orchard Knob. Its strategic value was small, except for the fact that the Confederate positions there had to be cleared before any advance could be made on Missionary Ridge. Thomas moved Granger's corps — two divisions commanded by Wood, who was to make the attack — and Sheridan into formation as if he were conducting another of the parade reviews so often held in the previous month. This time, however, the troops didn't stop. Wood's men, supported by Sheridan, rammed ahead until they had swept the enemy from Orchard Knob. In the years which followed, Thomas' seizure of Orchard Knob seemed only a minor skirmish when compared to larger and more significant battles, but it cost Wood 190 killed and wounded. However, it also provided an advance Federal position for the attacks to come.

On November 24, at two o'clock in the morning, General Giles A. Smith was given the delicate task of leading Sherman's divisions across the Tennessee. Smith was a quick-thinking Illinois officer, whose position in the months prior to his appointment in the army was that of an innkeeper in Bloomington, Illinois. Truly, it was strange how the art of war found willing students from such varied backgrounds. Smith maneuvered his 116 boats loaded with men across the river, surprised the Confederate pickets there, and commenced to build his boats into a bridge. Within several hours he

[11] Grant, II, 70. Boatner, 144–145. *Official Records*, Ser. I, Vol. XXXI, Pt. 2, 664.

had his pontoons linked, and Sherman's men began to cross the river.

Once across the Tennessee, Sherman formed his troops for the assault upon the end of Missionary Ridge. Morgan Smith's division was placed on the left, John E. Smith's division was stationed in the center, and Hugh Ewing's division was placed slightly to the right. Throwing out a heavy skirmish line, the columns moved ahead quickly, managing to throw three brigades upon the northern tip of the ridge before being discovered, but was stopped by an unexpected ravine at Tunnel Hill. Sherman entrenched and readied for the next day.

While Sherman had been carrying out his duties on the eastern end of the Union line, Hooker was busy in the west. That commander now had an odd assortment of divisions under his control. Osterhaus' division of the XV Corps, which contained the 13th Illinois, had been unable to cross with Sherman due to a weakening of the pontoon bridge, and was therefore assigned to Hooker. Besides retaining control of John W. Geary's division of the XII Corps, "Fighting Joe" also had Charles Cruft's division of the XIV Corps, which consisted of the brigades of Whittaker and Grose. The last-named officer, a stout fighter from Ohio, commanded six regiments, three of which were from Illinois. One of Whittaker's regiments was from Illinois. Thus it was that the admixture of men under Hooker's command contained regiments from the three major Union armies, those of the Cumberland, the Tennessee, and the Potomac.[12]

The four Illinois regiments which made up part of Cruft's division were organizations which had substantial reputations. In Grose's brigade were the 59th, Philip S. Post's old regiment from western Illinois; the 75th, a Whiteside and Lee counties regiment, commanded by Colonel John Bennett; and the 84th, another western Illinois regiment, commanded by Colonel Louis Waters. In the brigade of W. C. Whittaker, one of the staunch rescuers of Thomas at Horseshoe Ridge, was the 96th, a Jo Daviess and Lake counties regiment, under Colonel Thomas E. Champion.

[12] Grant, II, 63–76. G. A. Smith was wounded on the afternoon of November 24. The information concerning Smith's position as an innkeeper comes from *Historical Encyclopedia of Illinois*, 486. *Official Records*, Ser. I, Vol. XXXI, Pt. 2, 94, 188–189, 251, 314–315.

The morning of November 24 was, as one soldier was to remember it, a real "Scottish morning," the air being "dim with mist." At the same moment that Sherman was getting his divisions across the river farther to the east, Hooker was marching Geary's division of eastern troops and Whittaker's brigade of Cumberlanders across the Wauhatchie ford of Lookout Creek. Here there was some exchange of musketry with Confederate pickets, which roused Cheatham's men on the summit of the mountain. Coming quickly down the slopes, the Confederates filled the rifle pits near the base. By eleven o'clock the defenders faced two divisions of Union troops, those of Cruft and Geary. Now Hooker gave the signal for the attack to begin.[13]

As the Federal charge up Lookout Mountain developed impetus, an unbroken line of troops from the 59th, 75th, and 84th Illinois, all of Grose's brigade, surged to the front. Enemy musketry which, under different circumstances, might have proved difficult, today was not. The greatest problem which faced the advancing regiments was that of the climb itself—a step-by-step rigorous advance through gullies and ravines, and over fallen trees and rocks. This, coupled with the natural tension of the attack, could have been accomplished only by a young army.

By late afternoon Hooker had carried the enemy positions, and was able to report that his hold upon the mountain was impregnable, although he was not yet on the crest. Grant took no chances, however, and sent William Carlin's First Brigade of the First Division, XIV Corps, for the purpose of reinforcing Hooker against a possible enemy counterattack. Carlin's movement, in which Hapeman's 104th Illinois was engaged, experienced some heavy fighting near Craven House.[14]

The taking of most of Lookout Mountain, except the very crest, was accomplished in a surprisingly easy manner. Yet, along with Thomas' stand at Chickamauga, it ranks as one of the thrilling moments of the war. Soldiers of the Army of the Cumberland standing in line far below upon Orchard Knob could hear the sounds of artillery and musketry as they echoed down through the falling mist. Only occasionally, as the fog momentarily rose,

[13] *Ibid.*, 154–155. Lathrop, 233. Taylor, 39, 43. Dodge, 116.

[14] Calkins, 172. Craven House was often referred to by the troops as the "white house." *Official Records*, Ser. I, Vol. XXXI, Pt. 1, 462–463, 466–467.

could the men below see the flashes of light from the guns of the advancing troops. In the ranks of the 123rd Illinois most of the men pessimistically viewed the charge up the mountain as a "forlorn hope" and thought that it would not be successful. Then, for one heart-stopping instant, the colors of a Federal regiment were seen waving from near Craven House. The band of the 123rd immediately broke out in a quickstep version of "Hail to the Chief," and in the ranks of the Illinois regiment not a few were emotionally affected. Far to the right of the Federal line, the "awful glory of the spectacle" was similarly revealed to the men of the 34th Illinois. The fog near that side of Lookout had completely blown away, revealing the brilliant regimental colors of the 13th and 75th Illinois. And, when the sun went down and dusk fell over the mountain, the long string of campfires of the Federal troops, glowing like lava from an active volcano, indicated to an entire Union army the success of Hooker's men.[15]

While his troops bedded down for the night, Grant began the work which only a commanding general of vast armies must do. Recognizing the President's concern over Chattanooga, he sent a message to Washington which told of Hooker's achievement, with assurances that the fight was progressing "favorably." Later, at midnight, he telegraphed Burnside at Knoxville, encouraging that general to hold on as long as possible. Then orders of the coming attack upon Missionary Ridge were written. Sherman and Hooker were ordered to move at daylight; Thomas was instructed to hold his corps on the plains near Orchard Knob until the other generals had accomplished their missions on the Confederate flanks.

In detail, Grant's plans for the morning of November 25 were deceptively simple. Hooker's divisions were to continue moving toward Rossville Gap, which amounted to nothing less than an assault upon the enemy left. Sherman's veterans from the Army of the Tennessee, given the choice plum of the battle, were asked to work southward past Tunnel Hill and against the main Confederate works. Thomas' Cumberlanders, held in abeyance until the completion of the first two assignments, would then advance up the center of Missionary Ridge. It must have seemed obvious to

[15] *Three Years in the Army of the Cumberland,* 150–159. Payne, 87.

Thomas that Grant greatly distrusted the fighting ability of the IV and XIV corps. Even the simplest private in the Army of the Cumberland would realize that few Confederates would remain in the center of Missionary Ridge if their army were outflanked both on the left and the right.[16]

There are intangibles in war, however, and if Sherman didn't know it at the beginning of this long day, he was about to find it out. In the assault of November 24, when his XV Corps had moved up the northern slopes of Missionary Ridge, it had been halted before nightfall by a previously unknown fact of geography. Separating the Union troops from the main part of the ridge was a low ravine, or depression, further enhanced as a defensible position by a wagon road and a railroad tunnel. Bragg had added to these natural advantages three and a half parallel lines of entrenchments. The first of these was along the base, near the depression, the second was halfway up the slope, and the third was along the ridge. Along the last was a formidable collection of artillery, appropriately depressed so as to rake Sherman's troops as they advanced down the detached hill. Nor was there a lack of troops to man these positions. Bragg had massed no fewer than 14 brigades at this end of the ridge.

Sherman's attack began as scheduled, at dawn. Leaving the brigades of J. A. J. Lightburn, J. I. Alexander, and Joseph R. Cockerill to hold the hill taken the day before, he sent Morgan L. Smith's division along the east side of Missionary Ridge. Along the western slope he sent a brigade commanded by Colonel John M. Loomis of Chicago, and supported by two brigades from John E. Smith's division. Between the troops of Loomis and Morgan L. Smith moved Ewing's division, including the brigade of General John M. Corse.[17]

These advancing units were made up to a large extent of Illinois regiments, and in many instances it was Illinois soldiers who took the lead. Loomis' brigade, for instance, consisted of several Indiana regiments plus the 26th and 90th Illinois, the former being Loomis' own regiment. The 26th, from scattered counties in central Illinois, was a low-numbered regiment which had had

---

[16] Grant, II, 73–76. *Official Records*, Ser. I, Vol. XXXI, Pt. 2, 33–34.

[17] *Report of the Adjutant General*, III, 172; V, 643. *Official Records*, Ser. I, Vol. XXXI, Pt. 2, 572–573. Boatner, 145.

surprisingly little battle experience by November of 1863 in comparison to other veteran regiments. The 90th, a regiment from Cook and Will counties, had been tested at Vicksburg, but beyond that had seen very little action.

John E. Smith's two brigades, which advanced to Loomis' rear, were also well stocked with Illinois regiments. The 56th, which would lose so many men off Cape Hatteras, the 63rd, led by Colonel Joseph McCown of Camargo, Illinois, and the 93rd, a hard-fighting regiment from Bureau and Stephenson counties, were part of the line moving along the west side of the ridge.

Corse's brigade, which experienced the most vicious fighting of the day at the center of Sherman's line, contained a number of Illinois troops. Two regiments, in particular, were heavily engaged in the early-morning hours. The first of these was the 40th Illinois, a Hamilton, Wayne, and Clay counties regiment, commanded by Lieutenant Colonel Rigdon S. Barnhill of Fairfield. These men had been well tested on the field at Shiloh and in the Vicksburg campaign. The second was the 103rd Illinois, a regiment almost wholly raised in Fulton County and commanded by Colonel Willard A. Dickerman of Liverpool, Illinois. The 103rd had participated in the Vicksburg campaign, but had done little else.

On Sherman's left, where Morgan L. Smith's division advanced, were three more Illinois regiments. They were the 55th, a cantankerous, hard-fighting regiment from northern Illinois, best known for its great stand at Shiloh; the 116th, a Macon and Christian counties regiment under the command of Colonel Nathan Tupper of Decatur; and the 127th, a comparatively new regiment from Kane and Kendall counties, commanded by Lieutenant Colonel Frank S. Curtiss of Chicago. Though carrying high numbers, the last two regiments had taken part in the Arkansas Post and Vicksburg campaigns.[18]

As Sherman's attack on the morning of November 25 developed, it was Morgan L. Smith's troops who gained the initial success of the day. Carrying their advance up a more gentle slope, they managed to move to a position near the railroad cut on that side of the ridge. Corse, attacking at the center, was to experience much greater difficulties, however. Gaining a position on high

[18] Taylor, 57–58. *Report of the Adjutant General*, II, 387.

ground in its initial assault, the brigade, led by Captain William Walsh and his company from the 103rd Illinois, got to within 50 feet of the Confederate works before it was thrown back. Walsh, who came from Fairview, Illinois, was killed, and the Federal troops were driven back down the slope. A second assault, brought to bear by the 40th Illinois, actually carried into the enemy positions, but was unable to hold. Then Corse himself was badly wounded. The viciousness of this two-hour battle on Sherman's end of the ridge is shown by the casualties suffered by the 103rd Illinois. Mustering 237 men on the morning of November 24, the regiment was reduced in number to 148 by the next evening.[19]

Loomis, meanwhile, had only fair results from his attack on the Confederate left. Since Corse's attack was the most significant, and since the crest of the ridge had to be taken before the flanking movements could succeed, Loomis could advance only so far. Still, he ran into hard fighting. Both Illinois regiments in his command were hit hard by casualties. Lieutenant Colonel Robert A. Gilmore of Chicago, the ranking officer of the 26th, and three of his subordinates were killed or wounded. The 90th Illinois was even harder hit. Its popular colonel, Timothy O'Meara, was killed almost immediately; his successor, Lieutenant Colonel Owen Stewart of Chicago, was wounded; and three other officers of the regiment were killed or wounded. The 93rd Illinois, fighting in one of Smith's supporting brigades, also suffered heavy casualties as well as the loss of its commanding officer, Colonel Holden Putnam of Freeport.

Much of the Federal history of Missionary Ridge is written about the successful events which occurred late in the afternoon of November 25. Yet in the morning and early afternoon of that same day, Sherman's men of the XV Corps had about all they could really want in the way of fighting. Opposed by the dogged Confederate veterans of Pat Cleburne, they got into the hardest conflict many of them were ever to see. Pinned down by accurate fire which increased as Cleburne brought up regiment after regiment in support, Corse's and Loomis' men could do very little. The 90th Illinois, for instance, was brought under a most galling fire. In all of this there was sufficient bravery, though not enough to overcome the fact of impossible odds. Colonel Putnam of the

[19] *Ibid.*, V, 643. Grant, II, 76–80.

93rd Illinois, for example, was cut down while waving the regimental colors before his men in an attempt to get them to continue their advance. All was useless, however, and Sherman's black-hatted veterans of the Vicksburg campaign began to comprehend some of the difficulties which had faced the Army of the Cumberland for some time.[20]

From his position on Orchard Knob, Grant watched the growing failure of Sherman's assault with increasing apprehension. Seeing columns of Confederate regiments massing to the assistance of Cleburne at the north end of the ridge, he sent Howard's two divisions from the XI Corps to assist on the Federal left. Turning then to Thomas, he directed that general to prepare his corps for a movement upon the Confederate center. By shortly after three o'clock the Army of the Cumberland was ready to advance.

At the moment when Grant directed Thomas to prepare for an attack upon Missionary Ridge, the condition of the Federal line presented a balance of achievements and failures. Hooker had occupied the crest of Lookout Mountain, evacuated by the Confederates, and had moved a regiment into Rossville Gap. Detained in crossing Chattanooga Creek longer than anticipated, he was now moving Cruft's division, consisting principally of Illinois troops, on Grant's right along the ridge. Osterhaus' division, which contained the 13th Illinois, marched to the left of Cruft, and Geary's veterans of the Army of the Potomac moved to the right. On the far left of Grant's grand army, Sherman was still struggling valiantly to break Cleburne's hold on that end of Missionary Ridge, with little success. In the center, four divisions of Thomas' troops prepared for a movement upon the first line of Confederate rifle pits. From left to right their commanders were Baird, Wood, Sheridan, and R. W. Johnson.

It was sometime between three and four o'clock in the afternoon when the six cannon shot signifying the beginning of Thomas' assault were fired. At the first loud boom, the men of the Army of the Cumberland, according to one Illinois officer, began to fall in and dress without command. By the time the fifth report was heard, the men were moving forward without command.

---

[20] *Report of the Adjutant General*, II, 387; V, 312. *Official Records*, Ser. I, Vol. XXXI, Pt. 2, 573–576.

When the sound of the sixth shot echoed along the ridge, the bands began to play and the colors of each regiment were unfurled. There were no other sensations, wrote that officer of the 123rd Illinois, but that of enthusiasm.[21]

No sooner had the assaulting troops left their forward positions than the Confederates opened fire. Union artillery now opened a barrage along the ridge in support of the advancing line of battle, and one of the first shots to be fired exploded an enemy caisson, sending a sheet of flame into the air. This brought a cheer from the Federal soldiers, who, now halfway to the Confederate rifle pits at the base of the ridge, increased their pace to the double quick. Then, in almost an instant, another great cheer swept along the length of Wood's and Sheridan's divisions. The blue line had reached the enemy trenches.

This was the point at which Grant had asked the advancing divisions to halt and reorganize. But between orders and their execution there are often unforeseen developments. From his position atop Orchard Knob, Grant could see the long blue line enter the Confederate trenches and appear immediately on the other side. As an Illinois officer was to write years later, flag bearers began to vie with each other in order to keep their colors in the lead, and their comrades were in happy pursuit. Some flag bearers moved so fast that they became exhausted and fell to the ground, but when this happened the substitute bearer picked up the banner and waved it challengingly at his regiment. It was a picture which defied reality: the Army of the Cumberland seemed to be taking matters into its own hands.

A hundred years later, it is still not easy to explain the magnificent events of that November day. Among the veterans themselves, it became almost a legend that a mistaken interpretation by Sheridan's division of a gesture of its commander led the soldiers to charge beyond the extent of their orders. That colorful little Irishman had been a target for enemy sharpshooters and cannoneers from the moment the attack started. Now, as he paused with his troops near the base of the ridge, he took a flask of whiskey from his pocket and waved it jauntily at his tormentors. This

[21] *Ibid.*, 34–35. Grant, II, 77–83. *Three Years in the Army of the Cumberland*, 150–159.

action, some have written, was interpreted by the troops as a command to continue the attack beyond the trenches.[22]

Beyond the legend, however, there is something else. The Army of the Cumberland was an exasperated and frustrated giant, scorned by Grant in his selections for the main assaults upon the ridge. Now, as the burden of this eventful day fell upon its soldiers, they struck with a vengeful fury. Putting Sheridan's whiskey story where it belongs, it is much easier to believe the historian of the 73rd Illinois when he tells the story of that regiment's attack upon the Confederate trenches. Having stopped momentarily to await further orders, the regiment was approached by Sheridan himself, who said: "I know you; fix bayonets and go ahead." Down the line, in Johnson's division, General Carlin had the same idea. Riding through the ranks of the 104th Illinois, he shouted to the troops of his brigade: "Boys, I don't want you to stop until we reach the top of that hill. Forward!" It was then that the whole line, its flag bearers waving their banners in front as if to tantalize the men, swept forward in one great wave.

What followed constituted one of the great moments of the war. Carlin's brigade, fighting on the right end of Thomas' line, moved rapidly up the slope in the face of rigorous enemy fire. The 104th Illinois, flanked by two Indiana regiments, scrambled frantically behind its flag bearer as he ran at full tilt over fallen logs and through high brush. As the soldiers of this Illinois regiment reached the halfway point of the climb, they could hear the Confederate officers above them encouraging their own men to stay in line. Above the shouting and the sound of rolling musketry could be heard cries of "Chickamauga, Chickamauga" from up and down the line of Union soldiers. A solitary taunting shout at first, it soon became a chant, answered feebly and infrequently by the cry of "Bull Run" from above. Not even the wounding of the 104th's most popular junior officer, Lieutenant Orrin S. Davison of Evans, Illinois, could stop the advance of that regiment. Davison, who would die a month later from his injuries, fell to one knee and shouted to his men of H Company: "Go on boys, and take the hill and attend to me afterward." [23]

---

[22] *Ibid. Official Records*, Ser. I, Vol. XXXI, Pt. 2, 34–35. *Three Years with Grant*, 150. Taylor, 68.

[23] Calkins, 180–181. Newlin, 272–273.

Not too far away, the 19th Illinois, also in Johnson's division, carried their attack at the same rapid pace. Jumping over the first line of Confederate rifle pits, the regiment followed its commanding officer, Colonel Alexander Raffen, in a steady drive up the hill. Even so, there were still some regiments ahead of the 19th. Far up the hill, the flag bearer of one Illinois regiment was pulling himself up a steep incline, one hand on his flag, the other clinging to the underbrush. Finally that solitary hero sank exhausted behind a fallen log and waved his banner defiantly at the men below. Truly, as one Illinois officer was to write a few days later, the whole army was "drunk with excitement."

To the left, in Sheridan's division, the charge was being led by Colonel Francis T. Sherman's brigade, which included the 36th, 44th, 73rd, 74th, and 88th Illinois, the first three of which headed the charge. Sherman, who came from Chicago, found the ascent up the ridge to be much more difficult than did other troops involved in the attack. Gallant little Colonel Silas Miller from Aurora, the precisely dressed commanding officer of the 36th, was wounded shortly after his regiment left the base of the hill. Later on his regiment, caught in a sharp oblique fire halfway in its charge, suffered a large number of casualties.

But the "Fox River Regiment," like all those participating in the attack, was not to be denied. Private Walter Reeder of Aurora, knocked off his feet by a shot which in time would prove to be mortal, took his handkerchief from his pocket and gallantly waved his fellows on. Another private of the 36th who was wounded at this point of the charge was one who had shown cowardice at Chickamauga. Proud of his injury, he slanted his charge over to his commanding officer and proudly exhibited the proof of his new courage. Nearby, in the 73rd Illinois, the flag bearer became so exhausted from carrying his heavy burden up the steep incline that he collapsed with sheer fatigue. How could such an army be deprived of victory? [24]

Farther to the left in Hazen's brigade of Wood's division, the troops of which had outdistanced all others in the race to the top, an Ohio soldier sat behind a fallen tree in order to catch his breath. Looking down the long line of blue, from left to right, he

[24] *Three Years in the Army of the Cumberland*, 150–159. Newlin, 265. Taylor, 191. Bennett and Haigh, 532–533.

viewed a sight which he would remember for the rest of his life. The whole Federal line of battle had become a collection of inverted V-shaped formations, each one being a regiment strung out behind its regimental colors. As he recalled years later, the onlooker was impressed by the number of Illinois flags well on their way toward the crest of the ridge. There, as far as the eye could see, were the colors of the 25th, 33rd, 89th, 100th, 22nd, 27th, 42nd, 51st, 79th, 36th, 88th, 74th, 73rd, and the "dashing 19th" Illinois. Focusing his view upon the colors of the 27th Illinois, the regiment which had fought so well at Stone's River with Roberts' brigade, he watched the flag disappear three times from view as its exhausted carrier fell to the ground. On each occasion, however, the brilliant banner came up once again, and the regiment resumed its scrambling climb to the top. Farther down the line, he watched the 88th Illinois run into a brisk enfilading fire which knocked its flag bearer to the ground. Then the commanding officer of that regiment, Colonel George Chandler of Chicago, picked up the flag, waved it quickly in front of his men, and challenged them to follow him to the top. This was an example of the raw courage which brought Chandler to his death within a year.[25]

That soldier from Ohio was not the only capable observer of the great charge of Thomas' army. A mile or so away, Major James A. Connolly of the 123rd Illinois watched the assault from an appropriate spot on the slope of the ridge. A few days afterward, in a most literate manner, he would write his wife of his impressions of that moment:

> One flag bearer, on hands and knees is seen away in advance of the whole line; he crawls and climbs toward a rebel flag he sees waving above him, he gets within a few feet of it and hides behind a fallen log while he waves his flag defiantly until it almost touches the rebel flag; his regiment follows him as fast as it can: in a few moments another flag bearer gets just as near the summit at another point, and his regiment soon gets to him, but these two regiments dare not go the next twenty feet or they would be annihilated, so they crouch there and are safe from the rebels above them, who would have to rise up, to fire down at them, and so expose themselves to the fire of our fellows who are climbing the mountain.[26]

[25] Taylor, 57–58, 70–71.

[26] *Three Years in the Army of the Cumberland*, 150–159.

For as long as the veterans of the Army of the Cumberland lived, there were arguments as to which regiment reached the top of the ridge first. Many authorities, years later, were ready to credit the men of Hazen's brigade, mostly Ohio soldiers, with that achievement. Yet it is likely that the summit was reached by a half-dozen regiments at the same time. The aforementioned Major Connolly, whose memory most certainly was fresh when he wrote his description of the battle, remembered seeing a series of flags being planted upon the crest of the ridge at almost the same instant. When he himself got there, he found no less a person than Montgomery Meigs, the Quartermaster General of the Army, "wild with excitement" while turning a captured cannon upon the retreating foe.

Another claim to being first was lodged by the 73rd Illinois, whose commanding officer, Colonel James Jaquess of Quincy, was wounded in the last surge to the top. The flag bearer of the 88th Illinois, which was in the same brigade, John Cheevers of Manlius, Illinois, jumped into the Confederate rifle pits with his banner just as his enemy counterpart was leaving. In the 36th Illinois, Sergeant Leverett Kelley of Udina, Illinois, scrambled into the Confederate breastworks, waved his hand to his regiment to follow him, and then turned to accept the surrender and sword of a Confederate officer. In the decades which followed the war, the 36th was another of the many Federal regiments to claim primacy upon the crest of Missionary Ridge.[27]

There is little doubt that Sheridan's division, which included the 73rd and 36th, reached the top of the ridge in one grand surge that swept everything before it. Harker's brigade, which had in it a sprinkling of Illinois regiments, moved into the Confederate rifle pits so quickly that individual soldiers were able to hold brief conversations with the departing enemy. An officer of the 42nd Illinois, Lieutenant Alfred Johnson of Chicago, though suffering from a wound which was to bring him death two weeks later, reached the top of the ridge just as a Confederate sharpshooter was drawing careful aim on the commanding general of the brigade. "Who the h—l are you shooting at?" Johnson shouted, as he clubbed the Confederate with his pistol. There was sufficient reason then for Sheridan and his brigadiers to be

[27] *Ibid.* Taylor, 70–71, 72–73. *Civil War Medal of Honor Winners*, 8.

proud of the performance of their men. "Soldiers, you ought to be court-martialed, every man of you," one of them was reputed to have said. "I ordered you to take the rifle-pits and you scaled the mountain!"[28]

Truly there was a multitude of heroes scattered through the ranks of Illinois soldiers who made that historic charge on the late afternoon of November 25. The 19th Illinois, for example, that superbly conditioned Zouave regiment from Chicago, carried a vicious charge into the enemy works on the Federal right. One of its regimental officers, Captain David Bremner of E Company, snatched a falling flag from a wounded bearer and carried it to the top despite the blood which streamed from a wound on his own face. In the ranks of Osterhaus' division, which was working its way down the flank of Missionary Ridge, the tough old 13th Illinois of Chickasaw Bayou fame also got in its licks. Led by Sergeant Simeon Josselyn of Amboy, Illinois, who captured a Confederate flag and waved it triumphantly from a high rock on the crest, the regiment was one of the first to plant its colors in a place which signified victory. And in Mitchell's brigade of Cruft's division, the farmboys of the 78th Illinois, a hard-foraging regiment which had earned its spurs on Horseshoe Ridge, made sure to place affairs in their proper perspective. When the Confederate left collapsed with the speed of a bursting balloon, the men of the 78th, remembering the hard days behind them, rounded up three pigs from a nearby farm and herded them in the charge up the hill.[29]

In all of this, there must have been a lesson for Geary's and Howard's well-dressed Pennsylvanians and New Englanders from the Army of the Potomac. Watching the slouching black hats of Sherman's western regiments hurl themselves at an almost unbreakable defense on the Confederate right, and witnessing the emotional charge of the Army of the Cumberland up the incline of Missionary Ridge, these eastern commanders suddenly became aware of a side of the war too uncommon in the theater from

[28] Bennett and Haigh, 529–533. The 36th captured the guns of a New Orleans battery. Taylor, 75, 72–73.

[29] Lathrop, 233. The 59th Illinois, in Grose's brigade, also claimed to have reached the summit first. *Report of the Adjutant General*, II, 147. W. J. Jefferson, *Battles of Chattanooga* (Milwaukee, Wis., 1886), 62. *Civil War Medal of Honor Winners*, 8. Diary of John Batchelor, 40–41.

which they had come. Western soldiers were in the war to win. "I knew that Western men would fight well," Howard was reputed to have said after the battle, "but I did *not* know that they went into battle and stormed strong works like men on dress parade." Yet within the ranks of western troops themselves there was an even stronger admiration for those who followed the banners of Illinois regiments. An Ohio soldier, impressed with the numbers of Illinois men throughout the brigades of Beatty, Willich, G. D. Wagner, Harker, and Francis Sherman, came to an emphatic conclusion as to the fighting qualities of the troops from the Prairie State. They could, he wrote, be described by one word: they were "MEN!"[30]

When it was all over, and Bragg had withdrawn his army into Georgia, the ordinary Illinois soldier reached the quick and modest judgment that the tremendous victory of the Army of the Cumberland had been the result of a great deal of high-powered strategy among the general officers who commanded them. "Poor old Braxton Bragg!" an Oquawka veteran was to comment. "Who could stand against such a combination as this: Hooker at Lookout Mountain; Grant, Thomas, and Sheridan at the center, and Sherman on the left." Yet, in all fairness, the victory had been won through the sheer courage and audacity of men who took matters into their own hands. The strategy, what there was of it, had not sprung full blown from the brows of Grant, or Thomas, or anyone else. It came basically from a simple desire to give the devil his due, and to make some sort of atonement for those who still lay unburied at Chickamauga. Once that area had been left by Bragg, soldier after soldier of the Army of the Cumberland went back to see where he had fought on that September day. There they searched out the bones of their fallen comrades — the 78th Illinois, for example, found the bones of their Major Broadus exactly where they had left him on Horseshoe Ridge — and they buried them, and marked their graves with wooden boards.[31]

Revenge had not been won without cost; battles at this stage of the war never were. Orchard Knob, Lookout Mountain, and Missionary Ridge ran to a grand total of 6,667 casualties for the Confederates, 5,824 for the Federals. Among the latter, the largest

[30] Taylor, 37–38.

[31] Jamison, 202. Eby, 100–103.

loss by a single regiment was that of the 15th Indiana in Sheridan's division, which counted 24 killed and 175 wounded. The largest Illinois losses were to be found among those regiments which fought with Sherman. The 90th Illinois had a total of 117 casualties; the 26th counted 93; the 93rd suffered 93; the 103rd had 89. When one considers the fact that, at this stage of the war, most Illinois regiments had been depleted in size to between 200 and 300 men, the losses at Chattanooga placed the above-listed organizations virtually out of commission.[32]

Thus Grant had achieved a major triumph. The enemy had been driven from Chattanooga and, within a few days, would be chased from the siege at Knoxville. Another turning point of the war was reached.

---

[32] Thomas L. Livermore, 106–108. Fox, 443.

CHAPTER IX

The Invasion of Georgia

Grant's victories at Chattanooga and the onset of winter helped to bring a number of months of comparative inactivity to the theater of war in southeast Tennessee and northwest Georgia. With the coming of 1864, a series of significant developments took place. Grant was promoted to the rank of lieutenant general, and on March 10, 1864, was officially appointed to the position of general-in-chief. With his departure from the West, Sherman was given the command of the Military Division of the Mississippi, and shortly thereafter was given orders to move into Georgia against the Confederate army now commanded by General Joseph Johnston, who had replaced Bragg.

There was another reason for military inaction in the West. No further major campaigning could begin in Georgia until it was determined whether or not Sherman would have an army large enough to carry out such an effort. Three-year enlistments of some Union regiments were coming to a close and there was some worry as to whether many of the veteran campaigners in them would once again enter the service for another term. In order to persuade many of the doubtful to re-enlist in the army, Congress passed the so-called Veteran Volunteer Act, which provided that any soldier who signed for further service in the armed forces of the nation would be given a month-long furlough, transportation home, and a bounty of $400.

The announcement of the Veteran Volunteer Act, with all of its inducements, did not immediately strike a responsive chord among the Illinois regiments serving in the West. A great many of them, in fact, were filled with men who wished to go home to stay at the end of their three-year enlistments. An Illinois soldier of the 7th, a truly veteran regiment, wrote in December of 1863, for instance, that there was no question but that almost all of the young men in his organization were ready and anxious to return home and to allow others to take up the burden of war. What was true in regard to the 7th Illinois was also true of other veteran regiments. The troops, at least many of them, had had their fill of marching and fighting.[1]

The outstanding case of an Illinois regiment which objected to re-enlistment was that of the 55th, a really experienced regiment which had seen hard campaigning at Shiloh, Vicksburg, and Missionary Ridge. Raised by Colonel David Stuart from the "Douglas Brigade" and the "Canton Rifles" in northern and western Illinois, it had been commanded by a number of incomparably inept officers. Stuart, greatly disliked by the regiment because of his insistence upon using such outmoded tactics as the hollow square, was eventually promoted out of the unit and succeeded by Lieutenant Colonel Oscar Malmborg of Chicago, an equally incompetent officer. Though the regiment had made a glorious record in combat by January, 1863, it was generally attributed by the troops to their own courage and not to the ability of their commanders. Consequently, when their three years of service ran out, they simply refused to re-enlist if they would have to serve under the same incompetents again.

Finally, after a tremendous amount of pressure—even from the divisional commander, the highly respected Morgan L. Smith—most of the troops of the 55th agreed to sign for another term of service, provided that they be allowed to choose their own regimental colonel. This concession was tacitly granted by Smith though never placed in writing. The troops of the 55th then organized two political parties: the "Church and State" party, which supported the candidacy of Chaplain Milton Haney of Bushnell, Illinois, and the "Council of Kent" party, which supported the incumbent Malmborg. In an election held in true democratic tradition, Haney, who was one of the heroes of the western regiments, won in a landslide. This unusual chaplain never filled the

[1] Blanchard, 107.

position of commanding officer of the 55th, however, for as soon as the regiment had re-enlisted, the original agreement which was made with the troops was forgotten. Malmborg eventually resigned in September, and the regiment was placed in charge of Lieutenant Colonel Charles Andress of Mendota. It may be added, nevertheless, that the 55th Illinois made a strong case for itself in 1864, and almost every soldier in the West admired this highly independent regiment for its desire to rid itself of its unpopular field commander.[2]

The problem of the re-enlistment of troops in western regiments never became an extremely serious one, but it did cause some concern among the commanding generals of the various armies. Tremendous pressures of all types were placed upon the more reluctant soldiers to sign for another term of service. A member of the 20th Illinois, for instance, wrote later that almost his entire regiment wished to go home for good, but then General James B. McPherson appeared and spoke to the men in a "most patriotic" manner, the drums were beaten, bonfires were built, songs sung, and a generous supply of whiskey handed out. This was the method, according to the reminiscent veteran, by which the men of the 20th Illinois were "pledged to stand by the flag and their names enrolled." A soldier of the 61st Illinois, that regiment so inexperienced at Shiloh that it was immediately swept from the field, wrote after the war that it was hard to "veteranize" the Illinois regiments in 1864 because of the intense desire of the troops to go home. The problem of the 61st Illinois itself was solved by the emotional pleading of its commanding officer, Lieutenant Colonel Daniel Grass of Lawrenceville, Illinois. "Stand by the old flag, boys!" argued Grass, who was greatly liked by his men. "Let us stay and see this thing out!" Far into a cold and raw evening, the men of the 61st heard the pleas of their colonel. Then they marched back to their tents, unbuckled their cartridge belts, and walked down to the adjutant's tent to re-enlist.[3]

It would be a mistake to assume that every soldier in each regiment signed up for further service in the army, of course. In fact, a study of the muster rolls for regiments coming from Illinois indicates that a considerable number of men from that state left

---

[2] [Crooker *et al.*], 306–310. *Army Life of an Illinois Soldier*, 224.

[3] Blanchard, 107. Stillwell, *Story of a Common Soldier*, 186–188.

the service late in 1864. The motives of those who did become veteran volunteers differed, however, in accordance with circumstances which faced each regiment, or each individual in each unit. Many signed again from purely patriotic instincts or from a sense of comradeship born of long and arduous months of service together. In attempting to explain the reason for the almost total re-enlistment of the 53rd Illinois, Lieutenant Charles Brush of that regiment wrote his father back in Ottawa: "The boys have been in a long time, crowded the rebellion till already tottering for a fall. Now I say if they feel like it, let them go in and have the honor of closing up the war." [4]

The effect which the simple factor of comradeship had upon the re-enlistment of Illinois soldiers should not be underestimated. A soldier of the 34th Illinois for instance, Sergeant Edwin Payne of Whiteside County, pleaded with his girl friend not to judge him "too harshly" because he had signed in for another term of service with the army. "The truth is our Regt, or a sufficient number of them have enlisted as veterans for the Regt to go home as an organization to recruit," he wrote. "I could not resist the opportunity, or rather could not see my old comrades going again and myself remain behind." An officer of the 103rd, a Fulton County regiment which had a record of high desertions in 1863, wrote that the re-enlistment of his regiment was just about the "grandest thing of the war." Out of a strong sense of loyalty to each other, almost all of the men of the regiment had placed their names once again upon the muster rolls. And a member of the 40th Illinois, writing realistically about the behavior of ordinary soldiers, stated that "about 15 of us were talking about it [enlistment] and cussing it, until every son of a gun of us concluded to, and did re-enlist." Thus it was that the 40th Illinois, a regiment which had proved itself at Shiloh, found its own particular reasons for offering itself again to the service of its country.[5]

It must be added, however, that many an Illinois soldier re-enlisted because of the privileges allowed by the Veteran Volunteer Act. The size of the bounty, $400, was a considerable inducement for that time, and the chance to go home as a "veteran"

[4] Brush to his father, Jan. 25, 1864, Brush Family Papers.

[5] Payne to Miss Kim Hudson, Dec. 26, 1863, Edwin W. Payne Papers. *Army Life of an Illinois Soldier*, 210.

soldier had tremendous psychological appeal to the men. A kind of "veteran fever" ran through various Illinois regiments, and, as a member of the 10th Illinois phrased it, the call of home and money was too much for many a campaigner to resist. David Givler, a bugler with the 7th Illinois, summarized the effect of those appeals in a letter written to a friend back in the home state in July, 1864. Givler, who in the previous December had indicated to the same correspondent that he would not re-enlist under any circumstances, wrote: "Seven months has passed since the *veteran and green back* fever got us fast for another term in the army."[6]

In the early months of 1864, trains traveling between Illinois and the military camps of the South were filled with regiments going on or returning from furlough. In either instance, the troops were allowed to disembark at Cairo so that they might eat and rest in the Soldier's Home, a long rambling frame structure well known by western soldiers. Warm and well lighted, nicely furnished with tables and benches, it was favorably regarded by troops which had visited it. If the regiments were returning home to northern Illinois, they were once again reloaded on the trains and taken to Chicago, where, after being given another meal at the Soldier's Rest in that city, they were allowed to travel on to their individual towns.

The reaction of the troops to their return home after having been gone for so long varied. In most cases their behavior aboard the trains, particularly while heading toward Illinois, was somewhat less than restrained. The 7th Illinois, for example, very likely the first regiment to return on veteran's furlough, became involved in a serious altercation with the provost guards, and had to be severely disciplined. One young soldier recalled after the war that once the train had entered Illinois the troops of his regiment became almost giddy with emotion. When the conductor aboard his particular car announced in a stentorian voice that the train was about to stop at "My-candy" (Makanda, Illinois), the troops of the returning 61st Illinois began to roar with laughter, and to chant the name of each town passed.

Since each soldier was given a rather sizable bonus before boarding the train, there was much gambling. A veteran of the

[6] Ephraim A. Wilson, *Memoirs of the War . . .* (Cleveland, 1893), 287. Givler to a friend, Dec. 9, 1863, July 21, 1864, Givler, 106, 112.

10th Illinois remembered years later that his regiment, traveling home on freight cars, maintained a continuous game of chuck-a-luck. Many of the soldiers were to lose their "comfortable roll" of greenbacks before the train reached the disembarkation center.[7]

Each village, hamlet, and city generally turned out in celebration to welcome their returning heroes. A member of the 50th Illinois was to remember with some emotion that almost every settlement and "neighborhood in Adams county was lighted up with a welcome." The 7th Illinois, for instance, received a tumultuous reception upon its return to Springfield early in 1864. The 33rd Illinois, the "Teacher's Regiment" was marched down the streets of Bloomington to Roger's Hall, where it was welcomed by the faculty of the Illinois State Normal School, given a fine meal, and presented with a patriotic program. The master of ceremonies of the celebration, after a series of appropriate remarks, called for three cheers for the flag, three hisses for the Confederacy, and spirited singing of some patriotic songs. Then the boys were allowed to go home. The aforementioned 50th Illinois received comparable treatment. There the veterans of Donelson, Shiloh, and Corinth were forced to listen to a collection of patriotic airs sung by a bevy of ladies, and then were led by the commanding officer, Colonel Moses Bane of Quincy, in a rendition of a mournful song entitled "Home Again." There followed a long harangue from Bane in which each soldier was asked to act as a recruiting sergeant for the regiment during the regimental furlough. Then the men were allowed to see their families.[8]

For some, the time at home became a "sweet dream . . . thirty short days of unalloyed enjoyment." Many of the soldiers married girls with whom they had corresponded through the previous three years, and others began friendships with the opposite sex which would culminate in the same way two years later. One would suspect, however, that for a great many others the return home was similar to that experienced by young Leander Stillwell of the 61st Illinois. Arriving at Grafton, he walked the last few

[7] Stillwell, *Story of a Common Soldier*, 171, 172. Jamison, 211. Payne, 99–100.

[8] Charles F. Hubert, *History of the Fiftieth Illinois Volunteer Infantry . . .* (Kansas City, Mo., 1894), 256. Way, 273.

miles down a country lane, surprising his parents, who had not expected him. The next few days were spent in walking about old haunts and in seeing old friends. Then there was the sudden realization that nothing was really the same. Between 1861 and 1864, manhood had come to Stillwell, and home was not really home. He had lived too long a different kind of life, with comrades who were really now his friends. A veteran campaigner of the 36th Illinois would have agreed with Stillwell: within days after his return, he felt an "eager longing for the hardtack and army ration of the front." Nor was the sensation any different for Lieutenant Peter Weyhrich of the 44th Illinois. Writing a friend who was already back at the front, he described an "uneasiness at home, a feeling of being in 'hot water,'" and a desire to rejoin his companions. "However," he concluded, "you know what one's feelings are after being away from the regiment for such a long time."[9]

With the return of the troops from their veteran furloughs, Sherman began his long-delayed movement against Johnston's army in Georgia. The Union force consisted of Thomas' Army of the Cumberland, which contained General O. O. Howard's IV Corps, Palmer's XIV Corps, Hooker's XX Corps, and General W. L. Elliott's Cavalry Corps; the Army of the Tennessee, under McPherson, containing Logan's XV Corps, General Grenville M. Dodge's XVI Corps, and General Francis P. Blair's XVII Corps; and the Army of the Ohio, under General John M. Schofield, which consisted of the latter's own XXIII Corps, plus George Stoneman's cavalry.

A number of Sherman's commanders and troops came from the state of Illinois. Palmer and Logan, both corps commanders, came from the Prairie State; General Schofield also came from Illinois. Born in New York, he was brought by his family to Bristol in Kendall County at the age of 12. Two years later, in 1845, his parents moved to Freeport, from which town he entered West Point. In business in Missouri at the beginning of the war, he had reentered the army from that state.

Scattered among the various corps of Sherman's grand army were 70 veteran regiments from Illinois. Compared to the num-

---

[9] *Ibid.*, 136. Stillwell, *Story of a Common Soldier*, 174–175. Bennett and Haigh, 554. Weyhrich to D. C. Smith, April 24, 1864, Smith Papers.

ber from that state which had taken part in the attacks on Lookout Mountain and Missionary Ridge, this represented a drop of over five regiments, and it indicated the substantial number of men who had failed to muster in for a second term of service. Such regiments as the 19th and 35th Illinois, for example, both regiments which had been reduced by a lack of re-enlistments, were now missing; those who had signed on again were amalgamated into other regiments.[10]

Sherman's advance into Georgia started on May 7, almost the same time at which General George G. Meade's Army of the Potomac went on the offensive in the East. In his movement against Johnston, Sherman sent Thomas' Army of the Cumberland, led by Grose's brigade, in a frontal assault upon the Confederates. Grose's command consisted of two Indiana regiments, one Ohio regiment, and three from Illinois: the 75th, under the command of Colonel John Bennett of Morrison, the 80th, led by Colonel Andrew F. Rogers of Upper Alton, and the 84th, commanded by Colonel Louis Waters of Macomb. Schofield's Army of the Ohio was ordered to make a flanking movement to the left, and McPherson's Army of the Tennessee was sent to the right or south through Snake Creek Gap in an attempt to flank Johnston at Resaca. Pinning Johnston near Rocky Face Ridge, Thomas forced the Confederate commander to fight a heavy engagement at that spot, while the mountains and poor weather hid the flanking movements. Other regiments from Illinois engaged in the heavy fighting near Dalton besides those under Grose included the 36th, the "Fox River Regiment" which had seen action at Missionary Ridge, the 42nd, the 44th, the 59th, the 73rd, the 79th, the 88th, and the 107th.[11]

Johnston quickly realized the threat as nearly all of Sherman's army moved to Snake Creek Gap and withdrew in the direction of Resaca. Here, once again, heavy fighting took place, as Sweeny's division, consisting mainly of Illinois troops led by an Illinois commander, made a wide sweep behind the town of Calhoun,

[10] Jacob D. Cox, *Atlanta*, Vol. IX of *The Army in the Civil War* (New York, 1885), 245–249. *Historical Encyclopedia of Illinois*, 469, 551–571.

[11] *Official Records*, Ser. I, Vol. XXXVIII, Pt. 1, 63–64. Dodge, 127, 132–134. *Reminiscences of the Civil War from Diaries of Members of the 103rd Illinois Volunteer Infantry*, ed. Regimental Committee (Chicago, 1904), 52.

and the three Federal armies moved upon Johnston frontally and to his flanks. Once again the Illinois regiments of Grose's command were involved in bitter skirmishing, as were other regiments from the same state. The 9th Illinois was heavily involved, as was the 66th Illinois, which was hard hit by casualties as it attempted a crossing of the Oostanaula River. So intense did the conflict become at Resaca that the troops of the 105th Illinois, after taking a prisoner whose arm was tattooed with the words "Fort Pillow," bayoneted him on the spot. The highest losses in the conflict were suffered by General Dan Butterfield's division of the XX Corps, of which the 102nd Illinois was a part. Following Johnston's withdrawal from Resaca the night of May 15, another sharp engagement took place at Adairsville. Here the 36th Illinois played a significant role, being engaged on the field for 12 straight hours without relief.[12]

Following his victory at Resaca, Sherman advanced upon a broad front, throwing his cavalry out in a series of deceptive flanking movements. By May 20 he had forced Johnston back to a very strong defensive position at Allatoona Pass. Resting his army for three days, Sherman began to outflank Johnston, sending McPherson's Army of the Tennessee in an enveloping sweep from the west and Schofield's Army of the Ohio in an arc to the east. Thomas was given the task of attempting to pin the Confederate army with a frontal movement. The result of Sherman's strategy was a savage several-day battle at Dallas, or New Hope Church, in which attacks and counterattacks were made by the contending armies. Sweeny's Second Division of the XVI Corps, which included the 48th Illinois, a southern Illinois regiment commanded by Colonel Lucien Greathouse of Elizabethtown, the 52nd Illinois, a Kane County regiment commanded by Colonel Edwin Bowen of La Moille, and the 66th Illinois, the old "Birge's Sharpshooters," commanded by Lieutenant Colonel Andrew Campbell of Paris, suffered heavy losses once again. The hero of the battle was the leader of the XV Corps, John A. Logan, who fulfilled

---

[12] *Ibid.* Robert Hale Strong, *A Yankee Private's Civil War* (Chicago, 1961), 16. The Fort Pillow "massacre" occurred April 12, 1864, and involved the killing of Negro soldiers by victorious Confederate soldiers after the Negroes' surrender. Fox, 447. Bennett and Haigh, 588. The 36th Illinois never really forgave their corps commander, O. O. Howard, for keeping them in line of battle so long.

that role to perfection. This southern Illinois general was rapidly becoming a legendary figure throughout Sherman's grand army. During the fighting at Dallas, when the 103rd Illinois was finding itself hard pressed to hold in the face of a Confederate attack, Logan appeared on the scene to cheer his troops on. With his ruddy complexion, which some Illinois soldiers attributed to whiskey, and with his large sweeping mustache, he was easy to recognize. Nor was he one to mince words, as he shouted to the beleaguered men of the 103rd: "It's all right, damn it, isn't it?" "It's all right, General," replied the commanding officer of the Illinois regiment. Then, to cap the day, Logan mounted his large black horse and led a stirring charge upon an enemy battery.[13]

The victory for Sherman at Dallas was, to a large extent, an Illinois one. "Blackjack" Logan and "Bulldog" Sweeny played substantial roles in bringing the main two-day fight to a successful conclusion, and over 30 Illinois regiments were engaged in the conflict at one time or another.

Johnston's strategy, designed to draw Sherman deeper into Georgia, where the Confederate commander could fight on his own terms, was not without merit. As Sherman moved toward the new enemy positions to the east of Cassville, there were more than a few Federal officers who felt concern for the future of the Union army and who entertained a great deal of respect for the clever Confederate commander. Philip S. Post of Galesburg, Illinois, now commanding a brigade in the Army of the Cumberland, indicated such thoughts in a June letter home. There was not, he wrote, the "slightest sign of demoralization on the part of the enemy." Furthermore, he added: "No army could possibly have fallen back taking everything with them more clean than they have." Two weeks later Post wrote again – a worried, tempered letter which predicted misfortune for Sherman in the weeks to come. "The enemy have a good position and excellent works and I fear our troubles are but just fairly commencing," he stated. Then, indicating more concern over the morale of the opposing army, he concluded: "The prisoners we take are more defiant than ever, and they are evidently prepared to fight desparately."[14]

---

[13] *Report of the Adjutant General*, III, 495, 621–622; IV, 422–425. Dawson, 54. *Army Life of an Illinois Soldier*, 251–252.

[14] Post to Miss Mary Post, June 9, 24, 1864, Post Papers.

Post's worries were proper ones in a great many ways. Johnston, after his retreat from Allatoona Pass, and after New Hope Church, had taken up positions on Lost, Pine, and Brush mountains to oppose the new Federal move on the left back to the Chattanooga and Atlanta railroad. Sherman's operations, slowed by bad weather and supply difficulties, were not sufficient to force Johnston to retreat until the middle of June, when the Confederate commander moved part of his army to Kennesaw Mountain. Considerable fighting took place during these maneuvers. Pine Mountain, Gilgal Church, and Big Shanty were a few of the spots at which heavy skirmishing occurred. Though separate or partly isolated engagements, they were all part of the developing line of conflict which ran between the two great armies over and to both sides of Kennesaw Mountain.

As for all Union troops under Sherman, these middle days of June, 1864, were trying ones for the regiments from Illinois. The 34th, for instance, was heavily engaged near Marietta, taking a large number of prisoners. Colonel Fred A. Bartleson of the 100th Illinois was killed while leading a skirmish line near the base of Keenesaw on June 23. This brave and much-loved officer, who came from Joliet, lost an arm at Shiloh, and had just returned to his command after a lengthy imprisonment at Libby Prison in Richmond, Virginia. He was only one of the many casualties of a two-week period which, according to Lieutenant Edwin Payne of the 34th Illinois, was filled with "continual pop, pop, popping all along the line" interspersed with "an occasional ear splitter from the batteries."

The experienced Major James Connolly of the 123rd Illinois, confirming Payne's impressions of the fighting, informed his wife back in Charleston, Illinois, that the cannonading around Kennesaw Mountain was the heaviest he had ever heard. The infantry, as usual, suffered the worst of the discomforts. Fighting around Big Shanty, for instance, was particularly hard, and several Illinois regiments became lost and confused when trying to move upon Confederate positions there.[15]

---

[15] Payne, 134. *Army Life of an Illinois Soldier*, 304. Bennett and Haigh, 611. *Joliet* (Ill.) *Republican*, July 9, 1864. Payne to his wife, June 4, 16, 1864, Edwin W. Payne Papers. *Three Years in the Army of the Cumberland*, 222.

The entire reason for Sherman's direct assault upon Johnston's entrenchments on Kennesaw is still a matter of conjecture after a hundred years. The unfavorable weather, which made a continuation of the successful flanking movements hazardous, and the feeling that the Confederate position was weakly held may have been among his reasons. Further, a severe defeat inflicted upon Johnston at this place would have opened the way for a quick conquest of Atlanta. Sherman also mentioned the "moral effect" of a direct assault. Whatever the background for Sherman's judgment, he began preparing for the attack on June 24. The attack would begin at nine o'clock on the morning of June 27.

As planned, the main effort of the Army of the Cumberland was led by John Newton's Second Division of the IV Corps and by J. C. Davis' Second Division of the XIV Corps. Newton's division was composed of three brigades: C. G. Harker's, which consisted of Ohio troops; G. D. Wagner's, which contained mostly Indiana regiments; and Nathan Kimball's, which included a scattering of state regiments, among them the 100th Illinois.

Davis' division was composed of two brigades; Colonel Dan McCook's, which included among its five regiments the 85th, 86th, and 125th Illinois, the last named commanded by Colonel Oscar F. Harmon of Danville, Illinois; and Mitchell's, which contained another Illinois regiment, the 78th, the western Illinois organization which had fought so well at Chickamauga.[16]

The main effort of the Army of the Tennessee was led by Morgan Smith's Second Division of the XV Corps. This command contained the 55th Illinois, the unit which had demanded a change of officers before its troops would re-enlist; the 116th, a Macon County regiment commanded by Major Anderson Froman of Decatur; the 127th, a Cook and Kendall counties regiment led by Lieutenant Colonel Frank S. Curtiss of Chicago; and the 111th, a Marion and Logan counties regiment commanded by Colonel James S. Martin of Salem.

Smith's veterans of the Army of the Tennessee managed to get their attack off early and with some small success. The division commander had aroused his men early and had spoken to them frankly of the nature of the assault. Told to strip down in order

[16] *Official Records*, Ser. I, Vol. XXXVIII, Pt. 1, 68. Newlin, 312. [Crooker *et al.*], 322–335. Aten, 185–186.

to better climb the mountain, the men consumed their breakfast heartily, but in an atmosphere in which "sportiveness was rare or spasmodic." These were really veteran soldiers, and regiments such as the 55th Illinois, which had fought in every major battle in the West, knew the odds of attacking such a hill against a determined foe. Notes were written out by the individual soldiers to their families back home and deposited with the regimental cooks for forwarding in case of death.

Despite the fact that Logan was once again on hand to cheer the men of his XV Corps on by riding up and down in front of the lines, his long black hair fluttering in the breeze, Smith's assault went only to the first line of enemy trenches. There his men stayed, unable to go farther, yet close enough to hear Confederate officers ordering their men to stand fast.[17]

The attack on Thomas' end of the line was begun by the firing of a single artillery piece. The men of the 85th Illinois moved out steadily through the open fields at the base of the mountain and then charged in a ragged assault up the slopes. Not far away, also in Dan McCook's brigade, the 86th Illinois struggled manfully through the brush and briars in their area of the mountain. And in Mitchell's brigade, the 78th Illinois, which had started its climb in good order, soon settled into an exhausting disorganized charge.

The heat was terribly intense. The color bearer of the 85th Illinois, struggling to reach the enemy trenches with his handful of followers, did so only to collapse before he had planted his flag. The 34th Illinois, fighting in support of McCook's troops, had started its charge up the slope with a "whoop and a run," only to run out of steam halfway up the mountain. This was the regiment which, only a few hours previously, had complained to its division commander, Davis, about always being chosen to fight in front of the army. Davis' reply was an admission that it was an honest complaint, for he had asked for the 34th to lead the charge since it was one regiment which did not fall back until ordered. Once the position of the regiment was confirmed, the Illinois troops began to make wagers on the outcome of the day. "The bet on one side," wrote Lieutenant Edwin Payne of the 34th,

[17] [Crooker *et al.*], 322–335. Dawson, 56–57.

"was that our skirmish line wouldn't drive the rebel skirmishers from their rifle pits."

Those who placed their money against the 34th were losers. The regiment carried its charge to the Confederate trenches, where it took seven or eight prisoners. One member of the same regiment managed to climb to the second row of defensive works, only to run into a rock-throwing barrage. The first missile knocked off the hat of the Illinois private; the second, a 20-pound boulder, hit him in the midsection and rolled him back down the slope.[18]

Newton's division, which attacked Hardee's right and center, suffered calamitous losses in its charge up the hill. General C. G. Harker, the Ohio brigadier, was mortally wounded while attempting to lead his troops beyond the first row of Confederate trenches. Kimball's and Wagner's men were also repulsed. Only one man of Newton's entire division reached the secondary defense line — the color bearer of the 100th Illinois, who was bayoneted just as he planted his regimental flag.

As appropriately described by an officer of the 86th Illinois, Captain Allen Fahnestock of Lancaster, Illinois, it was truly a "bloody Monday." To an Oquawka soldier of the 10th Illinois, it held the same meaning — a "dark, sad day." McCook, the dreamy-eyed Ohioan, was mortally wounded, and his successor, Colonel Oscar L. Harmon, was shot directly through the heart. Both fell just short of the Confederate *chevaux-de-frise*. Harmon, whose record in the war was exceptional, had written his wife a farewell note the night before the attack. McCook, likewise, had experienced forebodings about the coming day, meeting with his officers on the evening of June 26 in order to warn them of the dangers in the assault.[19]

If courage alone could have won the day, then victory would have been an early result. Confederates who fired directly into the oncoming assault troops could not help admiring their unfortunate foes. Colonel Caleb C. Dilworth of Havana, Illinois, bravely took command of McCook's brigade and made a gallant but unsuccessful attempt to keep the attack going. Colonel Silas

[18] Civil War Diary of Allen Fahnestock, Aug. 7, 1863–Nov. 18, 1865, ISHL, 89. Payne to his wife, July 9, 1864, Edwin W. Payne Papers.

[19] Civil War Diary of Allen Fahnestock, 88. *Quincy Daily Whig and Republican*, July 8, 1864. Jamison, 248.

Miller, the dapper commanding officer of the 36th Illinois who had just recovered from a wound inflicted at Missionary Ridge, was shot down again – and this time he died as a result of his injuries. In the 86th Illinois, a musician, Alanson Webber from Saratoga, Illinois, joined his regiment's charge voluntarily, and when his fellows were repulsed with heavy losses he covered their retreat by maintaining a standing steady fire at their tormentors. A young soldier of the 10th Illinois lost his hand at the wrist when it was torn off by a Confederate shell. Wrapping his coat over the stump, he lay on the ground and patiently awaited medical attention while fanning flies from helplessly wounded men with his good hand. Nor was the courage on one side alone. The 78th and 86th Illinois, both of which had carried their charges to within a few paces of Confederate trenches, were showered with spades, rocks, and clods of dirt by the sturdy defenders.[20]

The Federal attack was neither a failure nor a success. The blue-coated soldiers, only yards away from success, could go no farther, and some of them could not safely retreat. Regiments such as the 34th Illinois dug rifle pits with bayonets and bare hands and clung stubbornly to the steep slope despite the rocks and taunts thrown at them by the Confederates. Davis' and Newton's men held on to what they had gained, and a peculiar kind of siege, three-quarters of the way up the mountainside, began. A day or so later, a careless soldier of the contending armies ignited the dry brush on the mountainside, beginning a fire which endangered the wounded who still lay untended between the trenches. A "soldier's truce" was arranged, the men coming out of the defensive works to gather up the dead and wounded and to put out the fire. Here occurred one of those strange concidences of conflict. An officer of the 75th Illinois, Captain William Parker of Dixon, was able to meet with his brother, a member of Cheatham's division, during this brief interlude of peace.[21]

In the strange manner of war, once the truce was ended the troops went back to their positions and continued the fight, the

[20] Thomas L. Livermore, 120–121. Fox, 452, 510. Fox points out that the 125th Illinois led the storming column up Kennesaw. Bennett and Haigh, 611. *Civil War Medal of Honor Winners*, 10. Jamison, 248.

[21] E. W. Payne to his wife, June 28, 1864, Edwin W. Payne Papers. P. S. Post to Mary Post, June 28, 1864, Post Papers. Payne, 134.

Union soldiers inching their works forward to within 27 paces of the defenders, the latter continuing to rain rocks, dirt, and an occasional spade upon the sapping parties. In the veteran 59th Illinois, the troops employed a trick they had learned from the old Vicksburg campaigners of Sherman's army. Filling a barrel with dirt and rolling it in front of their trenches, they were able to dig and move with safety. The troops of the 78th, 86th, and 125th Illinois were not so fortunate, however. Besides the bullets, rocks, and other missiles which were aimed at them from time to time, these Illinois soldiers were tormented by "turpentine balls," balls of cloth soaked in turpentine, lighted, and thrown down the slopes.[22]

The dangers implicit in all of this, plus the intense heat of midsummer, were too much for a few of the Federal soldiers. One young veteran soldier of I Company, 34th Illinois, Private Edward O'Donnell of Mount Carroll, became momentarily mentally distraught, and wandered into the Confederate lines carrying a coffee pot and a frying pan. O'Donnell, listed on the company rolls as a deserter, was made a prisoner and later died at Andersonville in Georgia. Another soldier of the 86th Illinois suffered the same affliction, and calmly strolled up the mountain with a tin bucket in his hand. The latter incident was the last straw for the opposing Confederate soldiers. Why had the 86th sent that "——— damn fool over to them?" they shouted over the parapet. Didn't the Illinois regiment know that the man was "insane?"[23]

With all of the difficulties, the Federal troops held on and were even able to throw back several attacks designed to drive them off the mountainside. Finally, on the night of July 1, Sherman returned to his former strategy by sending McPherson's army to the right of Kennesaw Mountain toward the Chattahoochee River. Johnston, once again outflanked, was forced to withdraw from the positions which he had so carefully prepared.

The battle of Kennesaw Mountain was over, and the penalty for Sherman's rashness in attacking frontally was duly paid. Of the 16,225 Federal soldiers directly engaged in the assault, over

---

[22] Herr, 231. Civil War Diary of Allen Fahnestock, 91.

[23] Payne, 134–135. The story of the demented men at Kennesaw Mountain is told in several regimental histories. *Three Years in the Army of the Cumberland*, 228, also carries interesting material on the attack.

2,000 were killed, wounded, and declared missing. Only 450 Confederate troops fell under the same classifications. Among Illinois regiments engaged in the fighting, the 125th, fighting with McCook, lost 47 killed, 52 wounded, and 5 in the missing category. In the same division, the 86th Illinois had a total of 116 casualties. The 74th, in Newton's division, suffered 89 casualties; the 103rd, fighting with the XV Corps, had 73. Among all Federal regiments involved in the attack upon Kennesaw Mountain, the 40th Indiana had the longest casualty list with 34 killed, 125 wounded, and 10 missing.[24]

By the end of the first week in July, Johnston had fallen back to the Chattahoochee River, where, once again, Sherman turned the flanks of the Confederate army and forced it to retreat. The Fabian tactics employed by Johnston in refusing to fight Sherman unless it be on his own terms posed many difficulties for the Union commander, but were even more exasperating to the Confederate government, which had hoped for a more aggressive defense. On July 17 Johnston was relieved by John Bell Hood, whose willingness to fight at every opportunity was known by friend and foe alike. All of this was not lost on the ordinary Confederate soldier, who was torn between the sensibility of Johnston's patience and the emotional appeal of Hood's more aggressive strategy. He knew, with a kind of stoic fatalism, that fighting would be done sometime and somewhere. There was an illustration of this on the banks of the Chattahoochee. Once, while the armies faced each other across this turbid stream, a solitary picket of the 105th Illinois spotted his opposite number on the other side and shouted: "How many men has Johnston got?" "Oh, about enough for another killing," was the reply.[25]

The army which Sherman was so expertly handling in its campaign through Georgia was, in a sense, a composite of troops from all parts of the nation. There were regiments from virtually every loyal state in the Union including those in New England and the border area between the Confederacy and the North. The Army of the Cumberland, for instance, contained units which had been withdrawn from the Army of the Potomac the previous

[24] Fox, 452. Thomas L. Livermore, 120–121.

[25] Strong, 119.

November and dispatched to the Chattanooga area under the command of Hooker. Both the Army of the Tennessee and that of Thomas included regiments from Kentucky and Tennessee, as well as from Kansas and Missouri.

In a way, however, each soldier under Sherman's command generally considered himself one of two types — an easterner or a westerner. And westerners classified themselves as serving either in the Army of the Cumberland or the Army of the Tennessee. This association between men from different sections of the country, and from different armies, naturally led to comparisons. Westerners, generally, were quite likely to stand together, for no matter how bad relations became between McPherson's and Thomas' men, each considered the other part of the second-best army in the nation. Always, men from the West tended to look upon those from the East as having poorer fighting qualities, an attitude which often was cause for quarreling and violence between regiments from the two sections of the Union. "The 11th and 12th Corps Potomac men, and ours never meet without some very hard talk," wrote a Canton, Illinois, officer of the Army of the Tennessee. It goes without saying that the hard talk was followed by fisticuffs in some cases.[26]

Furthermore, most western soldiers greatly resented having to serve under officers imported from the Army of the Potomac. Part of this reaction stemmed from a natural distrust of such men as a result of the succession of military defeats which had taken place in the East. "They are either totally unfit for their positions or they are traitors," an Illinois officer once wrote of eastern officers in general. "I cannot account for our reverses in any other way." Nor could the western soldier accept the eastern officer's concept of maintaining discipline. In 1864, for example, the 103rd Illinois, a Fulton County regiment, while marching toward Atlanta, passed before a general who had recently served with the Army of the Potomac. "Bring out your Potomac horse," shouted the Illinois soldiers; "Advance to Washington"; "Fall back on your straw and fresh butter."[27]

The remarks of the 103rd, flippant as they were, reflected an

[26] *Army Life of an Illinois Soldier*, 218.

[27] W. W. Orme to his wife, Oct. 3, 1863, Orme Papers. *Reminiscences of the 103rd*, 46.

over-all attitude which the rangy westerners had toward their eastern comrades. The "Potomac horse," a method of disciplining troops in the Army of the Potomac, could not be applied in the West. Most soldiers of Illinois or Iowa regiments were perfectly willing to admit that eastern regiments were better drilled, while denying that the latter came anywhere near the standard of western soldiering. As a soldier of the 33rd Illinois phrased it, "they [the easterners] wore more feathers and less dust than those from the West. . . ." Furthermore, the same soldier concluded, there just wasn't that friendly association between men and officers that existed in the troops that had just come down the river. The "Pilgrims," as many Illinois soldiers called them, might have used a little more of the independence and contrariness which such regiments as the 55th Illinois showed upon occasion.[28]

Between the Army of the Cumberland and the Army of the Tennessee there was also a sense of separation. The latter organization had fought under Grant and Sherman for so long that it had absorbed the characteristics of both men. Its soldiers were slouchy, careless in dress and behavior, capable of covering long distances each day, and proud of a successive string of victories in savage battles. The Army of the Cumberland, likewise, had taken on the character of its own commander, "Pap" Thomas. It was ponderous on offense, grudging on defense, calculating, and courageous. Its victories had been hard won; its defeats had been crushing. Given time and good guidance, it would demolish the very armies which had inflicted hardship upon it.

The two armies, much in the manner in which Grant and Sherman worked with Thomas, only tolerated each other. It was as described by a member of the 103rd Illinois, a regiment of the XV Corps. The Army of the Tennessee, he said, got along but barely with the divisions of the Army of the Cumberland – "much in the spirit of a dog chewing a bone, allows another to come within ten feet." Yet among the competitive westerners there were even further classifications. Illinois soldiers, quite naturally proud of their feats at Shiloh, Vicksburg, and Stone's River, considered the regiments of their home state to be the best. The troops from Michigan, wrote a Fulton County officer, could be considered equal only to "Jeff Thompson's scalawags." "The Illinois boys

[28] Way, 47–48.

and the Iowaians coalesce more readily," he concluded, "and seem to have more family feeling between them than at least either of these state's troops have for those of other states." [29]

Despite the less than fraternal association between armies or parts of armies, Sherman's marching men developed, in the days preceding the battles around Atlanta, a supreme confidence both in themselves and in their commander. As one Illinois officer expressed it, there was but little question that Grant would whip Lee, and that Sherman would beat Johnston. A southern Illinois private of the 111th Illinois phrased it more colorfully, writing: "They say there is no danger of Sherman going to Hell, for he will outflank the devil and go to heaven." As far as the army itself was concerned, it felt a special sense of supremacy over anything which the Confederates might throw in its path. As it was written by one veteran Illinois campaigner—"they *can't whip* this army; we are like the big boy, 'too big to be whipped.'" [30]

A major factor in the development of this superb body of fighting men was that of time. Time had winnowed out the incapable and the inept; it had sent the weak-willed back to Illinois, Ohio, or Iowa, and it had retired the old to civilian positions. The veteran regiments, now re-enlisted, were rarely up to full complement. Two or three hundred men in number at the time of Sherman's grand march to Atlanta, they were commanded by extremely young men. Philip S. Post, for example, a brigadier in the Army of the Cumberland, was 31 years old; General Giles A. Smith, the division commander who came from Bloomington, Illinois, was 34. The officers in the lower ranks were quite generally men who had earned their positions through the real respect of their subordinates. It was, without a doubt, an army flushed with youth, and challenged with the enormity of its task.[31]

Confidence had given it a courageousness which, if sometimes foolish, was always welcome. An eastern Illinois officer of the 123rd Illinois could note the change. A year before, he wrote, the men of the Army of the Cumberland were nervous and upset be-

---

[29] *Army Life of an Illinois Soldier*, 218, 66–67.

[30] *Three Years in the Army of the Cumberland*, 240. Private R. G. Ardrey to his brother, June 12, 1864, "Civil War Letters of Robert G. Ardrey."

[31] Aten, 243. Post, a lawyer before the war, was born in New York in 1833. Smith, who owned a hotel in Bloomington, Illinois, was born in 1829.

fore battle; now they were constantly "laughing, singing, whistling, making jocular remarks about the Johnnies. . . ." An insensibility to danger and death could be found everywhere in the ranks. Captain Levi Ross of the 86th Illinois, writing his father back in Princeville in May, told how men of his regiment had become indifferent to the sound of bullets. Furthermore, he stated, they thought the army to be invincible, and that Sherman and Thomas knew which "cards were trumps and how to play them advantageously." A seasoned trooper of the 10th Illinois admitted to only one fear during the campaign; that was the "tick, tick, tick" of shell fragments as they winged through the leaves of the trees. Philip S. Post, the officer from western Illinois, wrote that he never ceased to be amazed at the insouciance which his men of the 59th and 74th Illinois showed toward enemy fire. The cannonading, he wrote just before the battle at New Hope Church, was vicious and constant, and there was a continuous "whir-r-r-ring" of shell fragments in the air, and the constant "phe-w-ph-e-w" of Minie balls. Yet, he concluded: "It is perfectly marvelous with what utter indifference our old Regiments regard these death dealing missiles and though every few minutes some of their number is stricken down their jests flow just as glibly, and the more narrow the escape, the sharper the comments." [32]

Sherman's army soon proved, while marching into Georgia, the truth in the claim that war breeds a callousness to misfortunes of all types. By the time the spires of Atlanta came into view, the army had become a hardened and massive collection of professional soldiers which, when "well handled," as one Illinois veteran phrased it, could "whip the devil." Nothing seemed really to matter to them except victory and defeat. Once, when the 103rd Illinois saw a regimental surgeon fall off his horse and into a muddy ditch just before Atlanta, the soldiers of that regiment "consoled him with a clear 1,000 cheers, groans, and sharp speeches." "Anything short of death," stated one western Illinois officer, "is a capital joke. I have seen them make sport of a man lying by a roadside in a fit." A soldier of one northern Illinois regiment confided to his diary a perfect illustration of the emergence of a real

[32] *Three Years in the Army of the Cumberland*, 224. Ross to his father, May 11, 1864, Ross Papers. Ephraim A. Wilson, 323. Post to Miss Mary Post, June 1, 1864, Post Papers.

fighting man. He had been sitting earlier in the day by a young soldier who had been boasting about his apparent imperviousness to enemy bullets. Suddenly a musket ball struck the young man frontally in the forehead. "He fell across my lap . . . ," wrote the first Illinois soldier, "and his brains and blood ran into my haversack, spoiling my rations. So I took his."[33]

The toughness and resilience spilled over into every phase of life in Sherman's army. A western Illinois soldier noted that the men of his brigade were covered with scars from insect bites received a year before along the Big Black. But, he contended: "I never heard less complaining, or saw troops in better spirits." The same soldier could have added that at times even the higher officers felt the effects of that supreme and easy optimism. On one occasion, when General Peter J. Osterhaus, a division commander, rode into the camp of the 103rd Illinois, he was greeted with cries that "kraut by the barrel" had arrived from army headquarters. Osterhaus blew up and angrily chastised the commanding officer of the regiment, Lieutenant Colonel George W. Wright of Lewistown, for maintaining poor discipline. After having been given a few tough assignments, the 103rd was quick to conclude that "Yelping 'sauer kraut' at a German is a poor way to gain his favor."[34]

With it all, however—the casualness toward death and violence, and the casualness toward rank—it was an army filled with some of the most courageous fighting men ever to serve one nation. There was sufficient reason why eastern officers who commanded them marveled at their qualities. And among them all, "Fighting Joe" Hooker was willing to admit, the men from Illinois led all the rest.[35]

In the days between May of 1864 and the end of the year, a radical change occurred with respect to the attitude of Federal soldiers toward the property rights of southerners. As Sherman's supply lines lengthened, the troops began to supplement their rations, which were slender at times, with food from nearby farms.

---

[33] *Three Years in the Army of the Cumberland*, 168. *Reminiscences of the 103rd*, 47. Strong, 20.

[34] *Three Years in the Army of the Cumberland*, 260, 309–310.

[35] Brush to his father, July 31, 1864, Brush Family Papers. Hooker told young Brush that he was profoundly impressed with Illinois troops.

The desire for food was only one of the factors in the growing disregard for the concerns of the people of the conquered areas, however. More and more, advanced Union cavalry units began to come across the bodies of blue-coated foragers who had been killed by revengeful southerners, and to whose bodies had been pinned signs reading: "Death to all foragers." A study of diaries, letters, and reminiscences indicates that such incidents were not uncommon, and that the whole of Sherman's army soon became aware of them when they happened. Two members of the 40th Illinois were so treated, for instance, and within days all of the regiments from that state had heard of the deaths of the men.[36]

Western soldiers in Georgia soon assumed the attitude, therefore, that the conquered had few if any rights. Poultry of all kinds, cattle, and fruit fell to the invading army – and the depredations would become worse. "Because I am in the army," wrote a soldier of the 55th Illinois to his family, "you need not think that I am suffering – even away down here in Georgia." The food was simply unbelievable, continued young Lieutenant Thaddeus H. Capron: beefsteak, potatoes, cabbage, peaches and cream, and "blackberries and good doughnuts," all with the help of Georgia farmers. A soldier of the 36th Illinois was able to write that his regiment had smoked good Georgia tobacco and had eaten fine Georgia peanuts over half the face of that state. And a private of the 52nd Illinois, whose little group of associates in the regiment titled themselves the "Hyena Mess," related that he and his friends were "luxuriating on stewed green apples, and beef hearts, livers and tongues," a "favorable change" from the previous week's diet of "fat and greasy pork." Another Illinois soldier wrote to his wife that he had seldom seen such a surfeit of fruit, Georgia peaches, cherries, apples, and mulberries. And years later, an Oquawka, Illinois, soldier would remember with pleasure eating many sweet potatoes on the long march to Atlanta.[37]

---

[36] *Three Years in the Army of the Cumberland*, 208. Jamison, 312. The Illinois State Historical Library contains several accounts of the killing of foragers.

[37] "War Diary of Thaddeus H. Capron, 1861–1865 . . . ," *Journal*, XII, No. 3 (October, 1919), 385. Bennett and Haigh, 580. "Diary and Personal Memorandum Book of Private James P. Snell, 52nd Illinois Volunteers" (unpublished transcript, ISHL), 2. *Three Years in the Army of the Cumberland*, 216. Jamison, 280.

Along with their changing attitude toward southerners, the soldiers developed also a deeper identification with the aims of the war and an increasing intolerance for those who opposed those aims — the Copperheads. Early in 1864, several veterans were killed in a series of riots involving Copperheads and veterans on furlough in Charleston, Illinois. News of these incidents spread rapidly among the Illinois regiments in Sherman's grand army. "Illinois seems to be blackning her fair name by war in her own borders," wrote Lieutenant Charles Brush of the 53rd Illinois; "it is a burning shame and an insult to her soldiers fighting for the whole country." Other Illinois soldiers were willing to go beyond Brush's mild sentiments. Captain Levi Ross of the 86th Illinois, a regiment which had taken part in McCook's valiant charge up Kennesaw Mountain only a month before, wrote his family back in Ottawa that he wished the nation would draft 500,000 Copperheads. Sherman's army, he strongly asserted, was going ahead; no subversion in the rear was going to hinder its conquest of the South. An Illinois chaplain, whose task was to give Christian comfort to a Prairie State regiment in Sherman's army, was more explicit in his remarks. "I mean now Copperheads," he wrote; "yes Cowardly sneaks, Dirty Slipperry Slimy nasty Copperheads, Pore pukes, the back of my hand to them." [38]

There was, as can be seen, little question about the political sentiments of these veteran volunteer regiments. Those who had opposed the principles of the administration had long since gone home, leaving only the stronger supporters of Lincoln and his policies. In regiment after regiment holding mock elections in the summer of 1864, Lincoln stood clearly as the soldiers' choice over General McClellan, the Democrat candidate. The 34th Illinois, for instance, which a year before had shown anti-administration sentiments, now gave 241 votes to Lincoln and only 11 to his opponent in a trial election held by that regiment. An officer of the 123rd Illinois noted the same intense feeling; almost every regiment he saw in midsummer of 1864 indicated strong support for

[38] "Coles County in the Civil War 1861–1865, ed. L. M. Hamand, *Eastern Illinois University Bulletin*, No. 234 (April, 1961). This pamphlet contains a reprint of "The Charleston Riot, March 28, 1864," by Charles H. Coleman and Paul Spence. Brush to his father, Aug. 7, 1864, Brush Family Papers. Ross to his father, July 21, 1864, Ross Papers. *Diary of James T. Ayers*, 10.

the President. Sergeant Leander Stillwell of the 61st Illinois saw an even more interesting development among Illinois soldiers in that same period. His regiment, recruited in the Carrollton area, had consisted almost solely of Democrats at the beginning of the war. Now, in 1864, virtually every one of these same soldiers was ready to support the Union ticket of Lincoln and Andrew Johnson. It was the same everywhere, Stillwell found. And James T. Ayers, the Illinois chaplain who expressed himself so strongly on the issue of Copperheads, was almost as emotional in his feelings on the political race between Lincoln and McClellan. "Well," he told his diary, "my vote will be cast if I live for Father Abraham For President and Andy for vice President and Oglesby for Govenor and in short my vote will be Union all through sure as life." [39]

It was the first week in July, 1864, when an officer of the 123rd Illinois stood on the banks of the Chattahoochee River with generals Thomas and Sherman, and viewed for the first time the spires of Atlanta in the distance. Somehow, the young Illinois soldier felt that a turning point of the war had been reached. Apparently "Pap" Thomas thought so too. Standing on the edge of the river like a "noble old Roman," the commanding general of the Army of the Cumberland turned to the Illinois officer, Major James Connolly, and ordered that several Parrott guns be brought up. In quick fashion, the rifled cannon were rolled forward, and only minutes later a Federal shell burst "beautifully" on the other side of the river. Sherman had begun his final effort to capture Atlanta.[40]

The great Union army moved upon the Georgia railroad center from the north and east. McPherson's Army of the Cumberland made a grand envelopment in the direction of Decatur, with Dodge's XVI Corps moving to a position directly east of Atlanta. Schofield's Army of the Ohio came down upon the city from the northeast, and Thomas' Army of the Cumberland moved ponderously toward Peachtree Creek from the north. It was at this last place that Hood, on July 20, decided to hit hard at the advancing Federal army.

---

[39] *Three Years in the Army of the Cumberland*, 293. Payne, 162. Stillwell, *Story of a Common Soldier*, 229–230. *Diary of James T. Ayers*, 61.

[40] *Three Years in the Army of the Cumberland*, 235.

The sun which rose on the morning of July 20 revealed a typical July day—hot and dry. Thomas had thrown his corps across Peachtree Creek. But there was a gap between Thomas and Schofield. The Army of the Cumberland offered an inviting target. Hood's strategy was to take advantage of this fact: he would push a sharp attack upon Thomas when his army was isolated and crush the right wing of the great Federal army.

It was early afternoon when the Confederates began their assault, first against Newton's division on the east flank and then down the line to Geary's eastern troops. Among the Illinois regiments which were to see hard fighting on this intemperately hot day were the 74th, a Winnebago County unit, commanded by Colonel Thomas Bryan of Durand; the 79th, an Edgar and Douglas counties regiment, commanded by Colonel Allan Buckner of Arcola; the 82nd, a northern Illinois regiment, commanded by Colonel Edward Solomon; and the 104th, the La Salle County regiment, under the charge of Colonel Douglas Hapeman.

Solomon's regiment, the 82nd, had an interesting history. Originally organized as the "Second Hecker Regiment," it was composed principally of Germans from Chicago. Shortly after its mustering-in it was sent to the East, where, after joining the Army of the Potomac, it fought at Fredericksburg and Gettysburg. Now, on July 20, 1864, it found itself in a place far removed from Marye's Heights and the Little Round Top. In General Alpheus S. Williams' division of Hooker's corps the 82nd was participant in and witness to some of the more savage Confederate attacks of the day. Alongside Geary's division, the Illinois regiment poured a terrible flanking fire into the ranks of the attackers, killing a considerable number of Hood's finest troops.

The 104th Illinois, fighting in Colonel Anson McCook's brigade, also became heavily engaged in repelling Hood's assault upon the Army of the Cumberland. This Illinois regiment was most expertly handled by Hapeman during the day, and came off with relatively few casualties. For this, and for his courage in the face of enemy fire, the young commanding officer of the 104th was awarded the Medal of Honor.[41]

The hard fighting of July 20 did not finish Hood, of course.

[41] *Official Records*, Ser. I, Vol. XXXVIII, Pt. 1, 156–157. Aten, 200. *Report of the Adjutant General*, IV, 593–598; V, 48–49, 120–124. *Historical Encyclo-*

Two days later, on July 22, he once again hurled his army at Sherman's men, this time against the XVI Corps of McPherson's division, commanded by Grenville M. Dodge, which was positioned far to the Union left. It was noon before Hardee's men, having just finished a lengthy roundabout night march from Atlanta, were able to strike at the XVI Corps. The surprise of the assault was only a momentary one, however, for Dodge quickly made adjustments in his line of battle to meet the situation. To a member of the 55th Illinois, a regiment not directly involved in the early fighting, the "battle was grand"; the Confederates, he would write later, were killed almost as if they were in a turkey shoot. The Confederates continued the attacks, however, making an unfortunate error in directing them against an area of the field held by the 64th Illinois, the old "Yates Sharpshooters," commanded by Colonel John Morrill of Dayton, Illinois. Morrill had armed his men with Henry repeating rifles which enabled the 64th not only to throw off the Confederate assaults and inflict heavy losses, but also to mount a successful counterattack. This last maneuver recovered the position in which the commanding general of the Army of the Tennessee, McPherson, had been killed only an hour before.[42] Logan succeeded McPherson on the battlefield, but O. O. Howard later was named commander, a move which caused some bitterness among those who believed Logan deserved the post.

At three o'clock in the afternoon, just as Hardee's attacks were coming to a close, Hood sent Cheatham's corps and General G. W. Smith's 5,000 Georgia militia troops in a frontal attack upon Logan's XV Corps. It was a situation made to order for the southern Illinois general. A member of the 55th Illinois, standing near Logan at the time, recalled years later that his face actually seemed to light up as he strode up and down the lines shouting: "Hold them! steady, boys, we've got them now."

Despite Logan's supreme confidence, the situation developed an aspect which could have proved dangerous for the Federal army. Manigault's Confederate brigade, driving down the At-

---

pedia of Illinois, 561. Calkins, 222. *Civil War Medal of Honor Winners*, 7. Fox, 453. Fox indicates that the hardest fighting of the day was done by Pennsylvania, Ohio, and other eastern regiments.

[42] "War Diary of Thaddeus H. Capron," 389–390. *Report of the Adjutant General*, IV, 340.

lanta to Decatur railroad, managed to insert itself between Logan's line and the Army of the Ohio, enveloping the right flank of the XV Corps. Four 20-pound Parrott guns of H Battery, 1st Illinois Light Artillery, were taken, and Morgan Smith's old division, now commanded by General J. A. J. Lightburn, was driven back. Lightburn's regiments included a number of units from Illinois, but one of them in particular, the 55th, played an important role in the recovery of Logan's right wing. Once again it was the popular Chaplain Milton Haney who became the hero of the regiment. This time, finding the 55th being hard pressed, he picked up a rifle and led it in a stirring counterattack which helped to stabilize the Federal line and throw back Manigault's troops.[43]

Illinois provided a number of other heroes in this Battle of Atlanta. Logan himself was all over the field, having replaced his old battle cry of "remember the blood of your mammies! give 'em hell!" with "McPherson and revenge!" One young Illinois soldier, writing in his diary a few days later, was able to record a number of colorful impressions of the day's fighting and of Logan: "A little after dinner the fun commenced—rebs having been reinforced by the whole of Hardee's Corps, they felt confident of using up our army—were sadly disappointed . . . lively time rebs charging our works—handsomely repulsed every time. saw Gen Logan about 4 p.m. was in the best of spirits [some alcoholic too] damning the rebels etc. . . ."[44]

The 55th and 64th Illinois were not the only regiments to improve upon their already sturdy reputations on this day. The 20th and 31st Illinois, fighting with the division of Giles A. Smith, the former Bloomington innkeeper, took a particularly hard beating from attacks by Cleburne's and George E. Maney's Confederate divisions. The first of these units, raised in and around Champaign County, was commanded by Colonel Daniel Bradley of Champaign. The 31st, the old "dirty-first," which was raised originally by Logan himself, came naturally from southern Illinois. By mid-afternoon, both of these Illinois regiments found

[43] "War Diary of Thaddeus H. Capron," 387–388. [Crooker *et al.*], 346. *Civil War Medal of Honor Winners*, 7.

[44] *Report of the Adjutant General*, II, 575. Dawson, 65. "Civil War Diary of William C. Titze" (unpublished manuscript and partial transcript, ISHL), 70.

themselves fighting off Confederate attacks coming at them from both sides of their breastworks. Holding their positions, they inflicted heavy casualties upon the oncoming troops. A member of the 103rd Illinois who visited the area of the fighting shortly after the end of the battle found that the bodies of enemy soldiers lay "as thick on one side of the works, as the other. . . ."[45]

Hood's casualties were enormous, 8,000 out of the approximately 37,000 troops engaged. Among the 30,500 Union troops who found their way into action, 3,722 were declared to be killed, wounded, or missing. The heaviest single regimental loss suffered by Federal troops in the fighting on July 22 was that of the 13th Iowa, in the XVII Corps, which counted 25 killed, 188 wounded, and 93 missing. The largest losses by Illinois regiments were suffered by the 31st, with a total of 163 casualties; the 64th, the regiment of the XVI Corps with the repeating Henrys, with losses of 122; the 111th, in Lightburn's division, with 154 casualties (86 of that number missing); and the 66th, Sweeny's division of the XVI Corps, with losses of 76.[46]

By July 25 Sherman had invested Atlanta on the north and east. The only line of communication which Hood still maintained out of the city was the railroad to the south. On July 26 Sherman sent General George Stoneman and three brigades of cavalry in a five-day raid upon the Confederate retreat toward Macon to cut Hood's remaining line of supply from the south. One of Stoneman's brigadiers was Colonel Horace Capron of Durand, Illinois, and two of his finest regiments were the 14th and 16th Illinois Cavalry. The raid was unsuccessful in achieving its objective, for Stoneman was captured and a large portion of his command was lost after heavy fighting with Joseph Wheeler's Confederate cavalry.[47]

On July 28 another savage battle was fought near Ezra Church west of Atlanta, when Howard's Army of the Tennessee made another attempt to cut Hood's supply line to the south. Much of the fighting here was done by Logan's XV Corps; among Illinois troops, fighting was done by the 9th, 12th, 66th, and 127th regi-

---

[45] *Reminiscences of the 103rd,* 108. Blanchard, 130–131.

[46] Thomas L. Livermore, 122–123. Fox, 453.

[47] *Historical Encyclopedia of Illinois,* 569. Most of the 14th and 16th regiments were saved, however.

ments. Once again Sherman's attempt to envelop Atlanta from the south met failure.[48]

For many Illinois soldiers this was the hardest part of the Atlanta campaign thus far. Regiments had been decimated by the almost constant fighting from Rocky Face Ridge to Ezra Church; in some regiments not a single day had passed without a casualty. One young soldier, Private William C. Titze of West Salem, Illinois, questioned in his diary how long his own regiment, the 66th, could keep itself in service. It had suffered numerous casualties and its horses were giving out under the heavy duty. Every Illinois regiment in Grose's brigade of the Army of the Cumberland, the 59th, 75th, 80th, and 84th, had lost one third of its complement since the end of May. Some Illinois regiments, the 20th for instance, had suffered so many casualties in the campaign that they were never reconstituted. The growing doubts of Sherman's men about the capture of Atlanta are illustrated in the diary entry of young Sergeant James P. Snell of the 52nd Illinois: "I do not look for the triumph of our arms, and the occupancy of the city, for at least 60 days, and hardly then, *unless we have reinforcements*. We have not, to-day got one-half the guns in our battle front, we had at Resaca and Dallas. In the two months more of active service, without accessions, scarce a 'corporal's guard' will remain to tell of the victories and glories won in Georgia! May God help the right!" [49]

Part of the trouble seems to have been that the Federal troops had no difficulty seeing the prize for which they had so long fought. It was visible from almost every position, though assistance from nature was needed in some cases. "Several of our boys have been having a 'sly look' at 'ye city of Atlanta,'" wrote Sergeant Snell of Aurora, Illinois, "from the top of a tall pine tree, near the graveyard, not far from our camp." Philip S. Post, writing his sister back in Galesburg on the day after the battle of Ezra Church, described most graphically his impressions of the be-

[48] *Official Records*, Ser. I, Vol. XXXVIII, Pt. 1, 78. "Diary of James P. Snell," 38–39. *Civil War Medal of Honor Winners*, 4, states that Robinson Murphy, a musician with the 127th Illinois, took over leadership of two regiments and led them into battle at Ezra Church. For this he was awarded the Medal of Honor.

[49] "Civil War Diary of William C. Titze," 64. "Diary of James P. Snell," 59. Herr, 290.

sieged city and the fighting around it. "My brigade," wrote Post, "occupies a line of works more than a mile long. The fire goes on night and day without the slightest intermission, and the booming of the cannon at night and the fires which nightly illuminate the sky from burning houses in Atlanta will always be retained by our soldiers among their most vivid and melancholy recollections. . . ." The cannonading was continuous, Post stated; the Confederate shells at night looked like "camp Kettles," and exploded like thunderclaps.

Later Post wrote of looking at Atlanta through a telescope and spoke of

> a beautiful city spread out before you assailed and defended by one hundred and fifty thousand combatants with all the destructive engines known to modern warfare. The landscape would, at any time, have been very striking, but it never presented so many attractive features as it does now and while the graceful smoke which puffs out and curls heavenward (but seldom interfering with the prospect) claimed the eye the rattle of musketry and roar of artillery would not fail to impress the ear, and the pleasure of the whole thing is seasoned by a slight sense of insecurity of human affairs of which you are ever and anon reminded by the whirr of the bullet or scream of a shot or shell en passant.

Few Illinois soldiers would have disagreed with Post's prediction that the memories of those July and August nights would prove unforgettable. And very likely they would have agreed with Post's own rationalization about the horror of it all. Falling back upon a quotation from Alexander Pope, he carefully told his sister: "Whatever is, is right." [50]

While Post was seeking an essence of truth in the flames of war, young Private James Snell made another entry into his diary. "It is whispered around (a little bird sang in my ear) in official circles, that a big *move* commences this p.m. the two corps on our left (4th and 20th) to move to the right, tomorrow morning." Further details in the rumors which passed from soldier to soldier were a little vague. Nobody really knew where the attack was going to take place, though the military grapevine had it that Montgomery in Alabama might be the goal.

Snell's version of Sherman's next big move was a typical pri-

[50] "Diary of James P. Snell," 3. Post to Miss Mary Post, July 29, Aug. 18, 1864, Post Papers.

vate's one: it was only partially right. It was obvious to the commanding general of the great Federal army around Atlanta that the key to the final capture of that city was the cutting of the railroad to the south. Other moves had failed, but Hood himself gave Sherman one more opportunity. The Confederate general sent the bulk of his cavalry on a wide sweeping raid toward Dalton, which was good strategy had he had enough troops left in the area of Atlanta proper. He didn't, however, particularly cavalry, and Sherman was the first to recognize it. After the failure of Kilpatrick's Union cavalry to cut the railroad on August 20, Sherman regrouped his infantry divisions for a massive assault on the railroad town of Jonesboro.[51]

By August 30 Sherman had shifted a substantial part of his army directly south of Atlanta. Hood, recognizing the dangers of the move, quickly sent Hardee's corps to drive the Union forces back from Jonesboro. Arriving at two o'clock in the afternoon on August 31, the Confederate general immediately attacked, with but little success. "They charged," wrote Private Snell of the 52nd, "but our boys held their ground, and kept them at bay, with so little effort that they laughed at the Johnnies – cheered, as they came up – talked with them when they charged our line – and halloed after them as they retired toward their position." It was a tough and rugged army which faced Hardee's attackers, who were greeted with cries of "Wake 'em up Yanks!" and "No you dont! – Try again Jonny!" as they tried to cave in the Union line. "The air was resonant with spirited huzzahs," added Snell; "every man felt as though he was a phalanx– every command seemed to partake of the animation, and seemed anxious for a fray in which to work off their super-abundant enthusiasm."

Far to the right of the Federal forces, near Anthony's Bridge, General Hugh Judson Kilpatrick's cavalry, which included the 92nd and 123rd Mounted Illinois Infantry, opened an attack upon Cleburne's Confederate troops. Both regiments were armed with repeating Spencer rifles. Kilpatrick's attack, though diversionary, was fairly important. Cleburne was forced to change fronts to meet the Federal onslaught, which, after a considerable number

[51] "Diary of James P. Snell," 66. *Official Records*, Ser. I, Vol. XXXVIII, Pt. 1, 79–80. Boatner, 33.

of casualties, he managed to drive back. The 92nd Illinois distinguished itself by covering Kilpatrick's withdrawal across the bridge. One would suspect, however, that it was really the Spencers which did the trick. As Major James Connolly of the 123rd expressed it, each member of the regiment felt himself twice the man that an opposing Confederate was because of the gun. "We think our Spencers saved us," Connolly was moved to write, "and our men adore them as the heathen do their idols."[52]

At noon on September 1 the reinforced Federal army at Jonesboro began an attack of their own. William P. Carlin and Giles A. Smith, both Illinois generals, led significant assaults by their respective divisions against the Confederate breastworks. All went well. A sergeant of the 95th Illinois, Onley Andrus, would later describe fighting in a most matter-of-fact manner. "I had some very good shots," he wrote his wife, "as well as all of the Skirmishers who were all from our *Co*." Major Connolly of the 123rd Illinois looked at the battle in a different light. Writing his wife a few days afterward, he told of tears streaming from his eyes as a result of the emotional impact of the victory. "I could have lain down on that blood-stained grass, amid the dying and the dead and wept with excess of joy," he concluded. "I have no language to express the rapture one feels in the moment of victory, but I do know at such a moment one feels as if the joy were worth risking a hundred lives to attain it." Connolly had come a long way from a night four years earlier when he had lain in a Charleston, Illinois, hotel room attempting to comprehend the meaning of military tactics.[53]

The same could be noted about the men of the 78th Illinois. Almost 11 months earlier this untried regiment from western Illinois had marched at a forced pace in order to save Thomas' XIV Corps, which was being pushed off Horseshoe Ridge at Chickamauga. Now, on September 1, 1864, it had taken part in a beautiful envelopment of a Confederate brigade which resulted in the capture of General Daniel C. Govan. The achievement was

[52] *Official Records*, Ser. I, Vol. XXXVIII, Pt. 1, 81–82. "Diary of James P. Snell," 96–97. *The Ninety-second Illinois Volunteers*, 159. *Three Years in the Army of the Cumberland*, 83, 127.

[53] *Civil War Letters of Sergeant Onley Andrus*, 103. *Three Years in the Army of the Cumberland*, 258.

not without cost, however. The 78th suffered the largest losses of any Illinois regiment fighting at Jonesboro – 50 in all.

The Union victory at Jonesboro was, as anticipated by Major Connolly, the key which opened the lock at Atlanta. By nightfall of September 1 Hood was in hurried retreat from the besieged city. On the following morning the dusty blue-coated veterans of the long march south walked the last mile through the deserted redoubts and rifle pits. The road had been long and hard – Resaca, Dallas, Allatoona Pass, Kennesaw Mountain, and Atlanta itself; and 32,000 Union soldiers had been killed, wounded, or imprisoned along the way.[54]

[54] Fox, 546.

CHAPTER X

We Bring the Jubilee

The capture of Atlanta by Sherman was both an end and a beginning. Part of the Union army pursued Hood as far as Lovejoy's Station, a village south of Jonesboro, only to find the Confederates too strongly entrenched there. On September 8 Sherman returned his forces to Atlanta to recuperate and reorganize his army and to begin the fortification of the city so that it might be held by a small number of troops. To do this it was necessary, from Sherman's point of view, to evacuate the southern civilians from the city. It was not an easy order to issue, and its execution brought a bitter exchange of notes with Hood, who protested the "ingenious cruelty" of the Federal general. Sherman undoubtedly regretted the action as much as anyone. Some Union soldiers carried out the orders with great reluctance. "It is a sad sight to see them," wrote Lieutenant Charles Brush of the 53rd Illinois, "the citizens, leaving their homes of opulence and wealth and wending their way on foot—women and children in carriages, ambulances and wagons—out to the lines to go south, but such is war." Concluding with an obviously heartfelt prayer, the Ottawa, Illinois, officer added: "God grant that this one [war] may soon be closed and in such a way that we may never again see our country broken. . . ."[1]

[1] *Official Records*, Ser. I, Vol. XXXVIII, Pt. 1, 82–83; Vol. XXXIX, Pt. 1, 580–581. Alice M. Barker to Newell Brown, Oct. 22, 1864, Alice M. Barker Letter, ISHL. Hood's remarks are quoted in Earl Schenck Miers, *The General Who Marched to Hell . . .* (New York, 1951), 184. Brush to his father, Sept. 22, 1864, Brush Family Papers.

The army which Sherman was busily entrenching in the Atlanta area was greatly changed in many ways from that which had started the march from Chattanooga earlier in the year. General Hooker, whose ambitions always exceeded his superior's estimates of his ability, had become angry at Sherman's choice of Howard to command the Army of the Tennessee and had asked to be relieved. John Palmer, the Carlinville, Illinois, general, had run into the same kind of difficulty. Being placed in a position of having to take orders from Schofield, another Illinois general to whom he considered himself superior, he had asked for relief and had gone home. General Thomas W. Sweeny, the one-armed Irish "bulldog" who had organized the 52nd Illinois early in the war, also went his way, having become involved in a fist fight with his superior, General Grenville M. Dodge, in July. "The *devil* seems to be in our 'stars,'" wrote Sergeant James Snell, who was serving in Sweeny's old Illinois regiment. "We lost McPherson, by a lack of caution and prudence; Sweeny, through a drunken quarrel; Hooker, on account of jealousy and pride, because Howard took 'Mack's' place; and now Palmer swells the list, because for sooth he hated to report to Schofield, as a subordinate!" [2]

Finally old "Pap" Thomas was also sent away to Nashville—not because of any difficulty with Sherman, but because the operations of Forrest and Wheeler with the Confederate cavalry, and the preparations which Hood was obviously making at Palmetto, to the southwest of Atlanta, had convinced Sherman that the Confederates were making ready for a strike into Tennessee. What was left then at Atlanta was reorganized by Sherman into a well-equipped force consisting of two major armies. The first, the "Right Wing," commanded by O. O. Howard, the Bible-reading general who had lost an arm at Fair Oaks in 1862, consisted of Osterhaus' XV Corps (Logan would resume command here in January of 1865), and General F. P. Blair's XVII Corps. The "Left Wing," commanded by Henry W. Slocum, was composed of the XIV Corps, commanded by J. C. Davis, and the XX Corps, commanded by A. S. Williams. The cavalry was made up of two brigades under General Hugh Judson Kilpatrick, and two

[2] "Diary of James P. Snell," 51.

unattached units, the 1st Alabama Cavalry and the 9th Illinois Mounted Infantry.

Among the various corps and units in Sherman's army was a good representation of general officers and regiments from the state of Illinois. The Third Division of the XV Corps was commanded by General John E. Smith, the Galena officer, and the Fourth Division of the XVII Corps was commanded by Giles A. Smith, the Bloomington general officer. William P. Carlin, the Carrollton general who had compiled a rather brilliant record in the Missouri and Chattanooga campaigns, commanded a division in the XIV Corps. Another division in the same corps was under the command of General James Dady Morgan, who came from Quincy, Illinois. Morgan came into prominence early in the war as a courageous field commander of the 10th Illinois Infantry. A tough and colorful man, whose early life was filled with exploits on the high seas, he had risen through the various ranks to that of division commander. He was not the last Illinois officer who could be found in a position of authority and responsibility in Sherman's great army. One of Kilpatrick's cavalry brigades was commanded by Smith D. Atkins, a Freeport, Illinois general, whose role in the coming campaign would be a prominent one. Furthermore, in one of the real romantic episodes of the war, Atkins would symbolize the end of conflict in the South by finding a wife in the Carolinas.[3]

Of the 55,000 infantrymen in the great army poised at Atlanta, 45 regiments of them came from Illinois. One cavalry regiment from the same state composed part of the force of 5,000 cavalrymen at Sherman's disposal; further, a number of infantry units from Illinois, such as the 9th, 92nd, and 123rd, acted as mounted infantry, which actually amounted to cavalry. Out of the 2,000 artillerymen attached to the grand army, three batteries came from Illinois. Compared with other western states, the grand sum of nearly 50 regiments from the Prairie State is a significant one. Ohio provided 52 for the coming campaign; Indiana gave 27;

[3] *Report of the Adjutant General*, I, 103. *Historical Encyclopedia of Illinois*, 384. The story of Atkins' marriage is nicely told in John G. Barrett, *Sherman's March Through the Carolinas* (Chapel Hill, 1956), 263–266. Atkins married the daughter of the president of the University of North Carolina. *Official Records*, Ser. I, Vol. XLIV, 19–25.

Iowa, 15. New York led the contributions from the eastern states with 16 regiments.[4]

Sherman's plan of marching to the sea presented some danger, of course, though not nearly so much as one might have expected. The Union troops were opposed by no more than 13,000 Confederate troops at any one time. They were, moreover, second-rate soldiers—3,000 of them being members of General G. W. Smith's Georgia militia, certainly not in the class of the legions which Hood had taken north with him in his invasion of Tennessee.

But before any march to the sea could begin, Hood had to be dealt with. By October 1 the Confederates had moved north and westward, attempting to pull Sherman out of Atlanta by getting between him and Chattanooga. There was considerable fighting, and Sherman did draw back some troops to oppose Hood. Included in the action was the staunch defense of Allatoona Pass by General Corse on October 5. Illinois units involved in the sanguinary fighting included the 7th, 12th, 50th, 57th, and 93rd Illinois. Hood continued northwestward to Resaca and Dalton before turning into Alabama preparatory to his invasion of Tennessee. Sherman followed him to Resaca and then to Gaylesville, Alabama, on the Georgia line, before turning back to Atlanta.

Unlike many of the incidents or events of the American Civil War, the plan for the march to Savannah was a fairly well-kept secret even among the general officers of Sherman's army. By early November, however, even the lowest private was aware that an unusual occurrence was in the making. It was obvious that a new campaign was being planned, though few could guess correctly as to its destination. "Some mysterious work is in progress now," wrote a soldier of the 34th Illinois. "Sherman is destroying his own line of communications, and is evidently going to march to a new base of supplies—but is it the Gulf, the Atlantic, or where?" Even to Captain Levi Ross of the 86th Illinois, the plans of the high command seemed indiscernible. The Princeton, Illinois, officer knew that something important was in the air. The army would not issue an order that each man was to carry a new pair of shoes unless a great deal of marching was to be done.

[4] *Report of the Adjutant General*, I, 103. *Official Records*, Ser. I, Vol. XLIV, 7.

Beyond this, however, Ross could only report to his father that the men of the 86th were filled with consternation over the prospects and purposes of Sherman's preparations.

The great event began on November 15, when Sherman destroyed the military resources of Atlanta and sent his troops streaming off to the east. Major James Connolly of the 123rd Illinois could not help but be impressed by the opening of the campaign. There were "flags flying and men cheering," he wrote. Then, with a sense of the significance of the event, he added: ". . . we turn our backs on Atlanta, and our faces seaward."

Connolly's ideas were correct, but he had misread his directions. Slocum's wing of the army, to which the Charleston, Illinois, officer was attached, actually marched northward at first from Atlanta and across the old battlegrounds of the conflict of July 22. There, as Connolly was to discover, the fields of red Georgia clay were covered with the graves of the men of the XV Corps. The literate major concluded that none lay there "more thickly than the men of Illinois." What Connolly obviously saw was that spot of ground so savagely contested by the 20th and 31st Illinois.[5]

Slocum's Left Wing was following the route of the Atlanta to Augusta railroad through such towns as Decatur, Lithonia, Conyers, and Covington. Beyond the first of these places, the men of the 66th Illinois discovered an indication of the nature of Confederate resistance to Sherman's grand march. There, as Private William Titze of the 111th Illinois was to note in his diary, was a great supply of lances which the governor of Georgia had laid by for his militia. The men of the 66th, already equipped with rapid-firing Henry rifles, could only regard such weapons with the viewpoint of youth. They picked them up, and, in the way of the young, played at jousting and fencing, all in the spirit of fun. Days later, as Titze would write, "scores of them were carried around . . . giving the troops the appearances as though we were still living in the middle ages."[6]

The move which Slocum made toward Augusta was actually a feint. Once past the town of Madison, the Union general destroyed

[5] Payne, 163. Ross to his father, Nov. 5, 1864, Ross Papers. *Three Years in the Army of the Cumberland*, 304.

[6] "Civil War Diary of William C. Titze," 55–56.

the bridge which crossed the Oconee River, and then marched to the southeast alongside that stream. There was really nothing very difficult in all of this – no opposition except the interminable, red, slippery Georgia mud. It was mid-November, and the rains came often and hard. Marching along the country roads, it was not too uncommon to see a rangy veteran of Davis' XIV Corps, for instance, slide down an embankment and into a dirty bog hole. On an occasion when this happened near the ranks of the 52nd Illinois, a hardy regiment raised principally in Kane County, the troops of that unit were quick to raise a loud cry. "Dig him out," they shouted, "and see if he has any tobacco."[7]

While Slocum was marching at a steady but slippery pace along the Oconee, Howard's Right Wing was proceeding along the Atlanta to Macon railroad and to the rail junction of Gordon, just south of Milledgeville. There was little fighting along the way. Near Lovejoy's Station, on November 16, Kilpatrick's cavalry tangled briefly with two Confederate brigades from Wheeler's command. It was an easy victory for "Kill Cavalry's" men, for most of his force, the 92nd Illinois for example, were equipped with repeating Spencer rifles and trained to act as mounted infantry.

On November 22, near Griswoldville, just east of Macon, there was another effort by the Confederates to slow Sherman's advance. The Georgia militia, under G. W. Smith, made a brave but futile attack upon the advancing column of blue. The fight was a brief one. When it was all over, some of the Illinois soldiers who had taken part in the battle, particularly those of the 40th and 103rd regiments, were overcome with the sense of the futility of war. On the small field the bodies of the very old and very young men of the Georgia militia lay in sad little clusters. A Canton, Illinois, officer of the 103rd, weighed down with a feeling of guilt over the sight, walked back to his tent and carefully noted in his diary that the Federal army had "slaughtered those men."[8]

While Slocum and Howard were swinging in wide arcs in the direction of Milledgeville, capital of Georgia, Kilpatrick moved

[7] "Diary of James P. Snell," 104.

[8] Jacob D. Cox, *The March to the Sea: Franklin and Nashville*, Vol. X of *The Army in the Civil War* (New York, 1885), 27–31. Boatner, 509–510. *Official Records*, Ser. I, Vol. XLIV, 8–9. *Army Life of an Illinois Soldier*, 324.

through a series of fiercely fought actions with Wheeler's Confederate cavalry. The fighting at Ball's Ferry, Sandersville, and Waynesboro were victories for Wheeler. In a number of bitter skirmishes in early December, however, Kilpatrick pushed Wheeler about rather severely, inflicting numerous casualties upon the Confederate force.

Hugh Judson "Kill Cavalry" Kilpatrick was a strange and anomalous character whose traits were such that he could possibly have succeeded only in the art of war. While there was no question about his courage, there were many concerning his virtues. He liked women, he made much use of his power as a general officer to obtain them, and he didn't seem to care who knew it. There would be a time later, during the Carolinas campaign, when he would have to flee from the side of one favorite, clad only in a nightgown.

In late November and early December of 1864 in Georgia, there was property to be destroyed and there were Negro women to be liberated. The more judicious General Smith Atkins could do little to counsel his superior to remember his responsibilities as a soldier under the flag of the United States. As the historian of the 92nd Illinois would later write, the "female quadroons" who came into Kilpatrick's camp were "really very pretty," for they had "large, lustrous eyes, and pearly white teeth."

Kilpatrick called his subordinates, Atkins and the rest, together, to instruct them in the nature of this war. He interpreted Sherman's orders to destroy certain facilities. He wanted the total destruction of the enemy capacity and will to fight. It should have been no surprise to him when, after some of the more savage battles between himself and Wheeler, some of the men of the 92nd Illinois were found with their throats cut from ear to ear.[9]

What Kilpatrick was doing with his cavalry was an extreme of what Sherman's army as a whole was doing. Starting with only 20 days' worth of rations for his troops, the commanding general of the army ordered his soldiers to live off the land by foraging. This the army did with a will. Each regiment organized its own foraging party, which was to consist of 20 men and an officer. Soldiers from the ranks, unless they were in such parties, were under orders not to engage in any foraging activities.

[9] Barrett, 128. *The Ninety-second Illinois Volunteers*, 188, 216.

It is clear, however, that few regiments followed Sherman's dictum in regard to the 20-man squads. Because of the lack of Confederate opposition, there was little to prevent the ordinary soldier from organizing his own foraging parties. As Private William Enderton of the 34th Illinois recalled in the years following the conflict, the rules for obtaining food were seldom obeyed by his regiment, a hard-fighting Whiteside and Ogle counties unit. As this Sterling, Illinois, soldier put it, there was hardly a man in the entire organization who did not "forage from morning till night. . . ." The result was a surfeit of food in most Illinois regiments. As a western Illinois soldier of the 103rd remembered it after the war, the foraging details would return at the end of each day with wagonloads of vegetables and meat. The soldiers of the regiments who hadn't done their own foraging earlier would then gather about the wagons and carry off whatever they wished.[10]

As the days and miles of Sherman's march to the sea rolled by, southern farmers in advance of the armies began to receive forewarnings of what was in store for them and attempted to devise methods by which they could save their cattle and produce. A member of the 105th Illinois reported early in the campaign, for instance, that Union foraging parties began to come across a number of homes which flew the yellow flag, indicating the presence of smallpox. It was a ruse which worked only briefly. In time, the house which flew the yellow flag was always singled out first for search.[11]

Other southerners attempted to save food and valuables by hiding them. That too had only a brief success. As a member of the 105th Illinois described it, every Yankee invader soon learned to look for the telltale signs of overturned dirt and how to terrorize Negro slaves into informing upon their masters. In the years following the conflict, an Oquawka soldier of the 10th Illinois described the latter technique in detail. "What did you hide?" the Illinois soldiers would ask of one Negro. "Box clothes in de field," was the ordinary reply. "And what did you hide?" the troops would ask of his companion. "Books in de garden," would be the answer.[12]

---

[10] Payne, 166. *Reminiscences of the 103rd,* 141.

[11] Strong, 69–70.

[12] *Ibid.* Jamison, 285.

By the time Sherman's army was halfway to Savannah, it looked more like a combination of despoilers, pioneers, and masqueraders than a fighting machine. A member of the 64th Illinois would recall in the years which followed that his own regiment looked strange indeed, as each soldier had a piece of unskinned hog stuck upon the end of his bayonet, a skillet clanging from his belt, and his haversack filled with flour which spilled out and over his clothes. There may not have been a single kitchen utensil left in the areas traversed by the great army. They hung from the sides of horses and mules, and pealed dolorously from the backs of the regimental wagons. A Canton, Illinois, officer, caught up in the lighthearted atmosphere, wrote: "This is probably the most gigantic pleasure excursion every planned. It already beats every thing I ever saw soldiering. . . . I wish that Sherman would burn the commissary wagons. . . . Our men are clear discouraged with foraging. They can't carry half the hogs & potatoes they see right along the road." And a southerner, whose house was right on the path of the Union Left Wing, described the Federal advance as follows: "It was the 14th Corps that came through my place. They looked like a blue cloud coming. They had all kinds of music – horns, cow-bells, tin-pans, everything they could pick up that would make a hideous noise. . . . They burned everything but occupied dwellings. They cut the belluses at the blacksmith-shops. They took every knife and fork and cooking utensil we had." [13]

What was written by Major Charles Wills of Canton, Illinois, and the unnamed southerner clearly describes an army turned loose upon the land. More proof of this fact was presented by a soldier of the 64th Illinois, who wrote that little if any care was given to horses and mules along the line of march, for there were always more which could be requisitioned on the farms ahead. When an animal had worn out its usefulness, therefore, it was casually shot so that it might not fall into the hands of the Confederate army. The same soldier would note another strange episode which occurred as the long blue columns moved across the

[13] George Sharland, *Knapsack Notes of General Sherman's Grand Campaign* . . . (Springfield, 1865), 39. Sharland was a member of the 64th Illinois. Civil War Diary of Charles W. Wills, Nov. 14–Dec. 15, 1864, 6–7. Trowbridge, 502–503.

red Georgia clay. Some of the men of the 64th had come across a number of ancient but beautifully ornamented carriages and had confiscated them along with a herd of cows and countless Negroes. The cattle tied behind, they rolled in a strange procession; as described by a watching soldier of the 10th Illinois, the "skeleton remains of carriages of state, in which milord and ladies rode to the society functions of the Oglethorpe and earlier periods." Had the country ever seen such a conquering host? [14]

Vengeance was undoubtedly a great and motivating force throughout the ranks of the Federal army. "Everything must be destroyed," wrote Major James Connolly. "We have gone so far now in our triumphal march that we will not be balked." The same soldier would note the fires and smoke far to the left and right of his own column, indicating the presence of the various corps of the army. Southern farmers, he added, had a "paralyzed" look to them. Everywhere, wrote Connolly, were to be seen "Sherman's Sentinels," solitary brick chimneys that were all that remained of the burned tobacco, peanut, and fruit warehouses. A soldier of the 64th Illinois noted the same sight—the "cloudy pillar" which designated the advance units of each Federal corps. It was a sight which the individual soldier could never forget. "Our men burned all cotton gins and presses that have cotton in them . . . ," wrote a soldier of the 34th Illinois. "We see the smoke and flames of burning buildings all along the route. Oft times we feel the heat of the flames as we march past, where the buildings are close to the road." [15]

While many buildings were burned, most homes were spared destruction, but the contents were usually taken, of course. Food supplies were fed the advancing columns of troops, as if the army were a giant reptile which consumed as it moved. Still, it was not always possible to keep the great animal of the Federal army well supplied with provisions. Not far from Savannah, as a soldier of the 34th Illinois wrote, the daily ration fell sharply to a little hardtack and a few strips of bacon, until the head of the advancing column of the XIV Corps fell upon huge supplies of unhulled rice. The foraging party of the 86th Illinois found a ware-

---

[14] Sharland, 25, 15. Jamison, 290.

[15] *Three Years in the Army of the Cumberland*, 324, 314. Sharland, 34. Payne, 169.

house filled with such provender near the Savannah River and carried 60 wagons of rice back to the main body of the regiment. Other Illinois units experienced the same welcome change in diet. The 34th Illinois went on a daily ration of unhulled rice and fresh beef. The 10th Illinois, likewise, went through the daily routine of attempting to take the hulls off their rice allowance. In the latter case, Yankee ingenuity came to the fore. A western Illinois soldier of the 10th found a new use for an old-time well sweep — as a pestle — and the problem of unhusking the rice was solved.[16]

With the advancing army came swarms of Negro men, women, and children, freed by the army but with no place to go except with the conquerors. Major James Connolly's experience with them was a common one. Asking the unfortunate people what freedom was, the Charleston, Illinois, soldier got no answer; asking them where they were going, he was given a simple reply. "Don't know Massa," the Negroes told him, "gwine along wid you all." Lieutenant James H. Blodgett, an Amboy soldier of the 75th Illinois, told of his regiment's being followed by "thousands of contrabands . . . poor little children 'toting' their little bundles, footsore and weary, sobbing and limping. . . ." Private George Sharland, a Princeton soldier of the 64th Illinois, later described approximately the same sight. This rookie campaigner saw Negro women carrying bundles of cloth on their heads in the "mode of carrying peculiar to the South," and some with babies strapped to their backs. Other Negroes, he added, were burdened down with "plunder" from the homes of their recent masters. Some Federal soldiers saw the Negroes as a handicap. The 34th Illinois, the well-traveled "Rock River Rifles," found its route march slowed by the long lines of Negro men and women who straggled in front and behind each regiment.[17]

Nevertheless, wherever the blue uniform appeared, it was welcomed by these unfortunate people. Contrary to what Major Connolly thought, the freed Negro had a clear notion of the difference between slavery and freedom, even if he had difficulty in expressing himself concerning the two ways of life. Nor were the southern Negroes ignorant of the purpose and disposition of Sherman's

[16] Civil War Diary of Allen Fahnestock, 148. Payne, 175. Jamison, 287.

[17] *Three Years in the Army of the Cumberland*, 311. Blodgett to Newton Bateman, Feb. 21, 1865, Bateman Papers. Sharland, 14. Payne, 168.

various columns. No sooner had the Federal troops set out from Atlanta than they were cheered by bands of slaves who gathered alongside the roads. An Illinois chaplain marching with the army described them as emerging from the fields in droves, "frantic with joy" as they danced and sang for the troops. "God bress you, massa," a soldier of the 64th Illinois heard them call; "we're glad you come." As the historian of the 92nd Illinois would write some years later, they "knew the Yankees were their friends, and they warmly welcomed their deliverers from slavery." And a member of the 10th Illinois carefully noted the words of a little song which was sung by several runaway Negroes who appeared in the camp of his regiment. Rather expressively, they ran:

> Way down South in de land of gravel,
> Barefooted Yankees bound to travel.
> Look away! Look away! Look away! [18]

There is little question that many of the western soldiers in the Union army exceeded the normal bounds of behavior, even for a conquering army. This would be expected from an army of some 60,000 men, many of whom would have misbehaved in any society. Contrary to Sherman's instructions, private homes were entered and property was destroyed and taken. It was, in some cases, as described by Chaplain James T. Ayers of the 129th Illinois, in his own diary. "Many of our Boys will push into houses where only women are the inmates," he wrote, "and Steal and Rob all the Can Lay there unholy hands on and often treat women Rudely beside tareing up womens Dresses Bonnets and so on." "Well," concluded Ayers, "thease trifleling pukes are A disgrace to the great union Army and are found mostly Among those Substitutes and thousand doler men." [19]

What Ayers wrote and implied was true, but he left a good deal unsaid. This conquering army, and it was that, was not nearly as badly behaved at it might have been. Many commanders laid heavy punishments upon their men for more outrageous cases of foraging. Four members of the 10th Illinois, for instance, were hung by their thumbs for several days for exceeding the bounds of good behavior. Moreover, despite what was written in the years

---

[18] Civil War Diary of George Compton Beginning May 1st, 1865, ISHL, 5. Sharland, 17. *The Ninety-second Illinois Volunteers*, 188. Jamison, 316.

[19] *Diary of James T. Ayers*, 92.

immediately following the war concerning the treatment of southern white women by Federal soldiers, there were few if any cases of rape by Sherman's men. Other Confederate charges about the behavior of Union soldiers with compliant Negro women might merit answers concerning their own guilt. When an Illinois chaplain, George Compton, followed the Union army into the Carolinas several months later, he was amazed to see what he described as "so many examples of Southern Negro equality and amalgamation. . . ." Some of the products of this racial association, he noted, were almost white, and yet were maintained as slaves.[20]

Without a doubt, much of Sherman's official destructive hand fell upon property which might have helped the South survive as a rebellious force against the constituted authority. If there was any particular aspect of southern life upon which it came down with a greater weight, it was the railroad system. The railroads, Sherman felt, must be destroyed for reasons of his own safety, for he did not wish to have Hood's army suddenly appear to his rear. Far back at Lithonia, just east of Atlanta, on November 17, Sherman became so concerned about this phase of his campaign that he actually gave personal instructions to the 123rd Illinois on how it should be done. But if Sherman had his method, the ingenious Yankee soldier added his own art to the technique. In all of the literature concerning Sherman's great march to the sea, no finer description of rail twisting can be found than that written by Private George Sharland of the 64th Illinois. First, he wrote, the regiment stacks its arms alongside the track.

> This being done, some take axes and break off the heads of the spikes that fasten the rail to the ties; others get poles for levers, and with the same lift the irons from their beds; some get dry wood and rails to start the fires, while others pry up the ties, strongly inbedded in the soil from previous pressure. This being done, the next thing is, to pile the ties transversely, one upon the other, in layers of three, four, or five, as seems most convenient, making five or six layers in all, then piling two close together on the top, the irons are laid transversely on the top of same, so as to balance, then in like manner a tie or two is placed on the top of it, the stack being thus completed, dry wood and rails fill up the interstices, and the torch is applied. It does not take long for the raging flame with its subtle heat, to cause the ponderous iron to yield

[20] Jamison, 285. Miers, 229, quotes several sources concerning incidents of rape. Civil War Diary of George Compton, 4.

to its influence, and it can be seen gradually yielding itself in humble submission, the opposite ends gracefully touching the ground.[21]

Once the metal was softened, Sharland added, each company vied to twist the rails into the most intricate shape—bows, loops, and knots being among them. Beyond all these, however, was the "Lincoln Gimlet," a devilish and intricate design which defied any attempt at correction. This clever creation was widely used by the chief engineer of Sherman's army, Orlando Metcalfe Poe.[22]

As the *London Spectator* was moved to comment, the great march to the sea was an event "calculated to make men who are not Americans hold their breaths." Sherman had disappeared into eastern Georgia about the middle of the month. By November 28 Union soldiers were beginning to note Spanish moss dripping from the live oak trees. Mile after mile was passed by the winding columns with only the slightest opposition. The historian of the 34th Illinois later calculated that by November 29 his regiment had marched some 13 days and 221 miles. On December 1 Major James Connolly sat down to write his wife that his regiment, the 123rd Illinois, was exultant. It had crossed the Ulcofauhatchee, the Yellow, the Oconee, the Ogeechee, the Rocky Comfort, and the Buckhead rivers, and was still moving on. There was little the enemy could do, Connolly added, for Sherman kept his columns "careering" about the countryside in such a manner that they crossed and recrossed in front and behind each other.[23]

By December 3 Howard and Osterhaus' XV Corps were south of the Ogeechee near Scarboro, Slocum and his XX Corps had reached Buckhead Church, J. C. Davis' XIV Corps was moving toward Lumpkin's Station, and Sherman, now traveling with Blair's XVII Corps, had entered Millen. At the latter place, the Federal soldiers came upon the huts and caves which had constituted a Confederate prison for captured soldiers. Not a few of the bluecoated soldiers were convinced that the policy of open foraging of the South should be broadened to include the torch.

All the while, the North waited and wondered about the safety of the army. Where would Sherman emerge, or was his cause a

[21] *Three Years in the Army of the Cumberland,* 307. Sharland, 23.

[22] Barrett, 91.

[23] *London Spectator,* quoted in *Harper's Weekly* (N.Y.), Jan. 7, 1865. Payne, 167–168. *Three Years in the Army of the Cumberland,* 336.

"forlorn hope," as the newspapers of the day were fond of writing? Understanding the nation's concern, as Sherman neared his objective at Savannah he made an attempt to send news forward concerning the location of the army. The message was carried by Captain William Duncan and two privates, all of the 10th Illinois Cavalry. Floating down the Ogeechee River, the three men were carried past the guns of Fort McAllister, which guarded the harbor of Savannah, to the Union fleet, which stood by in the distance. "We have met with perfect success thus far," Sherman's message read; "troops in fine spirit and nearby."[24]

By December 8 Sherman's army had reached Pooler's Station, only eight miles from Savannah. The following two days were spent in investing the city: the XIV Corps to the left, and the XX, XVII, and XV corps stretching around to the right. By December 13 Sherman was ready to make his assault upon Fort McAllister, which barred Sherman's contact with the fleet. Hazen's division of the XV Corps, given the task, made a brilliant attack and took the Confederate works. A week later the Confederate army under Hardee evacuated Savannah.

Sherman's achievement was a spectacular march which destroyed Georgia as a base for Confederate military operations and placed a large Union army in a position from which it could march northward in support of Grant's campaign against Lee. In all of this, the cost had been amazingly slight. From Atlanta to the sea, the total number of Union casualties was less than 2,200.

It is easy, therefore, to understand the sentiments of the men of Sherman's army. Christmas time of 1864 was something special, for, as Sherman so aptly expressed it, they had presented the nation with the extraordinary gift of victory. For some, the sheer relief over having finished the long march was too much. On the night of December 24, for instance, the men of the 34th Illinois ran out into the warm moist air of the Georgia coast and began to fire their muskets in wild abandon. Finally, the officers of the regiment managed to regain control, disarming the troops and sending them back to their quarters. An hour later they were out

---

[24] *Official Records*, Ser. I, Vol. XLIV, 9. Miers, 258. Charles Howard, "Incidents and Operations Connected with the Capture of Savannah," in *Military Essays and Recollections* IV (1907), 432–433.

again, however. Making good-sized hand bombs by filling their canteens with powder, they set off continuous and terrific explosions which lasted until both of the ingredients for their explosives had disappeared.[25]

Fortunately others were better behaved. Some wrote letters to parents who had waited a long time for words of reassurance concerning the campaign. Captain Levi Ross of the 86th Illinois, for example, happily wrote his father back in Princeville that the army had finally arrived at Savannah and was hungry for news. Nobody seemed to know who had been elected as President of the nation – Lincoln or McClellan – but, said Ross: "we think *mighty strong* that Honest Abe will stay in the White House." Where the army would go from here Ross did not know. There was obviously no going back, for Georgia was a huge waste. So it must be South Carolina, Ross concluded, and if that were the case, the 86th Illinois was ready with a "bayonet in one hand and the torch in the other. . . ." And on the Sunday following the capture of Savannah, a few of the members of the 105th Illinois trooped dutifully off to church. There they patiently listened while the minister offered a prayer for the safety of the president and the armies of the Confederacy. It was too much for a soldier of the 105th, however, and he scribbled out a note and passed it forward to the pulpit. Would there also be a prayer for the President of the United States and its armies? "He then put up a powerful prayer that the life of the President of the United States may be spared to the close of this cruel war," wrote Private Robert Hale Strong of Du Page, Illinois, "in order that his eyes may be opened to the right. . . ."[26]

Despite the brief conflict of opinion between the 105th Illinois and the clergy, relations were fairly good between the citizens of the city and the victorious army. Captured food was returned to the city, and Sherman even solved the religious problem by allowing the local churches to omit prayers for President Lincoln, apparently upon the assumption that it was the other side which really needed the help anyway. In this background, most Illinois

[25] Payne, 182. *Official Records*, Ser. I, Vol. XLIV, 10–13. Cox, *The March to the Sea*, 52–53. Miers, 264.

[26] Ross to his father, Dec. 16, 1864, Ross Papers. Strong, 152.

soldiers were greatly taken with the languid and gracious ways of Savannah. "I have been most courteously treated by all of its citizens . . . ," wrote Major James Connolly of the 123rd Illinois. "Our whole army has fallen in love with this city. . . ."[27]

Meanwhile, preparations for the campaign into the Carolinas continued. Elements of the XIX Corps arrived in Savannah in January, 1865, relieving the troops of the XX Corps which had been garrisoning the city. Now Sherman's army was completely available to begin its march north. Bad weather held up the broadening of army movements until February, however, despite the fact that the various corps were poised for action throughout the late days of January.

The opposition to the Union advance northward would be far greater than those few troops who had sought to hinder Sherman's advance to Savannah. Hardee was present with two divisions totaling 8,000 men. There were also the tough Confederate cavalry under Wheeler, a corps from the Army of Tennessee, a division of South Carolina militia, and a scattering of troops from the Georgia militia and the Army of Northern Virginia. The entire Confederate army in the Carolinas, unorganized as it was, totaled at least 22,500 men. Before these troops and others could be gathered, however, Sherman marched into South Carolina, striking the Augusta to Charleston railroad by February 7. Here a number of regiments, including the 7th Illinois, were put to the task of destroying the track, which they did with great style and pride, bending the rails into twisted "Lincoln Gimlets."

Without a doubt, the Federal troops who moved into South Carolina were inspired with an extraordinarily intense spirit of revenge. This was the state which most soldiers credited with the cause of the war. As Chaplain James T. Ayers of the 129th Illinois phrased it in his diary: "I say go to it boys give her Jesse. She richly Deserves it. She is the mother of Harlots." The same sentiment was held by most of the blue-coated veterans, and its extremism was in no way lessened by the comments of such general officers as Kilpatrick. "In after years," stated the general to the troops of the 92nd Illinois, "when travelers passing through South Carolina shall see chimney stacks without houses, and the country

[27] Connolly, "Letters to His Wife," 375.

desolate, and shall ask, 'who did this?' some Yankee will answer, 'Kilpatrick's Cavalry.'"[28]

Kilpatrick's cruel concern about the future of his fame found comparisons through the ranks of Union soldiery. "My old boots – my old socks!" wrote a member of the 10th Illinois after considering the great amount of walking he had done in the South; "if I had old Jeff Davis here, I'd ram them down his dirty throat. . . ." The chaplain of the 129th Illinois had further thoughts on the subject of the president of the Confederate States of America. "He has made fatherless Children by tens of thousands and widows by thousands . . . ," commented James T. Ayers. "Hang him I say in A suit of some one of his Negro womens Close and Leave him on the Gallows for Crows and vultures to feed on."[29]

The presence of such emotions did not bode well for South Carolina. By February 11 various little towns along the Charleston railroad, McPhersonville, Hickory Hill, Brighton, Hardeeville, and Barnwell, mere whistle-stops, lay smoldering in ruins. In Hardeeville one of the larger wooden churches was torn down plank by plank until, in one big roar, its framework crashed to the ground. "There goes your d—d old gospel shop," shouted a member of the 102nd Illinois, a Knox and Mercer counties regiment which had seen little fighting before the Atlanta campaign. Chaplain Ayers was a witness to this little instance in the futility of war:

> In less than half hour all those buildings were tore down and piled in Rowes Ready to convert into Camps for Each Company. This being done then we Took the S[h]ingles and slivered planks and frames made fires and in no time was sipping Away at our Hot Coffee mixing up A little with Hard tack and sowbelly as composed as tho Hardeeville was Still Standing and in her great Glory. I was making some remarks on this scene. "Humph," says the boys, "this is nothing. The place is so Small we had not sea Room sufficient. If you had been with us on our big march you would have seen sights then." Well you see having Just Came into the sheepfold I am Green, yet but I'll soon get used to it no doubt.[30]

---

[28] *Official Records*, Ser. I, Vol. XLVII, Pt. 1, 17–19. Cox, *The March to the Sea*, 163–170. Boatner, 126–127. *Diary of James T. Ayers*, 74. *The Ninety-second Illinois Volunteers*, 211.

[29] Jamison, 317. *Diary of James T. Ayers*, 101.

[30] Stephen Fleharty, *Our Regiment: A History of the 102nd Illinois Infantry Volunteers . . .* (Chicago, 1865), 132. *Diary of James T. Ayers*, 74.

Not only destruction but also fire accompanied the Federal troops in their march through South Carolina. An Illinois soldier of the 104th regiment was moved to comment that there seemed to be so much use of the former that he wondered if Hell had not moved its location to the palmetto state. An Oquawka soldier of the 10th Illinois would remember after the war an incident in which the summer home of an important southern family, so influential that it was able to acquire northern medicines despite the war, was invaded by his regiment. Boards were ripped from the home for firewood, and the regimental wagons were loaded with furniture. Surely these men, whose faces were blackened from having marched through the smoke of burning resin pots and flaming pine forests, must have struck terror into the hearts of those few southerners who were courageous enough to stay with their homes.[31]

By February 12 the Union forces, flanked by Kilpatrick's 92nd Illinois, were well on the move. Confederate resistance was only sporadic. Wheeler's cavalry hit the mounted Illinois infantry regiment hard at Aiken, with a true cavalry melee resulting in which the 92nd fled in disorder to the safety of the advancing infantry. While this Illinois unit was getting its brief lesson on the necessity of alertness in war, the bulk of Sherman's army crossed the Edisto River, capturing and burning the town of Orangeburg. By February 15 the army was moving in the direction of Columbia and was only about eight miles south of the state capital. Two days later, Wood's division of Logan's XV Corps entered that Carolina city.

In the days preceding the capture of Columbia, events were building to a sharp climax. On February 15 the XV Corps had met a brisk contest while attempting to cross the Congaree River south of the city. There had been a tight little fight between soldiers of the 40th Illinois and the Confederate opposition, in which the chief spectacle was a hand-to-hand struggle near the bridge between an Illinois private and his enemy counterpart. Astride his opponent, and amidst the cheers of the 40th Illinois, the Union trooper choked the Confederate until he surrendered. That night, by way of revenge for the day's activities, Confederate batteries shelled Hazen's division all night, which irritated the

[31] Calkins, 287. Jamison, 296, 318.

men of the XV Corps considerably. Then, on February 16, Sherman's army marched past an abandoned prison for Federal soldiers on the outskirts of Columbia known as Camp Sorghum. The sight of the caves and shacks in which their comrades had lived, plus the bitter little fight of the preceding day, set the emotional tone for the Federal soldiers who entered Columbia.[32]

When the Third Brigade of the First Division, XV Corps, under the command of General George A. Stone, entered the capital of South Carolina, it found much to its surprise that it was not really the first Federal unit to enter the city. Flying above the statehouse was the flag of the 13th Iowa, and waving above the city hall were the colors of the 32nd Illinois. Both had been brought across at dawn by members of the two western regiments. The men of the Third Brigade, chagrined as they were, quickly hauled down the Iowa banner, but they were foiled by the foresight of the Illinois regiment. The latter had posted an armed guard in the tower over which the regimental flag waved, and had locked the trap door into the steeple from the inside.

Regardless of the contention over being the first to enter into Columbia, the men of Stone's brigade, the 13th Iowa, and the 32nd Illinois immediately became aware of one fact. Columbia was one vast storehouse of liquor. Negroes lined the streets offering bottles to the Union soldiers, and liquor stores, unfortunately not emptied before the capture of the city, offered tempting targets to any soldier who wished to smash down the doors. "Whisky and wine flowed like water," a soldier of the 103rd Illinois would write that night, "and the whole Div. is now drunk." Far up in the tower of the city hall, the color guard of the 32nd Illinois, fretting over their continuing duty, lowered the bell rope to the ground and shouted a request for a jug of liquor. It was happily fulfilled by the troops below, and soon the whole detachment of Illinois soldiers was drunk, amusing themselves the rest of the afternoon by firing into the crowded streets.[33]

There is no question but that conditions in Columbia on that

[32] *Official Records*, Ser. I, Vol. XLVII, Pt. 1, 19–21. *Reminiscences of the 103rd*, 182–183. Barrett, 59–62.

[33] *Official Records*, Ser. I, Vol. XLVII, Pt. 1, 21–22. Fenwick Y. Hedley, *Marching Through Georgia: Pen-Pictures of Every-Day Life in General Sherman's Army* . . . (Chicago, 1890), 370.

day, February 17, 1865, were conducive to acts of prime violence. Escaped Federal prisoners roamed the streets anxious to obtain revenge against their Confederate captors. Rabble from the local jails, local Negroes, and soldiers staggered about the town in various stages of drunkenness. All had cause to wish for retaliation against this Carolina city. In fact, the Iowa and Illinois soldiers of Logan's XV Corps had entered the city earlier in the day singing "Hail Columbia, happy land – If I don't burn you, I'll be damned." Later on the same day, a Canton officer of the 103rd Illinois was informed by a fellow member of his regiment that the city ought to be burned, but that he "would like to see it done decently."[34]

The fire did break out, and aided by a favorable wind it swept over the unfortunate town. Whatever the cause, for there is still debate on the subject after a hundred years, the night of February 17 was a bad one for the people of Columbia. Part of the Union troops quartered in the city attempted to put the fire out; part of them could be seen setting fire to different spots untouched by the flames. Buildings were looted, goods despoiled, and citizens driven from their homes. An Oquawka soldier of the 10th Illinois, remembering what he could of that night of fire, recalled a Carolinian highborn lady rushing about the streets crying: "The pee-an-nah! the pee-an-nah!" The same soldier would note that while generals Logan and Howard labored diligently to put out the flames, General Giles A. Smith could be seen riding about the streets, lifting his flask and crying "Damnation to the Confederacy." While Irish soldiers from Illinois regiments worked hard to save the convent in the town, and an Episcopalian officer of the 50th Illinois stood guard over the home of a minister of his faith, other Illinois soldiers despoiled a home of Catholic nuns, and the next morning General Logan, contrary to his actions on the night before, would curse over being denied the privilege of burning the same Catholic structure. It was truly a night of contradiction and evil, wherein the best and worst of humanity might be seen.[35]

As the night faded into dawn, the streets were filled with sol-

[34] George W. Pepper, *Personal Recollections of Sherman's Campaigns in Georgia and the Carolinas* (Zanesville, Ohio, 1866), 311. *Reminiscences of the 103rd*, 183–184.

[35] Jamison, 309–310. Barrett, 82–92.

diers and citizens and the sidewalks were "heaped with plunder." One Oquawka soldier remembered all of his life the little vignettes he encountered as he walked about the streets: a "soldier with a gorgeous silver platter of immense size," and a Negro, standing by his collection of loot, who said: "I dinks de Day ob Jubilee for me hab come." Soon, however, the soldiers of the tough 40th Illinois, the same regiment which had fought over the Congaree bridge a few days previously, were out on the streets, guns bayoneted, attempting to clear away the crowd of people. The stark, smoldering ruins presented a most unbeautiful sight to the morning sun. By noon the orgy was over. A soldier of the 103rd Illinois, after a midday walk through the town, was able to write: "I have just been through the streets . . . and it is as quiet as Sunday night in Canton."[36]

The Federal army moved on like a destructive flood. By March it had crossed the Wateree River and had entered Chesterfield. While Sherman directed his troops toward Cheraw, Hardee attempted a concentration of his own divisions at Fayetteville, in North Carolina. The Confederates were faced with all sorts of difficulties, however. Their rail connections were in bad shape, and much railroad equipment was being used to supply Lee's hard-pressed army in Virginia. By March 3 the Federal army had reached Cheraw, where it was to stay for three days, striking for Fayetteville on March 6.

The entrance of the Union army into North Carolina marked a definite change in the attitude of Sherman and lesser officers toward the depredations committed by northern soldiers. The commanding general of the army pointedly reminded his men that North Carolina was one of "the last states that passed the ordinance of secession," and that there were a large number of Union sympathizers within the borders of the state. Instructions went out even to Kilpatrick, the most ruthless of Union generals, ordering him to act with restraint toward the citizens of North Carolina. As Sherman crossed the border which separated the two Carolinas, he was heard to remark: "Boys . . . remember we are in the old North State now. . . ."[37]

---

[36] Jamison, 309–310. *Reminiscences of the 103rd,* 183–184.

[37] *Official Records,* Ser. I, Vol. XLVII, Pt. I, 22–23; Pt. II, 719. Trowbridge, 475.

By the evening of March 9, the XVII, XIV, and XX corps had reached the vicinity of the Lumber River. Very early the following day, Kilpatrick's cavalry, particularly the brigade which included the 92nd Illinois, became involved in a vicious little fight with Wheeler's men, the latter almost capturing Kilpatrick himself. Only the assistance of Mitchell's brigade of the XIV Corps, which included the 78th Illinois, allowed the Union cavalry to escape as easily as it did.

On March 11 Sherman reached Fayetteville. On March 15 the Union advance out of that city toward Goldsboro began, Slocum's army moving on the left and to the north, Howard's moving to the right. Kilpatrick's cavalry preceded the Federal Left Wing by skirmishing down the Raleigh road. By mid-afternoon of that day, Atkins' cavalry brigade got into a sharp action with Wheeler's rear guard once again, causing Slocum to order infantry troops forward in support. On the following morning, sharp fire between Confederate and Federal cavalry continued, with infantry being thrown in by both sides as the fighting became heated. Later in the morning, the Union forces went on the offensive, with Case's brigade of the Third Division, XX Corps, leading the attack.

General Henry Case was an Illinois officer who had come up through the ranks. At the beginning of the war he was only a first lieutenant in the 14th Illinois. Later he obtained the rank of captain in the 129th Illinois (Chaplain James T. Ayers' regiment). By 1864 he was a brevet brigadier. Now, near Averasboro, he led a smashing attack, along with the troops of the 105th Illinois, upon the enemy right flank. Moving at the double quick, the Illinois regiment dashed through a heavy thicket, and emerged in such a position as to allow for damaging volleys upon the opposing troops. By the afternoon Mitchell's brigade, including the 78th Illinois, famous from Chickamauga days, joined the fight on the left, driving the Confederate troops off the field.

The battle of Averasboro on March 16 was a surprisingly hard little struggle. Of the Federal forces engaged in the conflict, 682 were lost; of the Confederate divisions involved, about 865 were counted as casualties. Despite the important participation of various Illinois regiments in the battle, it was a New York regiment of the XX Corps which suffered the largest number of dead and wounded in the fighting. The 105th, strangely enough, only counted 6 dead and 16 wounded.[38]

On the following day, Slocum's wing of the army was once again on the move, this time in the direction of Bentonville. Davis' XIV Corps, and in particular General James D. Morgan's division, took the lead in that march. Morgan was that Quincy, Illinois, businessman whose life had been filled with adventure. On the morning of March 19 the First Division of the corps, commanded by General William Carlin, hit hard resistance in the form of Wade Hampton's cavalry. What Carlin and his superior Slocum did not know was that behind Hampton lay an entire Confederate army now commanded by Joe Johnston, Sherman's old opponent on Kennesaw Mountain. Consequently, when Carlin sent Harrison C. Hobart's First Brigade forward, it was done so upon the assumption that it was merely another Confederate rear-guard cavalry action. The Federal troops, moving through swampy land covered with brush, were thrown back with heavy losses, however. There followed a series of savage Confederate counterattacks. "Such incessant firing for three successive hours," wrote Surgeon John Hostetter of the 34th Illinois, "I have never heard." Morgan's division, which included the 16th and 34th Illinois, was particularly involved in the fighting of March 19, as was the 78th Illinois in Mitchell's brigade.

The fight near Bentonville continued through the next two days as well. Finally, on the night of March 21, Johnston withdrew his army in the direction of Smithfield. The three-day battle had involved 16,127 Federal troops, of which 1,646 were casualties, and 16,895 Confederate soldiers, of which 2,606 were considered to be lost. Among the Illinois units engaged in the conflict, the 16th counted the largest losses, 51 in all.[39]

By March 22 Sherman was on the move again toward Goldsboro. On the following day, the soldiers of the 26th Illinois moved into that town, scattering the rear guard of Confederate cavalry with a "first class yell." Soon the remainder of Sherman's two

[38] *Official Records*, Ser. I, Vol. XLVII, Pt. I, 23–25, 67, 125–130, 789. Barrett, 151–155. *Report of the Adjutant General*, V, 694. Fox, 548.

[39] Cox, *The March to the Sea*, 186–198. *Official Records*, Ser. I, Vol. XLVII, Pt. 1, 25–27. Payne, 202, 208–209. Fox, 460, 548, 551. Thomas L. Livermore, 144–145.

wings straggled into the small place, meeting the force of Schofield, the Freeport, Illinois, general, and were soon joined by A. H. Terry, the New York general officer, both of whom had come in from the coast.

The great Carolinas campaign was ended. It had been an arduous one, not so much because of the fighting at Averasboro or Bentonville, but because of the continuous struggle with the elements. There were few of Sherman's men who would admit, with all of the terrible foraging and burning committed in the two states, that this had been an easier march than that from Atlanta to Savannah. One would have to accept the words of the commanding general of the army himself, who wrote shortly after the capture of Goldsboro: "The march to the sea seems to have captivated everybody, whereas it was child's play compared with the other." [40]

[40] *Official Records*, Ser. I, Vol. XLVII, Pt. 1, 27–28. *Reminiscences of the 103rd*, 201. *The Sherman Letters*, 260.

CHAPTER XI

Two Victories in the West

Sherman's march to the sea and his Carolinas campaign were only part of the rapidly accelerating war effort in late 1864 and early 1865. Forced from Atlanta by the capture of Jonesboro in September, Hood retreated to the rail station at Lovejoy, where he stayed for several weeks, daring Sherman to come after him. Moving to Palmetto, he began to gather forces and supplies for a strike at Sherman's supply lines and at Tennessee. Forrest's operations in Tennessee were stepped up, causing Sherman to send Thomas and two divisions plus other troops to defend Nashville. The rebel will-o'-the-wisp successfully attacked a number of places including Athens, Alabama, September 23–24, and Johnsonville, Tennessee, November 3–5 — towns occupied by small Union garrisons. Early in December Forrest and other Confederate generals were striking at the railroads around Murfreesboro as part of Hood's invasion. A sharp little engagement was fought at Overall's Creek, three miles outside of the town, followed three days later, on November 7, by a larger skirmish on the Wilkinson pike. In both of these clashes, the major opposition to the Confederates was presented by the 61st Illinois, a regiment from Greene and Jersey counties commanded by Lieutenant Colonel Daniel Grass of Lawrenceville, Illinois. Fighting as part of a provisional force, the 61st led the successful defense of the railroad and supply depots around that strategic Tennessee town.[1]

[1] *Report of the Adjutant General,* IV, 236. Cox, *The March to the Sea,* 15–19, 103–104.

Forrest's attacks in Tennessee and Alabama were merely tactical maneuvers of the Confederate strategy. Hood hoped his invasion of Tennessee would force Sherman to withdraw from Georgia. It was a logical idea, and one which would naturally occur to Hood's audacious and free-ranging mind. If there were flaws in it, they rested on the fact that the Confederate commander just did not have enough men to perform such a risky task. Much of the old Confederate dash and élan were gone, and Hood was facing an army which not only had become a professional and resilient one, but which was defending any possible gateway to the north.

Hood had very little choice. He led his army from Palmetto, moving slowly in the direction of Marietta and Kennesaw Mountain. As he neared Marietta, he received information from his scouts that the Federals had established a huge supply depot at Allatoona, a few miles away. The importance of this news was quickly grasped by Hood, who realized that the capture of such vast stores, including over a million rations of bread, would be an enormously real and psychological victory for a flagging Confederate cause. To accomplish this task, therefore, he sent no less than an entire Confederate division under the command of General Samuel G. French.

French's career in the war was most untypical for general officers of the southern cause. He had held a series of desk jobs, ranging from chief of ordnance to commands of lesser districts. Placed in a more active role in 1863, he never seemed to grasp the changes which the war had brought about in the Union soldier. Federal garrisons may have surrendered earlier in the war without a fight, but in 1864 the ordinary Federal private in the West had undergone a tremendous evolution in temperament and fighting ability. The nature of this change was something which French was about to discover.

The Confederate movement toward Allatoona was not totally unobserved by Sherman's scouts. The original Federal garrison, which consisted of a brigade which included the 12th Illinois, was quickly supplemented by part of the Fourth Division, XIV Corps, commanded by a tough and forceful example of the new breed of Union generals, John M. Corse. These hurriedly entrained additions brought the total Allatoona defensive force to ten regiments, five of which came from the Prairie State. These last included the old and valiant 7th, equipped with repeating rifles; the 12th, which was originally organized by Colonel John McArthur; the 50th, the "Blind Half-Hundred"; the 57th, a northern Illinois regiment; and the 93rd, a western Illinois regiment which had fought courageously at Missionary Ridge. Of these Illinois units, the 7th, 50th, and 57th, along with the 39th Iowa, were part of a brigade commanded by Colonel Richard Rowett of Carlinville, Illinois. Like Corse, Rowett was part of the new breed, a sturdy little Englishman who had put aside his occupation of farming in Macoupin County at the beginning of the war in order to serve his adopted country.

As soon as French made his appearance at Allatoona on October 5, he demanded the surrender of the Federal garrison – as he phrased it, in order to avoid a "needless effusion of blood." Corse's reply was a stinging one, indicating his preparedness for a "needless effusion of blood" if it was "agreeable" to the Confederate general. Sherman, meanwhile, had reached Kennesaw Mountain, from which he could see that the Federal troops located at Allatoona were in trouble. In a message which contemporary journalists soon corrupted into "Hold the fort; I am coming," he urged Corse to hold on as long as possible.

At no time had Corse considered the possibility of surrender without a fight. He entrenched his troops along the railroads leading into the supply depot, using the embankments as a defensive line. The Confederate attacks fell mainly upon the 7th and 93rd Illinois and the 39th Iowa. Claudius W. Sears's Confederate brigade and W. H. Young's Texas troops made repeated assaults against Rowett's brigade, and the fighting not only became vicious but spectacular as well. The Carlinville officer was wounded twice, and later in the day Corse was laced across the cheek and ear with a musket ball, rendering him unconscious for over half an hour.

Just before noon, the weight of the Confederate assault became particularly heavy upon the 7th Illinois, which had previously inflicted heavy casualties with its Henry rifles. Finally Corse had to order his line to fall back into two redoubts built previously by

Union engineers. The retreat was not an orderly one, but it was covered by a courageous stand conducted by the 39th Iowa.[2]

French was rapidly learning about the growing professionalism of the Yankee soldier. He continued the attack past noon and until four o'clock, when he called off the useless conflict and hastily retreated after reports of Union reinforcements. Hood's gamble in attacking at Allatoona was costly for both sides: French's force lost 799 men and the Federals counted their losses at 707. The highest casualties suffered in the fighting were those of the 39th Iowa with 170. Not far behind was the 7th Illinois with 141 casualties, 16 per cent of the regiment being killed. The 93rd Illinois, which would suffer 446 casualties of all types before the end of the war, lost 83 men at Allatoona, 11 per cent of the regiment being killed.

The miscarriage of French's efforts failed to change Hood's strategy of attempting to pull Sherman out of Georgia by threatening Federal communications between Atlanta and the North. He moved in a leisurely fashion toward Rome, Georgia, in early October, while Sherman followed at the same casual pace through Marietta. All of this served to dissuade Sherman only momentarily from his great aim of raiding through Georgia. Hood had met an opponent with a greater "mental grasp and unbending will" than himself. Returning to Atlanta in early November, Sherman committed the army and the nation to a fateful decision. He sent Thomas the IV and XXIII corps and forwarded some portion of his cavalry to Nashville, where it was to be reorganized under James H. Wilson, the Shawneetown, Illinois, general who had just returned to the West from operations with Meade's command around Petersburg. It was now clear what Sherman's answer to Hood was to be. He was striking for the sea, leaving Hood for Thomas to handle.[3]

Through the late weeks of October and the early weeks of November, 1864, Hood spent his time repairing railroads in Mississippi and Alabama and in preparing his army for its movement into Tennessee. Thomas hastily gathered his troops for defense.

---

[2] Hubert, 310–311. Miers, 204–207. Cox, *Atlanta,* 227–232.

[3] William W. Cluett, *History of the Fifty-seventh Regiment Illinois Volunteer Infantry . . .* (Princeton, Ill., 1886) 82–83. Cox, *The March to the Sea,* 5. Fox, 456, 28. *Official Records,* Ser. I, Vol. XXXIX, Pt. 1, 580–584.

The IV Corps under General D. S. Stanley (later under General T. J. Wood) was concentrated along the Nashville and Decatur railroad at Pulaski, Tennessee. There were in this portion of the old Army of the Cumberland some 19 Illinois regiments, including such battle-tested troops as those of the 36th, the "Fox River Regiment," the 59th, and the 115th, the last named being the "Second Preacher's Regiment," commanded by the former Methodist minister, Jesse Hale Moore. Thomas H. Ruger's Second Division of the XXIII Corps, which included the 107th Illinois commanded by Colonel Francis Lowry of Monticello, was stationed in the vicinity of Pulaski. On November 15 General Jacob Cox's division of the same corps, which included the 65th and 112th Illinois, also arrived at that middle Tennessee city. And, at about the same time, the Freeport, Illinois, general, John M. Schofield, disembarked from his train to take command of the IV Corps and the part of the XXIII Corps now stationed around Pulaski at various strategic locations. This new command included about 25,000 infantrymen and about 5,000 cavalry.[4]

By the middle of November Hood was again on the move, striking north for Columbia from Florence, Alabama, in an effort to force Schofield from his works at Pulaski, and to arrive at the rear of Schofield before he could cross the Duck River. On November 22, Schofield, who never became hurried in his march northward, began the evacuation of Pulaski, moving virtually all of his forces along the Pulaski to Columbia pike. Only because he had a shorter distance to travel, and because Hood was unable to speed his march, was Schofield able to win the race to Columbia, where he arrived November 24, entrenching south of the Duck River at first, and withdrawing north of the Duck the night of November 27, upon Hood's arrival.

Hood's response to Schofield's tactics was once again to make preparations to turn his opponent's flanks. On November 28 Forrest's cavalry forced a crossing at Huey's Mill, about eight miles above Columbia, and on the following morning Hood's army began to build a pontoon bridge at that place. Wilson, whose cavalry had spotted these maneuvers, quickly anticipated an attempt by the Confederates to outflank Schofield by swinging their forces to the rear of the Federal army at Spring Hill, a little village be-

[4] Cox, *The March to the Sea*, 17–19, 218.

tween Columbia and Franklin. This southern Illinois general, already becoming one of the most respected of Union military leaders, passed his observations on this development to Schofield early on November 29 with the implied warning that inaction by the Union command might bring a catastrophic defeat.

Schofield was reluctant to move; he seemed to feel that Hood had other intentions due to Confederate troops still demonstrating at Columbia. Fortunately he did send Stanley with two Federal divisions to Spring Hill, 11 miles north of Columbia. T. H. Ruger's division, XXIII Corps, was also ordered north. One unit, the Second Division, IV Corps, commanded by General G. D. Wagner, contained in all 19 regiments, nine of which were from Illinois. This division got to Spring Hill first, the others being held up.

When Stanley, with Wagner, reached Spring Hill, he found that the ubiquitous Forrest had arrived near the place at about the same time. If Forrest was allowed to get hold of Spring Hill, and receive reinforcements, Schofield's retreat would be cut off and a whole Union army could fall into Hood's hands. Sharp fighting was soon in progress, involving Wagner's Third Brigade, which included the 42nd, 51st, and 79th Illinois, and commanded by Colonel Luther P. Bradley of Chicago, and Confederate infantry which had come in under General Pat Cleburne. Bradley's men hastily retreated after a brief skirmish, forming a line alongside Colonel John Q. Lane's Second Brigade, which was composed of six regiments, one of which was the 100th Illinois. Colonel Emerson Opdycke's First Brigade, seven regiments in all, five of which came from Illinois, was quickly brought up, stabilizing a Union line which held Cleburne's forces away from the Franklin pike. The action near Spring Hill was, as the following events proved, an important one, and if any one regiment was to be singled out for extra praise, it would be the 100th Illinois. This Will County regiment, under the command of Lieutenant Colonel Charles Hammond of Wilmington, Illinois, had distinguished itself at Stone's River and Missionary Ridge. Now, at Spring Hill, it executed a fine right-flank movement, attacked with fixed bayonets, and kept the door open for Schofield's retreat.[5]

While Wagner's division held its position near Spring Hill, there occurred one of those unaccountable events associated with

[5] *Ibid.*, 63–80. *Report of the Adjutant General,* V, 575–576.

war. Schofield marched his entire corps northward along the Franklin pike, only a half-mile or so from the campfires of Hood's unobservant pickets. When the Confederate commander suddenly became aware of what was happening, he made an attempt to stop the Federal movement, but it was late at night and the country was unfamiliar, consequently the effort failed. The entire story of just how and why Schofield was able to escape the Confederates at Spring Hill will probably never be known.

Hood was infuriated with his failure to trap the fleeing Federals, blaming the mishandling of the army upon his subordinates. Schofield moved quickly to Franklin the morning of November 30, where he immediately began to build works and make plans for a crossing of the Harpeth River.[6]

The village of Franklin rests on the south bank of the Harpeth, where that stream makes a deep bend to the east. Running southward from the town was the Columbia pike and the Nashville and Decatur railroad. Schofield's defensive arrangements included all of these natural and added features of the terrain, making on the whole a difficult position for Hood to assault. To the west of the town, with its right hinged upon the Harpeth, was Kimball's division of the IV Corps, which included Isaac M. Kirby's, Whittaker's, and Grose's brigades. These three units included 22 regiments, seven from Illinois. Among this latter grouping were the 21st, 38th, 75th, 80th, 84th, 96th, and 115th regiments, all with favorable reputations.

To Kimball's left was Ruger's division of the XXIII Corps, with its far flank resting near Carter House, a brick mansion just to the south of Franklin. Ruger's division had under normal circumstances only one Illinois regiment attached to it, the 107th, a regiment raised principally in DeWitt County. Today, however, a second Illinois regiment, the 72nd, having just arrived from Louisiana, was temporarily attached to that command; a fortunate development, for this fighting unit, commanded by Colonel Fred Staring of Chicago, was to have an important part in the developments of the day.

To the left of Ruger, and running south of Franklin to the Harpeth, was Cox's division of the XXIII Corps. This unit was

[6] Jacob D. Cox, *The Battle of Franklin* (New York, 1897), 83.

composed of 14 regiments, two of which, the 65th and 112th, came from Illinois. The first of these was placed in the front line; the 112th was held in reserve. North of the Harpeth was Wood's division of the IV Corps.

Because of the nature of the events of November 30, it is necessary here to deal with the disposition of the last of Schofield's units, Wagner's Second Division of the IV Corps. This force may be recalled as that which held the position at Spring Hill, and screened Schofield's withdrawal to the north. Now it was brought in as the rear guard: its three brigades were situated in various locations about the field. John Q. Lane's brigade, which included the 100th Illinois, was placed in an advanced position a half-mile south of Schofield's main army, and to the right of the Columbia pike. Colonel Joseph Conrad's brigade (formerly Bradley's) was situated in the same position, but to the left of the pike. Both, according to an officer of the 42nd Illinois, one of three units from that state in Conrad's brigade, were asked to hold a temporary line of defense behind "a very poor line of works." Wagner's instructions from Schofield were to retreat to the vicinity of Carter House at the first show of Confederate strength. As it developed, Wagner's interpretations of these orders were general ones. He himself remained at Carter House to the rear, too far from his division to command and transmit orders properly.

The last of Wagner's brigades was that of Opdycke, consisting of seven regiments, five of which came from Illinois. Once again, because of the significance of Opdycke's brigade in the fighting at Franklin, it is necessary to understand the makeup and disposition of that unit. Besides the 24th Wisconsin and 125th Ohio, the brigade was composed of the following Illinois regiments: the 36th, the "Fox River Regiment," commanded by Lieutenant Colonel Porter Olsen of Newark, Illinois; the 44th, consisting of seven Illinois and three Michigan companies, commanded by Colonel Wallace Barrett of Michigan; the 73rd, the "Preacher's Regiment," commanded by Colonel James Jaquess of Quincy; the 74th, a Winnebago County regiment, commanded by Colonel Thomas Bryan of Durand; and the 88th, the "Second Board of Trade Regiment," commanded by Lieutenant Colonel George W. Smith of Chicago. All of these men were placed in reserve by

Opdycke, whose last orders from Wagner, informally given, were to "fight when and where you think best; I may not see you again." [7]

November 30 was, as Captain James Sexton of the 72nd Illinois remembered it, a "bright, invigorating Indian summer day." Schofield, having moved his trains across the Harpeth, where they were being shepherded by Wilson's cavalry, watched and waited as Hood's generals paraded their men into attack formation. General Jacob Cox, who played an important role in placing the troops, wrote after the war that he could not recall another battlefield "so free from obstruction to the view." "Bands were playing," added Cox, "general and staff officers were riding in front of and between the lines, a hundred battle flags were waving in the smoke of battle, and bursting shells were wreathing the air in great circles of smoke. . . ." At his headquarters down the Columbia pike lay Hood, exhausted from his long ride, his head on a grounded saddle, transmitting orders to his subordinates. One may well conjecture about the source of this one-armed and one-legged general's will. Inside Carter House, at the center of the Union line, the Carter family, including a son and four daughters – huddled in the cellar while Confederate shells screamed over their home. Down the road, wearing a gray uniform, was one of the Carter boys, and before the end of the following day he would die in his own house.[8]

It was after three o'clock in the afternoon before Hood was able to mount his attack, striking first at Wagner's detached brigades on the Columbia pike. This force, whose commander had been ordered to withdraw at the slightest show of strength, failed to do so, engaging in a furious exchange of fire with the advancing Confederates. Momentarily the assault was checked, but then Cleburne's division moved rapidly by Lane's flank, throwing the Federals into confusion. Conrad's flank was also turned. There

[7] *Ibid.*, 61–62, 54–55. *Report of the Adjutant General*, IV, 546–548; VI, 47–49. Cox, *The Battle of Franklin*, 73–79. *Official Records*, Ser. I, Vol. XLV, Pt. 1, 342.

[8] James Sexton, "The Observations and Experiences of a Captain of Infantry at the Battle of Franklin," in *Military Essays and Recollections*, IV (1907), 473–476. Cox, *The Battle of Franklin*, 90, 93–94. The story of the Carter family comes from different sources. Cox, in *The March to the Sea*, 95–96, deals with it. The house still stands on the outskirts of Franklin, and is maintained by a local historical society.

was a hasty retreat, the two "hapless brigades" streaming to the rear as a disorganized crowd; the Confederates followed them, their officers shouting "Go into the works with them." [9]

The men of French's, Cleburne's, and John C. Brown's Confederate divisions hit Ruger's and Cox's commands hard, as the Federal soldiers hesitated to fire for fear of hitting Wagner's routed brigades. The 44th Illinois and 72nd Missouri, plus the Ohio and Indiana troops of Silas A. Strickland's brigade, were swept back from their works near Carter House. Only the 72nd Illinois, that recently arrived regiment from the Army of the Tennessee, now attached to Ruger's command, could be seen maintaining their position, their black hats bobbing up and down as they loaded and reloaded their rifles. A time of crisis was now at hand.

As indicated before, because of its exhaustive part in the rear-guard action at Spring Hill, Opdycke's brigade had been placed in reserve about a hundred yards behind Carter House. The men of these seven regiments, not having eaten since breakfast, were given permission by their brigade commander to build fires and make coffee. When this was done, the soldiers remained at rest, huddled in small groups, smoking and eating. It was at this moment, at about four o'clock in the afternoon, when they heard the cheers and shouts indicating a Confederate success on the other side of the house.

Even after a hundred years, and with all the accounts and stories of the incident, it would be hard to determine the sequence and exact events which followed. Opdycke's men, mostly Illinoisans, seemed to realize instinctively the serious implication of the Confederate cheers. They leaped to their feet, unstacked their rifles, and moved on the double quick to the south side of Carter House, with Opdycke's orders to charge following them.[10]

It was probably Lieutenant Colonel G. W. Smith of the 88th Illinois who moved his regiment forward first, followed quickly by the men of the 74th Illinois. Young Private Stewart Hoskinson of Rushville, in G Company of the 73rd Illinois, recalled years later the shock of battle as Opdycke's brigade hit the triumphant Confederates head on. "I well remember what a badly demor-

[9] Cox, *The Battle of Franklin*, 156.

[10] Newlin, 462–473.

alized mob [Lane's and Conrad's men] we met just in the yard at the Carter House," he wrote; "it was a fight, nearly, to get to the front, they wildly struggling to the rear, and we crowding to the front." Hoskinson and his comrades soon made their way through the retreating Federals. The little Rushville soldier spotted a Confederate private about to club a fallen Union officer and shot him right in the "breadbasket." [11]

Hoskinson's hard and cynical reference to the death of an enemy soldier really indicates the nature of the fight at Franklin. It was later written by Captain Sexton of the 72nd Illinois, and with a good deal of truth, that the battle near Carter House was a "private soldier's battle, the sum of its strategy being to hold and occupy a few square feet upon which the soldiers stood to the last." The Chicago officer could have found any number of supporters for his statement. "There was no side-stepping or fiddling," another Illinois soldier would write: "it was simply a free fight, on an open field." [12]

There is no finer example of the initiative of the Union soldier in the entire war. The historian of the 73rd Illinois recalled, years later, that Opdycke's order to move forward came long after the men had picked up their guns, and with a "yell and a bound" had begun to climb the high fence around Carter House and move into the fighting. The same writer again recalled with some malicious humor how his own regiment, the "Preacher's Regiment," flung out epithets at Wagner's retreating men, and bayoneted and clubbed their way into the melee. General Cox, farther to the Union left, noted that Opdycke's men "looked as if breasting a furious gale with strained muscles and set teeth." The brigade commander himself was a model of bravery and courage. After his shouted order to "move forward to the lines," his horse was shot out from under him, and he was pitched forward directly into the path of the advancing Confederates. Acrobatically, he rolled over, grabbed a musket from an enemy soldier's hands, and clubbed him with it. "At this juncture," commented an Illi-

[11] *Ibid.*, 440.

[12] Sexton, "Observations and Experiences at the Battle of Franklin," 483. Thomas E. Milchrist, "Reflections of a Subalteran on the Hood-Thomas Campaign in Tennessee," in *Military Essays and Recollections*, IV (1907), 459.

nois soldier some years later, "the muskets were empty, no one could stop to load — no shots were fired; the fight was now hand to hand, breast to breast, and the cold, gleaming, pitiless bayonet was the instrument of death."[13]

The above recollection was only that, however — a memory of a brief moment when there was no gunfire, only the thudding of musket butts against flesh, and the cries of pain, anger, and encouragement. In time the Illinois units involved in the fighting, which amounted to no less than half of those regiments in the vortex of the conflict at Carter House, managed to load their weapons and commence firing once again. So did the Confederates. Still, much of the fighting remained at close range. The 44th Illinois, for instance, managed to recapture a Union battery and turn it upon the onsurging enemy. The 36th Illinois fought a terrible close-range battle with Cleburne's men, and lost its commanding officer, Lieutenant Colonel Olsen, early in the fight. Not only did the 36th lose a number of its officers, but it lost also a considerable portion of its noncoms and flag bearers. The determination of the latter groups to hold their regimental banner was best exemplified by Private Charles W. Sears of Aurora, Illinois, who fought a hand-to-hand struggle with an enemy private. "No you don't," shouted Sears as he clutched the flagstaff; "not unless you take me with it."[14]

To the Federal right, in Ruger's division, the savagery of the conflict reached a similar level. The colors of the 107th Illinois, the DeWitt County regiment, were being carried off by a triumphant Confederate soldier, but Private Bailey Walker, a southern Illinoisan in G Company, leaped a fence, shot the enemy private, and brought back two other Confederate standards besides that of his own regiment. The 72nd Illinois continued fighting in the position it had held at the beginning of the conflict. Like the 107th, it paid a price for its constancy. Lieutenant William Stokes of Champaign, in G Company, and Lieutenant Albert Packer of Salem, Ohio, in I Company, were both killed while firing their pistols at the charging Confederate battle line only 20 feet away. One black-hatted member of the 72nd, blood streaming from his

[13] Newlin, 462–463. Cox, *The Battle of Franklin*, 98–99. Herr, 320.

[14] Cox, *The Battle of Franklin*, 257. Bennett and Haigh, 650–663. *Official Records*, Ser. I, Vol. XLV, Pt. 1, 246.

face, angrily charged the same advancing line with a pickax which he had picked up from the Union works. In D Company of the same regiment, a determined private, John Harbridge of Chicago, saw a Confederate colonel struggling mightily to climb over the Union works. He placed his musket against the midsection of the enemy officer, shouted "I guess not," and fired. A horrified onlooker in the 72nd, Captain James Sexton, remembered the rest of his life that the blast from the muzzle of the musket "actually let daylight through the victim." [15]

Opdycke's defense of Carter House only saved the Union lines from the first attack by the Confederates. To the right of the center of the Confederate assault, in Cox's position, Silas A. Strickland's brigade of Indiana and Ohio soldiers were driven back from their works, and hard fighting continued in that sector for hours. On this left of the Union line, a courageous stand by John S. Casement's brigade, containing the 65th Illinois, the "Second Scotch Regiment" commanded by Colonel William Stewart of Chicago, and Israel N. Stiles's brigade, containing the 112th Illinois, a Henry County regiment commanded by Colonel Thomas Henderson of Toulon, saved the breach from being widened. During the conflict at this spot, over 200 Confederates fell in front of the 65th, and the colors of the 15th Mississippi were captured by the Illinois regiment. The 112th was to merit special attention in the battle reports. Inserted into the break caused by Strickland's defection, it fought a dismal but rewarding struggle with Cheatham's men before the latter retreated.[16]

Thrown back twice, Hood's divisions came on again and again. Captain Sexton of the 72nd would write afterward of the roar of musketry quieting at times to an "almost absolute silence," and then rising to the "loudest fury." Always, he added, one could hear the constant cry along the Union works for "Cartridges! Cartridges!" General Cox, some 30 years later, would remember with feeling the still atmosphere of the late afternoon, when the

[15] *Reports of the Adjutant General*, VI, 48. Sexton, "Observations and Experiences at the Battle of Franklin," 478–479. Sexton remembered the name as Arbridge. The names of the two unfortunate officers were obtained by scanning the muster roll of the 72nd regiment in *Report of the Adjutant General*, IV, 518–545.

[16] Cox, *The Battle of Franklin*, 118. *Report of the Adjutant General*, IV, 368–369. Cox, *The March to the Sea*, 93–94.

smoke from the constant gunfire lay like a fog over the field. Firing was so continuous and heavy that the IV Corps alone would expend over a hundred wagonloads of ammunition. One can easily understand, then, the reasoning of one writer who would declare in time that the battle of Franklin was the "greatest drama in American history. . . ."[17]

It was a drama to which there were many facets. There was a loyal, brave, and accomplished Confederate army directed by the embittered cripple Hood, who strangely could not come to the conclusion that he should end his assault. There was the savage aspect of that first Confederate drive, when Opdycke's heroics changed the tide of battle. And there was the tremendous casualty list among the general and ranking officers of both sides. Early in the assault, the Federal general David S. Stanley was wounded and taken out of the fight, plus large numbers of regimental commanders. Along the Confederate battle line, general officers charged and died with their men almost as if they were inspired by a death wish. The brilliant Pat Cleburne was torn from his horse by a musket ball on the second attack of the day, and directly in front of the 36th Illinois. General John Adams pitched off his horse and died in the ranks of the 65th Illinois. Otho F. Strahl and States Rights Gist were killed in front of the 72nd and 107th Illinois, and Hiram B. Granbury fell in front of Opdycke's Illinois troops. J. C. Carter was mortally wounded. J. C. Brown, A. M. Manigault, William A. Quarles, Francis Marion Cockrell, G. W. Gordon, and Thomas Scott, all Confederate general officers, were wounded during the day. Among the lesser-rank Confederate officers wounded was Captain Theodoric Carter, a member of the family about whose house the battle was fought. At sunset, when the fighting had ceased, the family found him on the battlefield. He was carried home by his father and three sisters to die.[18]

As Van Horne, the historian of the Army of the Cumberland, wrote after the war: "The battle of Franklin, for its proportions, was one of the grandest of the war." He was able to conclude this

[17] Sexton, "Observations and Experiences at the Battle of Franklin," 473–476. Cox, *The March to the Sea*, 94–95. Stanley F. Horn, *The Army of Tennessee* (Indianapolis, 1941), 402–403.

[18] Cox, *The Battle of Franklin*, 200–201, 213–214. Van Horne, II, 203. Cox, *The March to the Sea*, 96–97. Herr, 325. General Carter, mortally wounded, was not a member of the Carter House family.

because of the preponderance of the Union victory there. Though it was a clear victory for its duration (some seven or eight hours), it was as terrible a struggle as any in the war. Of the 27,000 Confederates engaged, there were 6,252 casualties, a loss which, in every way, Hood could ill afford. Of the 28,000 Union soldiers on the field, losses were only 2,326. The heaviest single regimental loss among the Federal units was suffered by the 44th Missouri in Ruger's division, which tallied 34 dead, 37 wounded, and 92 missing. Among the Illinois regiments, the newly arrived 72nd led all the rest, losing 9 of its officers and 150 of its 325 men. Wagner's 51st Illinois lost 154. Once again the 36th Illinois also came in for its share of punishment, losing 62.[19]

Most indicative of the extent of the Union victory at Franklin, however, was the number of battle flags taken at the Federal breastworks. Thirty-two such banners were captured by the defending troops; Opdycke's brigade of Illinois soldiers captured ten of them during that first bayonet defense at Carter House. With all of this, the deaths of the Confederate generals, the heavy losses suffered by Hood, and the dashing of all of that general's hopes, one may little doubt the recollections of one Illinois soldier concerning the events of November 30, 1864. As the cannon finally ceased firing, and their sounds were replaced by the moans and pleas of the wounded who lay before the Union parapet, he listened as two Illinois officers discussed the character and importance of the dying day. "We ought to remain here and wipe hell out of 'em," stated one of them. The reply of the second, carefully thought out and phrased, was: "There is no hell left in them. Don't you hear them praying."[20]

Following the Confederate repulse at Franklin, Schofield took his army across the Harpeth, and marched the last 19 miles toward Thomas' defensive position at Nashville. In no way did the Federal soldiers regard the retreat as a defeat, for even the lowest among them realized the havoc which they had wrought among Hood's army. The march along the Franklin pike was more in the nature of a casual parade, in which certain of the regiments

[19] Van Horne, II, 202–203. Thomas L. Livermore, 131–132. Cox, *The March to the Sea*, 96–97. Fox, 458. Sexton, "Observations and Experiences at the Battle of Franklin," 481.

[20] Cox, *The March to the Sea*, 94. Milchrist, "Reflections of a Subalteran," 461.

managed to incorporate a great deal of fancy foraging. The 115th Illinois, for instance, by this time most inappropriately carrying the title of the "Second Preacher's Regiment," found an elegant and untouched mansion just south of Nashville. Before sunrise of December 1, several of the companies from that regiment pounded their way into the house, fried their pork and hardtack in the kitchen, drank wine out of elegant goblets, and made use of silver teaspoons and plated forks. An army traveling at a pace slow enough to allow these excursions would not be a hard-pressed one.[21]

Stung by his losses on November 30, Hood vainly pursued his dream of victory by bringing his troops into position south of Nashville. What he hoped to attain by continuing the campaign is difficult to discern. From his own statements, one may assume that he envisioned reinforcements from such an unlikely place as Texas, or that he imagined that Thomas in some uncharacteristic way would launch an ill-concerted attack. Nevertheless, he built his defensive line: his right flank, commanded by Cheatham, was anchored on the Murfreesboro road; his center, commanded by S. D. Lee, was astride the Franklin pike; his left, commanded by A. R. Stewart, bent around to the Hillsboro pike.[22]

In his slow but positive manner, Thomas began to build up the Union forces in Nashville. General A. J. Smith's three divisions of the XVI Corps began to arrive from Missouri on November 30, the same day on which Schofield was making his heroic stand at Franklin. The first of these divisions was commanded by General John McArthur, who had first come into the war as the organizer of the 12th Illinois. McArthur, a Scotsman by birth, came to Chicago in 1849, where he subsequently became the owner of a boiler factory. He rose quickly in the service, having fought with distinction at Donelson and Shiloh. The division of the Detached Army of the Tennessee which he commanded at the time of the defense of Nashville contained only one Illinois regiment. This was the 114th, a Cass and Sangamon counties regiment.

The Second Division of the XVI Corps, commanded by General Kenner Garrard, did contain a large number of Illinois troops.

---

[21] Royse, 233.

[22] *Official Records*, Ser. I, Vol. XLV, Pt. 1, 658. Cox, *The March to the Sea*, 109.

These regiments from the Prairie State included the 49th, a regiment raised principally in Washington County; the 58th, a De Kalb and Cook counties regiment; the 117th, from southwestern Illinois; the 119th, an Adams and Schuyler counties regiment; and the 122nd, a Macoupin County regiment.

The Third Division of the XVI Corps consisted of only two infantry brigades, seven regiments in all; three were from Illinois. They were the 72nd, the "First Chicago Board of Trade Regiment," which had arrived in time to take part at Franklin; the 81st, a southern Illinois regiment which was truly battle-tested; and the 95th, under the charge of Colonel Leander Blanden, who also commanded the brigade to which his regiment belonged.

The 9 infantry regiments and 2 artillery batteries from Illinois within the XVI Corps, added to the 3 regiments in the XXIII Corps and the 20 regiments in the IV Corps, brought the total number of Illinois units attached to the main body of Thomas' command to 34. This figure does not include the four Illinois cavalry regiments serving with James H. Wilson, the 3rd, 6th, 7th, and 9th; or I Battery of the 1st Illinois Artillery under the same command.[23]

Much to the irritation of Grant, Thomas took his time in arranging his attack upon Hood's line. Part of the delay was caused by his concern in finding an adequate supply of horses for Wilson's cavalry. Furthermore, troops continued to arrive, and appropriate arrangements had to be made for them. On December 1, General James B. Steedman, best remembered for his part in the battle of Chickamauga, showed up with 5,000 more infantrymen, primarily Negro troops of the District of the Etowah.

All of this could not be understood by President Lincoln, Secretary of War Stanton, or Grant. There was considerable distrust of Thomas in high places. On December 6 Grant flatly ordered his subordinate to attack at once, and Thomas made preparations to obey two days later. But on the morning of December 8 the Union soldiers awoke to find the fields and roads covered with sheets of ice, and the attack was once again postponed. Too far removed from the scene to understand, Grant worked himself into a quiet fury over what he felt was an unnecessary delay. Could the general-in-chief so easily have forgotten how he himself had been

[23] *Ibid.*, 222–226. *Historical Encyclopedia of Illinois*, 358.

misunderstood by Halleck at such a great distance? Nevertheless, Grant decided to remove Thomas, first considering Schofield, and then settling upon John A. Logan for the position. The latter was ordered to Nashville, but as fate would have it, he never made it. Thomas attacked on December 15.[24]

Thomas, whose battle eye was as good or better than that of any other general in the war, made his plans for the assault with the usual care. Steedman's colored troops were placed on the Federal left opposite Cheatham. Wood's IV Corps was detailed to press the Confederate position on Montgomery Hill; A. J. Smith's XVI Corps was ordered to move to the right of that promontory; and Schofield's XXIII Corps was directed to remain in the works of Nashville in reserve. James H. Wilson was ordered to proceed with his cavalry down the Hardin pike and around to the Confederate rear.

Steedman's Negro brigades, pushing down the Murfreesboro road under the cover of a gray December fog, were the first to move on the morning of December 15. The action here was a feint, however, for the XVI Corps was to make the main effort of the day. Because of the mud, ice, and fog, an unfortunate combination, McArthur was slow to move his division across the Hardin pike, delaying Wilson's cavalry strike to the west. Nevertheless, the latter eventually saw McArthur move from his front, and then commenced to drive Hood's troops from a set of detached works near Richland Creek.

The XVI Corps, led by McArthur's division, continued its pressure to the right of Montgomery Hill through the remainder of the morning, forcing two Confederate brigades from their entrenched position on the Hillsboro pike. There was, no doubt, a considerable amount of consolation for the veterans of the Red River campaign in this achievement. Schofield, called out of reserve, sent his XXIII Corps in the broad envelopment of the Confederate position, Darius N. Couch's Second Division, containing the 107th Illinois, moving sharply to take an important ridge to the west of the Granny White pike.

During the maneuvering of the XXIII Corps, Wood's IV Corps, which contained no fewer than 20 Illinois regiments out of its

---

[24] *Official Records*, Ser. I, Vol. XLV, Pt. 1, 34–37; Pt. 2, 54, 55, 70, 97. Catton, *This Hallowed Ground*, 366–367. Cox, *The March to the Sea*, 99–123.

total complement of 54, launched its own attack upon the main Confederate defenses at Montgomery Hill. The assault here was spearheaded by Colonel Philip S. Post's brigade of the Third Division, which included the commanding brigadier's own regiment, the 59th Illinois. Both Post and the 59th had come a long way from Pea Ridge and the sturdy defense against Stand Watie's Indians.[25]

The attack by Post's brigade at Nashville was a lesser version of the overwhelming of Missionary Ridge almost a year earlier. Headed by the 59th Illinois, once started the brigade couldn't stop. It assaulted the first line of Confederate works with a "bold dash," leaped over them, and surged pell-mell into the second line of trenches. Kimball's division of the same corps, which included no fewer than seven Illinois regiments, supported Post's effort, working its way toward the Franklin pike. The 96th Illinois, under the command of Major George Hicks of Galena, made a brilliant charge into the enemy breastworks, capturing a battery of Confederate Napoleons. Grose's brigade, which contained the 75th, 80th, and 84th Illinois, struck at a salient held by the Confederate command of General G. D. Johnston. Grose's attack, led by the 80th and 84th regiments, was concluded with a ten-minute struggle within the Confederate redoubt, and a rout of the defending troops. Like Post, Grose had considerable difficulty in restraining his men from continuing their charge beyond the assigned limits.[26]

The morning delay, occasioned by McArthur's inability to move his troops across the Hardin pike, caused the day to come to an end without a definite decision to Thomas' attack upon Hood. The latter, fighting a battle to which he should never had committed himself, and committing himself to continue it long after he should have retreated, built a new defense line overnight. These works stretched from what the Federals called Overton Hill on the right, a sharp incline to the east of the Franklin pike, to Shy's Hill on the Confederate left, east of the Granny White pike. Thomas, on the other hand, gave few specific orders to his subordinates that night, allowing the implication of a renewed attack to stand, and continuing preparations.

[25] *Ibid. Official Records*, Ser. I, Vol. XLV, Pt. 1, 37–39. Herr, 334–335.
[26] *Ibid.* Dodge, 197.

The morning of December 16 began like that of the preceding day. Steedman's colored troops moved up on the far Confederate left, and continued to press Cheatham's division to the east of Overton Hill. Wilson's cavalry worked its way in a wide envelopment of the Confederate left. Thomas, meanwhile, convinced by an earlier reconnaissance conducted by Colonel Post, ordered the brigade of that Illinois officer to move ahead directly against Overton Hill. About three o'clock in the afternoon, Post's men, including the 59th Illinois, stripped down for the assault, leaving their haversacks and heavier equipment behind. With the 59th leading the charge, the brigade closed column by column and began its movement up the slope. Somehow, the inexplicable imponderables of war effected the result of this courageous effort. Steedman's inexperienced Negro troops became entangled with Post's brigade, Post himself fell wounded (he would be awarded the Medal of Honor for his gallantry), and the enemy grape, canister, and musketry became "terrific." The assault on Overton Hill became stalled.[27]

Wilson's envelopment continued to have a grand success on the Confederate left. The Shawneetown general's troops had dismounted, and with their repeating rifles were carrying the fight to their opponents. It rapidly became obvious to Wilson, undoubtedly one of the great cavalry commanders of the war, that there "was no longer any uncertainty as to which flank" the Federal attack should move upon. After capturing a dispatch from Hood which indicated grave concern about the Confederate left, Wilson urged his fellow Illinoisan, Schofield, to broaden his attack in that area, with no immediate result. The young cavalry commander then left his troops and rode the two miles behind Post's beleaguered troops to Thomas' headquarters. There he pointed out to the commanding general in no uncertain terms the guidons of his own cavalry "in plain sight moving against the left and rear of the enemy's line."

It was not in Thomas' character to hurry. Wilson later recalled his superior raising his field glasses and "coolly" scanning the scene as if he doubted the information. Then, "as calmly as if on parade," he turned to Schofield, standing nearby, and ordered the

[27] *Official Records*, Ser. I, Vol. XLV, Pt. 1, 39–40. Dodge, 147. Herr, 334–335.

Freeport, Illinois, general to move with his entire corps. Smith also moved against the enemy's works.[28]

The drive upon the Confederate left was the determining factor in victory. Stiles's brigade, which included the 112th Illinois under the command of Lieutenant Colonel Emory Bond of Cambridge, moved sharply to the right of Shy's Hill. W. L. McMillen's brigade of the Detached Army of the Tennessee, containing the 114th Illinois commanded by Lieutenant Colonel Samuel Shoup of Springfield, followed with a brilliant assault to the left of the same slope. During the maneuver of the latter regiment, Captain John M. Johnson of Beardstown, in charge of A Company, captured a Confederate battery and, with the "involuntary assistance compelled from some captured rebs," brought the cannon to bear upon the retreating foe. Far to the left of Shoup's troops, the 59th Illinois, fighting with Post's brigade, heard the cheers of Stiles's and McMillen's veterans, and the effect was a "magnetic" one. Post's brigade was quickly reformed, and it swept like an irresistible tide over Overton Hill.[29]

The crushing of the Confederate left was the final blow, and Hood's entire defense collapsed like a bursting balloon. It was Missionary Ridge all over again, with a race between various Union regiments to bring their colors to the crest of the two hills before the others. "It was the biggest *stampede* I ever saw," wrote one Illinois soldier. "The ditches were full of guns and other abandoned material and from almost every tree and stone wall were shaking white rags." Private William Moore, C Company, 117th Illinois, from Lebanon, ran so briskly over Shy's Hill that he became separated from his regiment. Continuing on, he stumbled across a Confederate battery which he charged singlehandedly and captured. Onley Andrus, a pessimistic and solemn sergeant of the 95th Illinois, fighting with the XVI Corps, at last found something to cheer about. "The road all the way from the battlefield is strewed with guns clothing Haversacks . . . ," he happily informed his wife.[30]

---

[28] Wilson, *Under the Old Flag*, II, 114–115. *Official Records*, Ser. I, Vol. XLV, Pt. 1, 40.

[29] Herr, 334–335. *Report of the Adjutant General*, VI, 223.

[30] James H. Blodgett to Newton Bateman, Feb. 21, 1865, Bateman Papers. *Civil War Medal of Honor Winners*, 4. *Civil War Letters of Sergeant Onley*

If there was any real resistance offered to the advancing Union regiments, it was felt by the 114th Illinois. Leading a triumphant charge by W. L. McMillen's brigade over Shy's Hill and down the Granny White pike, it came upon a large farmhouse (probably the Granny White house itself), which had among its outbuildings an inviting smokehouse. In the character of the Army of the Tennessee, the Sangamon County soldiers made a quick strike at the sides of bacon and hams therein. "The lady of the house courageous and with a long board smites ye Yanks right and left making several ears ring . . . ," wrote Harrison Chandler, the quartermaster of the 114th. "The boys yell," concluded the Chandlerville, Illinois, soldier, "but let her pound at will. . . ." An astonishing victory and a rasher of bacon were worth a few buffets, felt the men of the 114th.[31]

The battle of Nashville was a personal vindication of both Thomas and those elements of the Army of the Cumberland which were still attached to his command. Grant had given this loyal, modest, and uncomplaining general an immense amount of discomfort, and only once had Thomas given way under the pressure. This had happened five days before the victory over Hood's forces, when Thomas called his corps commanders to his headquarters for a conference. After dismissing the others, the commanding general restrained James H. Wilson from leaving, saying to him with much feeling: "Wilson, the Washington authorities treat me as if I were a boy. They seem to think me incapable of planning a campaign or of fighting a battle, but if they will just let me alone till thawing weather begins and the ground is in condition for us to move at all I will show them what we can do. I am sure my plan of operation is correct, and that we shall lick the enemy, if he only stays to receive our attack.[32]

Hood had stayed and was soundly whipped, whipped even worse than Bragg at Missionary Ridge, when Thomas' Army of the Cumberland had stormed the slope uncontrolled. Now, in the

---

Andrus, 112. The reader may remember Sergeant Andrus from preceding chapters as a dour and cantankerous complainer about the army.

[31] "Civil War Diary of Harrison Chandler, June 22, 1864–Jan. 1, 1865, Section V" (unpublished transcript, ISHL), 7. Note that Chandler very likely came from the family after which his town was named. The conclusion that the 114th struck at the Granny White house comes from a study of maps.

[32] Wilson, *Under the Old Flag*, II, 116.

waning daylight of December 16, 1864, when far off in Georgia Sherman had marched unopposed to the coast, Thomas' men pursued the Confederates through the wet and mud south of Nashville. "Dang it to hell, Wilson, didn't I tell you we could lick 'em?" Thomas shouted at his subordinate in the righteous indignation to which he was entitled. Nor were his men to miss the sense of deliverance which victory implied for them. Given the task of guarding the gateway to the north, the men of the IV Corps and their companions could not help their feelings of elation. Lieutenant James H. Blodgett, an Amboy soldier of the 75th Illinois, probably expressed such sentiments as well as anyone when he wrote his friend, Newton Bateman, State Superintendant of Public Instruction of Illinois: "Then the great north which had given Grant's army a Thanksgiving turkey and was preparing to give Sherman's army a Christmas one . . . suddenly found that Thomas was somebody and that he too had an army."

Wilsons' cavalry followed Hood's shattered divisions late into December, when torrential rains brought the pursuit to an end. The Confederate invasion of Tennessee had also come to an end. Schofield's savage defense of Franklin, implemented by the sturdy defense of the five Illinois regiments in Opdycke's command, had torn the heart out of the invading army, slaughtering its best divisions and field generals. The effect of Nashville was different. Hood's killed and wounded were exceedingly small, probably not much more than 1,500 men, but he lost 4,462 captured. Thomas' amounted to slightly more than 3,000. Nevertheless, Thomas had destroyed the organization of the Confederate army. He had smashed it so that it would never again effectively fight as a separate army. That is all that could be asked of any commanding officer.[33]

[33] *Ibid.*, II, 126. Blodgett to Bateman, Feb. 21, 1865, Bateman Papers. Cox, *The March to the Sea*, 126–129. Thomas L. Livermore, 132–133. Horn, 417.

CHAPTER XII

Illinois and Other Campaigns

During the course of the war, Illinois regiments, lesser units, and general officers fought in a variety of widely separated areas and campaigns. Almost every major and minor episode of the conflict, from Gettysburg in Pennsylvania to Prairie Grove in Arkansas, had one or more participants from the great Prairie State. Illinois men stormed Fort Wagner at Charleston, South Carolina, in 1863, and sweated out the long summer of 1864 in Brownsville, Texas. There were over a thousand Illinoisans in the United States Navy, fighting on the interior rivers such as the Tennessee and the Mississippi, and upon the high seas as well.

There were a number of strange assignments for Illinois soldiers, such as that fulfilled by the so-called "Sturgis Rifles," a special company raised and equipped with Sharpe's rifles by Solomon Sturgis, a wonderfully patriotic merchant from Chicago. As a youth, Sturgis served alongside Francis Scott Key as an army volunteer in the War of 1812. When the Civil War broke out, he contributed over $120,000 to the cause, buying government bonds and raising the special company. Despite the nobility of his intentions, however, the "Sturgis Rifles" never really did anything but act as a special bodyguard for General George B. McClellan. A few members did fight at Antietam, however. Finally, in November, 1862, it packed up its unused rifles and came home.[1]

To cover the activities of all Illinois units and the general of-

[1] *Historical Encyclopedia of Illinois,* 511–512.

ficers who commanded them would require a more detailed and extensive study than is possible here. Illinois gave to the nation not only such well-known figures as Grant, Logan, Schofield, and Palmer, but also many other personalities who played their own special roles in the great war. The participation of John Alexander McClernand in the early battles of the war and in the raising of troops has been discussed. The parts which Benjamin Prentiss and Stephen Hurlbut played in the battle of Shiloh were touched upon, though each contributed more than that solitary deed to the winning of the war. There was General Mason Brayman of Springfield, Illinois, who not only served through Belmont, Fort Donelson, and Shiloh, but also held district occupation commands through the rest of the war, being raised to the rank of brevet major general in 1865. There was John Franklin Farnsworth of St. Charles, Illinois, who organized the 8th Illinois Cavalry, fought through the Peninsular and Antietam campaigns, and then resigned to become a staunch radical Republican politician in the middle of the war. Farnsworth's nephew, Elon John Farnsworth, was to attain an even greater fame. This young cavalryman of the 8th Illinois not only attained a general officer's rank but probably participated in more battles and skirmishes than any other officer in the war, from Mechanicsville to Gettysburg, where he was killed in one of the most courageous and disastrous attacks of the entire conflict.

Nor was Farnsworth the only Illinois soldier to participate in that significant battle. The troops of General John Buford, the half-brother of General Napoleon B. Buford of Rock Island, fought a bitter rear-guard action near McPherson's Ridge, setting the stage for the fighting on Little Round Top. General Wesley Merritt, famous 30 years later in the Spanish-American War, was another Illinois officer who performed heroically in that most famous of Civil War battles, as well as elsewhere, especially under Sheridan.[2]

One could go on and on recounting the deeds of Illinois soldiers from 1861 to 1865. The 82nd Illinois, a regiment raised principally in Cook County, fought at Fredericksburg, Gettysburg, and in

[2] *Ibid.*, 59, 162, 371. Boatner, 97. Merritt, who came from Salem, Illinois, commanded American land forces in the Philippines during the Spanish-American War.

the Chattanooga and Atlanta campaigns. The 23rd Illinois, also raised in Cook County, campaigned not only in Missouri but in the major eastern movements as well, ending its war service at Appomattox. The 8th and 12th Illinois cavalries ran the gamut of fighting in the East, participating in the hardest battles in that theater of conflict.

The areas of conflict participated in by Illinois troops, besides those discussed in previous chapters, fall into three broad categories. They are the military movements in Louisiana and Texas and the Red River campaigns; the eastern theater of war, including the fighting in Virginia, Maryland, and Pennsylvania; and the Mobile campaign. In all of these, as shall be indicated below, Illinois soldiers fought from the beginning to the end, and took part in their most bitter phases.[3]

Following the capture of Vicksburg in July of 1863, the luckless XIII Corps, which consisted mainly of Illinois regiments and which, under McClernand, had been given some of the most difficult tasks of that campaign, was separated from the main body of Grant's army and sent to operate against the Confederate defense of Jackson, Mississippi, conducted by General Joseph E. Johnston, at this time almost a year and a half from his trials in Georgia. The march of the XIII Corps, now commanded by Ord, was conducted under the most uncomfortable conditions, intense heat and dust and, as one would suspect, skillful handling of the Confederate enemy by Johnston himself.

As the siege of the Mississippi capital continued through the early days of July, other Union troops were brought forward from the Vicksburg encampment, including the IX Corps, composed mainly of eastern troops; the XV Corps, later to be distinguished in the Georgia campaigns; and two divisions of the XVI Corps, one of these commanded by General Jacob G. Lauman, an Iowa officer.

On July 12 the First Brigade of Lauman's division, under the

[3] *Report of the Adjutant General*, II, 276–278; V, 120–122; VIII, 155–157, 376–378. It was not possible to deal with the special mission of Colonel James Jaquess within the boundaries of this work. In 1864 Jaquess undertook to carry certain papers to Jefferson Davis on behalf of the President of the United States. For a complete account of this occurrence, see Clarence P. McClelland, "An Illinois Colonel's Visit to Jeff Davis in 1864; His Contribution to Lincoln's Re-election," *Journal*, LV, No. 1 (Spring, 1962), 31–44.

charge of Colonel Isaac Pugh of Decatur, Illinois, and including the 28th, 41st, and 53rd Illinois, was ordered to a position near the Pearl River on the Union right wing. Pugh, who later rose to the rank of brevet brigadier, moved his brigade forward, entrenching it in a set of substantial and defensible works. Within the hour, however, Lauman committed a horrible mistake by ordering a direct charge upon the heavily manned Confederate position. The slaughter was almost unbelievable. The 41st Illinois, a central Illinois regiment commanded by Lieutenant Colonel John Nale of Decatur, lost two-thirds of its complement, 202 altogether, including its popular major, Francis M. Long of Taylorville. The 53rd, a La Salle County regiment, lost 162 men in all, including its colonel, Seth Earl of Ottawa, its lieutenant colonel, John McClanaham of Lacon, and eight officers who were wounded or killed. The 28th, a western Illinois regiment commanded by Colonel Amory Johnson of Petersburg, a hero of Shiloh, had 68 casualties. All in all the losses were enough to bring a quick end to the career of Lauman. He was promptly removed and sent home by Sherman.

The fighting around Jackson was fairly continuous between July 9 and 16. On July 13 there was severe skirmishing involving the 33rd Illinois, the "Teacher's Regiment," particularly after Sherman began to draw his lines tighter around the Mississippi city. It was in this action that a future governor of Illinois, Private Joe Fifer of McLean County, was severely wounded and taken off the field. Three days later Johnston withdrew his army from Jackson, and the city fell to the Federal army.[4]

Following the fall of Jackson, the XIII Corps was assigned to the Department of the Gulf, commanded by General Nathaniel P. Banks. This politician-general, fresh from the successful campaign against Port Hudson, below Vicksburg, had been given the task of leading a Union force into Texas. Part of the XIII Corps was moved to New Orleans and then to Bayou Teche, where it chased a Confederate army under General Richard Taylor in a march through New Iberia and Opelousa. There was a great deal more foraging than fighting done by Banks's troops. Poultry was brought in to Union encampments by the wagonload. One Illinois

[4] *Official Records*, Ser. I, Vol. XXIV, Pt. 2, 534–536. Way, 46, 49. Fox, 440.

regiment, the 33rd, was able to boast that it never carried a cooked chicken during any of the campaign. The whole march was one to be remembered with great amusement by Illinois troops participating in it. While trudging through New Iberia, for instance, the 33rd Illinois was "taken with one of those freaks of howling and yelling which often came upon it, and kept it up at such a rate that the natives were frightened well nigh out of their senses." So dismayed were many of the residents that virtually every town in the area was heavily decorated with French flags in an attempt to indicate that popular loyalty was not necessarily to the Confederacy.

From Jackson in Mississippi to Opelousa in Louisiana, the XIII Corps had an easier time than it had ever had or would ever have again. From the 50 barrels of rum foraged from a train in Mississippi to the roasted poultry of Louisiana, the whole march was a "lark." Eventually almost the entire corps returned to New Orleans, where, for the first time, boys from backwoods Illinois towns were able to become acquainted with the mysteries of the great gulf city. The young men from McLean County and elsewhere roamed through the French quarter, drank the famous beverage of the coffee houses, stood in silence before the statue of Henry Clay, and took boat rides on Lake Pontchartrain. As many of the same men were to discover, this was the last of the free and easy life. Just a few months later, under N. J. T. Dana, such regiments as the 33rd Illinois would be on a campaign aimed at Brazos Island at the mouth of the Rio Grande and at the capture of Fort Esperanze, near the mouth of Matagorda Bay. There they would remain, or at Brownsville or on Matagorda Island, while Banks made his plans to advance up the Red River in 1864.[5]

When the scheme for the latter campaign reached a point of execution, it was initiated by a shifting of a good many of the troops and generals in the Department of the Gulf. McClernand, finally clearing the "unfortunate misunderstanding" between the administration and himself, was once again given the control of the XIII Corps. Though inactive for almost six months, the Illinois general had lost none of his flair for politics and histrionics.

[5] Way, 47–53.

Senator Lyman Trumbull was persuaded to send appropriate remarks to Banks, so that commander might not underestimate McClernand's appeal to the people back home. "Our people think well of him," wrote the senator, "and I understand his old corps think well of him." And when McClernand arrived at the headquarters of his old command, he could not resist the temptation to issue a flamboyant general order. "Comrades!" he proclaimed. "New fields of duty and peril are before us. Let us hasten to make them historic with the valor and success of American arms." It is not known whether Grant, busy in the East, ever took the time to read the remarks of his old antagonist. If so, he must have suffered a slight twinge of nostalgia for the hills of Vicksburg.[6]

By 1864 other changes had been made in Banks's command. Troops of the XIX Corps, formerly attached to the Army of the Potomac, were brought west to bolster the western regiments of the XIII and XVI corps. These shiny and well-drilled soldiers had not lived in the same world as that of the men of the latter two units. They were, in fact, so shocked by the rough bearing and shabby appearance of the Illinois, Iowa, and Michigan regiments with which they would have to campaign, that it would require a number of incidents to convince them of the "soldierly" qualities of their new comrades. The first of these, a long route march in which the eastern soldiers dutifully carried their rifles as per army regulations, should have been enough to have accomplished this. The southern Illinois soldiers of the 18th and 81st Illinois made the whole long distance in record time, holding their rifles at "rest arms," parallel behind the neck, and by restricting their stride to only the barest formation. When, at the end of the day, the Connecticut and Rhode Island men of the XIX Corps collapsed on the ground in sheer exhaustion, the two Illinois units were prepared to continue the march for several more hours.

A second incident may have been a real convincer, however. The 3rd Rhode Island, a swaggering Irish regiment, made the mistake of testing the courage and fighting ability of the 33rd Illinois in a drunken brawl. Heavily outnumbered, the "Teacher's

[6] Trumbull to Banks, Feb. 6, 1864, Nathaniel P. Banks Papers, ISHL. General Order No. 14 to XIII Army Corps, Feb. 23, 1864, Turner Papers.

Regiment" virtually pulverized their comrades from the eastern state.[7]

If the differences within the Federal army in Louisiana and Texas had been all on the lower levels, the Red River campaign might have begun on a better footing. Such was not the case, however, for the variances found between such regiments as the 3rd Rhode Island and the 33rd Illinois existed in a comparable way among the general officers in that area. The men of the XIX Corps, for instance, were commanded by a glistening and precise regular by the name of William Buel Franklin. This general officer had come out on the minus side of the Army of the Potomac, having earned not a few demerits for his conduct at Fredericksburg. Nor were the rest of Banks's easterners gifted with higher reputations. Admiral D. D. Porter, an easterner who had spent most of his time in the western theater of war, was to describe them as men who looked as if they had "spent the winter in the gay saloons of the St. Charles [a famous old hotel in New Orleans]. . . ." One could, therefore, scarcely compare them to such men as Lawler, the brawling champion of the Big Black, or that sterling officer from Farina, Illinois, Thomas E. G. Ransom.[8]

Nor were the differences between the general officers missed by the soldiers in the ranks. Banks's eastern generals, for instance, were regarded by Illinois soldiers as little more than "headquarter's Pimps." McClernand, they argued, was buried by Banks in a rear assignment because the latter feared both the Illinois general's rank and ability. Consequently, the ordinary Illinois veteran felt that there were only two adequate commanders in the field — the aforementioned Ransom, whose courage was respected by all, and General A. J. Smith, a sturdy regular well known by western soldiers.[9]

By March Banks's campaign was well under way. Seven Illinois regiments, the 47th, 49th, 58th, 95th, 117th, and 199th, all from Smith's Detached Army of the Tennessee, parts of the XVI and XVII corps, participated March 14, 1864, in the capture of Fort De Russy, a Confederate stronghold near Alexandria on the Red

[7] Newsome, 113. Duncan Ingraham to his niece, Jan. 31, 1865, Ingraham Papers.

[8] Porter, 219. Boatner, 303–304.

[9] Bentley, 249, 261.

River. The next day the navy occupied Alexandria, which had been evacuated by the Confederates. The XVI Corps pushed the Confederates back at Bayou Rapides March 21, capturing a number of guns. On March 25 Banks arrived to take command — a calamity in itself.

By April 7 Banks's advance units were at Wilson's Plantation, near Pleasant Hill, where a brisk cavalry fight occurred. On the following day a severe engagement was fought by the contending forces at Sabine Cross Roads or Mansfield, Louisiana.

The Battle of Sabine Cross Roads was probably more vicious than any fought in the entire Red River campaign. "Dick" Taylor had entrenched his Confederate troops so as to form an obvious trap — obvious, that is, to everyone except Banks, who ordered two divisions of the XIII Corps to advance directly into it. Ransom, who commanded the latter two units, protested vociferously against the directions of his superior, arguing that such an assault would "finish" his troops.

Ransom was correct, of course. Regiments were committed one by one by Banks, and one by one they were defeated. Finally an attack by a Texas division on the Union left unhinged the whole Federal line, and the XIII Corps was routed. The 77th Illinois, which lost severely in the battle, 170 men in all, was deprived of its field commander, Colonel Lysander Webb of Peoria, early in the fight. The 130th Illinois, from Bond and other scattered counties, found itself caught in a savage crossfire, and its ranking field officer, Major John B. Reid of Greenville, was wounded through the lungs. Leaderless, the regiment continued the fight for only a short time longer before surrendering to the onrushing Confederates.

The rout of the XIII Corps was almost like that suffered by the Federal right at Stone's River. Ransom himself was wounded. The "Chicago Mercantile Battery," and other Illinois artillery units as well, lost every one of their guns as mules and horses careened to the rear minus their caissons and wagons. Banks lost 2,235 in dead, wounded, and missing, as well as 20 guns and 250 wagons.[10]

The effect of the battle of Sabine Cross Roads was catastrophic

[10] *Official Records,* Ser. I, Vol. XXXIV, Pt. 1, 177, 305–307. Ludwell H. Johnson, *Red River Campaign: Politics and Cotton in the Civil War* (Baltimore, 1958), 95–97, 136, 140. Bentley, 246–258. The men of the 77th felt

as far as the XIII Corps was concerned. The 130th Illinois, its losses totaling 260 (232 of whom were missing or captured), illustrates the point. One private reported for duty on the following day. The 77th Illinois, defending one of Banks's wagon trains, was decimated. The corps, its morale destroyed, was ordered by Banks to the rear. An Illinois soldier of the 117th regiment, Sergeant Sidney Zebina Robinson of Paddock's Grove, fighting in Smith's corps, sympathized with his Illinois comrades. The XIII Corps, he wrote, was "as fine a Corps as is in the field." But fighting under these "eastern generals," how could anything be accomplished, he remarked. Robinson's conclusions were bitter ones. He simply could not put down on paper the extremities of hatred which Illinois troops had for Banks and his staff.[11]

Young Robinson might have added, however, that the Illinois troops of the XVI Corps did manage to obtain revenge for the defeat of their comrades by meeting Taylor's men on April 9, the day following the defeat of Sabine Cross Roads. Banks had hurriedly withdrawn his army to Pleasant Hill, where Smith's Detached Army of the Tennessee was in bivouac. The Confederate commander, trailing the Federal retreat too closely, ran full tilt into the XVI Corps and W. H. Emory's division of the XIX Corps, with serious fighting resulting. The latter unit, composed of eastern troops, collapsed before the Confederate assault, but Joseph A. Mower's division of the XVI Corps did not, and, for a brief time, it was breast-to-breast fighting on the part of the combatants. Midway through the battle, a Confederate division drove a gaping hole in the Union line, pushing back the 58th and 119th Illinois with a savage charge. In the rear, hidden by tall underbrush, was the 117th Illinois, a Madison and St. Clair counties regiment commanded by a former McKendree College professor, Colonel Risdon Moore. Coming from their hiding place with "a most hidious yell," as Captain David McFarland of O'Fallon, Illinois, described it, the 117th formed a line supported by the 58th and 119th, and drove the enemy from the field. It was in this furious action that Sergeant John Cook of the 119th left his quartermaster

the battle to be far harder than any in the Vicksburg campaign. Mary Livermore, 397–402. Fox, 444. Bryner, 103.

[11] Fox, 444. Robinson to his family, April 13, 1864, Sidney Zebina Robinson Papers, ISHL.

post and led his company into the teeth of the enemy defense. For this the Ellington, Illinois, soldier would receive the Medal of Honor.[12]

Though the battle of Pleasant Hill was a victory for the Federal forces, Banks did not act as if it were. Troops lay wounded on the field all night, and when A. J. Smith requested a chance to aid them Banks refused and ordered a retreat. The language of the commanding officer of the XVI Corps, according to Sergeant Robinson of Paddock's Grove, was grand and inspired. Smith was not the kind of man who retreated in the face of victory. Nor was McClernand, who was on a sickbed back at Grand Ecore. When he heard of the Federal victory at Pleasant Hill, he defied a rampaging fever and led the remaining divisions of the XIII Corps forward in order to clinch the Confederate defeat. Banks ordered the movement halted, but the Illinois general disobeyed, pretending that he had never received the message. Twice more Banks repeated the order, however, and finally McClernand, along with Smith, retreated with angry and disgusted troops.

The Federal losses at Pleasant Hill were 1,369, less by over a hundred than those of the Confederates. Yet this was little consolation to the western troops of the Federal army, for they had developed such an intense hatred of Banks that nothing less than his resignation would have satisfied them. Captain David McFarland, the O'Fallon, Illinois, officer who would die a month later at Alexandria, expressed the typical Illinois soldier's contempt for the leadership of the army. "I think they [William Buel Franklin and Albert L. Lee] are dead as Genls.," he wrote. "Their becility [*sic*] and stupidity in allowing themselves to become the easy pray to the rebles should never be forgivin." Sergeant Sidney Robinson of the 117th Illinois had similar feelings. "The boys are mad, disheartened and discouraged on account of the way this expedition has been managed," he complained, "and Banks is a hiss and a byword for all of the Western troops here. . . ." The young Paddock's Grove soldier had further thoughts on the matter: "Banks has acted the part of a coward, has brot disgrace and

[12] *Ibid. Official Records*, Ser. I, Vol. XXXIV, Pt. 1, 341–350. McFarland to his wife, April 13, 1864, David McFarland Papers, ISHL. McFarland's letter is a fine account of the battle of Pleasant Hill. *Civil War Medal of Honor Winners*, 10. See also Bentley, 311, 262–263.

contempt on the American arms and one of my happiest days will be when we leave this department." Sergeant Duncan Ingraham, a soldier of the 33rd Illinois who hailed from the crossroads hamlet of Robin's Nest, Illinois, expressed the same sentiment in a slightly more literate manner, being a member of the "Teacher's Regiment." "We are living in the land of plenty," he stated, "yet on the worst commissary stores we ever had – wormy crackers and stinking beef and pork." "*Something is rotten*, too besides rations, for Gen. Franklin was badly defeated at Sabine Pass."[13]

Even the capable A. J. Smith fell victim to the ill temper of the troops, being hissed by the members of the 81st and 95th Illinois during a loading incident on one of the rivers. Smith's reaction was no uncertain one, however, for he threatened to place the two regiments on a boat and send them to "H—— a warm place if they wished."[14]

Banks did continue his unsuccessful campaign along the Red River, retreating clear to the Mississippi, although, it must be added, with fewer Illinois troops than he had had before. The XIII Corps, that valiant orphan of the war, was disbanded in June, 1864, and most of its Illinois regiments were sent to participate in the campaign against Mobile. McClernand had gone home long before then, having become disabled with malaria early in 1864. The XIII Corps was not the only body of troops which managed to escape Banks's inept command. The Detached Army of the Tennessee, including the XVI Corps, was fortunate enough to head north to Missouri and then went to Nashville in support of Thomas. There, as indicated previously, it was to have a prominent part in the smashing of Hood's invasion of Tennessee.

Yet even to the end of the Red River campaign, there were Illinois troops fighting in that area. At Yellow Bayou (Bayou de Glaize) on May 18 the largest Federal losses were suffered by the 58th Illinois, a Cook, Kane, and DeKalb counties regiment commanded by Colonel William Lynch of Elgin. And to the end, the Illinois troops who served under Banks retained a bitterness which time would never erase. As the campaign neared its end, the

[13] McFarland to his wife, April 18, 1864, McFarland Papers. Robinson to his mother, May 4, 1864, Robinson Papers. Duncan Ingraham to his niece, Sept. 20, 1864, Ingraham Papers. Thomas L. Livermore, 109.

[14] Newsome, 122.

Macomb Eagle expressed the entire sentiments of a state which had seen many of its soldiers sacrificed by that incapable commander. "It is possible," commented the *Eagle*, "that if he had indulged less in champagne he might have made a better campaign."[15]

While the Illinois troops of Banks's command were undergoing the frustrations of serving with that general, other Illinois soldiers were contending with similar problems in the East. There were, as has been indicated before, several Prairie State regiments which fought through the arduous campaigns in Virginia, Maryland, and Pennsylvania. The 82nd Illinois, organized by Colonel Fred Hecker in Chicago, and consisting mainly of Germans, played an important role in the battles of Fredericksburg, Chancellorsville, and Gettysburg before being brought back to the West. At Chancellorsville, when Joe Hooker was cut to pieces by Lee and Jackson, this Illinois regiment suffered one of the highest regimental losses in that conflict—155 in all.[16]

Another Illinois regiment which struggled manfully in the East was the 23rd, the "Irish Brigade," which was raised and commanded by Colonel James A. Mulligan. After the capture and exchange of the regiment at Lexington in Missouri, Mulligan took it to Virginia, where it participated in 17 different engagements, including Second Kernstown and fighting around Petersburg. At Second Kernstown the casualties of the 23rd were second highest among the Union regiments involved in the fight, totaling 114 in killed, wounded, and missing. Mulligan, who became a division commander, was killed at Second Kernstown on July 24, 1864.[17]

A third Illinois regiment which served in the East was the 39th, the "Yates Phalanx," a northern Illinois unit which was commanded by Colonel Thomas Osborn of Chicago during most of its duration. This regiment fought at First Winchester in 1862 and at Fort Wagner in the Charleston, South Carolina, harbor in 1863. Following its re-enlistment in 1864, it was sent to Bermuda Hundred and then to Drewry's Bluff, where, in May of 1864, it suffered

[15] Bentley, 314–316. Fox, 448. *Macomb Eagle*, May 7, 1864.

[16] *Chicago Tribune*, Nov. 22, 1863. This paper gives an excellent account of the participation of the 82nd Illinois in the battle of Gettysburg. Fox, 436.

[17] *Ibid.*, 453.

122 casualties. It fought at Deep Bottom in 1864 and at the assault on Petersburg in April, 1865. In the latter place the 39th lost 61 of its remaining 150 men. Out of the nine color bearers which the regiment had in this assault, seven were shot down. And in the final campaign to Appomattox, the 39th was present, suffering 72 more casualties in this final phase of the war.[18]

There was, with all of this bloodletting, little pleasure to serving with the Army of the Potomac or the Army of the James. As Private Ransom Bedell, a Cook County soldier of the 39th Illinois, noted, it was not uncommon for a general officer of those commands to call upon his few western regiments to lead the various assaults. There was sufficient reason for this, Bedell added, for when the 39th charged, it moved like an "avalanche." For this reason and others, most Illinois soldiers in Virginia or Maryland would have preferred to serve in the West. A sergeant of the 12th Illinois Cavalry, Ashley K. Alexander of Cherry Valley, Illinois, implied such sentiments when, after the debacle at Fredericksburg, he wrote his sister back in Illinois that the war would be lost. Alexander was willing to go even further; he would bet a hundred dollars on the ultimate decision. Eastern generals were so poor, he added, that "our men have been slaughtered like hogs." Another Illinois soldier, writing to his girl friend back home, indicated that he too had had his fill of serving with such men as Butler and Burnside. Furthermore, he concluded, all of his regiment was "fast to go to Springfield. . . ."[19]

One of the most interesting of the Illinois regiments serving with the eastern commands was the 29th U.S. Colored Infantry. The state of Illinois had commenced the raising of this unit in the late months of 1863, when Governor Yates finally resolved himself on the issue of the Negro soldier and issued an executive order defining the terms under which a colored regiment was to be raised. The 29th was raised slowly, however, for a multitude of reasons, among which were low pay and mistreatment of captive Negro soldiers by the Confederates.

The regiment's A company, brought together in the Quincy

[18] *Ibid.*, 447, 457, 461, 364. See also W. H. Jenkins, "The Thirty-ninth Illinois Volunteers, Yates Phalanx," *Transactions, 1914*, No. 20 (1915), 130–137.

[19] Bedell to his cousin, Aug. 24, 1864, Ransom Bedell Papers, ISHL. Alex-

area, was filled in the early months of 1864. The remaining companies, up to and including K Company, were recruited slowly but gradually from all sections of the state, including those of "little Egypt." The official date of the mustering-in of the regiment, that is to say the moment at which the organization was officially accepted for service, was April 24, 1864.[20]

Noncommissioned officers of the 29th were drawn from the ranks and were, therefore, colored. Officers, following the regulations and custom of the time, were white. When President Lincoln first gave official sanction to the formation of Negro volunteer regiments, the War Department quickly set up procedures by which the latter could be chosen. This involved the establishment of the so-called Bureau for Colored Troops, which, in turn, created various selection boards for the commissioning of white officers for Negro regiments.

In the beginning it appeared as though it might not be easy to obtain an adequate number of suitable officers, since there was, for a time, a stigma to serving along with colored troops. But, as one Negro historian phrased it: "Ambition, as ambition will, smothered many a white man's prejudice and caused more than one West Pointer to forget his political education."

Soon there was a veritable flood of letters from applicants for commissions to state governors and to the Bureau for Colored Troops. Many of these men were sincere and battle-trained officers, anxious only to gain the increase in rank which such appointments carried. Others were illiterate and unprincipled men, desirous of obtaining the commissions only for reasons of personal gain. Among the latter, for example, was Milton Littlefield of Jerseyville, Illinois, who began his military career as a captain of the 14th Illinois. By 1863 he was a colonel in the 21st U.S. Colored Infantry, and by 1864 he was a brevet brigadier. This strange soldier of fortune would become known as the "Prince of Carpetbaggers."[21]

---

ander to his sister, Jan. 17, 1863, Ashley K. Alexander Papers, ISHL. R. T. Prentice to Lovina Eyster, Nov. 3, 1861, Reuben T. Prentice Papers, ISHL. See also *Illinois State Journal*, May 23, 1865.

[20] Cornish, 178. *Quincy Herald*, Dec. 8, 1863. *Report of the Adjutant General*, VIII, 777–805.

[21] Cornish, 208. Joseph T. Wilson, 125. For a study of Littlefield's career, see Daniels.

The 29th U.S. Colored was extremely fortunate in the officers which commanded and led it. Its organizing officer was Lieutenant Colonel John A. Bross, a former captain of A Company, 88th Illinois. Bross, who came from Chicago, had both the appropriate military background for his new command, having fought in the cedars at Stone's River, and the political connection necessary to obtain the appointment. His brother was an editor of the *Chicago Tribune*, and became the lieutenant governor of Illinois following the war. Unfortunately the family tie was enough to cast some doubt upon Bross's ability shortly after his appointment. "Who is Col. Bross," wrote one minor Illinois politician. "Is he some political hack manufactured for the occasion or is he a *man* who has been doing yeoman's service in the army. . . ." Time proved that Bross was a man who was capable of both inspirational leadership and sublime courage. The same would hold true for the other officers of the 29th, for five of them were to be killed or wounded before the regiment was mustered out of the service.[22]

So it was that the 29th U.S. Colored Infantry was accepted for service on April 24, 1864. The regiment was immediately assigned to the Fourth Division, IX Corps, the first Negro division to serve with the Union army in Virginia. The division was commanded by General Edward Ferrero. Ferrero's record in the army was a questionable one, and it became even more so in the months to come. The IX Corps in general had been gifted with unfortunate officers. This "wandering corps," whose troops were entitled to wear the emblem of the shield crossed with anchor and cannon, was to reach perhaps a low point in that respect in April, 1864, just when the 29th U.S. became a part of the organization. At that time General Ambrose E. Burnside reassumed command of the corps.

Despite the misfortunes of the IX Corps, both in commands and assignments, it did have a fine record of regimental racial tolerance. As a Negro historian was to write some years later, the treatment of colored soldiers by white "was tempered by humanity, and pregnant with a fraternal feeling of comradeship."

On April 25 the 29th U.S., along with other units of the Fourth Division, was marched down 14th Avenue in Washington, D.C.,

---

[22] *Historical Encyclopedia of Illinois*, 61. William Strawn to J. B. Turner, Nov. 18, 1863, Yates Papers. *Report of the Adjutant General*, VIII, 777–805.

to board the train for the front. During this parade a strange extemporaneous review of the division was conducted by President Lincoln. The President was also traveling down 14th Avenue, and an accidental meeting between the new Negro soldiers and their "benefactor" took place. It was reported that the faces of the soldiers took on an appearance of awe and pride as they passed the man about whom they had refused to hear anything but good. Raising their hats, the troops shouted "Hurrah, hurrah, hurrah for Massa Linkun! Three cheers for the President!"[23]

On May 6 the 29th U.S., along with other regiments of Ferrero's division, joined the Union army in Virginia. Here the division was temporarily attached to the VI Corps, commanded by General John Sedgwick, who was to die May 9 at Spotsylvania. The unit had been given the task of protecting the supply trains to the rear of the grand assault upon Lee's army. Almost immediately, however, the 29th found itself in action. On the night of May 6 the Confederates launched an attack upon the trains which the Negro soldiers promptly threw back. With Grant moving the main army through the Wilderness in the direction of Spotsylvania, the task of the 29th became even more difficult, for the lifeblood of the entire Federal offense flowed through the supply lines to the rear, and there were constant attempts by Lee's cavalry to destroy them.

With the Army of the Potomac now moving rapidly through the Wilderness, Spotsylvania to Cold Harbor and thence to Petersburg in broad-flanking maneuvers to the left, the 29th U.S. Colored Infantry was often forced to undergo long daily marches in order to maintain its position with respect to the supply trains. The regiment spent some time in defending a vital plank road stretching from Banks' Ford on the Rappahannock to Todd's Tavern in the Wilderness, and then marched to Salem Church near Fredericksburg, where another attack was made by Lee's veterans upon the rear lines of communication. The 29th then took part in the movement to the North Anna, crossed the Pamunkey, marched by stages to Bethesda Church, and then crossed the James on June 17. This was hard soldiering, and the new Negro regiment did it so well that a "strong feeling of pride and *esprit de corps*" welled up among its troops. On June 18 the Fourth Di-

[23] Joseph T. Wilson, 412, 381–384.

vision returned to the IX Corps. When the unit reached the second line of trenches to the left of Petersburg, where it remained inactive until mid-July, the soldiers began to chafe "with eager ambition" to do real fighting along the front line. Their wishes, unfortunately, would soon be realized.[24]

As the Petersburg siege settled into an impasse that threatened to go on and on, General Grant began to consider seriously an idea which had originated in the ranks of the 48th Pennsylvania, a regiment composed of former coal miners. The plan, as proposed to the general-in-chief by Lieutenant Colonel Henry Pleasants, the commanding officer of the Pennsylvania regiment, called for the digging of a series of galleries beneath the Confederate lines. These would be filled with explosives, set off at a given time, and followed by an assault designed to exploit both the hole and the confusion which would develop in the enemy entrenchments. The plan was reluctantly accepted by Grant, and digging was commenced in late June and continued through the early part of July.

Meanwhile Grant, who had once before at Vicksburg seen such an explosion fail to achieve its purpose, ordered General Burnside, commanding officer of the IX Corps, to select and train particular regiments of his command for the attack. That general officer, cognizant of the low state of morale among his troops and the wear and tear which the war had inflicted upon them, chose Ferrero's division of colored soldiers to lead the assault. Through the hot days of July the men of the 29th, along with their comrades of other regiments, were trained to meet the conditions of the proposed attack.

It was only a few days before the deadline for the assault that the troops were told of their strange mission. As one would suspect, the comparatively new troops immediately recognized the responsibility which they carried upon their shoulders. Colonel Henry G. Thomas, ranking officer of the Second Brigade, which included the 29th U.S., recalled several years later that the soldiers promptly huddled in small groups after being given the information about the assault. Suddenly one soldier, followed by others, began to sing a song which in all of the long months after

[24] *Official Records*, Ser. I, Vol. XXVI, Pt. 1, 987–990. Joseph T. Wilson, 386–387, 407–408. *Official Records*, Ser. I, Vol. XL, Pt. 1, 594–596.

the assault they would never sing again. It ran: "We-e looks li-ike me-en a-a-marchin' on — We looks li-ike men-er-war."

The underground tunnels were cleared on July 29, the attack being scheduled for the following morning. Only hours before the charge, the commanding general of the Army of the Potomac, George G. Meade, made a decision which was to affect the course of events. Somehow Meade had reached the conclusion that the Negro troops of Ferrero's division were too inexperienced and too untried, and that they could not possibly head the attack. Burnside, the commander of the corps responsible for opening the hole in the Confederate line, argued vehemently, claiming that his white troops were simply not up to another frontal charge. Meade was a stubborn man, however. He took his case to the general-in-chief, and received Grant's concurrence on the matter. Thus the die was cast; General James H. Ledlie's First Division of the IX Corps, consisting of white troops, would be the first to move once the mine had been exploded. Ferrero's Negro division was scheduled to follow.

The method by which Ledlie was chosen to head the assault was indicative of the point of view which Burnside now held toward the success of the plan. The corps commander most certainly had other white divisions, but Ledlie's was picked simply because Burnside called the commanding officers of his white divisions together and asked them to draw straws. The commanding general of the First Division pulled the short one. How could victory be achieved by this process of preparing an attack?[25]

Burnside's plan for the day called for the mine to be exploded before dawn on the morning of July 30. The troops were up early; the men of the 29th U.S. ate the standard pre-assault breakfast of hardtack and salt pork. The hour for the explosion passed with no occurrence. There was some problem with setting off the charge. Finally, close to five o'clock, the air was rent with a tremendous sound. A reporter who witnessed the sight which followed was to describe it thus: "In a moment the superincumbent earth, for a space forty by eighty feet, was hurled upward, carrying with it the

[25] William H. Powell, "The Battle of the Petersburg Crater," in *Battles and Leaders of the Civil War*, ed. Larned G. Bradford (New York, 1956), 559–561. Henry G. Thomas, "The Colored Troops at Petersburg, in *ibid.*, 573–576. Boatner, 647–648.

artillerymen with their four guns, and three companies of soldiers. As the huge mass fell backwards it buried the startled men under immense clods — tons of dirt. Some of the artillery was thrown forty yards toward the enemy lines."[26]

Once again there was a long delay. Ledlie, cowering behind a protective bombproof shelter allegedly well-provisioned with liquor, was reluctant to begin the charge. Finally he ordered his brigadiers forward, he himself remaining behind. There now followed a tragic comedy of errors. By the time the white division reached the crater all organization was lost. Regiment after regiment piled into the gaping hole, became separated from their officers, and were unable to move forward. At six o'clock Meade ordered all troops in the assaulting force, both "white and black," forward and into the crater. Ferrero's division received its orders to attack; the First Brigade, under Colonel Joshua Sigfried, consisting of the 27th, 30th, 39th, and 43rd colored regiments, took the lead. The Second Brigade, consisting of the 19th, 23rd, 28th, 29th, and 31st and commanded by Colonel Henry G. Thomas, followed. General Ferrero, who as divisional commander was ordered to direct the movement, didn't. He got only as far as Ledlie's bombproof shelter, where, in joyful conviviality with his superior, he remained for the rest of the day.[27]

Down into and around the crater went the First Division, Sigfried's brigade veering to the left, Thomas' to the right. The Illinois soldiers of the 29th led the latter maneuver, Lieutenant Colonel Bross out in front. Bross, overcome by that peculiar sense of doom which had pervaded the whole plan, had dressed in his complete uniform. Thomas, his superior, described him later as being "conspicuous and magnificent in his gallantry." Bross, who carried the regimental colors himself, lasted only a few moments, however. As he fell, mortally wounded, the colors of the 29th were picked up by a regimental lieutenant, who was also quickly shot down. The uproar was fantastic. At first the Federals were partially successful but soon were forced back into the crater. Confederate Alabama soldiers who had fought their way to the

[26] Thomas, "The Colored Troops at Petersburg," 575. Joseph T. Wilson, 415, quoting the *Philadelphia Times*, January, 1883.

[27] *Official Records*, Ser. I, Vol. XL, Pt. 1, 595–599. Joseph T. Wilson, 415–416. Thomas, "The Colored Troops at Petersburg," 577.

lip of the crater, and were firing down into the center of the milling soldiers, were surprised to note that not all of the colored soldiers fell back. The Alabamians quickly concluded that the white Federal officers below must have been chosen upon the basis of courage, for both they and their colored subordinates fought "with desperation."

As the fighting in the crater continued, cries of "no quarter" could be heard coming from the Negro soldiers, and the conflict almost became a hand-to-hand one. It was a lost cause as far as the Federal troops were concerned, however, and it could only be a matter of time before they would be overwhelmed. As one Confederate account of the fighting ran:

> Bayonets, swords and the butts of muskets were used. The deafening roar of artillery and musketry, the yells and imprecations of the combatants, drowned the commands of officers. A negro in the crater attempted to raise a white flag, and it was instantly pulled down by a Federal officer. The Federal colors were planted on a huge lump of dirt, and waved until Sergeant Wallace, of the Eleventh Alabama, followed by others, seized them and tore them from the staff. Instantly a white flag was raised, and the living, who were not many, surrendered. The crater was won.[28]

Thus it was that, shortly after one o'clock, the Petersburg mine assault came to an end. The casualties of the Fourth Division were heaviest of all such units taking part in the attack, totaling 1,327 killed, wounded, and missing. The 29th U.S. suffered its share of that number with 11 officers killed or wounded, 19 enlisted men killed, 47 wounded, and 47 captured or missing, for a total of 124. A study of the muster rolls shows that few of those captured at the Petersburg Crater ever returned home.

There was a tendency in the early reports of the attack to place the blame for the Federal failure upon such Negro regiments as the 29th U.S. A close analysis of the facts shows, however, that the faults in the execution of the plan lay not so much with those who were asked to carry it out but with those given the responsibility of leadership. As the death of the gallant Bross proved, no amount of courage could overcome a hopeless situation. Meade, who forced Burnside to lay aside his original plans for the attack, should have shouldered a good deal of the blame. Burnside him-

[28] *Ibid.*, 577–578. Joseph T. Wilson, 413–419. *Official Records*, Ser. I, Vol. XL, Pt. 1, 595–599.

self was partially responsible, as was Grant, who, once the attack had failed, shoved the responsibility upon the shoulders of the cowards Ledlie and Ferrero. The only fault for which the soldiers of the 29th U.S. and their comrades could be blamed was that of having too much courage to run for safety or being unable to get out of the crater as soon as they found that the attack had no chance of success.[29]

The problem of the 29th U.S. was now one of rebuilding itself for future campaigns. During the late months of 1864, all of the Negro regiments of the armies of the Potomac and James were brigaded together in the newly formed XXV Corps. The Illinois regiment was formed with the Third Brigade, Second Division, commanded by General William Birney. That winter found the 29th playing a role in the Petersburg siege operations and occupying secondary trenches near Chafin's Farm and Fort Burnham. Once again it was bitter soldiering, for the troops had to contend not only with the unceasing cold of the winter, but also with continuous fire from Confederate riflemen.

On March 26, just as the spring thaws began to fill the streams, the 29th, along with the rest of Birney's division, was ordered to break camp and cross the James River. Marching across a pontoon bridge, the 29th moved quickly to Hatcher's Run. There the Illinois regiment bivouacked and built new breastworks.

Several days later General Philip Sheridan led a large force to Five Forks, where, on April 1, he inflicted a calamitous defeat upon Lee's troops. This event signaled the breakup of the Petersburg siege. In the pre-dawn of the following day, the 29th U.S., with the rest of its division, paraded in attack formation. Casings were taken from the regimental flags. The command of "forward! guide centre! march!" was given, and the Illinois troops moved toward the Confederate trenches. These works were promptly breached, and the Negro troops soon marched into Petersburg, their long legs moving to the tune of "John Brown's Body."

Birney's division moved through the Virginia town and to its outskirts on the other side, where the troops once again went into bivouac. The significance of the great development taking place in these days of early April was well illustrated by the reaction

[29] *Ibid.*, 248. Cornish, 273–276. The figures indicating the losses of the 29th are a result of my own tabulation from *Report of the Adjutant General*, VIII, 777–805, plus the reports in *Official Records*.

of the farmer on whose land the Negro troops were quartered. The old man was shocked at the sight of colored men in the blue Federal uniform. "Poor old Virginia! poor old Virginia!" the Illinois Negroes heard him cry, "that I should have lived to see this day!"

By April 6 the 29th had reached Sayler's Creek. Three days later it was at Appomattox. Now the end was near. In one last convulsive struggle, Lee made an attempt with cavalry to force the part of the Federal line at which the Illinois soldiers were located. It failed, and the surrender came.

For most of the white soldiers in Grant's great army, the war was almost finished. The same was not quite true for the XXV Corps, however. On May 18 Grant ordered the whole corps to prepare for embarkation to Texas. By May 24 it was on the high seas, and by the early part of June it had reached its new quarters. The 29th U.S. Colored Infantry was stationed at Brownsville, near the Mexican border. Here the unit remained until November, 1865, when it was finally mustered out.[30]

Though not as high as certain other Negro regiments in the war, the total casualty list for the 29th certainly rates it as a fighting unit worth reckoning with. Not including the large numbers of men who lost their lives in Confederate prisons, almost 158 soldiers of the regiment were killed and wounded, or died of disease. Despite the poor pay, which amounted to less than that for white soldiers, and the poor conditions of service, the total number of desertions in the 29th came to only 49.

Nor were the colored soldiers of the 29th the only Negroes from Illinois who fought in the Federal forces. Actually there were Negro recruits in 21 other U.S. regiments, in artillery units, and in various regiments from half a dozen states. This fact showed that the American Negro truly understood the meaning of the war and its implications of freedom for himself. There was, therefore, an extra meaning in a cartoon printed by *Harper's Weekly* only a week or two following the death of Lincoln. Two soldiers, one white, the other colored, and both wounded, face each other. The white veteran extends his hand, saying: "Give me your hand, Comrade! We have each lost a leg for the good cause; but thank

[30] Joseph T. Wilson, 455–467. *Report of the Adjutant General*, VIII, 777–805.

God, we never lost HEART." The title of the drawing is: "A Man Knows a Man."[31]

While the Illinois soldiers of the 29th were contributing their part to the final defeat of Lee's army, other regiments from the same state were participating in the so-called Mobile campaign. These latter troops consisted principally of those from the ill-fated XIII Corps, including such Illinois regiments as the 8th, 11th, 28th, 33rd, 37th, 58th, 75th, 76th, 81st, 91st, 94th, 97th, 99th, 108th, 114th, 117th, 119th, 122nd, and 130th. Under the command of General Edward R. S. Canby, the Federal army moved upon Mobile from the east, capturing Spanish Fort on April 8, 1865. On the following day Canby made a massive attack upon the Confederate works at Fort Blakely, capturing it before sundown. The assault was brilliant. Sergeant George F. Rebbmann, B Company, 119th Illinois, a Brown, Adams, and Schuyler counties regiment, earned a Medal of Honor for his gallantry here. The same was true of Captain Patrick H. Pentzer of the 97th Illinois and Private John H. Calahan of the 122nd Illinois, both of whom came from Macoupin County. In this, almost the last major battle of the war, the long-tried 8th Illinois lost 64 more of its brave men, and the 76th Illinois, a Champaign and Kankakee counties regiment, lost 98.[32]

By April 12 the Federal army was in Mobile. Within a few weeks Montgomery also fell into Union hands. The war was essentially over. Yet one cannot help but picture the antics of various Illinois regiments as they entered the city which considered itself the heart and soul of the Confederacy. The 33rd, for instance, moved itself, rifles and all, into the gleaming white statehouse. There, in the assembly halls, it elected its own senate and passed its own laws. It was loudly suggested that Jefferson Davis be hung for high treason, that the army rations be changed from hardtack to roast beef and turkey with cranberries, and that each volunteer's pay be changed to $100 a month. The war, indeed, was over.[33]

---

[31] *Ibid.*, 806–812. Figures concerning the 29th are a result of my own tabulation from *Report of the Adjutant General*, VIII, 777–805. The cartoon appears in *Harper's Weekly*, April 27, 1865.

[32] *Official Records*, Ser. I, Vol. XLIX, Pt. 1, 96–98. *Historical Encyclopedia of Illinois*, 551–571. *Civil War Medal of Honor Winners*, 4, 9, 6. Fox, 461.

[33] Way, 59.

CHAPTER XIII

Confederate Prisons--The Return Home

The sturdy Yankee defense at Allatoona, along with similar incidents elsewhere, pointed up one fact in the last two years of the war. Union soldiers were ready to resist capture by their Confederate enemy to the utmost. These stands were not entirely due to courage or bravery alone, or to the growing professionalism of the Union army, but also involved was the widespread knowledge within the ranks of conditions which reportedly awaited the individual soldier should he be taken prisoner. As early as November, 1863, and as late as January, 1865, for example, the *Chicago Tribune* ran soul-stirring pieces upon the plight of the inmates of Confederate prisons. The paper even reported that most soldiers were determined to die on the field rather than be taken. Nor was it uncommon for soldiers themselves to come across evidence which gave them proof of the horrible conditions awaiting them upon capture. In 1864 the men of the 52nd Illinois, a Kane and Whiteside counties regiment, came across a copy of the *Richmond Whig* which claimed that one Confederate prison presented sights "surpassing description." Union soldiers occasionally escaped from these enemy enclosures, making their way to freedom. Sergeant James P. Snell, an Aurora soldier of the 52nd Illinois, was one of many who witnessed such incidents. On one occasion a Union scout staggered into the camp of the 52nd, bringing a tale of having escaped from Confederate irons by artfully fashioning a key for the lock. At another time, several members of the 9th Illinois wandered into the same camp, carrying a "sorry tale" of conditions at Andersonville, Georgia, the most notorious of the Confederate stockades. Such stories were bound to have an effect. Writing after the war, Private Henry Eby, a Mendota soldier of the 7th Illinois Cavalry, described a narrow escape from capture by the enemy. Trapped by a company of Confederate troops, he spurred his horse to a gallop, defying their shouts of "Halt, halt, you Yank!" As Eby phrased it, this "Yank wouldn't halt worth a cent."[1]

Although Andersonville was the most famous and infamous of Confederate prisons, there were many others in which Illinois soldiers were to find themselves imprisoned. They included Castle Thunder in Richmond, another prison by the same name in Petersburg, and Cahaba Prison in Alabama, all three of which were converted commercial buildings. Another of the same type was Libby Prison for Union officers, located on the James River in Richmond. Not far from Libby was the notorious Belle Isle, which gave the enlisted men within its confines the privilege of sleeping out in the open, unless they were fortunate enough to have tents.

Somewhat similar to Belle Isle were the numerous stockade prisons throughout the South. These included Andersonville (officially Camp Sumter); Camp Lawton in Millen, Georgia, where the prisoners made their huts from the branches of trees; and Camp Ford and Camp Groce in Texas. The last two, possibly the best of all Confederate prisons, approximately ten acres in size, were surrounded by stockades of oak timber. Other stockades, less important but nevertheless having unsavory reputations, were located at Salisbury in North Carolina, at Macon in Georgia, and at Charleston, Columbia, and Florence in South Carolina. The last named, though not nearly so famous as Andersonville, had a savage death rate, due not only to the poor conditions within the stockade but also to its unspeakably cruel camp commander.

Despite the intentions of Union soldiers, many of them became prisoners after 1863. A Confederate charge made at a dis-

[1] *Chicago Tribune*, Nov. 12, 1863, Jan. 12, 1865. "Diary of James P. Snell," 123. Eby, 237.

advantageous time or men lost fighting in strange country and wandering into Confederate picket lines brought large numbers of Illinois campaigners into captivity. The experiences of the newly captured men were as varied as one could imagine. Private Henry Eby, who escaped seizure once, wrote that his eventual capture at Chickamauga was followed by a long march to a distant railhead. Eby and his captured companions were then packed into a freight car "almost as thick as sardines in a box. . . ." The trip from Dalton, Georgia, to Richmond, Virginia, took eight days, and only infrequently were the men allowed to disembark and stretch their legs. "This was the worst experience I ever had in railroad traveling," Eby wrote after the war. "We were obliged to stand up or sit on the floor, and fold up like a jackknive with our hands clasped around our knees to keep our backs from breaking."

Much different was the introduction to captivity of Private Lewis F. Lake, a Rockford soldier of Taylor's Battery B, 1st Illinois Artillery, who was taken captive in Cheatham's charge at Atlanta on July 22, 1864. He and his fellows were marched double-time into the besieged city, where, to their own amazement, they were given refreshments by the ladies of Atlanta. Within days, however, Lake was to witness the other face of the Confederacy. A week later, and with only a few moldy crackers to eat in that time, he was marched into the stockade at Andersonville.[2]

Members of the 73rd Illinois who were captured at Stone's River received similar treatment. Loaded aboard a train, they were given biscuits until they reached Chattanooga, where, in an abrupt change, inedible and half-cooked food was offered to them. Like Private Lake, these soldiers of the "Preacher's Regiment" were taken to Andersonville. Private John McElroy, a Chicago soldier of the 16th Illinois Cavalry, described a variation of this theme after the war. Following his capture, he was taken to a nearby farmhouse and exhibited as a curiosity before a roomful of southern girls, who made caustic remarks concerning his appearance and dress. "Make him sing!" they demanded. "Make him sing!" McElroy was to live through the horrors of Anderson-

[2] *Ibid.*, 131–133. Lewis F. Lake, "My War Service as a Member of Taylor's Battery, Company B, 1st Illinois Light Artillery" (unpublished manuscript and typed transcript, ISHL), 10, 12.

ville and record them later with great clarity, yet it was this one little moment in his entire captivity which gave him the most embarrassment.[3]

It is probable that some accounts by prisoners were exaggerated and embellished and that one copied from another. It is now impossible to extract the actual from the imagined in a good many cases. Conditions in southern prisons were certainly often appalling, as they were in northern prisons. On the other hand, in many cases the men had the same food as the guards, conditions in the South being what they were, especially late in the war.

One of the finest fighting units of the entire Union army was the 92nd Illinois Mounted Infantry. Because of the nature of the regiment, its constant opponent in the last year and a half of the war was the Confederate cavalry commanded by General Joseph Wheeler. In 1864, during the Atlanta campaign, a number of the men of the 92nd were taken prisoners by Wheeler's men, and had the ill fortune to witness one of the real atrocities of the war. Several of them were beaten about the head with revolvers and two or three were shot on the spot without cause. The survivors were taken to Andersonville by train. When they disembarked in the little town, which consisted of some eight or nine houses, they could see and smell the famous stockade some distance away. Escorted to the gates by no less than the commandant of the prison, Henry Wirz himself, the men of the 92nd suddenly saw human beings "as black as negroes," a reflection of what they themselves would be in two or three months. The inmates, their faces discolored by the pitch pine fires about the camp, greeted the newcomers with cries of "fresh fish." But of all of the descriptions of that fatal moment when a Federal prisoner entered the gates of Andersonville, none is more compelling than that written by Private McElroy of the 16th Illinois Cavalry. This Chicago soldier, brought to the stockade at night, wrote:

> Five hundred weary men moved along slowly through the double lines of guards. Five hundred men marched silently along towards the gates that were to shut out life and hope from most of them forever. A quarter of a mile from the railroad we came to a massive palisade of great squared logs standing upright in the ground. The fires blazed up

[3] *This Was Andersonville: The True Story of Andersonville Military Prison as Told in the Personal Recollections of John McElroy . . .*, ed. Roy Meredith (New York, 1957), xxxii-xxxxiii. Newlin, 563–570.

and showed us a section of these. Two massive wooden gates, with heavy iron hinges and bolts, swung open as we stood there, and we passed through into the space beyond. . . . We were in Andersonville.[4]

The lives of the captives differed with the nature of the military prison in which they were kept. Colonel Fred A. Bartleson of the 100th Illinois, a Joliet officer who was later exchanged, only to be killed at Kennesaw Mountain, wrote that his imprisonment at Libby was marked by only a few "eventful" days. The rest, he complained, were "most monotonous and of an even tenor of routine." Henry Eby, the 7th Illinois cavalryman who was captured at Chickamauga, wrote later of spending his time in Smith Prison near Richmond "skirmishing" for lice, a technique which involved holding one's clothes in a knitting position and cracking the vermin with the fingernails. Colonel Bartleson described his monotonous routine: "I go to bed about ten, get up a little after daylight for roll-call, then breakfast. Read, write, walk and talk and grumble for a while. At two p.m., roll-call, then have dinner. Read, write, walk, talk and grumble till bedtime."[5]

Those who were incarcerated in Libby Prison could consider themselves a little more fortunate than the inmates of other Confederate prisons. The prisoners here were, in the main, a cosmopolitan group. As Bartleson noted, there were officers of all nationalities. One could learn French or German if he wished, study fencing from an expert, become acquainted with life in Constantinople from a Turk, pick up facts about the geography of east Tennessee, or participate in either spontaneous or planned concerts. And, as one might suspect, there was continuous gambling — cards, checkers, chess, or whatever one wished. As the historian of the regiment would write, even the members of the 73rd Illinois who were prisoners took part in this latter activity, a strange pastime for the "Preacher's Regiment."[6]

In other Confederate prisons, life differed in accordance with the problems of survival. Members of the 36th Illinois, imprisoned at Atlanta, were faced with no difficulties in obtaining ra-

[4] *The Ninety-second Illinois Volunteers*, 308–310. *This Was Andersonville*, 5.

[5] *Letters from Libby Prison . . .*, ed. Margaret W. Peelle (New York, 1956), 15, 57. Eby, 148.

[6] *Letters from Libby Prison*, 69. Newlin, 566.

tions — there was all the cornmeal they wanted to eat, and it was occasionally mixed with meat which should have "exacted reverence from any man who looked at it." There were, however, the endless hours of boredom. "What time we could not use up playing cards, sledge, euchre, etc.," wrote one member of the regiment, "was spent in reading light literature." An officer of the 81st Illinois, Captain Edmund Newsome of Murphysboro, faced the same situation. "One great trouble," he wrote after the war, "was that he had nothing to do, and no tools to do anything with. . . . I found an old razor blade, all gapped except one inch to the point, with that, I made wooden forks and spoons, and engraved letters on bone set in handles." [7]

Of all of the Confederate prison camps, the one most noted for fairly good treatment was that of Camp Ford, located near Tyler, Texas. As many Illinois veterans explained after the war, there seemed to be a great natural affinity between themselves and their Texas captors. The battle of Sabine Cross Roads had brought to the prison virtually all of the 130th Illinois and a good portion of the 77th. Under the command of Captain Joseph M. McCulloch of Cazenovia, Illinois, the prisoners were allowed to exchange goods for food. There were hardships, of course, a shortage of clothes and widespread scurvy during the winter and spring of 1865. Yet in comparison to Andersonville or Belle Isle, there were few deaths among the 4,700 prisoners, most of whom came from Illinois. When they did become ill, the men were fairly well treated in Confederate hospitals located at Marshall, about 40 miles away. Prisoners were allowed to collect wood outside of the stockade each day, and rations were supplemented by produce from gardens which prisoners were permitted to keep. Mail facilities were adequate, and the men spent much time writing letters to the folks at home. The stockade had a newspaper, the *Camp Ford News*, there was a "main street" on which were located a barber, a baker, and a shoemaker, as well as various "factories" of one kind or another. Prisoners were allowed to carve combs and trinkets from the horns of cattle, and one Illinois prisoner actually saved $600 by selling such merchandise to his fellow inmates and to Texans who visited the camp. So well did some Illinois pris-

[7] Bennett and Haigh, 398. Newsome, 188.

oners do in this respect that they were able to bribe their way to freedom.[8]

Whatever the prison, the primary problem was food. At Libby and Belle Isle prisons in Richmond, the rations were of fairly good quality until the fall of 1863. Up until that time, the inmates could supplement their diet of flour, salt pork, and bread by purchases of fruit, eggs, and molasses from the outside. But in the late months of the same year there was a radical change. Private Henry Eby, who arrived at Richmond at this time, recalled afterward that his rations at Belle Isle consisted principally of pressed unsifted cornmeal in small quantities, occasional beans and meat, and water drawn straight from the James River. Once in a great while, he added, the men were given a watery bean soup so laden with bugs that the prisoners referred to it by the unappealing name of "bug soup."

Three memories of Belle Isle remained with Eby for the rest of his life. One was of the time his bean ration consisted of only 15 seeds, another was of the time a stray dog wandered into camp and was quickly dressed and eaten, and the third was of his constant hunger. Whenever he was fortunate enough to receive a full ration, Eby noted, he could not keep his mind off it. "It seemed as though the little morsel was magnetized," he wrote. "I would take a few bites of my bacon and hardtack (the bacon I was obliged to eat raw as I had no way of cooking it), and after eating just enough to aggravate me, would be obliged to stop or have none left for the following two or three days."[9]

Eby's experiences at Belle Isle were similar to those of other Illinois soldiers imprisoned at Libby, only a short distance away. Officers of the 36th Illinois later remembered rations consisting of two tablespoons of black beans, two of rice, six ounces of mule meat pickled in brine, and three slices of bread. Were it not for packages sent by relatives, the death rate at both prisons would have been much higher. Not all of the packages which were sent reached their destination. As Colonel Bartleson and other Illinois soldiers discovered, many of the Sanitary Commission and War

[8] Bentley, 280–306. Large numbers of the 77th and 130th Illinois regiments were captured at Sabine Cross Roads. Mary Livermore, 403–407.

[9] Eby, 135–136, 143.

Department supplies were "pillaged" by hungry guards, and their would-be recipients were left to fend for themselves.[10]

If the rations at Libby and Belle Isle could be considered poor, those at Andersonville would have to be termed horrible. Diaries and records kept by Illinois soldiers imprisoned here tell the same unvarnished story. Ground meal, half corn and half cob, was given as a steady diet to the prisoners; as a result, most of the men sooner or later contracted dysentery. Those fortunate enough to obtain money could buy food from the Confederate commissary or from individual enemy soldiers, but the prices were almost prohibitive. After the war, members of the 55th Illinois, one of the hardiest regiments from the state, remembered paying $2 a pint for salt and 30¢ for an egg. Wood had to be purchased from the guards, or obtained from work gangs who cut it from nearby pine forests. The burning of such wood led to the peculiar appearance of the inmates, all of whom were covered with a dark resinous substance. "Face, neck and hands became covered with a mixture of lampblack and turpentine," wrote one Illinois prisoner, "forming a coating as thick as heavy brown paper, and absolutely irremovable by water alone." Even when a prisoner was fortunate enough to have food and firewood, he sometimes found himself missing a third item necessary for cooking – a pan or utensil. These were indeed rare at Andersonville. The canteen proved to be invaluable to the men within that terrible stockade. Broken in half, it provided two separate plates or cooking utensils, which could also be used to dig a well or tunnel.

The instinct to survive led the men at Andersonville to mend and make do, to devise and create. Boots were used as water tanks, and coats were the best means of carrying rations. As one Illinois soldier pointed out, however, one's real chance for survival depended greatly upon the nature of the partnership which existed between himself and a companion. If true and sincere, it allowed for a sharing of rations and supplies, and the nursing of one by the other if he became ill. Such a relationship was that of Private Jack North and Private Chester Hayward, both of Prairie

[10] Bennett and Haigh, 402–404. *Letters from Libby Prison,* 33. For further information on the possible stealing of supplies, see *Official Records*, Ser. II, Vol. VI, 570–571, and "Civil War Diary of Flavius Philbrook" (unpublished and incomplete manuscript, ISHL).

City, Illinois. According to the recollection of Private John McElroy of Chicago, both men looked after each other with such admirable devotion that each was able to return safely to his home. But in the case of the death of one partner, as a member of the 55th Illinois wrote, the surviving soldier viewed his own future with a practical inclination. The death of the deceased was always kept a secret as long as possible so that the remaining veteran might continue to draw two sets of rations.[11]

Conditions in officers' prisons such as that at Macon never quite reached the low level which existed at Andersonville in midsummer of 1864. The Macon stockade, for instance, had a far better water supply than that provided by the horrible and well-described creek at Andersonville, and the rations, though never plentiful, were slightly better and often included a slice of bacon or pork. Furthermore, the better financial situation of the officers and the higher educational and social level of their families back home normally provided for a supplement to the daily ration. Mail often brought money vouchers of one kind or another, allowing for the purchase of food which was generally shared with others. Furthermore, it was usually more possible for officers to establish cordial relationships with their captors. The Murphysboro officer, Captain Edmund Newsome of the 81st Illinois, would remember from his experience in one Carolina officers' camp that the "Masons of Raleigh brought down a good dinner for their brethren amongst the prisoners, and they had a fine time of it." A similar incident was recalled by an officer of the 115th Illinois, the regiment which fought so well at Chickamauga. Suffering from starvation in one officers' camp, he was rescued by a Captain Cooper of the Confederate army, a brother Mason, who gave him $20 in Confederate money with which he was able to buy food.[12]

Generally, when officers were removed from Macon in Georgia to camps in South and North Carolina, their treatment improved immeasurably. Captain Newsome, for instance, witnessed in a South Carolina camp a table so full of food that "it seemed more

[11] *The Ninety-second Illinois Volunteers*, 310–312. [Crooker *et al.*], 376. *This Was Andersonville*, 28–29, 9, 127–128.

[12] Newsome, 179–180, 222, 270. Newsome writes: "Didn't the rest of us wish we were Masons?"

like fairy-land" than anything he had ever seen. And in North Carolina, where war sentiments were tempered with both moderation and humanity, Union officers were given treatment which seemed comparatively regal when compared to that rendered at Macon.[13]

Macon, an officers' prison, had bad conditions, as did Libby and Belle Isle in Richmond. At the latter place, the death rate reached a level of ten a day by the end of 1863, many of the deceased being soldiers from Illinois. Diarrhea was rampant, and it was reported that some of the members of the 112th Illinois actually became so weak from the ailment that they died from suffocation caused by maggots crawling about the face. Drinking water from the James River was itself no small factor in the large death rate. There were few blankets in camp; after a northern chaplain visited the ranks of the 112th Illinois to distribute coats to the soldiers, many of the men were forced to trade them for food.[14]

As indicated several times previously, no Confederate prisons could compare to that at Andersonville in Georgia. Properly named Camp Sumter, it was brought into existence late in February, 1864, near the small village which eventually gave its name to the place. About 60 miles from Macon, and on a rickety railroad running from that town to Albany, the camp consisted of 16½ acres, eventually enlarged to 26. As it was planned, the grounds of the stockade were cut in half by a small but unpredictable stream from which the camp's water supply would come. No sanitary facilities were provided, and the wash from the dirty slopes poured directly into the creek. Upstream, as if inspired by some satanic cunning, were located the latrines for the Confederate guards.

The over-all command of the Union prisoners in Georgia resided in the hands of General John H. Winder, while the immediate responsibility for the Andersonville stockade was that of Major Henry Wirz. Both men came to inspire a tremendous hatred in

---

[13] *Ibid.*, 207–208.

[14] William B. Hesseltine, *Civil War Prisons: A Study in War Psychology* (Columbus, Ohio, 1930), 117–120. Bradford F. Thompson, *History of the 112th Regiment of Illinois Volunteer Infantry* . . . (Toulon, Ill., 1885), 460–470.

the minds of Illinois soldiers who were imprisoned within the infamous stockade, and with sufficient reason, although there were extenuating circumstances particularly in Winder's case. Private John McElroy, the Chicago soldier, was to describe Winder as a man whose sunken and gray eyes were "too dull and cold to light up" his "hard stony face." Furthermore, continued McElroy, he appeared to have a "thin-lipped compressed mouth" which was the "index to a selfish, cruel, sulky malignance." The same soldier concluded that Winder had the nature of "the coward of the playground, who delights in pulling off the wings of flies." It was reported by another soldier that on one occasion Winder boasted: "I am killing off more Yankees than twenty regiments in Lee's Army." And when Winder died in February, 1865, the standard joke among the Illinois soldiers imprisoned within the stockade at Andersonville was that the deceased general's last words were: "My faith is in Christ; I expect to be saved. Be sure and cut down the prisoners' rations." [15]

Wirz was a native of Switzerland; a small man who had first made his appearance in the war as a private of the Madison Infantry of the Louisiana Volunteers. Rapidly promoted thereafter, he made himself indispensable to Winder, and was given the immediate command of Andersonville prison in January, 1864. Called the "Dutch Sergeant" by many of the prisoners, he was described by McElroy as having "bright little eyes, like those of a squirrel or a rat," and as being of a "genus which lives on stealth and cunning, subsisting on that which it can steal away from stronger and braver creatures." His deeds, as shall be recounted below, were motivated, according to the testimony of Corporal John H. Goldsmith, a Petersburg, Illinois, soldier, by a sense of his own destiny. Goldsmith, who survived the rigors of the stockade only because he had the special and fortunate duty of distributing rations, once heard Wirz state that "he [Wirz] was doing more good than if he were in the field, and that he could whip more men than Johnston's army could." [16]

The terrible conditions within the Andersonville stockade have been extensively described by numerous historians and at least

[15] *This Was Andersonville*, xv, 7, 10–19, 264. Hesseltine, 63, 133–158.

[16] *Ibid.* N. P. Chipman, *The Tragedy of Andersonville: Trial of Captain Henry Wirz . . .* (2nd rev. and enl. ed., Sacramento, Calif., 1911), 277–278.

one novelist. The small acreage, on which at one time over 30,000 prisoners were camped, witnessed unspeakable filth and human degradation. The large number of inmates precluded sanitary discipline in the stockade. Latrines were placed almost everywhere on the slopes, and excreta was allowed to wash down into the narrow stream which was the sole water supply for many months. When rains came, conditions became even worse, for the topography of the camp forced the contents of the sinks or latrines to be washed over the whole camp. Only the appearance of the so-called "Providence Spring" in the camp of a young Illinois soldier served to alleviate the problem of drinking water in late 1864.[17]

Medical treatment at Andersonville was almost nonexistent, not because southern doctors were unwilling to treat the prisoners, but because of the overwhelming conditions in the stockade and the lack of medical supplies. Scurvy, diarrhea, dysentery, and gangrene were prevalent by midsummer of 1864. Teeth fell out, or at the least were loosened in most of the prisoners; glands became swollen from the poor diet; and the "smallest abrasion of the skin from the rubbing of a shoe, or from the effects of the sun, or from the prick of a splinter, or from scratching, or a mosquito bite . . . took on rapid and frightful ulceration and gangrene." From this, and the horrible diet of ground meal and husks, the men became "living skeletons." There was little for Confederate doctors to do but complain. Illinois soldiers of the 115th regiment who reported for sick call with gangrenous tissue were treated with an acid which burned some of the rotten flesh away. Private James Jennings, a Newark soldier of K Company, 20th Illinois, who reported for sick call in that same horrible summer of 1864, was given a dozen sumac buds as a treatment for scurvy. And it was reported among other Illinois soldiers after the war that the same doctors, in attempting to vaccinate for smallpox, accidentally induced syphilis in large numbers of prisoners, causing them to rot away with ulcerous growths.[18]

[17] *Official Records,* Ser. II, Vol. VII, 541, 546–550. Chipman, 484–485.

[18] *Ibid.,* 88–89. Royse, 273. James Jennings, "A Story of the Trials and Experiences of James Jennings, Late of Co. K, 20th Infantry at Andersonville Prison . . ." (unpublished typed transcript, ISHL), 8. *This Was Andersonville,* 305.

Nor was the lack of food or adequate conditions tempered by human kindness on the part of Wirz or the guards. Negro soldiers were badly treated, for instance; one Negro private was denied medical treatment, which would have taken only five minutes, for an injury which later proved fatal. Other Negro soldiers, it was reported by some Illinois soldiers, were shot by Confederate guards simply out of spite. In September, 1864, a Confederate guard fired wildly into the stockade with no provocation whatsoever, killing a soldier from an Illinois regiment. Other prisoners were fettered in irons, bucked and gagged, or placed in stocks. It was further reported in the postwar testimony of a Confederate surgeon that Wirz often pulled prisoners out of the ranks in order to hit them, or set hounds upon them.[19]

Of all the horrors of Andersonville, the filth, the dysentery, the food, and the mistreatment, the one most remembered by Illinois prisoners was that of the deadline. This was a mark or line within the stockade beyond which prisoners were forbidden to walk. It was reported among many Illinois soldiers that Wirz had given instructions to his guards to shoot first and ask questions afterward, and that sentries were ordered to fire upon any individual who placed so much as a hand across the fatal line. Deadline shootings increased rapidly in the fall of 1864 for a number of reasons. So many prisoners became demented from conditions in the stockade that they actually began to challenge the Confederate guards to shoot them. Further challenges of the deadline were made by spirited and reckless soldiers of Sherman's invading army who had been taken prisoners in the late months of the same year.[20]

The one case of a shooting at the deadline which virtually all Illinois prisoners seemed to remember was that of a poor demented prisoner who was known by the names of "Poll Parrot" or "Chickamauga," the one because of his incessant talking and the other because of the fact that he had lost a leg at Chickamauga. There is considerable doubt as to "Chickamauga's" real identity. Private McElroy, the Chicago soldier, remembered the man's name as Hubbard and that he was a soldier from the 38th Illinois. Yet there is no such person listed upon the muster rolls of that

[19] *Ibid.*, 34. Chipman, 283, 261, 119.

[20] *Ibid.*, 349. *This Was Andersonville*, 54–55.

regiment. Another prisoner testified afterward that the unfortunate man came from the 96th Illinois and that he had lived in the Galena area before the war. Whatever the identity and background of the soldier, the case became a famous one, for much of the testimony in the postwar atrocities trial of Wirz involved a discussion of the incident.

Several Illinois soldiers were present when "Chickamauga" came to his end. Private Hugh Snee, a Rockville soldier of E Company, 39th Illinois, gave postwar testimony that he was present at the time of the shooting. The omnipresent McElroy seems also to have seen the occurrence, writing afterward that "Chickamauga" had been accused by his mates of informing upon them, and was chased across the deadline by the vengeful soldiers. Though warned by the guard, McElroy stated, the cripple refused to recross the deadline, whereupon the Confederate fired, blowing the jaw off the Illinois soldier. Another account tells almost the same story:

> I walked down towards the gate and saw Captain Wirz on his gray horse inside the gate. I walked up towards the crowd. Just as I got there Captain Wirz came to the gate and I asked him what the trouble was, and he said that the boys were having some fun with "Chickamauga." I turned around to go back towards my tent, when I heard the report of a gun and saw the guard just drawing back his musket and I saw the smoke of the gun. I turned around to go back again near the dead-line, and saw this cripple lying just inside the dead-line. He seemed as if he was not quite dead; he was writhing in the agonies of death.[21]

A significant event which occurred inside the stockade at Andersonville was the hanging of the leaders of the "N'Yaarkers" or "Raiders," a gang which preyed upon other prisoners, by a vigilante group of western soldiers. The "Raiders" were not all from New York, nor were all of them Irish, as many Illinois prisoners claimed. They were, however, from the East, and they did compose a gang which stole from the "fresh fish" who were brought into camp, and sometimes murdered or informed in order to obtain food or special privileges.

Western soldiers put up with these depredations for several months until finally, in July of 1864, they began to organize for

---

[21] *Ibid.*, 30–31. Chipman, 280, 350.

mutual protection. The leaders of these so-called "Regulators" came from Illinois, and included Private Leroy L. Key and Private Ned Carrigan, both of whom came from Bloomington and were members of the 16th Illinois Cavalry; Private John McElroy, the Chicago soldier who came from the same regiment; a tough though unnamed fighter called "Egypt," who came from the 100th Illinois, and who provided much of the muscle for the group; and a sturdy veteran of the 67th Illinois who carried the nickname of "Limber Jim." Key, who took only western men into his organization and his confidence, finally struck in force at the "N'Yaarkers." Meeting the enemy near the small stream which flowed through the camp, the Illinois men tore them apart, arrested six of the leaders, and, with the permission of Wirz, brought them to trial. The hanging of the six, so well described in a recent novel, was followed by burial in a plot separate from the rest of those who were brought to death in the stockade. Thus, in a manner which they could have least expected, the gangsters and bullies of the Andersonville stockade attained a kind of immortality which they would not have had if they had been struck down under ordinary circumstances.[22]

Conditions in Andersonville were savage almost beyond description. The historian of the 92nd Illinois, in relating the chronology of 21 members of his regiment imprisoned within the stockade, writes that the deterioration of their bodies began within the first month of captivity. Gums softened, teeth began to fall out, and dysentery set in. Over half of the 21 were to die before the onset of fall. The pattern of such deaths within this most famous of all American military prisons was one which built up to a climax in midsummer of 1864. April, for instance, saw 576 of the inmates die; July provided 1,731 more deaths; and August and September served to bring down a total of 5,571 prisoners.

Of the poor unfortunates who could not survive the horrors of Andersonville, New York provided the greatest number. Close to 2,500 from that state were buried in the military cemetery nearby. Pennsylvania and Ohio soldiers came next with approximately 1,800 and 1,000 respectively. Over 900 men from Illinois fell vic-

[22] *This Was Andersonville*, 77–82, 89, 23–24. See also Civil War Diary of James H. Buckley, ISHL.

tims to the mistreatment, disease, and starvation which characterized the conditions of the stockade.

Although conditions at other Confederate prisons never reached the low point set at Andersonville, some of them were horrible enough. One authority has estimated that 15 out of every 100 Federal soldiers died during their imprisonment. Florence and Belle Isle provided their share of these. A total of 1,721, or eight-tenths of 1 per cent of Illinois soldiers, died in Confederate prisons, indicating that in all of the stockades, the specter of death walked with impunity.[23]

As Sherman moved deeper into Georgia, the imprisoned officers and men of Macon and Andersonville were transported to Savannah, where conditions were immeasurably improved. According to Captain Edmund Newsome, the Murphysboro officer of the 81st Illinois, the various inmates were given sufficient bricks and mortar to build fireplaces, an adequate quantity of food, and a great deal more of what may be termed as civilized treatment. There was not even the strict enforcement of deadline rules, Newsome added.

It did not last, however. Most of the officers were taken to Columbia in South Carolina, where conditions deteriorated, and the enlisted men were taken to Florence, in the same state, where the situation approximated that of Andersonville. The camp commandant here, a man by the name of Barrett, was perhaps even more vicious than Wirz; in the presence of one Illinois soldier he was reputed to have said: "By God, I'll learn these Yanks to be more a-feared uv me than of the old devil himself. They'll soon understand that I'm not the man to fool with. . . . Just hear'em squeal, won't yer?"[24]

Despite the understandably low morale among the inmates of such places as Andersonville, Florence, or Belle Isle, hope was never completely lost. The historian of the 104th Illinois, for instance, records the case of a mock election held in the Confederate prison at Columbia in which the inmates made their choice between McClellan and Lincoln. Only the eastern soldiers, ac-

[23] *The Ninety-second Illinois Volunteers*, 313–314. Chipman, 375, 381–382. Fox, 528. *This Was Andersonville*, xix, xx.

[24] Newsome, 187. *This Was Andersonville*, 248.

cording to that writer, showed an allegiance to the former, and Lincoln ran away with the votes by 884 to 143.

The same story repeats itself time and time again. In another incident described by the historian of the 115th Illinois, similar evidences of spirit were shown. In the terrible prison at Florence, it was a matter of routine for the prisoners to be lined up and told that Lee had "whipped General Grant and Great Britain has recognized the independence of the Confederate states. . . ." A Confederate sergeant would then ask if any prisoners wished to take an oath of allegiance to the new nation. At the end of the prisoners' stay at Florence, so wrote the member of the 115th, only 200 or 300 of the 15,000 inmates had betrayed the Union cause.[25]

The foremost evidence of the will to survive and win was best indicated by the continuous attempts by Union soldiers to escape from the various Confederate prisons. In fact, it became part of the philosophy of many within the stockades that one could scarcely lose by trying. Even if success was not achieved, there might still be a few days of freedom in which an escapee could overcome the effects of malnutrition by feeding off the countryside.

Escape from Libby, Belle Isle, or Castle Thunder, all in Richmond, was not difficult in the immediate sense. The real problem came in making one's way through the various cities toward the Union lines. Colonel Fred A. Bartleson of the 100th Illinois was privileged to witness one such casual escape when Major Erastus Bates, a Centralia officer of the 80th Illinois, and a Captain Porter, presumably from another Illinois regiment, calmly walked out the gate of Libby Prison. Both were back behind the prison walls within the week.[26]

An attempted escape by one Private Isaac Dalyrimple, an Osceola soldier of the 112th Illinois, met a similar fate. Dalyrimple sought to bribe his way past a Confederate guard who first took the money and then reported the incident to his superior. The Illinois soldier was then placed in solitary confinement in a room adjoining the camp bakery. Dalyrimple was a most enterprising young man, however. He cut a hole in the wall large enough to allow for nightly incursions upon the freshly baked bread. When

[25] Calkins, 239. Royse, 271.
[26] *Letters from Libby Prison*, 16.

Dalyrimple emerged from his confinement two months later, he was, to the amazement of his captors, the fattest man on Belle Isle.

The story of Dalyrimple is not yet finished, however. Along with large numbers of prisoners, he was moved to Andersonville in 1864, where, a month or so later, he managed to escape while cutting wood outside the stockade. Traveling at night, and living for 13 days upon the raw meat of a rabbit which he killed by throwing his ax, he eventually made it to freedom within the lines of Sherman's advancing columns.[27]

For others, escape from Andersonville was not so easily achieved. Private Elisha Lloyd, a Bristol soldier of the 36th Illinois, was one of those who made the attempt but failed. On the pretext of digging a well, Lloyd and some companions proceeded to work a tunnel to the outside, passing the dirt along hand to hand. For several weeks the work went along well, but then, as was often the case at Andersonville, one of Lloyd's accomplices informed in exchange for a loaf of bread. The Illinois soldier was brought before Wirz and punished by being bolted to a 50-pound ball and chain. Needless to say, he suffered immensely. His teeth fell out and his gums decayed from scurvy. When he was finally exchanged he was a stretcher case.

Slightly more successful was the escape attempt by Private James Jennings of the 20th Illinois. After the Andersonville prisoners were taken to Florence there was for some time a slight confusion on the part of Confederate authorities in arranging the guard for the new prison. Jennings, taking advantage of this, walked through the gate of the stockade one day, and continued on into the country. Receiving extremely kind treatment from Negroes along the way, he managed to travel for some time before being apprehended. Brought back to Florence, he escaped a second time. Guiding himself by the North Star and living on grapes and persimmons, he lived in freedom for almost another week before being captured and returned.[28]

The most successful method used by the Confederates to recapture escapees was the employment of bloodhounds. More than one young man was brought back into the Andersonville stockade

[27] Thompson, 470–476.

[28] Bennett and Haigh, 801–808. Jennings, 10–18.

with his face mangled or his ears torn off by the mastiffs. Once in a great while the hounds were eluded, however. In 1864 several members of the 92nd Illinois being transferred to Florence managed to escape by crawling into sections of a smokestack which lay about the depot at Columbus, Georgia. The five men avoided the hounds by walking for several miles in a shallow creek and by traveling only at night. Eventually the Illinois soldiers were recaptured, however, and placed aboard another train for Florence. At Blackshear, Georgia, the men again escaped, but once again their freedom was only temporary. This time the prison gate at Florence was latched behind them.

The prisons which Illinois prisoners found easiest to escape from were those located at Savannah and Columbia. At the former, where conditions were extremely good in a comparative sense, the guard was entirely inadequate and many prisoners made it to freedom. As one Illinois officer was to confide in his diary, not a small factor in such escapes was the aid given to the prisoners by either Negroes or Confederate members of the Masonic Order. At Camp Sorghum in Columbia, so called because sorghum was the principal item in the daily rations there, over 300 escaped from the camp. Still, as Captain Edmund Newsome recorded after the war, not all of those escapes were successfully terminated.[29]

It is entirely possible, however, that there might have been more attempts to escape from Columbia had it not been apparent that the war was coming to a close. Despite the facts of imprisonment, the stockade and such, the inmates of Confederate prisons were never without their sources of information regarding the progress of their cause. Negroes working about the camps often reported news to the prisoners at great risk. Captain Newsome reported an instance in which an elderly Negro, hitherto considered to be mentally deficient, shuffled up to several imprisoned members of the 81st Illinois and muttered: "Sherman is within thirty miles. He'll be here in a few days." Nor was it unusual for Confederate guards to pass along war rumors. One Illinois officer, confined at Savannah, confided to his diary that such gossip was the real spice of prison life. The prisoners, he related,

[29] Chipman, 246. *The Ninety-second Illinois Volunteers*, 321–326. Newsome, 198–200. Hesseltine, 165–167.

seemed to know the very conditions existing within the Lincoln cabinet.[30]

Because of the fight for survival which each prisoner was forced to make during his incarceration, adjustment to freedom whenever and however it came was not always easy. "We are strange, restless, discontented creatures . . . ," wrote a Joliet, Illinois, colonel after being committed to an exchange of prisoners. Private Henry Eby wrote that his own exchange seemed to be a dream which couldn't last. Once freed, Eby and his mates were treated by Union soldiers in a manner to which they could not adjust. Their clothes were stripped from them, picked up by pitchforks and thrown into a furnace, and each man was given a warm and unbelievably luxurious bath. So long had Eby and his friends scratched in order to live that they simply could not admit the existence of such kindness.[31]

Toward the end of the war, when Sherman's army was cutting a swath through North Carolina, most Confederate prisoners were simply given up by their captors and passed through the contending lines. Private John McElroy, the cavalryman of the 16th Illinois, wrote of this moment as the great experience of his life. His immediate reaction upon reaching freedom, he stated, was to eat far too much for his own good. In fact, he and his companions of the 16th Illinois actually became "positively drunk" on coffee, falling "helplessly into some brush." Nor was McElroy overstating the facts. The accounts of the exchange of the prisoners run to the same pattern. Each writer tells of relishing the "real" boiled beef and crackers, and of drinking the "*genuine coffee*" which freedom provided.

No better description of that indelible moment when a man regains freedom was ever put together than that written by Edmund Newsome:

We started on foot, led by a mounted Federal officer, and soon we came to our pickets, who presented arms. The road was very muddy, and my shoes were so bad that I could scarcely walk. Very soon we came to a turn in the road, and could see on a hill, our troops waiting for us, with the OLD STARRY FLAG in full view, and the band struck up

[30] Newsome, 215. "Civil War Diary of Major Jacob Muhleman" (unpublished typed transcript, ISHL). There are numerous references in this account to the rumors and gossip that went through the prison camp.

[31] *Letters from Libby Prison*, 80. Eby, 226–227.

"Red, White, and Blue." Then such a shout. We did not stop for mud or water, but ran to the river, and went pell-mell over the pontoon bridge, and into camp. . . . One went up to the flag, hugged and kissed the bearer, and wept.[32]

Some of the returning Illinois soldiers never made it, however. On April 27, 1865, near Memphis, the transport *Sultana*, greatly overcrowded, was wracked by a boiler explosion and fire. The *Sultana* sank in the Mississippi with casualties put as high as 1,900, including many Illinois men paroled from Confederate prisons.

The two great historical events of April, 1865, were, of course, the surrender of Lee to Grant at Appomattox, Virginia, and the assassination of President Lincoln. The former was met with expressions of joy which are typical for any news of that kind. The 36th Illinois, the "Fox River Regiment," which was stationed in Tennessee at the time, had just heard the bugles sound taps when the news of Lee's capitulation was passed along the line of tents by the sentries. A "wild delirium of joy" came over the Kane and Kendall counties men, and all began to fire their rifles into the air. Cannon were wheeled into position and soon every battery in Chattanooga was in play, shaking the foundations of the buildings with their reverberations. Even the giant Columbiads were fired, and the troops ran up and down the streets of the town shouting "When will we go home?"[33]

When the same glad tidings reached the headquarters of the 75th Illinois, a Lee and Whiteside counties regiment stationed in the same state, there was, according to Sergeant James Howlett, a Willow Grove soldier of that unit, a response appropriate to the occasion. At division headquarters not far away, Howlett noted, everybody became roaring drunk and there was high glee and handshaking everywhere. Happiness reigned in the headquarters of the 75th also, Howlett added, with one slight difference. "No one at these Head Quarters got drunk — care why?" the Willow Grove soldier asked of his diary; "nary a drop of whiskey!" And far away in North Carolina, in the ranks of the 129th Illinois, a Livingston and Scott counties regiment which had burned and scorched its way through the Carolinas, Chaplain James T. Ayers

[32] *This Was Andersonville*, 279. Newsome, 225–226.
[33] Bennett and Haigh, 710–711.

recorded that the Illinois men "Raised the yell," gathered all the hats in the camp and burned them, and began to be as merry "as the family did when the Prodigal Came home."[34]

The joy of victory was to be tempered, of course, with the death of the President only a few days later and the fact that the war continued briefly in some sections. "You can not imagine the depth of sorrow that weighed down the spirits of both officers and men," wrote Lieutenant Colonel Charles Brush, an Ottawa soldier of the 53rd Illinois, on hearing of the assassination. Writing to his father on April 19, Brush added that the impact of Lincoln's death upon the men was heartbreaking, and that his regimental major, Elisha H. Stumph of Ottawa, had cried like a child.

The death of the President had a far more personal meaning for the ordinary Illinois soldier, quite naturally, than it did for the troops from other states. "Did you ever hear minute guns?" Lieutenant Duncan Ingraham of Robin's Nest, Illinois, asked his father. "There is something inexpressibly solemn in their tone . . . ," continued this officer of the 33rd Illinois. "It may be weak and womanish but tears will come this and every time I think of our loved president. For *his* life I would have given my own." And Chaplain Ayers, far off in Moorehead, North Carolina, with the 129th Illinois, uttered a small prayer and a question, both as eternal as life itself. "God have mercy on us," wrote Ayers. "What is there man wont do."[35]

There were but few events left to the war. Sherman took his army on a hard but peaceful march through Virginia and to Washington, the pace being so forced that years later many Illinois veterans raged at the thought of it. Not a few Illinois troops collapsed on the march, and some actually died from the strain. Others, reveling in the emotions of a conquering army, were less affected. "This march is much like a holiday parade," wrote an Oquawka soldier of the 10th Illinois. Flags were displayed in many

[34] Civil War Diaries of James Howlett, entry for April 10, 1865, ISHL. *Diary of James T. Ayers*, 94.

[35] Brush to his father, April 19, 1865, Brush Family Papers. Duncan Ingraham to his family, May 26, 1865, Ingraham Papers. There is some evidence that the 33rd Illinois did not receive news of the President's death until two weeks later; see Civil War Diary of Thomas Chandler, ISHL, 103.

towns along the way, adding color to the already bright spring days, and the bands played incessantly as the armies streamed northward.

The occasion was the last and greatest military encampment of the war, the gathering of the armies of the Potomac, Tennessee, and Georgia in the city of Washington. In the days before the Grand Review, scheduled for May 23 and 24, Illinois soldiers, along with the others from the West, mingled with those of the Army of the Potomac. The mixing was like oil and water, and not a few fights resulted. As a rough veteran of the 105th Illinois saw it, "Sherman's Mules" were not about to give any ground to these "Feather Bed Soldiers" from the eastern states. Nor were the troops from the West about to compete with the latter in the area of military neatness and discipline. Ordered to wear new uniforms for the parade, the 105th, for instance, packed the new clothes in their blanket rolls and dressed in those which it had worn through Georgia and the Carolinas. The same was true of other Illinois regiments. "In discipline, in drill, in physique, *we are superior to the Eastern Army*," wrote Lieutenant Matthew H. Jamison, E Company, 10th Illinois, "but we shall not be so well dressed and will not appear so well to the superficial observer." "The Eastern people," Jamison pessimistically concluded, "think we are a rabble." [36]

Jamison and a few others were more than surprised, however. They watched the Army of the Potomac, white gloves and all, swing down Pennsylvania Avenue in perfect precision. Then, on the following day, the western armies had their moment. Tall, rangy, and supremely confident, Sherman's men overwhelmed those who viewed the parade. Lieutenant Colonel Brush, the Ottawa soldier, was one of those who felt the thrill of knowing that he was part of a host which was definitely superior. The following day, still overcome by the emotion of it all, he sat down and wrote his impressions to his father back home:

> I should judge there was nearly twice as many spectators out on the 24th as on the day previous, great enthusiasm prevailed — our march through Pennsylvania Avenue was one grand and continuel reception by the people . . . wreaths of flowers were showered upon the sol-

[36] Strong, 203. Jamison, 331, 337. For the reference to "Feather Bed Soldiers," see Strong, 210–211.

diers as they passed by, especially upon the general officers as we passed . . . every now and then some one would propose three cheers for Maj. Gen. Giles A. Smith. . . . It is acknowledged on all hands that we beat the world, the Army of the Potomac not excepted. The physique of our army is far superior to the eastern — our men *march* instead of trudge along. . . .[37]

While Sherman's men were quartered on the south bank of the Potomac, some of them were allowed to visit the capital and view, as David Givler, the Naperville soldier of the 7th Illinois, phrased it, things too "tedious to mention." In other areas, Illinois regiments made preparations for the long trip home. For some, the return did not come soon enough. Members of the 92nd, that hard-fighting regiment from Ogle and Stephenson counties, complained mightily about having to remain in service while other regiments, less affected by the war, were allowed to go home. It was the same old story— men who had spent so many months and years in an army at war now resenting a few more days in uniform with the nation at peace. Some ranking officers tried to keep their men occupied while the army was disbanded. The men of the 73rd Illinois, for instance, were marched almost continuously by their brigade commander, the war hero Colonel Emerson Opdycke. Yet drill and more drill could hardly suit impatient men. The soldiers of the "Preacher's Regiment" only became angry and swore at their regimental officers.

There were, however, more thoughtful Illinois soldiers who gave some brief thought to a future without rifles and cannon, or reveille and taps. A member of the 103rd Illinois, a Fulton County regiment, came to the conclusion that there was something to the army after all. He wondered what it might be like to have to work for wages again, allowing that it would go "sorely against the grain."[38]

That Fulton County soldier did return home in midsummer of 1865, as did most of the Illinois troops in the same year. For most regiments the time was a boisterous and red-blooded one, filled with the elemental passions of youth. Sergeant Leander Still-

[37] Brush to his father, May 25, 1865, Brush Family Papers. Almost every history of Illinois regiments participating in the Grand Review indicates that the westerners did well.

[38] Givler, 69. *The Ninety-second Illinois Volunteers*, 247. Newlin, 524. *Reminiscences of the 103rd*, 206.

well, the Otterville soldier of the 61st, would write later that once his regiment entered into "God's Country," it cheered mightily at every living thing it saw. The 105th Illinois came home with an even greater enthusiasm, engaging in a magnificent fight with the Chicago police. A Chicago woman would write that the regiments pouring through her city brought a multitude of pets – kittens, dogs, and parrots – and that vendors did a land office business in the area around the train station.[39]

Troops brought upriver from New Orleans had a variety of differing experiences. On one occasion, when it appeared to be the intention of army authorities to transport the 77th Illinois on the same boat with a load of mules, the soldiers objected and drove the animals off the vessel. The same boat ran out of fuel near Vicksburg, but the soldiers, impatient with the idea of waiting, quickly loaded it with coal and got the steamer under way once again. Boats and regiments raced each other to Cairo, Illinois, and wagers were freely made. The historian of that Peoria and Woodford counties regiment describes it as the most wonderful excursion of his entire life. And when the 59th Illinois, the battered western Illinois regiment, reached Cairo, it made a singular obeisance to a companion of many years. Members of the regiment scrambled to the flagstaff, hauled down the American flag, and hoisted a side of bacon in its place.[40]

For most of these regiments only two more steps stood between them and home: mustering out the regiment and riding the train to a regional city. The historian of the 73rd Illinois wrote touchingly of traveling by railroad through eastern Illinois, and the sudden cry of "We are at Camp Butler" from members of the regiment. There were parades, and a few days of listening to farewell speeches by various politicians. A soldier of the 59th wrote that the brief period was a time when soldiers were almost forced to become the prey of Springfield merchants. One local firm provided free rides into town for soldiers who indicated a willingness to buy a civilian suit from its store. As one bitter western Illinois soldier expressed it, the "love and patriotism" of such

[39] Stillwell, *Story of a Common Soldier*, 275–278. Strong, 215–217. According to Strong's account, the 105th threatened to burn down the city. Mary Livermore, 473.

[40] Bentley, 378–382. Herr, 460.

merchants were "exceeded by their innate desire to accomodate the soldiers with a forty dollar suit of clothes for one hundred and twenty-five dollars. . . ."[41]

The time of waiting did pass, however, and each regiment faced its moment of separation. The 77th, for instance, held a small "jollification" to celebrate the occasion. That night, in Camp Butler, the soldiers tied candles and torches to poles, sang songs, and quietly talked. "This was their last night in camp," wrote a member of the 77th, "the last time they would be together, and they made good use of it." The following day the regiment was taken to Peoria, where, at Rouse's Hall, they were to listen to one last series of speeches and sing one last round of songs. "We have written the last page, for our battles are all fought and our marches are all ended," the historian of the 77th would write in time.[42]

There were other words and other phrases, but none would be more eloquently written. The days of Pea Ridge, Donelson, Shiloh, Vicksburg, and countless other places of destiny would live only as afterthoughts, to be expressed in memory and recollection. There remained now only the returning, the last long walk down some city street, some shaded avenue in Decatur, Peoria, or Carbondale, or some dusty road through an isolated farm village. Perhaps it was Sergeant Leander Stillwell who told that story best. Arriving at Otterville at about sundown, his sword thrown back over his shoulder, he walked past the blacksmith shop and the local church. A dog came to the fence palings and barked, and a man sitting on the counter of the country store leaned forward to the window and peered. There was nothing more. Within days the young soldier was at his chores cutting corn; as he phrased it, "as if I had been away only a day or two, and had taken up the farm work where I had left off." For Stillwell the campfire was out, the bugles were silenced, and the long war was ended.[43]

---

[41] Newlin, 530. The historian of the 73rd states that the members of his regiment went swimming in the Sangamon immediately after their arrival. Way, 61. Herr, 354.

[42] Bentley, 383, 385–391.

[43] Stillwell, *Story of a Common Soldier*, 275–278.

Sources

Unpublished Material

"Biography of General John A. McClernand." 2 vols. Manuscript, possibly by Adolphus Schwartz, Illinois State Historical Library, Springfield.

Blanchard, Ira. "Recollections of Civil War Service with the 20th Illinois Infantry." Typed manuscript, Illinois State Historical Library, Springfield.

"Civil War Diary of Harrison Chandler, June 22, 1864–Jan. 1, 1865, Section V." Transcript, Illinois State Historical Library, Springfield.

"Civil War Diary of Major Jacob Muhleman." Typed transcript, Illinois State Historical Library, Springfield.

"Civil War Diary of Flavius Philbrook." Incomplete manuscript, Illinois State Historical Library, Springfield.

"Civil War Diary of William C. Titze." Manuscript and partial transcript, Illinois State Historical Library, Springfield.

"Civil War Letters of Robert G. Ardrey, 111th Illinois Infantry." Comp. Joseph L. Eisendrath, Jr. Typed transcript, Illinois State Historical Library, Springfield.

"Diary and Personal Memorandum Book of Private James P. Snell, 52nd Illinois Volunteers." Transcript, Illinois State Historical Library, Springfield.

Givler, David. "Intimate Glimpses of Army Life During the Civil War." Typed transcript, Illinois State Historical Library, Springfield.

Jennings, James. "A Story of the Trials and Experiences of James Jennings, Late of Co. K, 20th Infantry at Andersonville Prison During the Civil War." Typed transcript, Illinois State Historical Library, Springfield.

Lake, Lewis F. "My War Service as a Member of Taylor's Battery, Company B, 1st Illinois Light Artillery." Manuscript and typed transcript, Illinois State Historical Library, Springfield.

"Memoirs of Lemuel Adams." Typed manuscript, Illinois State Historical Library, Springfield.

Smith, Goerge O. "Brief History of the 17th Regiment of the Illinois Volunteer Infantry, U.S.A." Mimeographed transcript, Illinois State Historical Library, Springfield.

Newspapers

Chicago Daily Tribune
Chicago Times
Harper's Weekly (N.Y.)
Illinois State Journal (Springfield)
Joliet (Ill.) *Republican*
Jonesboro (Ill.) *Weekly Gazette*
Macomb (Ill.) *Eagle*
Macomb (Ill.) *Journal*
New York Herald
Quincy (Ill.) *Daily Whig and Republican*
Quincy (Ill.) *Herald*
Vicksburg (Miss.) *Daily Citizen*

Interview

Personal interview with Miss Olivia Dunlap, a relative of John A. McClernand. Jacksonville, Illinois, 1953.

Books

Army Life of an Illinois Soldier, Including a Day by Day Record of Sherman's March to the Sea; Letters and Diary of the Late Charles W. Wills, Private and Sergeant 8th Illinois Infantry; Lieutenant and Battalion Adjutant 7th Illinois Cavalry; Captain, Major and Lieutenant Colonel 103rd Illinois Infantry. Comp. and pub. by his sister [Mary E. Kellogg]. Washington, D.C.: Globe Printing Co., 1906.

Aten, Henry J. *History of the Eighty-fifth Regiment.* Comp. and pub. under the auspices of the Regimental Association. Hiawatha, Kan.: by the author, 1901.

Bacon, Alvan Q. *Thrilling Adventures of a Pioneer Boy While a Prisoner of War.* n.p., n.d.

Barber, Lucius W. *Army Memoirs of Lucius W. Barber, Company "D," 15th Illinois Volunteer Infantry, May 24, 1861 to Sept. 30, 1865.* Chicago: The J. M. W. Jones Stationery and Printing Co., 1894.

Barrett, John G. *Sherman's March Through the Carolinas.* Chapel Hill: University of North Carolina Press, 1956.

Bennett, L. G., and William M. Haigh. *History of the Thirty-sixth Regiment Illinois Volunteers, During the War of Rebellion.* Aurora, Ill.: Knickerbokker and Hodder, 1876.

Bentley, William H. *History of the 77th Illinois Volunteer Infantry, Sept. 2, 1862–July 10, 1865.* Peoria, Ill.: Edward Hine Printer, 1883.

Boatner, Mark Mayo, III. *The Civil War Dictionary*. New York: David McKay Co., Inc., 1959.
Brown, D. Alexander. *Grierson's Raid*. Urbana: University of Illinois Press, 1954.
Browne, Junius H. *Four Years in Secessia: Adventures Within and Beyond the Union Lines*. Hartford, Conn.: O. D. Case and Company, 1865.
Bryner, Cloyd B. *Bugle Echoes: The Story of the Illinois 47th Infantry*. Springfield: Phillips Bros., 1905.
Calkins, William W. *The History of the One Hundred and Fourth Regiment of Illinois Volunteer Infantry, War of the Great Rebellion, 1862–1865*. Chicago: Donohue and Henneberry, 1895.
Catton, Bruce. *Grant Moves South*. Boston: Little, Brown and Co., 1960.
———. *This Hallowed Ground*. Garden City, N.Y.: Doubleday and Company, Inc., 1956.
Channing, Edward. *A History of the United States*. 6 vols. New York: The Macmillan Co., 1912–25.
Charnwood, Godfrey R. B. *Abraham Lincoln*. (Makers of the Nineteenth Century, ed. Basil Williams.) 3rd ed. New York: Henry Holt and Co., 1917.
Chestnut, Mary Boykin. *A Diary from Dixie*. Boston: Houghton Mifflin Co., 1949.
Chipman, N. P. *The Tragedy of Andersonville: Trial of Captain Henry Wirz, the Prison Keeper*. 2nd rev. and enl. ed. Sacramento, Calif.: by the author, 1911.
Cist, Henry M. *The Army of the Cumberland*. Vol. VII of *The Army in the Civil War*. Subscription ed. New York: Charles Scribner's Sons, 1883.
The Civil War Letters of Henry C. Bear: A Soldier in the 116th Illinois Volunteer Infantry. Ed. Wayne C. Temple. Harrogate, Tenn.: Lincoln Memorial University Press, 1961.
The Civil War Letters of Sergeant Onley Andrus. Ed. Fred Shannon. Urbana: University of Illinois Press, 1947.
Civil War Medal of Honor Winners from Illinois. Springfield: Civil War Centennial Commission of Illinois, 1962.
Cluett, William W. *History of the Fifty-seventh Regiment Illinois Volunteer Infantry, from Muster in, Dec. 26, 1861, to Muster out, July 7, 1865*. Princeton, Ill.: T. P. Streeter, Printer, 1886.
Cole, Arthur Charles. *The Era of the Civil War, 1848–1870*. Vol. III of *The Centennial History of Illinois*. Ed. Clarence W. Alvord. 5 vols. Springfield: Illinois Centennial Commission, 1919.
The Collected Works of Abraham Lincoln. Ed. Roy P. Basler, Lloyd A. Dunlap, and Marion Dolores Pratt. 8 vols. New Brunswick, N.J.: Rutgers University Press, 1953–55.
Confidential Correspondence of Gustavus Vasa Fox, Assistant Secretary of the Navy, 1861–1865. Ed. Robert M. Thompson and Richard Wainwright. 2 vols. New York: De Vinne Press, 1920.

Cornish, Dudley Taylor. *The Sable Arm: Negro Troops in the Union Army, 1861–1865*. New York: Longmans, Green & Co., 1956.
Cox, Jacob D. *Atlanta*. Vol. IX of *The Army in the Civil War*. Subscription ed. New York: Charles Scribner's Sons, 1885.
———. *The Battle of Franklin, Tennessee, November 30, 1864: A Monograph*. New York: Charles Scribner's Sons, 1897.
———. *The March to the Sea: Franklin and Nashville*. Vol. X of *The Army in the Civil War*. Subscription ed. New York: Charles Scribner's Sons, 1885.
[Crooker, Lucien B., *et al.*] *The Story of the Fifty-fifth Regiment Illinois Volunteer Infantry in the Civil War, 1861–1865*. Clinton, Mass.: W. J. Coulter, 1887.
Crowder, James H. *Before and After Vicksburg*. Dayton, Ohio: The Otterbein Press, 1924.
Crummer, Wilbur F. *With Grant at Fort Donelson, Shiloh and Vicksburg and an Appreciation of General U. S. Grant*. Oak Park, Ill.: E. C. Crummer and Co., 1915.
Dana, Charles A. *Recollections of the Civil War with the Leaders at Washington and in the Field in the Sixties*. New York: D. Appleton and Co., 1898.
Daniels, Jonathan. *Prince of Carpetbaggers*. Philadelphia: J. B. Lippincott Co., 1958.
Davidson, Alexander, and Bernard Stuvé. *A Complete History of Illinois from 1673 to 1884*. Springfield: H. W. Rokker, 1884.
Dawson, George F. *Life and Services of Gen. John A. Logan, as Soldier and Statesman*. Chicago: Belford, Clarke and Co., 1887.
Dennett, Tyler. *Lincoln and the Civil War in Diaries and Letters of John Hay*. New York: Dodd, Mead & Co., 1939.
The Diary of James T. Ayers: Civil War Recruiter. Ed. John Hope Franklin. Springfield: Illinois State Historical Society, 1947.
The Diary of Orville Hickman Browning. Ed. Theodore C. Pease and James G. Randall. 2 vols. (Collections of the Illinois State Historical Society, XX, XXII; Lincoln Series, II, III.) Springfield: The Trustees of the Illinois State Historical Library, 1925, 1933.
Diary of Gideon Welles. 3 vols. Boston: Houghton Mifflin Co., 1911.
Dodge, Sumner. *The Waif of the War; or The History of the Seventy-fifth Illinois Infantry, Embracing the Entire Campaigns of the Army of the Cumberland*. Chicago: Church and Goodman, 1866.
Eby, Henry Harrison. *Observations of an Illinois Boy in Battle, Camp and Prisons, 1861–1865*. Mendota, Ill.: by the author, 1910.
Eddy, Thomas Mears. *The Patriotism of Illinois*. 2 vols. Chicago: Clarke and Co., 1865–66.
Edwards, William B. *Civil War Guns: The Complete Story of Federal and Confederate Small Arms: Design, Manufacture, Identification, Procurement, Issue, Employment, Effectiveness, and Post War Disposal*. Harrisburg, Pa.: Stackpole Co., 1962.
Fleharty, Stephen. *Our Regiment: A History of the 102nd Illinois In-*

fantry Volunteers with Sketches of the Atlanta Campaign, the Georgia Raid, and Campaign of the Carolinas. Chicago: Brewster and Hanscom, Printers, 1865.

Force, Manning F. *From Fort Henry to Corinth.* New York: Charles Scribner's Sons, 1882.

Fort Donelson National Military Park Pamphlet. Washington, D.C.: U.S. Government Printing Office, 1961.

Fort Henry and Fort Donelson Campaigns, February, 1862: Source Book. Fort Leavenworth, Kan.: The General Service Schools Press, 1923.

Fox, William F. *Regimental Losses in the American Civil War.* Albany, N.Y.: Albany Publishing Co., 1889.

Gracie, Archibald. *The Truth About Chickamauga.* Boston: Houghton Mifflin Co., 1911.

Grant, Ulysses S. *Personal Memoirs.* 2 vols. New York: Charles L. Webster & Company, 1885–86.

Gray, Wood. *The Hidden Civil War: The Story of the Copperheads.* New York: The Viking Press, 1942.

Hedley, Fenwick Y. *Marching Through Georgia: Pen-Pictures of Every-Day Life in General Sherman's Army from the Beginning of the Atlanta Campaign Until the Close of the War.* Chicago: Donohue, Henneberry and Co., 1890.

Herr, George W. *Nine Campaigns in Nine States.* San Francisco: The Bancroft Company, 1890.

Hesseltine, William B. *Civil War Prisons: A Study in War Psychology.* Columbus: Ohio State University Press, 1930.

Historical Encyclopedia of Illinois. Ed. Newton Bateman and Paul Selby. Chicago: Munsell Publishers, 1900.

Hobart, Edwin L. *The Truth About the Battle of Shiloh.* Springfield: State Register Printing House, 1909.

Home Letters of General Sherman. Ed. M. A. DeWolfe Howe. New York: Charles Scribner's Sons, 1909.

Horn, Stanley F. *The Army of Tennessee: A Military History.* Indianapolis: Bobbs-Merrill Co., 1941.

Howard, Richard L. *History of the 124th Regiment Illinois Infantry Volunteers, Otherwise Known as the "Hundred and Two Dozen," from August, 1862, to August, 1865.* Springfield: H. W. Rokker, 1880.

Howard, S. M. *The Illustrated Comprehensive History of the Great Battle of Shiloh.* Gettysburg, S.D.: by the author, 1921.

Hubert, Charles F. *History of the Fiftieth Illinois Volunteer Infantry in the War for the Union.* Kansas City, Mo.: Western Veteran Publishing Company, 1894.

Illinois Military Units in the Civil War. Springfield: Civil War Centennial Commission of Illinois, 1962.

Jamison, Matthew H. *Recollections of Pioneer and Army Life.* Kansas City, Kan.: Hudson Press, 1911.

Jefferson, W. J. *Battles of Chattanooga.* Milwaukee, Wis.: Wehner's Panorama Studio, 1886.

Johnson, Ludwell H. *Red River Campaign: Politics and Cotton in the Civil War.* Baltimore: The Johns Hopkins University Press, 1958.

Lathrop, David. *The History of the Fifty-ninth Regiment Illinois Volunteers.* Indianapolis: Hall and Hutchinson, 1865.

Letters from Libby Prison: Being the Authentic Letters Written While in Confederate Captivity in the Notorious Libby Prison at Richmond. Ed. Margaret W. Peelle. New York: Greenwich Book Publishers, 1956.

Life and Letters of Thomas Kilby Smith, Brevet Major-General, United States Volunteers, 1820–1887. Ed. Walter G. Smith. New York: G. P. Putnam's Sons, 1898.

Livermore, Mary. *My Story of the War: A Woman's Narrative of Four Years Personal Experience.* Hartford, Conn.: A. D. Worthington and Co., 1889.

Livermore, Thomas L. *Numbers and Losses in the Civil War in America, 1861–1865.* Bloomington: Indiana University Press, 1957.

McCormick, Robert R. *U. S. Grant: The Great Soldier of America.* New York: D. Appleton-Century Co., Inc., 1934.

Miers, Earl Schenck. *The General Who Marched to Hell: William Tecumseh Sherman and His March to Fame and Infamy.* New York: A. A. Knopf, 1951.

Military History and Reminiscenses of the Thirteenth Regiment of Illinois Volunteer Infantry of the Civil War in the United States, 1861–1865. Prepared by a regimental committee. Chicago: Women's Temperance Publishing Association, 1892.

Monaghan, Jay. *Civil War on the Western Border, 1854–1865.* Boston: Little, Brown and Co., 1955.

Moses, John. *Illinois: Historical and Statistical.* 2 vols. Chicago: Fergus Printing Co., 1889.

Newlin, W. H. *A History of the Seventy-third Regiment.* n.p.: Regimental Reunion Association, 1888.

Newsome, Edmund. *Experience in the War of the Great Rebellion by a Soldier of the 81st Regiment Illinois Volunteer Infantry from August, 1862 to August, 1865.* Carbondale, Ill.: by the author, 1880.

Nicolay, J. G., and John Hay. *Abraham Lincoln: A History.* 10 vols. New York: The Century Co., 1890.

The Ninety-second Illinois Volunteers. Ed. Committee of the Regiment. Freeport, Ill.: Journal Steam Publishing House, 1875.

Oldroyd, Osborn H. *A Soldier's Story of the Siege of Vicksburg.* Springfield: H. W. Rokker, 1885.

Palmer, John M. *Personal Recollections of John M. Palmer: The Story of an Earnest Life.* Cincinnati: The Robert Clarke Co., 1901.

Payne, Edwin W. *History of the Thirty-fourth Regiment of Illinois Volunteer Infantry.* Clinton, Iowa: Allen Printing Co., 1902.

Pepper, George W. *Personal Recollections of Sherman's Campaigns in Georgia and the Carolinas.* Zanesville, Ohio: Hugh Dunne, 1866.
Porter, David D. *Incidents and Anecdotes of the Civil War.* New York: D. Appleton and Co., 1885.
Pratt, Fletcher. *Stanton, Lincoln's Secretary of War.* New York: W. W. Norton & Company, Inc., 1953.
Private and Official Correspondence of Gen. Benjamin F. Butler, During the Period of the Civil War. Norwood, Mass.: The Plimpton Press, 1917.
The Rebellion Record: A Diary of American Events. Ed. Frank Moore. 11 vols. New York: G. P. Putnam, 1861–68.
Reminiscences of the Civil War from Diaries of Members of the 103rd Illinois Volunteer Infantry. Ed. Regimental Committee. Chicago: J. F. Leaming & Co., 1904.
Report of the Adjutant General of the State of Illinois. Rev. Brig. Gen. J. W. Vance. 8 vols. Springfield: H. W. Rokker, 1886.
Report of Proceedings of the Reunion of the 33rd Regiment. Bloomington, Ill.: Pantagraph Publishing Co., 1875.
Reunions of Taylor's Battery B, First Ill. Artillery. Chicago: The Craig Press, 1890.
Rich, Joseph. *The Battle of Shiloh.* Iowa City: Iowa Historical Society, 1911.
Richardson, Albert D. *The Secret Service, the Field, the Dungeon, and the Escape.* Hartford, Conn.: American Publishing Company, 1865.
Royse, Isaac Henry Clay. *History of the 115th Regiment Illinois Volunteer Infantry.* Terre Haute, Ind.: Windsor and Kenfield, 1900.
Sharland, George. *Knapsack Notes of General Sherman's Grand Campaign Through the Empire State of the South.* Springfield: Johnson and Bradford, Printers, 1865.
Sherman, William T. *Memoirs of Gen. W. T. Sherman.* 4th ed. New York: Charles L. Webster & Company, 1891.
The Sherman Letters: Correspondence Between General and Senator Sherman from 1837 to 1891. Ed. Rachel Sherman Thorndike. New York: Charles Scribner's Sons, 1894.
Stevenson, Alexander F. *The Battle of Stone's River near Murfreesboro, Tennessee, December 30, 1862 to January 3, 1863.* Boston: J. R. Osgood and Co., 1884.
Stillwell, Leander. *The Story of a Common Soldier of Army Life in the Civil War, 1861–1865.* 2nd ed. Kansas City, Mo.: Franklin Hudson Publishing Co., 1920.
Strong, Robert Hale. *A Yankee Private's Civil War.* Chicago: Henry Regnery Co., 1961.
Taylor, Benjamin. *Pictures of Life in Camp and Field.* 2nd ed. Chicago: S. C. Griggs and Co., 1875.
This Was Andersonville: The True Story of Andersonville Military Prison as Told in the Personal Recollections of John McElroy, Some-

time Private, Co. L, 16th Ill. Cavalry. Ed. Roy Meredith. New York: McDowell, Obolensky, 1957.

Thompson, Bradford F. *History of the 112th Regiment of Illinois Volunteer Infantry in the Great War of the Rebellion, 1862–1865*. Toulon, Ill.: Stark County News, 1885.

Three Years in the Army of the Cumberland: The Letters and Diary of Major James A. Connolly. Ed. Paul M. Angle. Bloomington: Indiana University Press, 1959.

Three Years with Grant as Recalled by War Correspondent Sylvanus Cadwallader. Ed. Benjamin P. Thomas. New York: A. A. Knopf, 1955.

Trowbridge, J. T. *The South: A Tour of Its Battlefields and Ruined Cities*. Hartford, Conn.: L. Stebbins, 1866.

Turchin, John B. *Chickamauga*. Chicago: Fergus Printing Co., 1888.

U.S. War Department. *The War of the Rebellion: A Compilation of the Official Records of the Union and Confederate Armies*. Prepared under the direction of the Secretary of War, by Bvt. Lt. Col. Robert N. Scott, Third U.S. Artillery. 70 vols. Washington, D.C.: Government Printing Office, 1880–1901.

Van Horne, Thomas. *History of the Army of the Cumberland: Its Organization, Campaigns, and Battles, Written at the Request of Major-General George N. Thomas Chiefly from His Private Military Journal and Official and Other Documents Furnished by Him*. 2 vols. Cincinnati: Robert Clarke and Co., 1875.

Villard, Henry. *Memoirs of Henry Villard: Journalist and Financier, 1835–1900*. 2 vols. Boston: Houghton, Mifflin and Co., 1904.

Wallace, Isabel. *The Life and Letters of General W. H. L. Wallace*. Chicago: R. R. Donnelly, 1909.

Wallace, Lewis. *An Autobiography*. 2 vols. New York: Harper & Bros., 1906.

Warfare Along the Mississippi: The Letters of Lieutenant Colonel George E. Currie. Ed. Norman E. Clarke, Sr. (Clarke Historical Collection.) Mt. Pleasant, Mich.: Central Michigan University Press, 1961.

Way, Virgil G. *History of the Thirty-third Regiment Illinois Veteran Volunteer Infantry on the Civil War, 22nd August, 1861, to 7th December, 1865*. Gibson City, Ill.: [Regimental] Association, 1902.

Whitney, Henry Clay. *Life on the Circuit with Lincoln*. Caldwell, Idaho: Caxton Printers, 1940.

Williams, George W. *A History of the Negro Troops in the War of the Rebellion, 1861–1865*. New York: Harper & Bros., 1888.

Williams, Kenneth P. *Lincoln Finds a General: A Military Study of the Civil War*. 5 vols. New York: The Macmillan Co., 1949–56.

Wilson, Ephraim A. *Memoirs of the War by Captain Ephraim A. Wilson of Co. "G," 10th Illinois Volunteer Infantry*. Cleveland: W. M. Boyne Co., 1893.

Wilson, James H. *The Life of John A. Rawlins, Lawyer, Assistant Ad-*

jutant-General, Chief of Staff, Major General of Volunteers, and Secretary of War. New York: The Neale Publishing Co., 1916.
———. *Under the Old Flag: Recollections of Military Operations in the War for the Union, the Spanish War, the Boxer Rebellion, etc.* 2 vols. New York: D. Appleton and Co., 1912.
Wilson, Joseph T. *The Black Phalanx: A History of the Negro Soldiers of the United States in the Wars of 1775–1812, 1861–'65.* Hartford, Conn.: American Publishing Company, 1888.

Articles and Periodicals

Atkins, Smith. "The Patriotism of Northern Illinois," *Transactions of the Illinois State Historical Society for the Year 1911*, No. 16 (Springfield: Illinois State Journal Co., 1913), 79–83.
Blodgett, Edward A. "The Army of the Southwest and the Battle of Pea Ridge," in *Military Essays and Recollections: Papers Read Before the Commandery of the State of Illinois, Military Order of the Loyal Legion of the United States* (4 vols.; Chicago: A. C. McClurg and Company, 1894), II, 289–312.
Burnham, J. H. "The Thirty-third Regiment Illinois Infantry in the War Between the States," *Transactions of the Illinois State Historical Society for the Year 1912*, No. 17 (Springfield: Illinois State Journal Co., 1914), 77–85.
Burr, Barbara. "Letters from Two Wars," *Journal of the Illinois State Historical Society*, XXX, No. 1 (April, 1937), 135–158.
Clausius, Gerhard. "The Little Soldier of the 95th: Albert D. J. Cashier," *Journal of the Illinois State Historical Society*, LI, No. 4 (Winter, 1958), 380–387.
"Coles County in the Civil War 1861–1865," ed. L. M. Hamand, *Eastern Illinois University Bulletin*, No. 234 (April, 1961).
Connolly, James A. "Major James Austin Connolly's Letters to His Wife, 1862–1865," *Transactions of the Illinois State Historical Society for the Year 1928*, No. 35 (Springfield: Phillips Bros., 1928), 217–438.
"Diary and Correspondence of Salmon P. Chase," *Annual Report of the American Historical Association for the Year 1902*, II (2 vols.; Washington, D.C.: Government Printing Office, 1903).
"The Diary of Colonel William Camm, 1861 to 1865," ed. Fritz Haskell, *Journal of the Illinois State Historical Society*, XVIII, Pt. 2, No. 4 (January, 1926), 793–969.
"Diary of Lieut. W. D. Harland, Company H, 18th Regiment, Illinois Volunteers and Thos. C. Watkins, Orderly Sergeant, Company H, 18th Regiment, Illinois Volunteers from June 17, 1861 to April 8, 1862," comp. Mrs. Clyde A. Hornbuckle, in *State of Illinois: Daughters of the American Revolution Genealogical Records 1940–*

41 (3 vols.; Illinois State Historical Library, Springfield), III, 268–284.

Dorris, Jonathan T. "Michael Kelly Lawler: Mexican and Civil War Officer," *Journal of the Illinois State Historical Society*, XLVIII, No. 4 (Winter, 1955), 366–401.

Eisendrath, Joseph L., Jr. "Chicago's Camp Douglas," *Journal of the Illinois State Historical Society*, LIII, No. 1 (Spring, 1960), 37–63.

Freeman, Henry. "Some Battle Recollections of Stone's River," in *Military Essays and Recollections: Papers Read Before the Commandery of the State of Illinois, Military Order of the Loyal Legion of the United States* (4 vols.; Chicago: The Dial Press, 1899), III, 227–246.

Howard, Charles. "Incidents and Operations Connected with the Capture of Savannah," in *Military Essays and Recollections: Papers Read Before the Commandery of the State of Illinois, Military Order of the Loyal Legion of the United States* (4 vols.; Chicago: Cozzens and Beaton Company, 1907), IV, 430–450.

Hunt, George. "The Fort Donelson Campaign," in *Military Essays and Recollections: Papers Read Before the Commandery of the State of Illinois, Military Order of the Loyal Legion of the United States* (4 vols.; Chicago: Cozzens and Beaton Company, 1907), IV, 61–82.

Jenkins, W. H. "The Thirty-ninth Illinois Volunteers, Yates Phalanx," *Transactions of the Illinois State Historical Society for the Year 1914*, No. 20 (Springfield: Illinois State Journal Co., 1915), 130–136.

Jenney, William. "Personal Recollections of Vicksburg," in *Military Essays and Recollections: Papers Read Before the Commandery of the State of Illinois, Military Order of the Loyal Legion of the United States* (4 vols.; Chicago: The Dial Press, 1899), III, 247–266.

McClelland, Clarence P. "An Illinois Colonel's Visit to Jeff Davis in 1864; His Contribution to Lincoln's Re-election," *Journal of the Illinois State Historical Society*, LV, No. 1 (Spring, 1962), 31–44.

Milchrist, Thomas E. "Reflections of a Subalteran on the Hood-Thomas Campaign in Tennessee," in *Military Essays and Recollections: Papers Read Before the Commandery of the State of Illinois, Military Order of the Loyal Legion of the United States* (4 vols.; Chicago: Cozzens and Beaton Company, 1907), IV, 451–465.

Nixon, Oliver W. "Reminiscences of the First Year of the War in Missouri," in *Military Essays and Recollections: Papers Read Before the Commandery of the State of Illinois, Military Order of the Loyal Legion of the United States* (4 vols.; Chicago: The Dial Press, 1899), III, 413–436.

Otis, Ephraim Allen. "Recollections of the Kentucky Campaign of 1862," in *Military Essays and Recollections: Papers Read Before the Commandery of the State of Illinois, Military Order of the Loyal*

Legion of the United States (4 vols.; Chicago: Cozzens and Beaton Company, 1907), IV, 122–147.

Paddock, George. "The Beginnings of an Illinois Volunteer Regiment in 1861," in *Military Essays and Recollections: Papers Read Before the Commandery of the State of Illinois, Military Order of the Loyal Legion of the United States* (4 vols.; Chicago: A. C. McClurg and Company, 1894), II, 253–268.

Partridge, Charles A. "The Ninety-sixth Illinois at Chickamauga," *Transactions of the Illinois State Historical Society for the Year 1910*, No. 15 (Springfield: Illinois State Journal Co., 1912), 72–80.

Powell, William H. "The Battle of the Petersburg Crater," in *Battles and Leaders of the Civil War*, ed. Larned G. Bradford (New York: Appleton-Century-Crofts, Inc., 1956), 559–570.

Putnam, Douglas. "Reminiscences of the Battle of Shiloh," in *Sketches of War History, 1861–1865: Papers Read Before the Ohio Commandery of the Military Order of the Loyal Legion of the United States*, ed. R. Hunter (5 vols.; Cincinnati: Robert Clarke and Co., 1888–1903), III, 97–111.

Seaton, John. "The Battle of Belmont," in *War Talks in Kansas: A Series of Papers Read Before the Kansas Commandery of the Military Order of the Loyal Legion of the United States* (Kansas City, Mo.: Franklin Hudson Publishing Co., 1906), 305–319.

Sexton, James. "The Observations and Experiences of a Captain of Infantry at the Battle of Franklin," in *Military Essays and Recollections: Papers Read Before the Commandery of the State of Illinois, Military Order of the Loyal Legion of the United States* (4 vols.; Chicago: Cozzens and Beaton Company, 1907), IV, 466–484.

Stillwell, Leander. "In the Ranks at Shiloh," *Journal of the Illinois State Historical Society*, XV, Nos. 1–2 (April-July, 1923), 460–476.

"The Story of an Ordinary Man," ed. Paul M. Angle, *Journal of the Illinois State Historical Society*, XXXIII, No. 2 (June, 1940), 212–232.

Thomas, Henry G. "The Colored Troops at Petersburg," in *Battles and Leaders of the Civil War*, ed. Larned G. Bradford (New York: Appleton-Century-Crofts, Inc., 1956), 573–578.

Wallace, Lewis. "The Capture of Fort Donelson," in *Battles and Leaders of the Civil War*, ed. Larned G. Bradford (New York: Appleton-Century-Crofts, Inc., 1956), 61–81.

"War Diary of Thaddeus H. Capron, 1861–1865, Extracts from Letters Written by Major Thaddeus H. Capron from September, 1861, to August, 1865, to His Father, Mother, Brother and Sisters, During His Service in the Fifty-fifth Illinois Infantry Volunteer Regiment in the Civil War," *Journal of the Illinois State Historical Society*, XII, No. 3 (October, 1919), 330–406.

Wardner, Horace. "Reminiscences of a Surgeon," in *Military Essays and Recollections: Papers Read Before the Commandery of the*

State of Illinois, Military Order of the Loyal Legion of the United States (4 vols.; Chicago: The Dial Press, 1899), III, 173–192.

Weinert, Richard P. "The Little Known Story of: The Illinois Confederates; They Lived in the North but Fought for the South," *Civil War Times Illustrated*, I, No. 6 (October, 1862), 44–45.

Wilkin, Jacob M. "Personal Reminiscences of General U. S. Grant," *Transactions of the Illinois State Historical Society for the Year 1907*, No. 12 (Springfield: Phillips Bros., 1908), 131–140.

———. "Vicksburg," in *Military Essays and Recollections: Papers Read Before the Commandery of the State of Illinois, Military Order of the Loyal Legion of the United States* (4 vols.; Chicago: Cozzens and Beaton Company, 1907), IV, 215–237.

Wilson, Bluford. "Southern Illinois and the Civil War," *Transactions of the Illinois State Historical Society for the Year 1911*, No. 16 (Springfield: Illinois State Journal Co., 1913), 93–103.

"With Grant at Vicksburg: From the Civil War Diary of Captain Charles E. Wilcox," ed. Edgar Erickson, *Journal of the Illinois State Historical Society*, XXX, No. 4 (January, 1938), 441–503.

Papers, Collections, and Diaries

Ashley K. Alexander Papers, Illinois State Historical Library, Springfield.

Nathaniel P. Banks Papers, Illinois State Historical Library, Springfield.

Alice M. Barker Letter, Illinois State Historical Library, Springfield.

Diary of John Batchelor, Illinois State Historical Library, Springfield.

Newton Bateman Papers, Illinois State Historical Library, Springfield.

Ransom Bedell Papers, Illinois State Historical Library, Springfield.

John C. Black Papers, Illinois State Historical Library, Springfield.

Orville Hickman Browning Transcripts, Illinois Historical Survey, Urbana.

Bruce Family Papers, Illinois State Historical Library, Springfield.

Brush Family Papers, Illinois State Historical Library, Springfield.

Civil War Diary of James H. Buckley, Illinois State Historical Library, Springfield.

Civil War Diary of Thomas Chandler, Illinois State Historical Library, Springfield.

Civil War Diary of George Compton Beginning May 1st, 1865, Illinois State Historical Library, Springfield.

Collin Cordell to his parents, March 7, 12, 1863, in possession of Mr. Howard Cordell, Tampa, Florida.

John C. Cottle Papers, Illinois State Historical Library, Springfield.

Crum Collection, Illinois State Historical Library, Springfield.

Henry G. Davidson Papers, Illinois State Historical Library, Springfield.

John C. Dinsmore Papers, Illinois State Historical Library, Springfield.

James F. Drish Papers, Illinois State Historical Library, Springfield.

Civil War Diary of Allen Fahnestock, Aug. 7, 1863–Nov. 18, 1865, Illinois State Historical Library, Springfield.
Charles H. Floyd Papers, Illinois State Historical Library, Springfield.
John G. Given Papers, Illinois State Historical Library, Springfield.
Samuel Gordon Papers, Illinois State Historical Library, Springfield.
Ulysses S. Grant Papers, Illinois State Historical Library, Springfield.
Humphrey Hughes Hood Papers, Illinois State Historical Library, Springfield.
Amos W. Hostetter Papers, Illinois State Historical Library, Springfield.
Civil War Diaries of James Howlett, Illinois State Historical Library, Springfield.
Edward H. Ingraham Papers, Illinois State Historical Library, Springfield.
Abraham Lincoln Papers, Illinois State Historical Library, Springfield (microfilm; originals in Library of Congress, Washington, D.C.).
Oliver Look Papers, Illinois State Historical Library, Springfield.
John A. McClernand Collection, Illinois State Historical Library, Springfield.
David McFarland Papers, Illinois State Historical Library, Springfield.
William Henry Marsh Papers, Illinois State Historical Library, Springfield.
Lyman K. Needham Papers, Illinois State Historical Library, Springfield.
Richard J. Oglesby Papers, Illinois State Historical Library, Springfield.
William Ward Orme Papers, Illinois State Historical Library, Springfield.
John M. Palmer Papers, Illinois State Historical Library, Springfield.
Lewis B. Parsons Papers, Illinois State Historical Library, Springfield.
Edwin W. Payne Papers, Illinois State Historical Library, Springfield.
Ira A. Payne Papers, Illinois State Historical Library, Springfield.
Philip Sidney Post Papers, Illinois State Historical Library, Springfield.
Reuben T. Prentice Papers, Illinois State Historical Library, Springfield.
Alexander Raffen Papers, Illinois State Historical Library, Springfield.
Logan U. Reavis Papers, Chicago Historical Society.
Sidney Zebina Robinson Papers, Illinois State Historical Library, Springfield.
Levi Adolphus Ross Papers, Illinois State Historical Library, Springfield.
James Monroe Ruggles Papers, Illinois State Historical Library, Springfield.
Edwin C. Sackett Papers, Illinois State Historical Library, Springfield.
Payson Z. Shumway Papers, Illinois State Historical Library, Springfield.
Elizabeth Simpson Papers, Illinois State Historical Library, Springfield.
D. C. Smith Papers, Illinois State Historical Library, Springfield.
James P. Suiter Papers, Illinois State Historical Library, Springfield.

Lyman Trumbull Transcripts, Illinois Historical Survey, Urbana.
Jonathan Baldwin Turner Papers, Illinois State Historical Library, Springfield.
Augustine Vieira Papers, Illinois State Historical Library, Springfield.
Wallace-Dickey Papers, Illinois State Historical Library, Springfield.
Philip Welshimer Papers, Illinois State Historical Library, Springfield.
John Wilcox Papers, Illinois State Historical Library, Springfield.
Civil War Diaries of Charles W. Wills, Nov. 14–Dec. 15, 1864; Jan. 9–March 23, 1865, Illinois State Historical Library, Springfield.
Richard Yates Papers, Illinois State Historical Library, Springfield.

Addendum to Sources

This addendum contains more recent or additional sources of information on the role of Illinois soldiers in the Civil War. In addition to biographies, autobiographies, memoirs, and military histories, there are collections of letters, diaries, and reminiscences about the war. On the whole, letters are a more reliable source than are diaries, unless the diary has been meticulously kept during the war itself. When the war ended and regimental associations were formed, one of the first actions of these groups was to publish a battle history of the regiment. Some of these are quite good and quite reliable; some are not. Their publication, however, did spur a great deal of postwar diary writing, which actually falls into the category of reminiscences.

The old adage that "old soldiers never die" is obviously incorrect, but it is clear that the memories of old soldiers sometimes lie. Years after the American Revolution, a group of citizens in Boston attempted to gather a set of reminiscences from the aging men who had taken part in the Battle of Bunker Hill. They turned out to be interesting accounts of the fighting there, but the problem was that each veteran, no matter what his location at the time of the conflict, saw himself as being in the center of the fight—an impossibility.

Memories grow dim. One's inclination is to slant events and to color them. The old veterans who sat out their lives in the parks of small towns talking of the past did not do service to the past. That is why diaries and recollections must be approached with some caution. Some are truly excellent, which is to be expected; some are slanted and biased, which is also to be expected. When some of America's leading Civil War figures could not escape their prejudices in postwar recollections (Jefferson Davis comes to mind, here), one could hardly expect the common soldier to do much better. Taken as a whole, however, these sources provide a basis for gaining insight into the role of the Illinois fighting forces.

Unpublished Material

Kerr, Kevin Gregory. "A History of the 124th Volunteer Infantry in the American Civil War." Thesis, Western Illinois University Library, Macomb, 1981.

Sanders, Raymond. "Men of Peoria in the Civil War." M.S. thesis, Illinois State Normal University, 1960.

Books

Ballou, Charles B. *Reminiscences of Charles B. Ballou.* Blandinsville, Ill.: n.p., 1925. Photocopy at Western Illinois University Library, Macomb.

Behrens, Robert H. *From Salt Fork to Chickamauga: Champaign County Soldiers in the Civil War.* Urbana, Ill.: Urbana Free Library, 1988.

Brown, Thaddeus C. S., J. Murphy, and William G. Putney. *Behind the Guns: The History of Battery I, 2nd Regiment, Illinois Light Artillery.* Carbondale: Southern Illinois University Press, 1965.

The Civil War Almanac. Ed. John S. Bowman. New York: Bison Books, 1982.

The Civil War Diary of Allan Morgan Geer. Ed. Mary Ann Anderson. Denver: R. C. Appleman, 1977.

Cooling, Benjamin Franklin. *Forts Henry and Donelson: The Key to the Confederate Heartland.* Knoxville: University of Tennessee Press, 1987.

Dear Eliza: The Letters of Mitchell Andrew. Ed. Mrs. M. B. M. Henderson, Mrs. E. J. M. Young, and Mrs. A. I. M. Nahelhoffer. N.p., 1976.

"Dear Friends": The Civil War Letters and Diary of Charles Edwin Cort. Ed. Helyn Tomlinson. N.p.: by the author, 1962.

Felty, Harold G. *Civil War Soldiers and Veterans, Hamilton County, Illinois.* Champaign, Ill.: Akiba Publishing Co., 1987.

Gerling, Robert. *Highland: An Illinois Community in the Civil War.* Highland, Ill.: Highland Historical Society, 1978.

A German in the Yankee Fatherland: The Civil War Letters of Henry A. Kircher. Ed. Earl J. Hess. Kent, Ohio: Kent University Press, 1983.

Hargrove, Hondon B. *Black Union Soldiers in the Civil War.* Jefferson City, Mo.: McFarland, 1988.

Historical Times: Illustrated Encyclopedia of the Civil War. Ed. Patricia Faust. New York: Harper & Row, 1986.

Howard, Robert P. *Illinois: A History of the Prairie State.* Grand Rapids, Mich.: William B. Eerdmans Publishing Co., 1972.

Jones, Douglas. *Elkhorn Tavern.* New York: Holt, Rinehart, and Winston, 1980.

King, James T. *War Eagle: A Life of General Eugene A. Carr.* Lincoln: University of Nebraska Press, 1963.

McDonough, James L. *James L. Schofield: Union General in the Civil War and Reconstruction.* Tallahassee: Florida State University Press, 1972.

McPherson, James M. *Battle Cry of Freedom*. New York: Oxford University Press, 1972.
Private Smith's Journal: Recollections of the Late War. Ed. Clyde Walton. Chicago: R. R. Donnelley, 1963.
Richard Yates: Civil War Governor. Ed. John H. Krenkel. Danville, Ill.: Interstate Publishers, 1966.
The Rough Side of War: The Civil War Journal of Chesley A. Mosman, First Lieutenant, Company D, 59th Illinois Volunteer Infantry Regiment. Ed. Arnold Gates. Garden City, N.Y.: Basin Publishing Co., 1987.
Sergeant Allen and Private Renick: A Memoir of the Eleventh Illinois Cavalry Written by Henry Allen, and, From the Papers of Mother Bickerdyke, a Three Volume Civil War Diary for 1862, 1863, 1864, Written by John H. Renick. Ed. Martin Litvin. Galesburg, Ill.: Wagoner Printing Co., 1971.
Simmons, Louis A. *The History of the 84th Regiment Illinois Volunteers.* Macomb, Ill.: Hampton Bros., 1866. Photocopy at Western Illinois University Library, Macomb.
Sword, Wiley. *Shiloh: Bloody April.* New York: William Morrow and Co., 1974.
Underwood, Larry. *The Butternut Guerrillas: A Story of Grierson's Raid.* Owensboro, Ky.: McDowell Publishers, 1981.
"Your Affectionate Husband": J. F. Culver's Letters Written During the Civil War. Ed. Leslie W. Dunlap. Iowa City: Friends of the University of Iowa Libraries, 1978.

Articles

Adams, David Wallace. "Illinois Soldiers and the Emancipation Proclamation," *Journal of the Illinois State Historical Society,* LXVII, No. 4 (September, 1974), 406–420.
Adolphson, Steven J. "An Incident of Valor in the Battle of Peach Tree Creek." *Georgia Historical Quarterly,* LVII, No. 3 (Fall, 1973), 406–420.
Anderson, Ken. "The Role of Abraham Lincoln and Members of His Family in the Charleston Riots During the Civil War," *Lincoln Herald,* LXXIX, No. 2 (1977), 53–60.
Bearss, Edwin. "Pvt. Charles E. Affeld Reports Action West of the Mississippi," *Journal of the Illinois State Historical Society,* LX, No. 3 (Autumn, 1967), 267–297.
Davidson, George. "Vicksburg, May 22, 1863," *Army,* XIX, No. 6 (June, 1969), 56–60.
Huffstodt, James T. "Lightning in the Evening Sky: The Story of an Illinois Regiment at the Memorable Siege of Vicksburg in 1863," *Lincoln Herald,* LXXXII, No. 2 (1980), 393–401.
______. "One Who Didn't Come Back: The Story of Colonel Garrett Nevius," *Lincoln Herald,* LXXXII, No. 1 (1980), 324–336.

Huffstot, Robert. "Post of Arkansas," *Civil War Times Illustrated*, VII, No. 9 (September, 1969), 10–19.
Lale, Max. "The Military Occupation of Marshall, Texas, by the 8th Illinois Volunteer Infantry," *Military History of Texas and the Southwest*, XIII, No. 3 (1976), 39–48.
McLean, James L., Jr. "The First Union Shot at Gettysburg," *Lincoln Herald*, LXXXII, No. 1 (1980), 318–323.
Merrill, James. "Cairo, Illinois: Strategic Civil War River Port," *Journal of the Illinois State Historical Society*, LXXVI, No. 4 (Winter, 1983), 242–257.
Morris, Roy, Jr. "The Sack of Athens," *Civil War Times Illustrated*, XXIV, No. 10 (October, 1986), 26–32.
Quinn, Camilla A. "Forgotten Soldiers: The Confederate Prisoners at Camp Butler," *Illinois Historical Journal*, LXXXI, No. 1 (Spring, 1988), 35–45.
Sterling, Bob. "Discouragement, Weariness, and War Politics: Desertions from Illinois Regiments During the Civil War," *Illinois Historical Journal*, LXXXLII, No. 4 (Winter, 1989), 239–263.
Swift, Lester L. "The Preacher Regiment at Chickcamauga and Missionary Ridge," *Lincoln Herald*, LXXII, No. 2 (1970), 51–60.

Papers, Collections, and Diaries

Henry C. Allams Letters and Unpublished Manuscript. Photocopy at Western Illinois University Library, Macomb.
Mason Brayman Papers, Chicago Historical Society.
Clement Moore Butler Papers, Illinois State Historical Library.
Peter Casey Correspondence, Chicago Historical Society.
George Compton Papers, Illinois State Historical Library.
Cornelius C. Courtright Diary, typed transcript, Chicago Historical Society.
Day Elmore Letters, Chicago Historical Society.
James Gaskill Collection, Chicago Historical Society.
Benjamin Grierson Papers, Illinois State Historical Library.
John A. Higgins Manuscript, Illinois State Historical Library.
David King Collection, Illinois State Historical Library.
Alexander Little Letters, Chicago Historical Society.
Jonathan Merriam Manuscript, Illinois State Historical Library.
John Merrilees Diary, Illinois State Historical Library.
James Adelbert Mulligan Collection, Chicago Historical Society.
William Culbert Robinson Papers, Illinois State Historical Library.
Henry Roe Collection, Chicago Historical Society.
William R. Rowley Papers, Illinois State Historical Library.
George Sawin Letters, Chicago Historical Society.
John Tallman Letters, Chicago Historical Society.
Martin Reuben Merritt Wallace Letters, Chicago Historical Society.
Samuel Willard Family Letters, Chicago Historical Society.

Sources for Illinois Regiments (in the Illinois State Historical Library unless otherwise stated)

The following sources for Illinois combat units in the Civil War were compiled from William L. Burton's excellent 1966 publication, *Descriptive Bibliography of Civil War Manuscripts in Illinois,* and from my wife's and my efforts to find materials that have surfaced or appeared since Burton's publication. For some regiments, like the 33rd Illinois Infantry, there are many available sources. The 29th U.S. Colored Infantry, which was raised in Illinois, unfortunately has no collections or articles pertaining to it (save the one I wrote for the *Journal of the Illinois State Historical Society,* autumn, 1963). The same can be said about some of the white regiments. It is important to note, however, that the Illinois State Archives in Springfield, Illinois, stores the files of the Adjutant-General of the State of Illinois during the Civil War, which contain muster rolls, documents, petitions, lists of promotions, and other items that may be of interest to the researcher.

ARTILLERY

Illinois Artillery, Chicago Board of Trade Battery

Lester, A. W. Diaries, March 18, 1862–August 1, 1865. 4 vols.*
Miller, Tobias Charles. Diary containing routine comments on war, plus a description of the Battle of Stones River. Chicago Historical Society.*
Nourse, John A. Diary and 315 items relating to his service in this unit. Chicago Historical Society.*

Illinois Artillery, Chicago Mercantile Battery

Brown, William L. Chicago Historical Society.
Roe, Henry. Chicago Historical Society.
Sickels, Thomas N. Letters to his family, 1862–65, on service in Louisiana.*

Illinois Artillery, 1st Regiment

Day, James Battersley
Gregg, Sarah
Hatch, Ozias M.
Hills, Edward Sherman. Biographical sketch by his grandson, 1968. 9 pp.*
Illinois Artillery, 1st Regt., Co. F
Lee, George Read. Letter, June 8, 1864, on a military execution. 3 pp., photostat.*
Sauter, Charles J. Chicago Historical Society.
Sherman, Jeremiah N. Chicago Historical Society.

Illinois Artillery, 2nd Regiment

Hatch, Ozias M.
Lanstrum, Christian Ernest. Papers, 1830–98, particularly 1862–65. He

* Denotes materials added since 1963.

was in an Iowa unit but was on detached service as a recruiter for some Illinois regiments.°
Strong, John D.

Illinois Light Artillery, 1st Regiment
Church, F. S. Application for bounty, with pen and ink sketch.°
Corbusier, William Henry
Day, James Battersley
Dickinson, Albert. Chicago Historical Society.
Lake, Lewis F.
McClernand, John A.
Taylor, Ezra. Chicago Historical Society.

Illinois Light Artillery, 2nd Regiment
McClernand, John A.

CAVALRY

1st Illinois Cavalry
Palmer, George H.

2nd Illinois Cavalry
Bateman, Newton
Hatch, Ozias M.
Lindsey, John Will. Papers, 1862–65. Civil War letters addressed from Springfield, Illinois; Bolivar and Memphis, Tennessee; Holly Springs and Vicksburg, Mississippi; New Orleans and Baton Rouge, Louisiana. Diary December, 1963–August, 1964, on service in Louisiana.°
Miller, George F. Diary, June, 1864–January, 1865, on duty in Louisiana and Mississippi. 60 pp., photocopy.°
Mudd, John J. Complaint in January, 1864, about inadequate provisions and the inability to secure an interview with General Banks.°
Parker, Zebulon. See for Spaulding below.°
Spaulding, John (Co. G). Letters, 1864–66, on Mississippi River and Texas campaigns. See Zebulon Parker, 50th Inf. Regt.°

3rd Illinois Cavalry
Coughenower, Henry B.
Hatch, Ozias M.
Herrick-Reasoner
Higgins, John A. Papers, 1860–78; Civil War letters to his wife about duty in Illinois, Missouri, Arkansas, Mississippi, and Louisiana. 102 items.°
Post, Thomas C. Civil War correspondence included in Post Family folder.°
Ruggles, James M.

4th Illinois Cavalry
Chapin, Alvin W. Correspondence, January, 1861–November, 1865, concerning duty in Tennessee and Mississippi, and family affairs.°
Dickey, Theophilus Lyle. Most of these important materials are in the Illinois State Historical Library; other items are in the Illinois Historical Survey, Urbana, and the Chicago Historical Society.
Gillett Family
Hatch, Ozias M.
Illinois Cavalry, 4th Regt. Miscellaneous items. Chicago Historical Society.
Lacy, Erasmus
Lanstrum, Christian Ernest. See Illinois Artillery, 2nd Regt.
McClernand, John A.
Smith, William
Stouffer, John M. Diary, February–August, 1862, describing duty at Pittsburg Landing (Shiloh) from April to May, 1862. 10 pp., typed.°
[U.S. Army] Dist. of West Tennessee

Wallace, Martin Reuben Merritt. Chicago Historical Society.
Wallace-Dickey
Wempel, Mindret (Maj.). See Gillett Family above.*
Wilson, Abraham. Illinois State University Library, Normal.

5th Illinois Cavalry

Ammen, Jacob
Burke, John W. Letters, May, 1862–November, 1864, on Pocahontas and Helena, Arkansas; Haines Bluff and Vicksburg, Mississippi.*
Hussey, Fenton
Illinois Cavalry, 5th Regt., Co. G. Muster rolls and home addresses of soldiers.
Packard, Thaddeus
Payne, Alonzo G.
Reece, Thomas Madison. See 118th Inf. Regt.
Roe, James H. Letters, 1861–64, about duties at Camp Butler, Illinois, and in Missouri; service and fighting at Pocahontas and Helena, Arkansas; and Vicksburg, Mississippi.*

6th Illinois Cavalry

Carmichael, Isaac
Corbusier, William Henry
Hatch, Ozias M.
Hurff, Augustus. "Reminiscences, 1862–1865, of 6th Illinois Cavalry and 103rd Illinois Infantry." 18 pp.*
Lippincott, Thomas W.
McClernand, John A.
Nixon, Madison G.
Wallace-Dickey

7th Illinois Cavalry

Eby, Henry H. Letters, May, 1861–August, 1864, on Civil War duty in Missouri, Mississippi, and Arkansas. He was a mounted orderly for General John Palmer and a prisoner of war.*
Forbes, Henry Clinton
Hatch, Ozias M.
McClernand, John A.
Macomber, William S. Letters, 1864–65, describing duty in Tennessee and Indiana, including hospital service in John Francis Hill Hospital in Evansville, Indiana.*
Oglesby, Richard

8th Illinois Cavalary

Bull, Carpenter
Esher, Jacob T. Chicago Historical Society.
Farnsworth, John F. Document, March, 1861. He was a former Congressman who organized the 8th Illinois Cavalry and the uncle of General Elon John Farnsworth, once of the 8th Illinois Cavalry, who was killed at Gettysburg.
Illinois Cavalry, 8th Regt.
Prentice, Reuben T.
Rogers, Elbert A. "Anecdotes of a Pioneer and a Soldier," circa 1942, describing the Civil War experiences of Frank A. Rogers. 58 pp.*
Sargent, John. Additions to this collection. Six papers, including letters of William H. Austin, 1861–64.
Van Patten, James S.
Weld, Hiram H. Chicago Historical Society.
Wheelock, Francis A.

9th Illinois Cavalry

Abbott, O[thman] A.
Brackett, Albert G.
Brown, Henry C. Civil War diaries, 1861–62; also Andrew Swanzy's diary, 1862, and record of Bureau County soldiers. 22 pp., microcopy.*

10th Illinois Cavalry

Atwood, Elbridge
Bateman, Newton
Greenwell Family

Illinois Cavalry, 10th Regt. Quartermaster returns, commissions, and correspondence.
Illinois Cavalry, 10th Regt., Co. I. Bounty, statement of enlistment.
Shaw, E. P. (Maj.). 1883 copy of his war memos of 1861–63 concerning duty in Missouri, Arkansas, and Mississippi. See Francis Springer Collection below.
Smith, Sardius. Diaries, 1862–63, on service in Missouri and Arkansas.*
Springer, Francis. Diary, 1863, on camp life and campaign in Arkansas. Collection includes Shaw memos above.*
Springer, John G.*

11th Illinois Cavalry

Allen, Henry A. Diary, 1842–64; memoirs on duty in Tennessee, Mississippi, n.d. Includes Allen's Civil War diary, 1861–64, and other materials Martin Litvin donated after editing the book *Sergeant Allen and Private Renick.**
Ingersoll, Robert G. Huge collection with remarkable correspondence.
Ingersoll Family Papers
Paul, Thomas (Capt.). War diary.*
Taylor, John G. Stephenson County Historical Society, Freeport, Illinois.
[U.S. Army] Dist. of West Tennessee
Walker, Charles. Letters and journal. 72 pp.*

12th Illinois Cavalry

Alexander, Ashley
Allen, Winthrop
Artlip, John V. See 11th Inf. Regt.
Chapin, Alvin M. See 4th Cav.*
Voss, Arno (Col.). Telegram on troop movements. Chicago Historical Society.

13th Illinois Cavalry

Behlendorff, Frederick
Bell, Joseph W. Chicago Historical Society.

14th Illinois Cavalry

Bailhache-Brayman
Capron, Horace. He commanded the 14th. Papers covering battles and campaign. Microcopy.*
Connelly, Henry C.
Greenwell Family
Hatch, Ozias M.
Quigg, David
West, Martin. Diary, 1863–64, describing camp life, troop movements, and skirmishes in Tennessee, North Carolina, and Georgia.*

15th Illinois Cavalry

Early, Jacob M.
Hallock, Almon P. Letters, 1862–65, on duty in Mississippi and Arkansas; photo album of soldiers with 15th Cavalry and 53rd Illinois Infantry Regiment.*
Koehler, Albright
McClernand, John A.
Tupper, Francis W.

16th Illinois Cavalry

Payne, Stephen E.

17th Illinois Cavalry

Hutchinson, Cyrus
McClernand, John A.

ILLINOIS INFANTRY REGIMENTS

7th Illinois Infantry Regiment

Foreman, Abner
Illinois Infantry, 7th Regt.*
Illinois Infantry, 7th Regt., Co. A
McClernand, John A.
Messick, Daniel W.

Norton, William Eldred. Diary, January–November, 1863, containing brief entries on camp life and hospital services while stationed in Tennessee.*

8th Illinois Infantry Regiment

Austin, William H.
Batterton, Ira A. Papers, 1848–94; Civil War letters, 1861–63, on secretarial duties to generals John A. McClernand, Richard Oglesby, and John A. Logan. Lengthy account of Vicksburg campaign in letters of May and June, 1863. He was editor of the *Vicksburg Daily Herald*. 430 items, microcopy.*
Davis, Reed
Forrest, Joseph
Griffin, John A.
Hatch, Ozias M.
Hinshaw, William
Illinois Infantry, 8th Regt.*
Leach, James
McClernand, John A.
Oglesby, Richard
Puffer, Richard R. Chicago Historical Society.
Simonson, Isaac*
Smith, Dietrich C.
Smith, John William. Diary, March–April, 1865. 1 vol.*

9th Illinois Infantry Regiment

Allen, William Anderson
Brown, Henry C.
Cox, Joseph R.
Dutschy, Joseph
Engelman-Kircher
Hatch, Ozias M.
Illinois Infantry, 9th Regt. Regimental Order Book, morning reports, and muster rolls.
Jenkins, Warren Y. Letters, 1861. See William McLean below.*
Jones, David W. One letter to sister, January, 1862.*
Kinzie, Arthur. Typed recollections of prison life. Chicago Historical Society.
Lander, Edward. Transcript. Illinois Historical Survey, Urbana.
McClernand, John A.
McLean, William A. Letters, 1861–65, 1874. Letters, April–July, 1861, about duty with the 9th Illinois Infantry Regiment at Cairo. Letters, 1862–65, on duty in the 117th Illinois Infantry Regiment in Alabama, Louisiana, Mississippi, and Tennessee, including duty near Memphis, November, 1862–November, 1863; Jefferson Barracks, Missouri, 1864; and the Battle of Nashville, December, 1864. Photocopy and typed.*
Ransom, Frederick E. See 11th Inf. Regt.

10th Illinois Infantry Regiment

Craig, Edward and Mary Ann (Posey). See for an 1862 letter from John W. Craig while he was a hospital steward at New Madrid, Missouri.*
Ferguson, John Hill. This important collection is in the MacMurray College Library, Jacksonville, Illinois.
Jansen, Theodore H. (Pvt.). Reminiscences, 1905, on Civil War duties in the western theater. 230 pp., typed, photocopied.*
King Family
McClernand, John A.
Ransom, Frederick E. See 11th Inf. Regt.
Swales, James

11th Illinois Infantry Regiment

Artlip, John V. (Co. M). Diary and letters, 1864. Microfilm.*
Atkins, Smith D.
Bell, Andrew J. Journal, "Brig. General Ransom's Expedition through

Kentucky." 23 pp. See David Rose Simpson, 77th Inf. Regt.°
Carrington, George Dodd. Diary with vivid accounts of camp life and engagements at Donelson, Shiloh, and Vicksburg. Chicago Historical Society.°
Hapeman, Douglas
Illinois Infantry. Photostats.
McClernand, John A.
Ransom, Frederick E. Sketch book of Civil War scenes. He was related to General Thomas E. G. Ransom, original organizer of one of the companies of the 11th. General Ransom, one of the most promising general officers in the army, died as a result of battle wounds.
Simpson, David Rose. See 77th Inf. Regt.
Wallace-Dickey
Woollard, James B. (chaplain)

12th Illinois Infantry Regiment
Andrews Family
McArthur, John (Col.). Chicago Historical Society.
McClernand, John A.
Mayer, Charles
Travis, William D. T. Sketch book, circa 1861–68, includes Birds Point, Missouri, landing of 12th Illinois Infantry.°

13th Illinois Infantry Regiment
Behlendorff, John A.
Illinois Infantry, 13th Regt. Regimental orders.
Marsh, William K.
Needham, Arnold T. Chicago Historical Society.

14th Illinois Infantry Regiment
Backus, Henry E. Diary, 1861–64. 7 vols., microfilm.°
Bruce Family
Early, Jacob M.
Grebe, Balzer. Autobiography; Civil War diary; letters; two notebooks.°
Hamman, George (Co. D). Journal, 1861–62, on Civil War duty in Missouri, Tennessee, and Mississippi. 18 pp., typescript.°
Harris, John L. War correspondence, 1861–68. 34 items.°
Hatch, Ozias M.
Illinois Infantry, 14th Regt., Co. A. Ordnance report.
Illinois Infantry, 14th Regt., Co. G.
Martin, Parkhurst T. Papers, 1857–1907; 83 letters; approximately 50 military documents, mostly quartermaster reports.°
Miner Family
Moore, John D. (Lt., Co. F). Papers, 1862–65, including quartermaster reports on the 49th Inf. Regt.°
Muhleman, Jacob R.
Post Family
Rice, Mortimer. Civil War diary, 1861–64.°
Shumway, Payson
Treadway, David R. Letters, 1864–65. Photocopies.°
Viera, Augustine
Weisner, Reuben E. Diary, May, 1861–January, 1862. Photocopy.°

15th Illinois Infantry Regiment
Curtiss, Frank S. Papers, 1859–1915, including army service.°
Hanaford, Frank. Civil War reminiscences, 1864–65, drawn from an interview circa 1914 on his capture at Ac[k]worth, Georgia, on October 4, 1864; his imprisonment at Andersonville and a prison camp about ninety miles southwest of Savannah; his escape with four other men in December, 1864; their journey through swamps and down St. Mary's River; their arrival at Fort Clinch on Amelia Island, Florida; and their voyage north. 22 pp.°

McClernand, John A.
Reid, William M. Diary, May 16–July 4, 1863. 22 pp.*
Rogers, George, Chicago Public Library.
Smith, Frederick A.
Wayne, Harley (Co. D). Letters, 1844–62. Typescript.*

16th Illinois Infantry Regiment
Hatch, Alexander S. Letters. See Hatch and Fessenden Families.*
Hatch, Ozias M.
Illinois Infantry, 16th Regt., Co. A. Record book.
Illinois Infantry, 16th Regt., Co. E. Physical descriptions of soldiers in the company.
King Family
Roe, John H. Chicago Public Library.
Russell, John

17th Illinois Infantry Regiment
Batterton, Ira A. See 8th Inf. Regt.
Griffin, John A.
Hale, Henry. Photostat.
Illinois Infantry, 17th Regt., Co. D
Illinois Infantry, 17th Regt., Co. I. Discharge papers.
Illinois Infantry, 17th Regt., Co. K
McClernand, John A.
Midler, Christopher C. Diary entries, containing a sketch. Chicago Historical Society.*
Parsons, Lewis B.
Ross, Leonard (briefly a general officer). Papers 1843–67, including Civil War letters, 1861–66.*
Smith, George O.
Vanuken, A. J. Diary, 1861–63, describing camp life and service in Cairo, Illinois; Missouri; Kentucky; Tennessee; Arkansas; Mississippi; and Louisiana. Interesting insights on war scenes.*

18th Illinois Infantry Regiment
Benedict, John W.
Brush, Daniel Harmon
Cogswell, L. A. Photostat.
Hatch, Ozias M.
Knowles, Leander. Civil War papers, 1861 and 1864, about camp life.*
Lawler, Michael K. Papers, 1819–79. Southern Illinois University, Carbondale. Microcopy at Illinois State Historical Library.
McClernand, John A.

19th Illinois Infantry Regiment
Bailhache-Brayman
Chandler, Knowlton H.
Christian, William. Chicago Historical Society.
Cox, Felix G.
Fenton, James
Johnston, Joseph S. Chicago Historical Society.
McClernand, John A.
Raffen, Alexander W.
Saunders Family Papers. Chicago Historical Society.

20th Illinois Infantry Regiment
Batterton, Ira A. See 8th Inf. Regt.
Blanchard, Ira. "Recollections of Civil War Service with the 20th Illinois Infantry, Company H," circa 1890. Typescript.*
Illinois Infantry, 20th Regt., Co. E
Jennings, James
McClernand, John A.
Wallace-Dickey
Ware, William

21st Illinois Infantry Regiment
Blackburn, David
Dodd, George W. (Co. F). Letters, 1861–63; diary, 1862–64.*
Hatch, Ozias M.
Illinois Infantry, 21st Regt., Co. F. Company book.
McMackin, Warren. Photostats.*
McMackin Family
Polk, William H. Letters on war duty in the 21st.*
Welshimer, Phillip

22nd Illinois Infantry Regiment

Adams, Lemuel

Austin, William M.

Hood, Samuel Bateman. Papers, 1861–63. Three volumes of military records of Co. I, 22nd Illinois.*

McClernand, John A.

Mulligan, James Adelbert. Large collection of letters, diaries, miscellanea. 1,000 items. Chicago Historical Society.

Neville, Harvey. Chicago Historical Society.

Paisley, Joel B. Letters, 1861–62. See also William McLean, 9th Inf. Regt.*

Ruppert, Charles

Travis, William D. T. See 12th Inf. Regt.

Woodward, Benjamin. Memorabilia, including a Bible.*

23rd Illinois Infantry Regiment

Hadden, Amaziah. Letters, January, 1862, from Camp Douglas.*

Nugent, Charles W. Loyola University Library, Chicago.

Nugent, James H. Chicago Historical Society.

Philips, Albert V.

24th Illinois Infantry Regiment

Dahlmer, Charles

McClernand, John A.

Mihalotzy, Geza

25th Illinois Infantry Regiment

Buckner, Allen. Memoirs, 1900, on service in the West, including battles at Shiloh, Chickamauga, Chattanooga, Missionary Ridge, and Nashville; also muster rolls and supply records. 48 pp.*

Parker, Lines L.

26th Illinois Infantry Regiment

Gould, Victor

Illinois Infantry, 26th Regt. Unidentified soldier's diary.

Mayer, John. Stephenson County Historical Society, Freeport, Illinois.

27th Illinois Infantry Regiment

Crippen, Edward W. Newberry Library, Chicago.

Dickerhoff, A. G. (assistant surgeon). Letter, April, 1863, concerning the need for military libraries.*

Glenn, John. Correspondence, 1861–64. 103 items.*

Illinois Infantry, 27th Regt. Newspaper clippings.

Jansen, Theodore H. (Corp.) See 10th Inf. Regt.*

Johnson, Andrew W. Letter, August, 1862, about camp life at Triscomby, Alabama. Photocopy and typed.*

McClernand, John A.

Northrup, Diedrick. Discharge, September, 1864.*

Onstot, William H. Fifty-eight letters, 1861–63, about Camp Butler and Cairo, Illinois, and his duties in Tennessee, Mississippi, and Alabama. Photocopy and typed.*

Ring, Dana B..

28th Illinois Infantry Regiment

Bateman, Newton

Gapen, Michael. Chicago Historical Society.

Illinois Infantry, 28th Regt.

Lanstrum, Christian Ernest. See Illinois Artillery, 2nd Regt.

McGrath, Hugh. Chicago Historical Society.

Merchant, Ira

Reese, George. Letters, 1861–64. 10 items.*

Sellon, Charles

29th Illinois Infantry Regiment
Bailhache-Brayman
Bozman, Richard M. See Bailhache-Brayman.
Carmichael, Isaac H.
Ferguson, James F.
Hatch, Ozias M.
Illinois Infantry, 29th Regt., Co. I. Muster rolls and payroll.
Kanady, Sanford B.
Lanstrum, Christian Ernest. See Illinois Artillery, 2nd Regt.
McClernand, John A.
Miller, Thomas F.

30th Illinois Infantry Regiment
Davis, John P.
Finley, Robert S. Promotion to quartermaster-sergeant, January, 1864, at Vicksburg.*
Hatch, Ozias M.
Illinois Infantry, 30th Regt., Co. D*
McClernand, John A.
Poak, David W. Seventy-five letters, 1861–64.*
Shedd, Warren. Mercer County Historical Society Museum, Aledo, Illinois.

31st Illinois Infantry Regiment
Culp, David
Force, M. F.
Frazee, Thomas J. See 73rd Inf. Regt.*
Hatch, Ozias M.
McClernand, John A.
McCoy, William P.
McIlrath, James. Letters, 1861–62, to Mrs. Jane McIlrath. Photocopies.*
Miller, J. T. See Thomas J. Frazee, 73rd Inf. Regt.*
Odum, Addison. Reminiscences on the Battle of Belmont, n.d. He was a civilian who took the place of his ill brother, Martin Odum.*
Ozburn, Lindorf

32nd Illinois Infantry Regiment
Crum Collection
Drish, James F.
Hussey, Jacob Y.
Illinois Infantry, 32nd Regt. Consolidated provisions returns.
Johnson, Francis Marion. Diary, 1862–63, of the principal musician of the 32nd and 133rd Illinois infantry regiments. Typescripts.*
Logan, John
McNair, Alfred. Letter, February, 1864, from Black River, Mississippi.*
Van Winkle, John H.

33rd Illinois Infantry Regiment (also known as the "Teachers" or "Normal" Regiment, which probably accounts for a larger number of collections.)
Ammen, Jacob
Bateman, Newton
Batterton, Ira A. See 8th Inf. Regt.
Bohrer, Florence Fifer
Capron, Albert. See Horace Capron below.
Capron, Horace. See 14th Cav.
Chandler, Thomas S.
Ela, George P. Illinois State University, Normal.
Fifer, Joseph. Later Governor of Illinois.
Fortney, John F. M.
Griffin, John A .
Holzkamp, Frederick. Diary, nearly all in German. Chicago Historical Society.*
Ingraham, Duncan G. and Edward H.
Ingraham, Edward H. (Co. B). Diary, January 1–December 31, 1862.*
Ingraham Family. Chicago Historical Society.
May, Edwin (surgeon). Illinois Historical Survey, Urbana.
Nixon, William M. See Newton Bateman above.
Pike, Edward M. Reminiscences of a skirmish at Cache River bridge, Arkansas, May, 1862.*

Williamson, Joseph B. Diary, 1862–64, detailing service in Missouri; skirmishes along the Mississippi; battles at Magnolia Hills and Vicksburg, Mississippi; troop movements in Louisiana; and experiences at Fort Esperanza, Indianola, Matagordo Island, and Pass Cavallo, Texas.*

34th Illinois Infantry Regiment
Hostetter, Amos W.
Illinois Infantry, 34th Regt. Records of Illinois Veteran Volunteers Association and diary of an unidentified soldier.
Payne, Edwin
Robinson, William C.

35th Illinois Infantry Regiment
Danmoor, Andrew. See Gillett Family below
Gillett Family. Includes two letters from a soldier of Co. G as well as letters from soldiers in other regiments.*
St. Clair, Hannibal C (Lt.). See Gillett Family above.
Smith, Gustavus A. Civil War documents, 1862–69.*

36th Illinois Infantry Regiment
Cavis, J. G.
Cummins, George A. Papers, 1860–64; letters, 1863–64; diary, 1860–64. Materials include the history of Co. F, mostly written after events but while Cummins was still in the regiment; battles of Chickamauga, Jonesboro, Missionary Ridge, Perryville, Resaca, Stones River, Atlanta, Chattanooga, and Tullahoma; and other duties while in the army.*
Elmore, Day. Chicago Historical Society.
Hogue, James C. Company description book, 1861–63; Order and Ordnance Book, 1862–65; muster rolls and other records.*
Koehler, Albright
Lapham, Edward (Co. D). One letter.*
Sackett, John H.

37th Illinois Infantry Regiment
Black, John Charles
Ketzle, Henry. Mercer County Historical Society Museum, Aledo, Illinois.
Messer, Erwin B. Military papers, some about the military prison at Springfield, Missouri, which he commanded in 1862–63; also letters and papers of the 37th Veterans Association.*
Payne, Eugene B.

38th Illinois Infantry Regiment
Bailhache-Brayman
Craig, Samuel
Fuller, Francis. Military papers on quartermaster duties.*
Morgan, Will. Letter, August, 1862, on camp life from a camp near Iuka, Mississippi.*
Patterson, William E.

39th Illinois Infantry Regiment
Bedell, Ransom
Brink, Samuel H. Knox College Library, Galesburg, Illinois.
Clark, Charles M. (surgeon). Chicago Historical Society.
Fuller, Henry (Sgt.). Discharge papers. See also 88th Inf. Regt.
Illinois Infantry, 39th Regt. Muster rolls.*
Illinois Infantry, 39th Regt., Co. G. Military papers.
Kendall, Neriah B. Diaries and papers, 1860–65.*

40th Illinois Infantry Regiment
Dillon, William L. Letters, 1861–65. He was in the Pittsburg Landing

(Shiloh) campaign in March, 1862, and was wounded and held prisoner for twenty-four hours at Shiloh.*
Elliott, William M. (surgeon). Miscellaneous military papers.*
Markle, Richard. Papers, July, 1863–January, 1865, on Civil War duties in Mississippi and South Carolina.*
Ross, Felix. Diary, 1861, April 24–October, 25, 1862. Photocopy.*
Ross, William H. Chicago Historical Society.

41st Illinois Infantry Regiment
Rickard, Robert W.

42nd Illinois Infantry Regiment
Baldwin, Thomas B.
Holt, Martin. Civil War memoirs, including a published edition. Some typed transcripts.*
Needham, Lyman K. (Co. K). Civil War letters. See also 92nd Inf. Regt.
Norton, David W.

43rd Illinois Infantry Regiment
Engelmann-Kircher
Goodwin, Samuel J. H.
McClernand, John A.

44th Illinois Infantry Regiment
Roush, George S. Stephenson County Historical Society, Freeport, Illinois.
Smith, Dietrich

45th Illinois Infantry Regiment
Corbin, Ida (Robinson). Unpublished biography of Nathan A. Corbin, in verse, of his Civil War duty in Mississippi, Tennessee, and Georgia.*
Gaskill, James R. M. (surgeon). Military records. Chicago Historical Society and the Illinois State Historical Library.*
Illinois Infantry, 45th Regt. Miscellaneous records and a petition of an election of officers.
McClernand, John A.
Miller, Joseph Warren
Taylor, William C. Chicago Historical Society.
Tebbetts, William H.
Wallace-Dickey

46th Illinois Infantry Regiment
Bankson Sisters. Letters, including several from soldiers of the 46th. Stephenson County Historical Society, Freeport, Illinois.
Blair, Jonathan. Three letters, 1861–63.*
Davis, John A. Stephenson County Historical Society, Freeport, Illinois.
Frazier, David. Chicago Historical Society.
Illinois Infantry, 46th Regt. Credit slips issued by sutler.
Woodring, John M. Illinois State University Library, Normal.
Woodring, Uriah. Illinois State University Library, Normal.

47th Illinois Infantry Regiment
Batterton, Ira A. Letters from men in other regiments. Microcopy. See also 8th Inf. Regt.*
Brent, George W.
Cole, William M. Civil War papers, 1865, strictly military. 4 items.*
Cole Family. See for letters from John D. Cole, Co. K.*
Cromwell, John Nelson
DeWolf, David. Letters to family from Missouri, Mississippi, Tennessee, and Georgia.*
Illinois Infanty, 47th Regt., Co. F. Payroll.*
Illinois Infantry, 47th Regt., Co. I. Company book.
Melick, Jacob A. (Co. D). Diary, October, 1863–64.*
Reed, Isaac P.

48th Illinois Infantry Regiment
McClernand, John A.
Wallace-Dickey

49th Illinois Infantry Regiment
Hatch, Ozias M.
McClernand, John A.
Moore, John D. See 14th Inf. Regt.°
Morrison, William Ralls.
Stewart, Levi. Letters to his sister-in-law regarding the death of Lewis Stewart at the Battle of Fort Donelson, Tennessee.°

50th Illinois Infantry Regiment
Cyrus Family. War letters of two Cyrus men.°
Floyd, Charles H.
Lease, Phebe Ellen and Sarah M. Letters from soldiers of the 50th.°
Parker, Zebulon. Civil War letters, 1862–65.°

51st Illinois Infantry Regiment
Smith, Benjamin T.
Walker, Samuel S.

52nd Illinois Infantry Regiment
Barto, Alphonso. Papers, 1862–64. Later Governor of Minnesota.°
Buchan, James E. Military papers.°
McClernand, John A.
Records of 52nd Illinois Volunteer Association.
Sackett, John
Snell, James
Van Fleet, John. Papers, 1865–1911, including miscellaneous memorabilia and materials on veterans' reunions.°
Wilcox, John S.

53rd Illinois Infantry Regiment
Brush, Henry Lyman
Buckley, James
Graham, William F.
Hallock, Almon P. See 15th Cav.°
Hitt, Daniel
Koehler, Albright
McClernand, John A.
Morning Reports

54th Illinois Infantry Regiment
Hatch, Ozias M.
James, Thomas P.
McClernand, John A.
Mitchell, Greenville M.

55th Illinois Infantry Regiment
Aagesson [Agerson], Nicholas S.
Holmes, David H. Letters, 1861. Photostats.°
Kennedy, William J. (Co. G). Letters to his wife regarding the Battle of Shiloh, advance on Corinth, Tallahatachie campaign, battles of Chickasaw Bayou and Arkansas Post, siege of Vicksburg, and other movements of the 55th; two letters to his wife concerning his death on June 22, 1863. He had been on the floating hospital *Nashville,* near Vicksburg, but died at Sayoso Hospital, near Memphis. 170 items.°
Roberts, Peter
Russell, George W. Civil War letters, 1862–65.°

56th Illinois Infantry Regiment
Bunn, David P.
Hatch, Ozias M.
Oliver and DeWitt Families. Papers, 1862. See for Lewis Oliver (fifer for the 56th Infantry Regiment).°

57th Illinois Infantry Regiment
Harford, John. Papers, 1862–65, on service as quartermaster at Corinth, Mississippi.°
Illinois Infantry, 57th Regt.
Williams, Jesse. Letter to his wife, January, 1862, from Camp Douglas, recounting he was recovering from fever, had no pay, and his regiment had received marching orders.°

Zearing, James Roberts. Letters to his wife and other correspondence, some of which is of especial interest regarding Shiloh, Corinth, and the Atlanta campaign. Chicago Historical Society.*

58th Illinois Infantry Regiment

Ammen, Jacob
McClernand, John A.
Sawin, George. Chicago Historical Society.
Weismantle, Matthew

59th Illinois Infantry Regiment

Calkins, Charles E.
Dougherty, Louis Cass
Fielding, Edward E. Letters, 1862–64, about Civil War duty in Arkansas and Tennessee.*
Post, Philip Sidney. Magnificent collection of letters, maps, and military papers. 1,300 items. Knox College, Galesburg, Illinois.
Wade, Edward H. Harper Library, University of Chicago.

61st Illinois Infantry Regiment

Ihrie, Warrene
Lawrence, James. Chicago Historical Society.
McClernand, John A.
Mitchell, William N. Southern Illinois University Library, Carbondale.
Moore Family

63rd Illinois Infantry Regiment

Compton, George N.
Illinois Infantry, 63rd Regt. Requisitions and provisions returns.

64th Illinois Infantry Regiment

Deskin, Enoch G.
Reid, George. Diary, 1864. Photostat.*
Smith, Charles E. Civil War diary, January, 1865–June, 1865.*
Woods, Robert M.

65th Illinois Infantry Regiment

Bradley, David Cleland (Adjutant). Letters to his mother. Mimeograph. Chicago Historical Society.*
Meinhard, Frederick. Letters, 1862–65, regarding Civil War duties in Virginia, Kentucky, Tennessee, Georgia, and Alabama. Typescripts.*
Parks, Robert B. Diary, March, 1862–February, 1865, regarding Civil War duty in Virginia, Kentucky, Tennessee, and Georgia, including a letter of March, 1863, on Camp Douglas.*
Sprague, Dudley D. (Sgt., Co. I). Diary describing service in Tennessee, Georgia, and Alabama, including Knoxville, Kennesaw and Lost mountains, and Jonesboro, Georgia.*

66th Illinois Infantry Regiment

Childress, George L.
Ransom, Frederick E.
Titze, William C.
Wilson, William. Letters, September, 1861–September, 1864, on duty in Missouri; Tennessee, including the battles of Fort Donelson and Shiloh; and Georgia, including the battle of Kennesaw Mountain. Entries include camp life and military affairs.*

68th Illinois Infantry Regiment

Illinois Infantry, 68th Regt., Co. C and Co. F. Muster-out payroll.
King Family
McClernand, John A.

70th Illinois Infantry Regiment

Reece, Thomas Madison. See 118th Inf. Regt.

71st Illinois Infantry Regiment

Illinois Infantry, 71st Regt. Special orders.

72nd Illinois Infantry Regiment

Dilla, John B. (Co. K). Letter, 1864.*

Hemingway, Anson T. Diaries, 1862, 1863, 1865–66, including Civil War service in Kentucky, Tennessee, Mississippi, and Alabama; later as a lieutenant in the 70th U.S. Colored Regiment; and duties with the provost marshall of the Freedmen's Bureau in Alabama, beginning July 25, 1865. He was the grandfather of Ernest Hemingway. Microfilm (check regarding restrictions).*

Holbrook, William B. Chicago Historical Society.

[McPherson, James B.] Orders to Colonel Frederick Starring to take command of the 72nd located at Richmond, Indiana.*

Maquire, J. N.

Seacord, Thomas S.

Starring, Frederick. See Bailhache-Brayman and also James B. McPherson above.

Stockton, Joseph

Weed, James. Chicago Historical Society.

73rd Illinois Infantry Regiment

Frazee, Thomas J. Four years of correspondence mentioning battles at Perryville, Stones River, Chickamauga, Resaca, Kennesaw Mountain, and Atlanta, and describing his experiences as a prisoner and parolee after his capture at Atlanta.*

Hatch, Ozias M.

Holmes, Alfred A.

Hoskinson, Riley M. Letter, October, 1863; journal, September–October, 1863, on duties in Chattanooga hospital service; capture by and escape from Confederates. Check University of Washington regarding permission to quote. 16 pp., microfilm.*

Kyger, Tilmon D.

74th Illinois Infantry Regiment

Heuston, William R. Civil War papers, 1862 and 1865.*

Whittlesey Family. Letters from Alfred Williams while on duty at Knoxville, Tennessee.*

75th Illinois Infantry Regiment

Blodgett, James

Howlett, James C.

Illinois Infantry, 75th Regt.

Lyman, Edson W. Microcopy.

Shaeffer, John W. Letters from Tennessee 1863–66, philosophizing about the war. Photostat.*

76th Illinois Infantry Regiment

Bartlett, Napoleon Bonaparte. Chicago Historical Society.

Busey, Samuel T. Diary on duty in Louisiana, Mississippi, Tennessee, Florida, and Alabama, including mention of Spanish Fort.*

Grether, Peter. Letter written in German complaining about wormy food, water, and lack of sleep. Chicago Historical Society.*

Tallman, John. Chicago Historical Society.

77th Illinois Infantry Regiment

Carroll, John W. (musician). Military papers, 1864–1903.

Miller, Henry H. Chicago Historical Society.

Parrett, Orange. Diary, 1863–65. Microcopy.*

Simpson, David Rose. Civil War correspondence, 1863–65, while stationed in Kentucky and Tennessee, including a 23-page journal by Andrew J. Bell (11th Inf. Regt.) on the Kentucky expedition.*

Smith, Joseph A. (Co. E). Medical ledger, 1863, entitled "Prescription Book, Diet Book and Diet Table."*

78th Illinois Infantry Regiment
Batchelor, John
Grubb, Perry D. Two letters, April, 1865, and four other undated letters describing his experiences as a prisoner in Augusta, Georgia, and Florence, South Carolina, after his capture at Louisville, Georgia, in November, 1864. Transcript.*
McNeil, James. Journal, 1862–64, on duty in Tennessee and Georgia. Photocopy.*

79th Illinois Infantry Regiment
Buckner, Allen. See 25th Inf. Regt.*
Harding, Jacob. Letters and miscellaneous items on J. Oscar Harding, 1863–93, regarding service in Tennessee and Andersonville Prison.*
Rives, Henry E.

80th Illinois Infantry Regiment
Crane, Albert F. Chicago Historical Society.
Cunningham, John R. (Co. H). Papers, 1863–66.*

81st Illinois Infantry Regiment
Hatch, Ozias M.
Hull, John A. Discharge papers.*
McClernand, John A.
McCullough, Arthur D. Diary, 1862–65. Microcopy.*
Roberts, Alexander. Diary, 1863.*
Trefftzs, Lewis

82nd Illinois Infantry Regiment
Haller, Gustav. Chicago Historical Society (in German).
Haller, John. Chicago Historical Society (in German).

83rd Illinois Infantry Regiment
Hatch, Ozias M.
McClernand, John A.
Moore Family
Palmer, George H.
Sawtell, Joseph C. Diary. 100 pp.*
Society of 83rd Illinois

84th Illinois Infantry Regiment
Fox, David. Quincy and Adams County (Illinois) Historical Society.
Suiter, James P.
Taylor, Benjamin F. Letters, 1862–64, on Tennessee and Georgia. Transcript.*

85th Illinois Infantry Regiment
Illinois Infantry. Photostats.
McClernand, John A.
Southwick, G. W. Letter, February, 1865, on a campaign in Georgia and duty in South Carolina. Photocopy.*

86th Illinois Infantry Regiment
Burkhalter, James L. Diaries, 1864–65. 4 vols.*
Dawdy, Lansing
Fahnestock, Allen L. Most of these important materials are in the Illinois State Historical Library, Springfield; other letters and materials are to be found in the Peoria (Illinois) Public Library and in the Quincy and Adams County (Illinois) Historical Society.
McClernand, John A.
Nurse, Henry H. Civil War letters, 1862–65, on Civil War service in Tennessee, Kentucky, Georgia, and North Carolina. Photocopy of transcript.*
Ross, Levi A.

87th Illinois Infantry Regiment
McClernand, John A.

88th Illinois Infantry Regiment
Fuller, Henry (Sgt.). Brief history, roster, and military activities of Co. C; letters 1863. See also 39th Inf. Regt.*

McClernand, John A.
Sherman, F. F.

89th Illinois Infantry Regiment
Hotchkiss, Charles T. Chicago Historical Society.

90th Illinois Infantry Regiment
Casey, Peter. Chicago Historical Society.
McClernand, John A.
Stuart, Owen (Col.). Civil War letters. Typescript.*

91st Illinois Infantry Regiment
Pankey, Thomas L.

92nd Illinois Infantry (Mounted) Regiment
Atkins, Smith D.
Becker, Egbert
Brown, William H. Papers, 1864–65, 1871–85, and others.*
Illinois Infantry, 92nd Regt., Co. G. Reports.
Needham, Lyman K. (42nd Regt.). See for Cyrus Eyster letters.
Winston, Thomas (surgeon, 92nd and 149th). Letters, 1862–65; diaries, December 1863–June, 1864, 1865, 1866. Photocopies.*

93rd Illinois Infantry Regiment
Baker, Lyman (Co. H). Memoirs, 1914. 56 pp., typescript.*
Buswell, Nicholas C.
Dunbar, Aaron. Diary, 1863–65. One microcopy reel.*
McClernand, John A.
Payne, Ira A.

94th Illinois Infantry Regiment
Gilmore, Jasper. Diary, 1863–65, on duty in Texas and Alabama. Copy with interpolations.*
McClernand, John A.
McMullen, William E.
Phillips, James E. (Lt. Col.). Papers, 1862–1904. 9 items.*

95th Illinois Infantry Regiment
Babcock, John B. Diaries, 1862–64; miscellaneous papers. Original and microcopy.*
Fletcher, John B.
Gilbert, Edwin. Papers, 1862–87; letters on Mississippi and Spanish Fort.*
McClernand, John A.
Winegar, Daniel G. Letters on duty in Tennessee, Mississippi, Louisiana, Arkansas, and Missouri, especially the battles of Vicksburg, Guntown, and Spanish Fort. Typescript.*

96th Illinois Infantry Regiment
Leekley, Jos[eph]
McClernand, John A.

97th Illinois Infantry Regiment
Eddington, W. R. (Lt., Co. A). "My Civil War Memoirs and Other Reminiscences. . . ."*
Illinois Infantry, 97th Regt., Co. C
Parker, Zebulon. See 2nd Cav. and 50th Regt.*
Willard, Samuel (surgeon). Chicago Historical Society.

98th Illinois Infantry Regiment
Kitchell, Edward (Lt. Col.). Diaries, 1862–64, on service in Tennessee, including the battles of Chattanooga and Missionary Ridge.*

99th Illinois Infantry Regiment
Dinsmore, John C.
Hatch, Ozias M.
McClernand, John A.
May, Edwin (surgeon).
Williamson, Joseph B. See 33rd Inf. Regt.

100th Illinois Infantry Regiment
Patterson, Anson

101st Illinois Infantry Regiment

English, William L.
Illinois Infantry, 101st Regt.
McClernand, John A.
Strong, John D. Correspondence regarding the Civil War. He was not a soldier.*

102nd Illinois Infantry Regiment

Armstrong, William (Capt.). See Josiah Kellogg below.*
Cochran, William. Letters and papers, 1860, 1863–65.*
Illinois Infantry, 102nd Regt.
Kellogg, Josiah. Letters, 1863–64, on camp life. Collection includes a letter from Captain Armstrong to Kellogg's wife regarding her husband's death.*
Sheahan, Daniel
Trego, Alfred. Chicago Historical Society.

103rd Illinois Infantry Regiment

Bordner, Harvey
Dickerman, Willard
Hurff, Augustus. See 6th Cav.*
Orendorff, Henry. Civil War papers. Microcopy.*
McClernand, John A.
Wills, Charles W. (Lt. Col.). Diaries, printed in part in his *Reminiscences of the Civil War from Diaries of Members of the 103rd Illinois Volunteer Infantry, and Army Life of an Illinois Soldier.*

104th Illinois Infantry Regiment

Brush, Henry
Courtright, Cornelius C. Chicago Historical Society.
Hapeman, Douglas
Hoge, Robert Perry. Chicago Historical Society.
Humphrey, William T. Chicago Public Library.
Marsh, George
Rowe, James L.

105th Illinois Infantry Regiment

Bender, George A. Chicago Historical Society.
Wheeler, Lysander. Letters, 1862–65, including material on duties in Kentucky, Tennessee, Georgia, with notes on the siege of Atlanta.*

106th Illinois Infantry Regiment

Brown, William V.
Campbell, George H. (Lt. Col.). Letters. See Gillett Family below.*
Chalfant, J. G. Letters. See Gillett Family below.*
Gillett Family. See 35th Inf. Regt.
Latham, Robert B. (Col.). Letters in Gillett Family Collection, in addition to his own collection in the Illinois State Historical Library.*
McClernand, John A.
Vanhise, David (Capt.). Letters. See Gillett Family above.*

107th Illinois Infantry Regiment

Illinois Infantry, 107th Regt.*

108th Illinois Infantry Regiment

Boals, Albert C. (Lt., Co. A). Diary, 1863, on service in Louisiana, Mississippi, and Tennessee, including accounts of the battles of Port Gibson, Champion's Hill, and Vicksburg.*
Bullock, Winfield A.
Illinois Infantry, 108th Regt., Co. E
Kellog, Price F.
Turner, Charles. Letters, 1864–65. Photocopy.*

109th Illinois Infantry Regiment (disbanded in 1863 for refusal to muster)

McClernand, John A.
Nimmo, Alexander J. Chicago Historical Society.

110th Illinois Infantry Regiment

Illinois Infantry, 110th Regt., Co. D
McClernand, John A.

111th Illinois Infantry Regiment

Dillon, Isaiah. Brother of William L. Dillon who served in 40th Illinois, he campaigned with Sherman through to Grand March in Washington, D.C. Letters also detail the burning of Columbia, South Carolina.°

McClernand, John A.

O'Bryant, Agustus W. See Abram Parker below.°

Parker, Abram C. Papers, 1865, including a description of his imprisonment at Belle Isle, Virginia.°

Peirce, Thomas (Capt., Co. C). Papers, 1862–1908; Civil War relics.°

Van Duesen, Thomas C. Forty-two letters, 1862–64, about service in Kentucky, Tennessee, Alabama, and Georgia.°

Woollard, John B. See 11th Inf. Regt.°

112th Illinois Infantry Regiment

Henderson, Thomas J. (Col.). Civil War diary, 1863–65; letters; unpublished history of the 112th, including reports on the battles of Franklin and Nashville.°

Illinois Infantry, 112th Regt., Co. D

Widney, John A.

113th Illinois Infantry Regiment

Ammen, Jacob

Bailhache-Brayman

Harper, John and Alexander. Letters, 1862–65, about duties in Nashville and Camp Butler.°

Russell, Frederick W. Letters to his mother, plus other family correspondence. Chicago Historical Society.°

114th Illinois Infantry Regiment

Beggs, Thomas B.

Brown, Albert

Bruce Family

Chandler, Harrison T.

Fish, Ezra. Journal, July 5–19, 1864, on Tupelo, Mississippi, expedition, including a report of the Battle of Harrisville. Photocopy of holograph transcript.°

French, Alvin. Transcripts. Illinois Historical Survey, Urbana.

Harding, William. Letter, September, 1863, about the Battle of Jackson, Mississippi.°

Hatch, Ozias M.

Judy, James. Records. 15 items.°

McClernand, John A.

Moore, John D. (Capt., Co. I). See 14th Inf. Regt.°

115th Illinois Infantry Regiment

Ammen, Jacob

Espy, Stephen B. Chicago Historical Society.

Herdman, John. Civil War letters. Photocopies.°

Illinois Infantry, 115th Regt., Co. I and Co. K

Loomis, Clark E. Miscellaneous papers.°

Martin, Elgin H. See Parkhurst T. Martin, 14th Inf. Regt.°

Philbrook, Flavius J.

Robinson, Gifford

Woods, John H. See Jacob Ammen above.

116th Illinois Infantry Regiment

Bear, Henry

Boyd, James P. (Lt. Col.). Diary, 1858–63, on duty in Arkansas, Louisiana, Mississippi, Yazoo River campaign, Arkansas Post, and siege of Vicksburg. He was fatally wounded in May, 1863. Statement on literary rights also available.

McClernand, John A.

117th Illinois Infantry Regiment

Ashley, William (musician). See Governor Charles S. Deneen Papers.°

Funk, Isaac

Hieronymus, Benjamin (Lt. Col, Co. A)
Hickman, Walker F. Letters, 1863 and 1865. See also William A. McLean, 9th Inf. Regt.°
Hood, Humphrey
Justice, Elihu
Look, Oliver C.
McClernand, John A.
McFarland, David
McLean, William A. See 9th Inf. Regt.°
Merriam, Jonathan (Lt. Col.). Papers, 1862–65. He campaigned in 1864 with the Army of the Tennessee at Red River and Fort Blakely.°
Messinger, John. See this collection for letters of descendants.°
Olden, William Parker
Robinson, Sidney Z. Transcripts. Illinois Historical Survey, Urbana.
Wilderman, David. Papers, 1862–65; "Descriptive Book" for Co. H, 1862–65.°
Wolf, Otto E. (musician, Co. F). Letters, 1863–65, about service in Tennessee, Mississippi, and Louisiana, including duty at Fort Pickering, Battle of Pleasant Hill, Tupelo campaign, and Battle of Nashville. Microcopy.°

118th Illinois Infantry Regiment
Cole, William M. See 47th Inf. Regt.°
Flick, Andrew. Transcript of diary, 1862–65, describing duty in Arkansas, Louisiana, and Mississippi; brief history of the Battle of Arkansas Post; roster and history of Co. F.°
Gordon, Samuel
Hamilton, Elisha B. Diary, 1863–64, on Civil War duty as a quartermaster-sergeant and lieutenant in Mississippi and Louisiana; thesis by Daniel Ryan on the diary. 91 pp., 1 reel microfilm.°
Hamilton, Elisha B. Quincy and Adams County (Illinois) Historical Society.
Illinois Infantry, 118th Regt. Journal and record books.
McClernand, John A.
Reece, Thomas Madison (surgeon).
Uhler, Andrew J.

119th Illinois Infantry Regiment
Bellchamber, John N. Drawings of troop movements, including one labeled "Banks' Army Crossing the Atchafallaya."°
Burke, Lemuel. Journal on the Red River campaign and duty in Tennessee, Louisiana, and Mississippi, including Spanish Fort. Typed transcript.°
Hambaugh, John H.
Hatch, Ozias M.
Illinois Infantry, 119th Regt.
McClernand, John A.
McCready, William A.
Pugh, Alexander G. Chicago Historical Society.

120th Illinois Infantry Regiment
Clark, William H. Chicago Historical Society and Illinois State Historical Library.
McClernand, John A.
Rilea, Joshua D. See 129th Inf. Regt.

121st Illinois Infantry Regiment
McClernand, John A.

122nd Illinois Infantry Regiment
Butcher, Jeremiah. Letters, March–April, 1864, about camp life and duty along the Mississippi River.°
Cox, Lansden
Crum Collection. See for John H. Crum's war letters.
Drish, James E.
Ibbetson, William H.
Illinois Infantry, 122nd Regt. Co. B
Peter, William H. and Samuel W.

123rd Illinois Infantry Regiment
Connolly, James A.
Connolly, James A. One letter filed with Bromwell Papers, Illinois Historical Survey, Urbana.
Garrison Family. See for Alva C. Garrison.°
Jones, Dumas
McClernand, John A.
Morgan, John. Letter, January 1, 1863, on Rosecrans's movements following Stones River. Photostat.°
Pepper, William A. Letters, 1862–63; diary, 1864–65, describing Civil War duties in Kentucky, Tennessee, Georgia, and Mississippi. Typed transcript.°

124th Illinois Infantry Regiment
Bartlett, Benjamin
Coder, Martin V. B. See for Marcus Lester's letters on Camp Butler.°
Given, John
Howe, Edward
Miller, Benjamin F.
Potter, Theodore (Lt.). Some Civil War papers.°
Randall, Cyrus. Thirty-five items, four of which concern his capture by the rebels. Photocopy. Chicago Historical Society.°
Smith, James W.

125th Illinois Infantry Regiment
Davis, David
Hunt, Oliver P. (1st Lt., Co. K). Papers, 1864–65, containing regimental records.°

126th Illinois Infantry Regiment
Anonymous (SC 1826). Poetry.°
Crowder, James H. Civil War papers and special orders concerning his asssignment in Arkansas.°
McClernand, John A.
Mechling, Jacob

127th Illinois Infantry Regiment
Curtiss, Frank S. See 15th Inf. Regt.°
Illinois Infantry°
Little, George W. Chicago Historical Society.
McClernand, John A.
Rickard, Robert W. Chicago Historical Society.

128th Illinois Infantry Regiment
McClernand, John A.

129th Illinois Infantry Regiment
Rilea, Joshua D. Journal, 1862–65, on Sherman's campaigns.°

130th Illinois Infantry Regiment
McClernand, John A.
Niles, Nathaniel. See for Col. John G. Reid.°

131st Illinois Infantry Regiment
McClernand, John A.

132nd Illinois Infantry Regiment
Pickett, Thomas Johnson

135th Illinois Infantry Regiment
Curtiss, Charles C. Diary commenting on weather, morale, an execution, guerrillas, local women, and a court martial for which he served as clerk. 183 pp. Chicago Historical Society.°
Johnson, Francis Marion. See 32nd Inf. Regt.

136th Illinois Infantry Regiment
Jones, A. J.
Telford, Samuel G. Military papers.°

137th Illinois Infantry Regiment
McClure, Elzy

139th Illinois Infantry Regiment
Smith, Dietrich C.

144th Illinois Infantry Regiment
King Family
Moore, John D. Papers, 1862–65.°

145th Illinois Infantry Regiment
Illinois Infantry, 145th Regt., Co. C

146th Illinois Infantry Regiment
Heath, W. F.

149th Illinois Infantry Regiment
Winston, Thomas. See 92nd Inf. Regt.*

150th Illinois Infantry Regiment
Deamude, Charles. See also Henry Bear microfilm.

151st Illinois Infantry Regiment
DeWolf, David. See 47th Inf. Regt.

152nd Illinois Infantry Regiment
McClure, Alexander H. Diary, February–July, 1865; papers.*

153rd Illinois Infantry Regiment
Heuston, William R.*
Smith, Gustavus A. Papers, 1841–1920, including some Civil War materials.*

156th Illinois Infantry Regiment
Hyde, John Ellington
Messer, Erwin B. Military papers.*
Terry, W. I. Four-page letter on the Civil War in Nashville.*

170th Illinois Infantry Regiment
Skinner, James G. Diary, April–May, 1864, on Red River campaign.*

Miscellaneous
Wallace, John M. Letters, mainly personal news, from a soldier serving in an Illinois regiment. Chicago Historical Society.*

Index

As used in this index, the initials *USA* stand for United States Army, *USN* for United States Navy. Both are applied to army or navy officers who did not come from Illinois. The initials *CSA* stand for Confederate States Army. Those officers who came from Illinois are denoted by the phrase "Ill. officer."

Note on the Author

Victor Hicken received his doctorate in history in 1955 from the University of Illinois. He taught at Western Illinois University from 1947 to 1981, holding the rank of Distinguished Professor for the last six years of that period. He also taught briefly at Knox College in Galesburg, Illinois. Besides this publication, he is the author of *The American Fighting Man* and *The World Is Coming to an End* as well as numerous articles. In 1967 he was president of the Illinois State Historical Society. Now retired, he resides in Macomb, Illinois.